P9-CAL-381

Hot from Harlem

Hot from Harlem

Twelve African American Entertainers, 1890–1960

REVISED EDITION

BILL REED

McFarland & Company, Inc., Publishers

Jefferson, North Carolina, and London

The present work is a revised and updated edition of a book self-published under the title *"Hot from Harlem": Profiles in Classic African-American Entertainment* in 1998.

All photographs are from the author's collection unless otherwise specified.

LIBRARY OF CONGRESS CATALOGUING-IN-PUBLICATION DATA

Reed, Bill, 1941–
 Hot from Harlem : twelve African American entertainers, 1890–1960 / by Bill Reed.— Rev. ed.
 p. cm.
 Includes bibliographical references and index.

 ISBN 978-0-7864-4467-0
 softcover : 50# alkaline paper ∞

 1. African Americans— Music — History and criticism. 2. African American musicians. 3. African Americans in the performing arts. I. Title.
 ML3556.R36 2010
 792.089'96073 — dc22   2009044035

British Library cataloguing data are available

©2010 Bill Reed. All rights reserved

No part of this book may be reproduced or transmitted in any form or by any means, electronic or mechanical, including photocopying or recording, or by any information storage and retrieval system, without permission in writing from the publisher.

Front cover: Hazel Scott, 1947; background ©2010 Shutterstock

Manufactured in the United States of America

McFarland & Company, Inc., Publishers
 Box 611, Jefferson, North Carolina 28640
 www.mcfarlandpub.com

To the memories of Dr. Beverly Robinson,
without whom this book could not have
been written, and Susan Le Vitus.

"You don't get *started* in show business ... you just start."
— Jackie "Moms" Mabley

Acknowledgments

For financial, moral or research support: Lorez Alexandria, L.T. Anderson, who told me I was a writer; Atlanta Historical Society, for help in locating the Whitman Sisters' relatives; Reid Badger, for help with Cook songography; Orin Borsten and his wonderful stories of Atlanta; Clora Bryant, for her recollections of Central Avenue; Chicago Historical Society, for leads on the Whitman Sisters; Peter Chinicci of the Marlborough School; Joan Cohen of Legwork Research; Dominique-René de Lerma of Lawrence University, Appleton, Wisconsin, helpful from the beginning; Drain Library, West Virginia State College, Institute, West Virginia; Judy Fireman, for answers to some sticky questions; JoAnn and Chet Gudger, whose stories about Demas Dean and access to his archives proved invaluable; Stephen Isoardi, for insight into black L.A. in the 1940s; Delilah Jackson, for the intro to Demas Dean; Olga James, a wonderful interpreter of Will Marion Cook songs and a big help with the Sammy Davis chapter; Herb Jeffries and his tales of Chicago; Ann Kenderson, University of Pittsburgh Library; Ernestine Lucas, the Whitman Sisters' great niece and keeper of the legacy; Marilyn Mahanand, Moorland-Spingarn Library; Nancy Marano, a great singer and good friend; Frances Nealy, whose memories of Central and L.A. in the '40s were essential; Fayard Nicholas; Thomas B. Reed, my nephew who helped me with genealogical research; Joan Rieger; Schomburg Center for Research in Black Culture (Mary Yearwood there was continuously helpful); Vera Miller Shapiro; Wayne Shirley, Library of Congress Music Division; Sister Fransescia Thompson, Eveleyn Preer's daughter, who answered questions for me; Vincent Virga, for help with photos; Simon Wiesenthal Center for Holocaust Studies, Los Angeles (their file on Valaida Snow was a boon); Frances E. Williams, who thought I should write this book; and Jay Kato and David Ehrenstein.

Table of Contents

Preface

When most people consider the early history of African American entertainment, the image that often springs to mind is that of the minstrel show with its attendant connotations of stereotypical mannerisms; however, nothing could be further from the truth. Starting in the mid–1800s, blacks began to invent what we know today as modern show business in all its varied forms.[1] Moreover, African American performers evidenced a subtlety and complexity of approach that was in every way unique. It is doubtful that any black comedian failed to touch — if only ever so lightly — on the subject of racism; or that there was ever a blues singer who didn't somehow manage to convey the sense that two-timing lovers weren't the *only* source of his or her woes.

"Try to picture the entertainment world without input from black performers, composers and writers," observed Bessie Smith biographer Chris Albertson. "The music of such composers as Ravel, Stravinsky and Shostakovich would be different, so would the paintings of Picasso and Braque, and Broadway musicals would certainly be less vibrant. There would be also be no jazz and blues, which means no rock and roll, no Gershwin, no Porter. And dance? Let's not even get into that."[2]

Recent research has indicated that even the Confederate anthem "Dixie" was actually written by blacks (a pair of Ohio brothers, Ben and Lew Snowden), only to later be expropriated by early white minstrel man Dan Emmett.[3]

In 1920, a veteran of black vaudeville, Mamie Smith, scored a coup with her recording of "Crazy Blues," marking the first time that anyone had made an authentic blues recording. The release sold in unprecedented numbers for the 37-year-old singer and was unquestionably the most modern sound anyone had heard in popular music up to that time.[4] It would be next to impossible to divine exactly how many of Smith's "Crazy Blues" sold to Caucasians and how many to blacks; however, at the time of her recording, most phonographs were owned by whites. Ironically, Smith's success followed directly in the wake of the "Red Summer" of 1919 that saw an unprecedented twenty-five race riots, hundreds of blacks killed and lynched by whites, and more than two hundred public KKK rallies.[5] *Après* Mamie came the deluge: Hun-

dreds of black female urban-blues singers were quickly signed up by recording companies to try and cash in on the success of her song with both white
and black record buyers alike. As much as a decade earlier, red hot and *white*
mamas like Sophie Tucker and Belle Baker had recorded their own versions
of something approximating jazz, but Smith and her "Crazy" tune offered up
the real thing. Yearning to learn some of the more rarified secrets of the art
of the blues, Tucker went so far as to send her maid to blues star Alberta
Hunter's dressing room to request a master class in how to sing "A Good Man
Is Hard to Find."

"I never did go," Hunter later recalled to her biographers Frank C. Taylor and Gerald Cook. "Something wouldn't let me. I think she would have
liked to learn my tricks and to take advantage of me by getting popular on
my style. But nobody can learn my style because I don't know it myself. It's
always changing."

"Finally," wrote Taylor and Cook, "Sophie sent her pianist, Ed Shapiro,
over to take down notes as he listened to Alberta sing."[6]

Such gestures were not without precedent: The first African slaves had
barely debarked from the vessels that brought them to America before their
masters began expropriating their songs and dances; these "Old World crossed
with New World" creations were shot through with responses to—and send-
ups of—the plantation owners' high-flown carriage and behavior.[7] By the
1840s this source material had been twisted by whites into the highly-styl-
ized performance ritual known as the Minstrel Show; so often referred to by
scholars as a "uniquely American art form." But minstrelsy—essentially nothing more than a parody of the Africans' response to their new homeland, i.e.,
a parody of a parody—was finally about as authentically American as a Swiss
yodel. The field hollers, buck dancing, call-and-response singing, and playing of the banjo (an instrument commonly believed to be of African origin)[8]
that minstrelsy drew upon so freely all harkened back to Africa, with the ele-
ment of mockery (i.e., blackface and distorted gesticulation) added by whites
out of detestation and fear of *the other*.[9]

The song titles of minstrelsy give some idea of the gruesome esteem in
which blacks were held by whites: "No Coon Can Come Too Black for Me,"
"The Man in the Moon Is a Coon," and the notorious "All Coons Look Alike
to Me" (sad to say, written by a black). Even Jerome Kern got into the act in
1909 with something called "Paris Is a Paradise for Coons."

Running parallel to such ostentatious displays of racial malice were serious attempts by black Americans to cultivate their own indigenous art. The
early 1870s saw the rise in popularity of Jubilee choral groups which specialized in singing slave hymns and spirituals (in part the very same African-
inspired source material that minstrelsy had so tragically debased). The
Jubilee vogue soon died down, ostensibly because it reminded many blacks
of a recent past full of suffering and despair.[10] What followed was a decade-

long lull in the growth of indigenous black musical culture, one which lasted until the emergence of ragtime in the mid–1880s. It was this relatively fallow period that found the first widespread participation by blacks in minstrelsy.

The immensely popular Primrose and West's Mammoth Minstrels, for example, offered a presentation consisting of a 60–40 mix of whites and blacks. It was, however, a perverse stripe of democratization that was served up: Since all the players appeared in blackface, the audience was scarcely in a position to detect racial difference. Fortunately, the blacks' reworking of the minstrel idiom's songs and jokes tended to be aesthetically much sharper and to represent an improvement upon what had theretofore been strictly a white pastime. The little good that had been added by whites was generally retained; the bad — the black neophyte troupers tended to discard. Soon there followed the first all-black (but white-owned) traveling minstrel shows such as the Ideal Minstrels, the Dudley Georgia Minstrels and M.B. Curtis' Afro-American Minstrel Company, one of a number of the all-black troupes — along with the Ethiopian Serenaders with nary a genuine Ethiopian in sight — that proved especially popular with foreign audiences.[11]

By the end of 1910 there were some 40,000 whistle-stopping performers employed in the U.S. (double the 1905 amount), including a disproportionate number of blacks consisting, in part, of some 6,000 musicians and 1,279 actors, many of whom had gotten their start in minstrelsy's main competition for audience favor during the period: the several hundred touring companies of *Uncle Tom's Cabin*.[12] Dramatizations of Harriet Beecher Stowe's famed polemical novel had begun barnstorming the country in the mid–1850s and came in every shape and size imaginable. In the 1860s, for instance, *Uncle Tom* companies had begun vying with each other for the sheer number of characters portrayed by *two* actors. The C.H. Smith Ideal Double Mammoth *Uncle Tom's Cabin*, for example, included two Topsys and two Markses (Sr. and Jr.), among others, along with three donkeys and ten mammoth Siberian hounds. Critics sarcastically referred to the venture as "C.H. Smith's Boston Alphabetical Quadrilateral Mammoth Double All-Star *Uncle Tom's Cabin* Combination"; nevertheless "doubling fever," as it came to be known, lasted for several seasons. Such bizarre transfigurations of Stowe's straightforward novel came about after sundry *Cabin* companies had been on the road for more than a decade and mere claims of "bigger and better" no longer proved automatic audience lure.[13]

For all the show's surefire popularity, notions of casting verisimilitude didn't strike Cabinmania until the 1870s when one producer got the idea of hiring an actual black man to play Uncle Tom. Up until then, all black characters in *Tom* productions had been portrayed by corked-up whites. The next thing you knew, "there went the neighborhood": Liza and Topsy also began to be played by actors who had no need for cork, and soon such casting became more the rule rather than the exception.[14]

The lengthy and distinguished theatrical career of the first African American member of Actor's Equity and Negro Actors Guild co-founder Leigh Whipper began by chance one day in 1900 when the struggling law student's attention was caught by a line of blacks standing in line in front of Philadelphia's Standard Theater. Investigating, he learned they were queued up to audition for a production of *Uncle Tom*. The next thing Whipper knew, he was dressed in slouch hat and overalls and singing "Old Black Joe," traveling with an integrated company of what has since come to be called "the world's greatest hit" and "our unofficial national play."[15] It is estimated that by 1912 the play had been performed in the U.S. at least 250,000 times; many of the artists who (like Whipper) had begun their careers in the Stowe classic, could still be found performing in black vaudeville of the 1920s.[16]

With the advent of modern vaudeville, consisting of non-ensemble performance and separate turns by specific artists, African Americans found themselves by and large cast outside the circle. By 1915, the rule of thumb on most white vaudeville circuits was one black act per bill — at the most. While the Jolsons, Jessels, and Cantors headlined in main stem vaudeville houses, such now-forgotten black stars as Hamtree Harrington, Gulfport Brown, and Stringbeans and Sweetie began appearing in theaters whites would never dream of setting foot in, especially in the South on the black Theatre Owners' Booking Association (T.O.B.A.) performance circuit. These same troupers, and hundreds more like them, also populated the world of all-black night clubs and films; some 800 shorts and features were produced between 1909 and 1950.[17]

The men and women profiled in this book represent a sampling of the African American entertainment professionals who managed to straddle the separate worlds of black and white show business. Nearly all of them were famous in their time — in some cases nearly as famous as such legendary "crossover" performers as Louis Armstrong and Duke Ellington. What *all* African American entertainers from this period have in common, however, is something that few if any of their white counterparts can lay claim to: a heroic dimension that was a concomitant result of the enormous freight load of inequities and indignities that was the lot of every black performer, regardless of professional status. Even among their own people, race became a weapon — a common denominator to level a crowded playing field. How many great black stars were introduced by vaudeville and night club emcees as being "hot from Harlem" even though they had never set foot in the "Negro Capitol of America"? In a culture that demands myth and disdains fact, only the simplistic and reflexive will do. That these performers managed to shoulder the burdens of racism two-shows-a-day and still get the job of entertainment done was a miracle. It didn't matter whether one was a renowned "crossover" performer like Ethel Waters or Nat "King" Cole, or one of the obscure thousands from the hermetically sealed world of all-black theaters and night clubs, there were always problems.

Sometimes trouble came in the form of an incident as humiliating as being arrested for appearing out of doors after dark. Certain cities in the South had such laws, making life hellish for black performers who, after all, began work at such an hour. Unscrupulous management and inadequate food and lodging were commonplace in black show business life.[18] And sometimes trouble came in a much subtler, more corrosive form, as when white critics referred to blacks not as the best in their particular field but rather the best *black* singer, the best *black* violinist, etc.

New words, phrases, comedy routines and dance styles created by black America from shortly after the end of the Great War until the advent of the Depression were assimilated into and remain a permanent part of the mainstream of American entertainment. Yet acknowledgment of this simple fact has often been slow in coming. Consider tap dance, begun on plantations as an outgrowth of African dance combined with a kind of subversive Morse Code between slaves.[19] Later it evolved by leaps and bounds in black vaudeville before strictly African American audiences. Finally it got taken up by whites such as Eleanor Powell and Fred Astaire, going on to become a unique form of dance expression thought of more as American rather than African American. This lack of distinction, extending to all forms of black entertainment, is unfortunate, for the fact of the matter is that from the mid–19th century onward, great numbers of African American performers were arguably superior to their white counterparts.

Bert Williams, to cite one example, was not just historically the first mainstream African American star, but in his heyday of the 20th century's second decade, an uppermost figure on Broadway who worked with and ranked alongside the likes of Eva Tanguay, Irene Franklin, Bert Leslie, Ed Wynn, and Leon Errol. On August 15, 1900, a major race riot erupted in New York City over a black man who had accidentally killed the white attacker of his wife. At the height of the riot, the cry went out to "get" Bert Williams, along with a handful of other prominent black performers of the day, including Williams' partner George Walker. Writes James Weldon Johnson in his *Black Manhattan,* "These seemed to be the only individual names the crowd was familiar with."[20] Williams survived unscathed, but the seemingly sure cure of fame had failed to protect him due to the color of his skin, and the incident is said to have haunted him for the remaining twenty-two years of his life. Williams was, in the words of W.C. Fields, "the funniest man I ever saw, and the saddest man I ever knew."[21] Similarly paradoxical pronouncements might be applied to many of the artists appearing in this book.

The testimony of those who witnessed the now all-but-forgotten Valaida Snow suggests a triple threat performer deserving of a place alongside Josephine Baker in the upper echelon of the all-time greats. Will Marion Cook changed the face of both musical comedy and jazz. Billy McClain attained major stage importance on three continents outside of North America. Singer-pianist Hazel Scott juggled a mainstream career with full-time social commitment. Mabel Whitman of the Whitman Sisters was a pioneering actress-manager. And yet nearly all — Sammy Davis, Jr., being a major exception*— have been pushed to the sidelines of history due to a combination of racial discrimination and a lack of documentation during their peak creative years by both the black and white press. Their artistry also tended to be inadequately or insufficiently captured on film or recordings.

Part One ("The Big Picture") of the book forms a chronological arc that moves from the very beginning of African American participation in show business up through the present age. Will Marion Cook and Billy McClain are discovered in action at the very dawn of black parity in the entertainment field; six chapters later, in the 1950s, the young Sammy Davis, Jr., is breaking through the invisible ceiling that has kept all those who came before him "in their place." In between, the likes of Valaida Snow, Nora Holt, Billy Strayhorn, Hazel Scott, Dinah Washington, and others can be found making incremental contributions to the fight against racism both in and out of the business. Every story is unique, but at the same time, each sheds light not just on the plight of entertainment professionals, but everyday African Americans as well, in the still-evolving, crisis-ridden history of U.S. race relations.

Part Two ("Zeroing In") examines the nuts and bolts of "the biz" — i.e., second-tier performers and behind-the-scenes figures — and also offers a brief overview of some long-forgotten figures. It also revisits three key cities that operated as ground zero(s) for black show biz in the early part of the last century.

This revised edition (the first was published in 1998) contains all of the text in the original edition, plus updates, including references to significant post-'98 tributes, documentaries, CDs, biographies, etc., dedicated to various personages contained herein.

---

*Since the publication of the first edition of this book and, specifically, because of the appearance of *Lush Life*, David Hajdu's 1996 biography of jazz musician Strayhorn, overall public awareness of Duke Ellington's invaluable musical cohort has grown considerably.

PART ONE

The Big Picture

1

The Birth of
the Black Musical
Will Marion Cook

The first decade of the last century saw numerous political, social and artistic milestones in Black America: In 1903, W.E.B. Du Bois published *The Souls of Black Folk*; a new young black fighter was taking on any and all contenders; and, spurred on by such figures as David Walker and Lemuel Haynes, the Back to Africa movement was beginning to take root. In music, this was the start of the jazz era. Scott Joplin was just putting the finishing touches on his first syncopated opera, *The Guest of Honor*. Jelly Roll Morton would take sole claim for jazz's invention, but in fact a number of musicians played nearly as great a role, including Freddie Keppard, Buddy Bolden, and long-forgotten Tony Jackson (see Chapter 12).

Work remained plentiful for African Americans in the rag-tag world of touring vaudeville presentations, thanks in great part to the continuing regional popularity of minstrelsy with its demeaning depiction of blacks. Even the twentieth economic depression in U.S. history wasn't sufficient to stem grass roots fascination with *Uncle Tom's Cabin*, which continued to offer employment to large numbers of African Americans. It is important to note that for black performers, minstrel and "Uncle Tom" shows offered a rare degree of (otherwise mostly unavailable) mobility and a means of migration out of the agrarian South. In the legitimate theatre, however, blacks were still lagging far behind their brethren in other entertainment realms. Even though the first serious black theatre group, the African Company, preceded the rise of minstrelsy by some forty years, the legitimate theatre — as exemplified by New York's Broadway district — was still pretty much a closed shop to blacks. But all that began to change in the early 1900s thanks to an aggressive group of African American playwrights and composers. Ragtime helped them get their foot in the door of New York's theatre world; but a number of them were college and conservatory-trained and even had a wider frame of musical reference. This gathering into the fold of Broadway marked the first significant acceptance of African-Art and its creators as a part of the broad mainstream of American culture. These men and women included: the performing-writing teams of Miller and Lyles, Cole and Johnson, and Tutt and Whitney; comedian-entrepreneur S.H. Dudley; Lester Walton (later United States minister to Liberia); and the most popular of all turn-of-the century entertainers, Sissieretta Jones, a.k.a. Black Patti (though she never quite made it to Broadway). (Such transitional figures are discussed in the Afterword.)

None made more of an impact than Will Marion Cook, the composer-producer-conductor who first brought black entertainment out of the boondocks and byways and launched it onto America's Great White Way.

Will Marion Cook, circa 1900.

Cook is the "Great 'Lost' American Theatrical Composer." The three, now all but forgotten Broadway musicals he wrote for the legendary comedy team of Bert Williams and George Walker in the early 20th century were huge successes. He also carved out a significant niche in the history of jazz; his 1906 outfit, the Memphis Students, was arguably the first-ever jazz big band.[1] Famous in his day, Cook has since been reduced to a footnote in theatre music and jazz surveys. But his artistic contributions should not be overestimated, for he played a pivotal role in the evolution of American popular music forms.

Duke Ellington called him "the master of all the masters of our people,"[2] Eubie Blake thought he was the reincarnation of Richard Wagner and the "most eccentric man I ever met,"[3] Frederick Douglass, early to recognize his talent, helped fund his European violin studies[4]; and James Weldon Johnson deemed him "the most original genius among all the Negro musicians."[5] Yet in all likelihood even the most avid devotees of American Popular Music have never heard of the man they are all talking about.

Born in 1869 and active until his death in 1944, Cook wrote and produced the first African American musical to ever appear on Broadway, and played a major role in bringing jazz to the concert arena. And yet, despite these and all of his other accomplishments, Cook has come to be known primarily to scholars. The reasons for this are many and complex, going beyond the racial discrimination experienced by others in this book; he was also undone by an inability to affect compromise of any sort. As an example, one need look no further than an incident that happened early in his career when Cook marched into the *New York Times* newsroom, stormed up to the paper's white music critic and began to berate the man who had just called him in print the world's greatest living "Negro violinist." Then Cook angrily lashed out, "What I've been trying to be is the greatest violinist, not the greatest Negro violinist." He then smashed his instrument on the writer's desk and stormed out, vowing never again to play it in public.[6] He kept his word. According to Cook's son Mercer, in a 1912 Clef Club concert at Carnegie Hall, his father only conducted but did not play. Another time, according to the son, he merely held the instrument and pretended to play, for which he received a fee of ten dollars. However, Cook did continue to practice the violin throughout his life.[7]

Measured against such fierce and preternaturally militant behavior, even the "Tiger Woman of Show Business"— Mabel Whitman of the next chapter — seems like a relative pussycat. Cook is recalled by many who knew him as "difficult" and set in his ways, with definite opinions concerning matters racial and otherwise. This fiercely proud black man had a capacity for spotting racial prejudice that was surely as finely tuned as his musical sense. However, during the most productive period in Cook's life, he had no connection with the various Back-to-Africa schemes and organizations, via which he could have conceivably vented his anger and frustration.[8]

The composite picture that emerges is of a man easy to respect but difficult to warm up to. He made many professional enemies, among the first of whom was his initial music publisher, Isadore Witmark. It was shortly after the 1898 opening of Cook's and Paul Laurence Dunbar's first musical *Clorindy* that the composer brought about a dissolution of his relationship with the powerful house of Witmark, charging that the company was cheating him on royalties.[9] Such behavior toward a white-run business by a black was considered completely unacceptable for the times, even from the point of view of most (understandably cautious) blacks. It was perhaps incidents such as this that led poet Dunbar to eventually state, "No, I won't do it. I just can't work with Cook; he irritates me beyond endurance," when asked why he had ceased collaborating with the composer.[10]

It has often been suggested that Cook's severely diminished renown over the years was a result not *just* of racism and changing fads and fashions in music, but also his irascibility and hard-nosed opinionation. In 1926, for example, he wrote an angry letter to the fashionable writer and primary patron of the Harlem Renaissance Carl Van Vechten, imploring him to "stop exploiting the unready poets, musicians and actors of my race. It only unfits them for the supreme test."[11] Always the defender of uniquely black art forms, he also wrote a letter that same year to the editor of the *New York Times* in which he correctly disputed theatrical impresario George White's contentions that he had invented the dances, the Charleston and the Black Bottom: "I have great respect for Mr. White, his genius as an organizer and producer of revues, but why do an injustice to the black folk of America by taking from them credit of introducing new and characteristic dances?"[12]

Yet, for all Will Marion's seeming prickliness, his son, the late Mercer Cook, a professor of romance languages at Howard University and American ambassador to Senegal, remembered his father as a man whose hard shell belied his essentially generous and compassionate nature. In 1944 in the NAACP publication "The Crisis: A Record of the Darker Races," he wrote, "I don't pretend to know all the people my Dad helped, nor would I intimate that all of his beneficiaries were forgetful of his favors. Because of his erratic temperament, it was not always easy to remain on close terms with him long enough to reciprocate."[13]

James Weldon Johnson's attitude toward his friend was perhaps best summed up in a confidential letter in which he wrote, "He has many of those personal peculiarities and eccentricities which we, no doubt, ought to expect and excuse in original geniuses."[14]

Cook's wife Abbie Mitchell, the soprano who originated the role of Clara in *Porgy and Bess*, echoed her son's sentiments that behind Cook's off-putting exterior there lay flexibility, generosity and kindness of immense proportions: "He would ask for and accept the criticism of the layman and profit by it. He was absolutely honest. Whatever he believed in he fought for. He was always ready to help anyone with talent whether he were Negro or white. His whole heart and soul and being were dedicated to making the Negro realize his possessions."[15]

So why was Cook's "problem" with racism so all-consuming? As a child prodigy, he had spent a large part of his teen years studying in Europe where the combined impact of his race and great talent resulted in his being treated almost like some exotic, perhaps superior being from another world. It follows that, when Cook finally returned to America at age 20 in 1889, he found himself totally ill-equipped to "accommodate" racial prejudice in any way, shape or form. At a time when perhaps even the most radical of African Americans saw the wisdom of occasional compromise, Cook would not, *could not* budge. Wrote one music historian:

> He had received cultured and humane treatment in Europe and refused to tolerate anything less in America. Faced with American prejudice and the normal frustrations and competitions of the professional music world, Cook became ever more suspicious of people's motives and more ill-tempered. Cook was not a loner by nature, but he tended to isolate himself, often moving quickly to insult or call into question others' motives. He was bound to run into trouble in a business that relied heavily upon personal contacts, friendship and mutual trust.[16]

*   *   *

The second of three sons, Will Marion Cook (christened Will Mercer) was born in 1869 in Washington, D.C. Both of his parents were from free black families, and graduates of Oberlin College. After getting his law degree from Howard University in 1871, Cook's father John Hartwell Cook became a professor and dean of the Law Department there, and was also the first black lawyer in the District of Columbia. John Cook died when Will was ten and the boy's mother, Marion, became responsible for support of the family. She was able to maintain her brood at a genteel poverty level during her sons' early years by teaching seamstress arts at Howard, and other related activities.

Will Marion had an aptitude for music from a very early age, and at 13 was sent off to live with an aunt in Ohio in order to attend Oberlin Preparatory School Conservatory. He matured rapidly as a violinist, was deemed a prodigy and soon was sent abroad to study with the help of a scholarship fund begun with a $2000 contribution by abolitionist Frederick Douglass. Aspects of his life were used as the basis of émigré Czechoslovakian writer Josef Skvorecky's 1987 novel *Dvorak in Love*, in which Will Marion appears as a major character.[17] The novelist's sources include an unpublished autobiographical fragment by Cook,[18] the proposed title of which was, fittingly, *A Helluva Life*. In the style of all of his exercises in fictionalized history, the Czech writer alternates actual facts with historical impressionism.

The first chapter of *Dvorak in Love*, "The Moor," is largely devoted to evoking the impression of exoticism made by a black man living in Europe in the 1880s. In Skvorecky's fanciful depiction of his subject's violin playing, there is an elusive sob — an emotional musical *attack* that more than makes up for any technical deficiencies. This ineffable "sound" is, of course, the early stirrings of a Hoo-Doo strain, the fabled Blue Note as it were, bubbling up from Cook's collective unconscious long before the jazz idiom even existed.[19]

During the three years Cook spent in Berlin, he lived in the home of his music teacher, world-famous violinist Josef Joachim; ill health caused him to return to America. After his arrival back in the U.S., 20-year-old Cook made his professional debut in Washington, D.C., and in 1891 was appointed director of the new (black) Fleetwood Orchestra, whose president was Cook's patron, Douglass.

In 1893, Cook, Douglass and Paul Laurence Dunbar formulated plans for an August 25 event at the Chicago World's Fair (the World Columbian Exhibition) to be known as Colored American Day. But the notion of according dignity to blacks in such a fashion was radical for its day and much belittled in the press. According to the picture painted in William S. McFeely's *Frederick Douglass*, the affair got off to a demeaning start, with vendors hawking watermelons. Things improved as the day wore on, with a Douglass speech; a musical performance by his grandson Joseph; a poem by Dunbar, "Colored Americans," written especially for the occasion; and a duet from an opera based on *Uncle Tom's Cabin* that Cook was then in the process of composing.[20]

Shortly afterward, Cook moved to New York City to pursue further musical training, and in 1894 began studying composition with the great Czech composer Antonín Dvořák who was in the U.S. teaching and lecturing at Manhattan's National Conservatory of Music. Cook lasted less than a year at the school — bad feelings arose between Dvořák and himself — and he abruptly abandoned the institution.[21] More significantly, he also began turning away from the classics entirely in favor of jazz music, just beginning to surface (at least in more avant garde quarters) as a seriously considered musical form.

Opinions differ as to the cause of Cook's abrupt career transition. One theory is that the falling-out with Dvořák precipitated the decision. Another has it that the circle of young forward-thinking black artists who befriended Cook in New York — including singer-composer Harry Burleigh, pianist-composer J. Rosamund Johnson, and the latter's brother James Weldon Johnson (teacher, poet and later U.S. consul to Venezuela) — might have also played a part by their urging him to experiment with indigenously American musical forms such as the newly emerging ragtime.[22] A determining factor might also have been the devastating experiences he had while with the Boston Symphony Orchestra early in his career. As a member of its string section, Cook came in line for the job of first violinist and was given the position ... literally. That is, he was allowed to sit in the first chair, but could not play solos because of his race. According to a man who knew him well, Arthur Briggs, first trumpet player with Cook's Southern Syncopated Orchestra, from then on Will Marion's attitude was, "If I can't get fame, I'd like to make money."[23] Perhaps to disguise the fact that he was now trafficking in less "respectable" musical forms, Cook told one and all that the project he was about to embark upon with partner Paul Laurence Dunbar was a one-act opera, to be known as *Clorindy: The Origin of the Cakewalk.* But the resultant musical comedy landed far off to one side of European opera tradition.

Prior to working on *Clorindy,* neither man had had much experience in writing for the stage; however, Dunbar was already well on his way to fame and acceptance as the most respected (by blacks *and* whites) African American poet in America, having been discovered and nurtured by fellow writer William Dean Howells. His *Lyrics from a Lowly Life* had recently been published and he was being widely praised as the black equivalent of white poet John Whitcomb Riley. Dunbar Societies began springing up in black communities all over the U.S. Many years later, Cook recalled the achievement of polishing off the show with Dunbar in short order:

We got together in the basement of my brother John's rented house on [Washington, D.C.'s] Sixth Street, just below Howard University, one night about eight o'clock. We got two dozen bottles of beer, a quart of whiskey, and we took my brother's porterhouse steak, cut it up with red onions and red peppers and ate it raw. Without a piano or anything but a kitchen table, we finished all the songs, all the libretto and all but a few bars of the ensembles by four o'clock the next morning.[24]

A few days after completing the marathon writing session, Cook was sitting at the piano going over what would become the most popular song from his forthcoming show, an irony-charged paean to the necessity of black economic independence, "Who Dat Say Chicken in Dis Crowd," when his mother, who had been cooking breakfast, came into the parlor with tears streaming down her cheeks. In an autobiographical fragment left by Cook, he recalls how she cried out to him for an explanation for his seemingly inexcusable about-face, for she was deeply ashamed of her son's debased musical ambitions. "Oh, Will! Will! I've sent you all over the world to study and become a great musician, and you return such a *nigger!*" she said, leading him to later reflect, "My mother was a graduate of Oberlin in the class of 1865 and thought that a Negro composer should write just like a white man. They all loved the Dunbar lyrics but they weren't ready for Negro songs."[25]

The guiding force behind *Clorindy* (which was soon to become the first black musical to ever appear on Broadway) was the popular comedy team of Williams and Walker—George Walker and his partner Bert Williams, who after Walker's death in 1909 would go on to become the first major African American star. Williams and Walker had given Cook the necessary money to get back to Washington to work on *Clorindy*, and when they heard the results they were impressed enough to advance him the funds to return to New York to try and get the show produced. In keeping with his grandiose self-confidence (even as a struggling songwriter), Cook started at the top. Back in New York he took *Clorindy* to M. Witmark and Sons, one of the great music houses of the time. After listening patiently to Cook audition for three-quarters of an hour, Isadore Witmark told him that it was crazy to think that any Broadway audience would listen to Negroes singing Negro opera; but as for the songs themselves, he loved them and was anxious to publish them. Still, that left the problem of getting the show produced. As described in *The Redd Foxx Encyclopedia of Black Humor*, it was an obstacle that Cook met in typical head-on fashion:

Trying for months to talk Edward E. Rice, the [Casino] theater's manager, into granting his company an audition, Cook was repeatedly refused. For over a month he nearly camped out in Rice's office, but to no avail. Finally, out of desperation, Cook took his well-rehearsed cast of twenty-six to an open audition. He had prepared a little surprise for Rice: When the manager entered the audition room, the entire cast broke into a rousing chorale number, "Darktown Is Out Tonight." Rice was swept up by the strikingly rhythmic beat and he booked the show into his theater."[26]

By 1898, the year *Clorindy: The Origin of the Cakewalk* premiered at the Casino Roof, there had already been a number of all-black cast pageants that had played in undistinguished settings throughout the country, including the mammoth *Black America* performed in Brooklyn three years earlier in 1895 (see Chapter Three). But a white Broadway audience had never been witness to such an event. Admittedly, the Casino was a rooftop location, but technically it qualified as a Broadway house (one which was patronized almost exclusively by whites), guaranteeing that, whatever its fate, *Clorindy* would receive major critical and audience recognition.

So bold was the concept of an all-black Broadway musical, producer-manager Rice was opposed to the extra-added novelty of Cook leading the orchestra. It was one thing for blacks to be able to sing and dance, but the role of conductor was an authority figure position. When Rice got wind of the fact that Cook was going to go against his wishes, he stormed into the theater. Rice's house conductor, Englishman John Braham, came to Cook's defense, lashing out at Rice, "Ed, go back to your little cubbyhole and keep quiet! This boy's a genius and has something great!"; Rice quickly backed off.[27] Opening night, Cook and his cast of theatrical upstarts faced a grim picture:

"When I entered the orchestra pit," Cook later recalled, "there were only about fifty people on the Roof [the Casino Roof Garden]."[28]

By the end of the opening chorus, however, "the house was," in Cook's words, "packed to suffocation. What had happened was that the show downstairs in the Casino Theatre was just letting out. The big audience heard those heavenly Negro voices and took to the elevators. At the finish of the opening chorus, the applause and cheering were so tumultuous that I simply stood there transfixed, my hand in the air, unable to move until [star Ernest] Hogan rushed down to the footlights and shouted: 'What's the matter, son? Let's go!' My chorus sang like Russians, dancing meanwhile like Negroes and cakewalking like angels, black angels! When the last note was sounded, the audience stood and cheered for ten minutes.

"I was so delirious," remembers Cook, "that I drank a glass of water, thought it wine and got gloriously drunk. Negroes were at last on Broadway, and there to stay. Gone was uff-dah of the minstrel! Gone the Massa Linkum stuff! We were artists and we were going a long, long way. We had the world on a string tied to a red-geared wagon on a down-hill pull. Nothing could stop us, and nothing did for a decade."[29]

The next day *Clorindy* was the major topic of the theatrical main stem; it ran throughout the rest of the summer and resulted in knockoffs springing up almost immediately around the Times Square area (although not technically on Broadway like *Clorindy*), such as Cole and Johnson's *Kings of Koondom* which opened in August of that year. Sad to say, it would take another half-century before an African American starring in a Broadway musical — Sammy Davis, Jr., in the 1950s' *Mr. Wonderful* (see Chapter 9) — would be dealt with more for reasons of sheer talent and ability, rather than in racial terms.

Clorindy came along at just the point in the evolution of popular music when minstrel shows were giving way to ragtime. It was part of Cook's greatness that he realized that there was a place for this music in the mainstream of the American Musical Theater, and not just stuck off to one side in regional vaudeville or in out-of-the-way theatrical venues such as was the case with other all-black shows.

After *Clorindy*, Cook worked on two other productions, *Jes Lak White Folks* (1899), described as a "one-act Negro operetto" with lyrics by both himself and Dunbar,"[30] and *The Casino Girl* (1900), a traditional all-white Broadway musical. He also contributed songs to two Bert Williams-George Walker touring shows, *The Policy Players* in 1900 and, two years later, *Sons of Ham*. Then in 1903 Cook provided nearly the complete score for another precedent-shattering undertaking, *In Dahomey*, the first full-length musical (as opposed to the one-act *Clorindy*) written and played by blacks to be presented at a major Broadway theater. The producers, however, were the all-powerful white team of Hurtig and Seamon whose initial full $15,000 backing of the show eventually netted them a 400 percent return, thus giving the lie to the prevailing notion of the day that black shows didn't make money.[31]

In Dahomey's basic plot, which concerned itself with a group of blacks who return to Mother Africa, was penned by J.A. Shipp, a well-known writer and performer who wrote the libretto for two subsequent Williams-Walker shows, *Abyssinia* and *Bandana Land*. Its primary lyricist Alex Rogers was also Cook's partner on these later productions. The idea for *In Dahomey* originated in experiences that Williams and Walker had while they were performing in proximity to real Africans when the two men worked at the San Francisco Mid-Winter Fair (or Exposition) some years earlier.[32] Because neither Shipp nor Williams and Walker really knew very much about Africa, most of the story's action was set in Boston and Florida with only the last act taking place on the "Dark Continent." (Dahomey was the West African French colony on the Gulf of Guinea that is now known as the nation of Benin.) To gauge the terror struck into the heart of the New York theater community by the coming of *In Dahomey*, one need look no further than the opening lines of a review of the production that appeared in the *New York Times*:

> A thundercloud has been fathering of late in the faces of the established Broadway managers. Since it was announced that Williams and Walker, with their all-negro musical comedy, *In Dahomey*, were booked to appear at the New York Theatre, there have been times when trouble breeders foreboded a race war.[33]

An almost wholly negative review of *In Dahomey* appearing in the old *Life Magazine* (not the Henry Luce publication) on March 13, 1903, echoed the *New York Times*: "[The Negro] may be a man and a brother all right, but when it comes to touching elbows with him for an entire evening, your New Yorker objects quite as strenuously as the Southerner. The management of the New York Theatre met this predicament by assigning seats for negroes [*sic*] in separate parts of the house."[34]

Despite all this racist controversy, Bert Williams was thrilled at finally getting a show on Broadway proper; he later wrote, "The way we've aimed at Broadway and just missed it in the past seven years would make you cry... I used to be tempted to beg for a fifteen dollar job in a chorus for one week so as to be able to say I'd been on Broadway."[35]

By Broadway standards *In Dahomey* was not a hit. It ran only 53 performances in the U.S., but there was life left in the show yet: As would prove to be the case with several other future Cook endeavors, *In Dahomey*'s greatest triumph was to be had on foreign shores. On April 28, 1903, *In Dahomey*'s entire company (including Cook) sailed for London where the show became the first all-black cast production to ever play the city when it opened at the Shaftesbury Theatre on May 16. It was loosely structured to begin with; by the time the production reached London, it was more like a vaudeville than a "book show." Wrote one reviewer, "[T]he wildly inconsequential abruptness of the way in which there was suddenly no more of *In Dahomey* about 11 P.M. on Saturday had to be seen to be believed."[36] The orchestra had to play "God Save the Queen" to signal the audience that the performance was indeed over.[37] The *Pall Mall Gazette* noted that the third act went "all to pieces in a manner which is little short of bewildering."[38]

Despite the on-stage confusion, the Williams-Walker extravaganza still managed to secure a set of almost uniformly positive reviews: "A welcome sensation of surprise" ... "There is a totally irresponsible sense of gaiety about the entertainment which graced the boards of the Shaftesbury Saturday night" ... "The large class of Londoners who are found of musical comedy will find a new sensation in [*In Dahomey*]." Others of this stripe are quoted by Jeffrey Green in a 1983 magazine article.[39]

The major dissenting voice, the evening newspaper *The Globe*, found a problem with the absence of "the negro (sic) in the rough" and "a composer [Cook] writing under white training, influence and inspiration." In other words, *In Dahomey* was found seriously lacking when it came to—in the words of Will Marion Cook describing his earlier *Clorindy* breakthrough—minstrel "uff-dah" and "Massa Linkum stuff." But, small matter: *In Dahomey* settled in at the Shaftesbury Theatre for what probably would have proved to be a mildly profitable run followed by a return to the U.S. had it not been for a tremendous publicity boost: a Command Performance request by the King of England to perform numbers from the show at Buckingham Palace as part of the young Prince of Wales' birthday celebration.[40] Overnight, *In Dahomey* went from mere hit show status to become the theatrical rage of London. George Bernard Shaw saw the show and afterward wrote to a colleague: "By far, the best acting now in London is that of Williams and Walker in *In Dahomey*. I shall certainly ask Williams to play Ftatateeta [Cleopatra's maid in *Caesar and Cleopatra*]." It is not known, however, whether Shaw actually approached Williams about the role.[41]

The troupe remained in London for a triumphant seven months and afterward toured throughout the British Isles for nearly a year, with Cook reporting back home that — with the exception of occasional problems with hotel accommodations (travelling Americans objecting to black performers ensconced in their hotels) — "the image in ivory recognizes the image in ebony as an equal and a brother."[42]

Midway through *Dahomey*'s British tour, Cook returned to America, drawn by the chance to collaborate with Broadway's top lyricist, Harry B. Smith, on the production *The Southerners*. Aside from the opportunity to work with a songwriter of Smith's caliber (he wrote the lyrics of such hits as "The Sheik of Araby," "Yours Is My Heart Alone" and the popular musical *Robin Hood*), what clearly also attracted him was the fact that *The Southerners* represented a shot at *another* first. Up until then, blacks had been seen on stage as chorus members in shows fronted by whites; *The Southerners* would be the first New York production to display both whites and blacks performing as characters.

Cook and Smith were surely one of the pioneering interracial Broadway songwriting duos, but you'd never have guessed it from looking at the program for the show when it finally opened on May 23, 1904, at the New York Theatre, the same house where *Dahomey* had premiered the previous year: Smith was listed as "Richard Grant" and Cook as "Will Mercer" (his actual middle name). If Cook's partner had been the only one to use a pseudonym, the assumption might have been that highly prolific Smith wanted to stave off increasing criticism that he was spreading himself too thin (he sometimes had as many as a half-dozen shows running on Broadway at any given time). Both men using *noms de plume*, however, suggests another possibility: that turn-of-the-century Broadway was not quite ready for the idea of an interracial songwriting team. Whatever the reason, *The Southerners* was a flop, closing after only 36 performances.

After its failure, Cook returned once more to the Williams and Walker fold. The resulting effort, *Abyssinia* (1906), was a much more opulent and, at the same time, artful show, and was indicative of George Walker's increasing interest in the *idea* of Africa, a place that was still as exotic and as otherworldly as the far side of the moon. As with *In Dahomey*, the libretto was by J.A. Shipp and the lyrics were primarily by the previous production's Alex Rogers.

In his *American Musical Theatre* writer Gerald Bordman outlines *Abyssinia*'s action as follows:

> After Rastus Johnson (Bert Williams) wins $15,000 in a lottery, Rastus and Jasmine (Walker) decide to visit the land of their ancestors which they have determined was Abyssinia. (The stage Abyssinia displayed real water pouring down a waterfall in a mountain pass, and a colorful bazaar with a "property lion and camel and real asses.") Their ignorance of foreign ways leads Rastus and Jasmine into several misadventures culminating before the throne of Abyssinia's iron-fisted monarch, Menelik. They are brought there as a court of last appeal after they "borrowed" a priceless vase. If Menelik sounds a gong three times, the "borrowers" must die, if he sounds it four times, they are pardoned. The long wait before the third and fourth gong provided a memorable scene, at once comic and terrifying.

Bordman adds, "One interesting feature of J.A. Shipp and Alex Rogers' libretto and lyrics was the way African blacks and American blacks were contrasted. Apparently, Shipp and Rogers wanted to suggest that coming to America marked a falling away from grace, if not perfection. The Africans speak the King's English. Indeed some of their dialogue and lyrics are so stilted they smack of parody. On the other hand the Americans speak lines straight out of minstrelsy."[43] *Abyssinia* had a short New York run but toured the U.S. for many months.

The third entry in the Williams and Walker-Will Marion Cook trilogy of Broadway productions was the only one to take place entirely on U.S. soil and contained the daring plot device of blacks putting one over on the white man when they strong-arm a railroad company into buying some property at a highly inflated price. *Bandana Land* opened at Broadway's Majestic Theatre on February 3, 1908, and received the best reviews of the three shows. It remained there for eleven weeks before setting off on the obligatory tour.

It would have been even more successful had it not been for illness befalling George Walker. Early on in the run, the comedian began to display very noticeable signs of paresis resulting from a long-untreated case of syphilis. He became incapable of satisfactorily completing performances and while on tour had to leave the company with his part being taken over by his wife, the popular Ada Overton Walker, who commenced to perform her husband's part in male attire.

Walker died the following year in a nursing home, bringing to an end the team of Williams and Walker as well as the production trio of Jesse Shipp, Alex Rogers and Will Marion Cook. These three, as well as Bert Williams, continued to successfully operate in the theater and in other areas of artistic endeavor with Williams' ten-year association with *Ziegfeld Follies* resulting in his becoming one of the most beloved and successful performers of the era.

After establishing himself with the Williams and Walker shows, Cook went on to become a prominent contributor to the artistic climate of black

New York and the first stirrings of the oncoming Harlem Renaissance of the 1920s. He brought together Negro choral societies, conducted "all-colored" composers concerts and wrote and gave lectures about African American art and music. In 1912 Cook was one of the founders of the Negro Players, a pioneer black stock company. Among its members were Henry Creamer, later of the songwriting team of Creamer and Layton ("Way Down Yonder in New Orleans," "After You've Gone"), wife Abbie Mitchell and actor Charles Gilpin, soon to originate the title role in Eugene O'Neill's *The Emperor Jones.*

* * *

"That's the man who taught me to conduct," Eubie Blake said of Cook. "I believe he was the reincarnation of Richard Wagner—looked like him too.... Cook never wore a hat because he was proud of his bushy hair. That was all that gave him away so you could know he was a Negro. Most eccentric man I ever met."[44] To illustrate, Eubie related to his biographer Al Rose an incident that took place early in Blake's career when Cook helped him sell a song to a music publisher. The deal was set, then offhandedly the publisher inquired about a certain peculiarity in Blake's piano playing.

"He's just curious," Eubie recalled. "Then suddenly Cook gets very indignant. He says, 'How dare you criticize Mr. Blake? He's a great artist. What do *you* know about genuine African music? *That's* genuine African music'— he's lyin' now. 'I insist that you apologize to him.'"[45] Cook ended up botching the deal.

Clef Club leader James Reese Europe was murdered in 1919 — stabbed to death by a mentally deranged musician whom the leader had reprimanded for ambling around the stage during others' performances— and Cook subsequently became more active as a conductor of the black musicians' union-fraternal organization's various activities. This included leading one of the first bands to perform on regular transmissions during the very earliest days of radio. These appearances constituted what must have been the very first live broadcasts of big band jazz.[46]

Cook's first experience with a large jazz music ensemble took place in 1905, when he acted as musical consultant, arranger and rehearsal conductor for the well-known ensemble, the Memphis Students. The outfit, not really students but an amalgamation of the finest black musical talent from all over the country, was put together by conductor Will Dixon and noted vaudevillian Ernest Hogan, who had starred five years earlier in *Clorindy.* Originally, Cook was not the official conductor of the Students, but from the very beginning the group reflected his distinct musical touch. A major contribution Cook made to the evolution of big band jazz while overseeing the Students was pointed out by Dave Dexter, Jr., in his book, *The Jazz Story*: "As far back as 1905, it is said that Will Marion Cook employed saxophones for the first time in a pop orchestra at Proctor's Twenty-Third Street Theater, a great vaudeville palace second only to the Palace on Broadway at Times Square."[47] And, as noted by author J.C. Thomas in a biography of John Coltrane, after Cook's early experimentation with the still-young instrument (invented in 1846), "It wasn't really heard from [again] until after World War I, and then mainly in a vaudeville context."[48]

The Memphis Students made history with their concerts of syncopated music at Proctor's and also at Hammerstein's Victoria Theatre on Broadway. In October of 1905, Cook and the group sailed for Europe where they filled a date at Paris' Olympia Theatre followed by stands at the Palace Theatre in London and at the Schumann Circus in Berlin. Abroad, the band was known as the Tennessee Students, more than likely to avoid a lawsuit from the original "Memphis" group's owner, Ernest Hogan, who claimed that Cook had absconded with his musicians.[49] The Students scored only modest success in Europe, but in the more than three-quarters of a century since then, they have come to be regarded as a cornerstone in the formation of big band jazz, with Cook viewed as the group's guiding spirit and primary artistic inspiration.

In 1912 Cook took part in an event given by the black musical fraternity, the Clef Club, at Carnegie Hall. Featuring his "Rain Song" and "Swing Along," it was the first jazz concert ever — although other kinds of music were also performed — staged more than a decade before white bandleader Paul Whiteman "officially" made musical history by presenting nearly the exact same kind of program at New York's Aeolian Hall in 1924 ("Rhapsody in Blue," etc.).[50] The sanctum of Carnegie had probably never seen, nor the full house in attendance had ever heard, the likes of what happened on that May 2nd evening in 1912: Conductor James Reese Europe's musical contingent consisted of approximately fifty mandolins, twenty violins, thirty harp-guitars (bandolines), ten cellos, one (!) saxophone, ten banjos, two organs, ten pianos, five flutes, five bass-viols, five clarinets and three timpani and drums.[51]

Typically, Cook sat in the violin section but did not play — keeping to his vow never to perform in public again. However, when he was recognized by the audience he came forward and conducted several selections.

Had he been able, Europe might have also indulged his fancy for an obscure wind instrument (name unknown) made out of the chinaberry tree which was, according to him, "something like a clarinet, and is made by the Southern negroes [sic] themselves." "Strange to say," the orchestra leader wrote in 1919 (some years after the Carnegie Hall affair), "it can only be used while the sap is in the wood, and after a few weeks' use has to be thrown away. It produces a beautiful sound and is worthy of inclusion in any band or orchestra. I myself intend to employ it soon in my band."[52] But only a few weeks after this was written — a month into a triumphant "Welcome Home" tour of Europe's U.S. Infantry Hellfighters Band — Europe was dead.

What the extraordinary Clef Club amalgamation of instruments (even minus the chinaberry device) sounded like in 1912 is almost impossible to imagine. However, on July 14, 1989, a scaled-down recreation of the event at Carnegie Hall, consisting of somewhat fewer than a hundred players (four pianos etc.), the Morgan State University Male Choir and the Harlem Boys' Choir, made a brave and successful attempt at approximating the sound of the 1912 concert. Just like at the original event, Cook's "Rain Song" and "Swing Along" were the undisputed hits of an evening that in more tradition-minded times might have passed for a historic occasion.

As for the way the presentation *looked*: Maurice Peress, who filled the shoes of Europe for the 1989 recreation, remarked in a NPR radio broadcast of the concert:

> I think there is some minstrelsy in the Clef Club event in Carnegie Hall; the way they set themselves up in the big half-moon circle. In fact, there's a photograph of the Clef Club which shows a kind of banjo, tambourine group on a little stage in the back of the Manhattan dance hall up on 155th Street where they gave that concert [shown in the photo]. I think there was certainly an effect on the Clef Club presentation from minstrelsy. It's not a bad word, you know. There were black minstrels and white minstrels and there were traditions that carried over and reached back.[53]

Besides Cook, other important African American contributors to the identical evenings of music (separated by 77 years) included J. Rosamond Johnson, Wilbur Sweatman, William H. Tyers and H.T. Burleigh.

In 1918, after a long stay in his homeland, Cook once again set about gathering together in one large orchestra a contingent of the very finest black instrumentalists and singers in North America for another tour of Europe. It was to be equipped to perform not just folk, pop and jazz, but the European classical repertoire as well. Thus, not only would his Southern Syncopated Orchestra (as the group was to be called) play Cook's own compositions and arrangements, but music by the likes of Brahms, Grieg, and African American classicist Samuel Coleridge-Taylor. For his star soloist, Cook secured saxophonist Sidney Bechet, even at this early stage in his career regarded as a master musician and improviser. And as such, he received a $500 advance — and four crates of toilet soap to offset his fear of a European soap shortage.[54]

If Will Marion Cook had done nothing else of importance in his professional lifetime, his having brought Sidney Bechet to Europe in 1919 would have secured for him a small but crucial niche in jazz history. The saxophonist became well-known during his initial tour of Europe with Cook (whom Bechet called "the old man"), and when he returned to France after World War II, the way was paved for his ascension to the status of a near-deity in that country.

Advertisements for the U.S. tour of the band exhorted its readers to "insist on your friends in both races to attend"; however, scattered appearances in Philadelphia and a few other cities did not draw a large audience of "friends" of either race, and in early June 1919 the musicians departed New York on the SS *Carmania* and the SS *Northland* for London. "We sailed in a cattle boat; the trip took fifteen days and we were all sick as dogs," Bechet later recalled.[55]

As was the case with *In Dahomey,* whose initial tepid U.S. reception was redeemed by European raves, Cook's Syncopators (more or less snubbed in the U.S.) were greeted with open arms and a boost from an important source, the eminent Swiss classical conductor Ernest Ansermet. It was at Philharmonic Hall that Ansermet first heard Cook's band and proceeded to write in the publication "Swiss Revue Romande": "The first thing that strikes one about the Southern Syncopated Orchestra is the astonishing perfection, the superb taste, and the fervor of its playing.... The musician who directs them and who is responsible for creating the ensemble [Cook] is, moreover, a master in every respect, and there is no orchestra leader I so delight in seeing."[56]

Ansermet's assessment of Cook's orchestra went on to become a historically important piece of jazz criticism, marking the first significant recognition of African American music in Eurocentric quarters (various portions of the Ansermet article have been reprinted in almost every significant book on jazz that has appeared since then).

The instrumentation of the Southern Syncopated Orchestra was highly unorthodox, revealing a West Indian influence in the choice of instruments which consisted of, in addition to a choir of twenty voices: two pianos, four bandolines, a drum, a tympanium, two basses, French horn, two trumpets, three trombones, cello, clarinet, flute, two saxes and two violins.[57] "It was really quite a show," writes Bechet in his autobiography *Treat It Gentle.* "One day Cook came up to me, that was in August of 1919, and very quiet-like told me there was to be a special performance at Buckingham Palace, a command performance.... It was the first time I ever got to recognize somebody [King George V] from his picture on my money."[58]

The musical organization was a large and unwieldy one, containing forty-two pieces, including twenty singers, and was soon beset by serious financial problems. Before long, many of its players and sections were being chopped away from the ensemble and sent off, piecemeal, back to America; however, many of the members remained in Europe to fan out across the British Isles and the continent to bring increased vitality to the transatlantic jazz scene.

Cook's wife Abbie was an important part of the "Syncopated" band, with Bechet remembering that once when she was performing "Un Bel Di" from Puccini's *Madama Butterfly,* he came forward without warning and suddenly began to *swing* Puccini's aria. The impromptu performance was a big hit; nevertheless, afterward Cook said to Bechet, "But, Sidney, why didn't you ask me?" Replied Bechet, "If I had warned you, you never would have allowed it."[59]

Only fourteen when she married Cook, Mitchell divorced him in 1906 after their second child was born. But the two continued to work professionally together as late as 1928 when he was her accompanist at a concert at New York's Lafayette Theatre.[60]

What the unrecorded Southern Syncopated Orchestra and Cook's music in general sounded like — although some of his scores survive — can be approximated by listening to such sources as: the early–20th century march music of John Philip Sousa (which also played a small but important part in the evolution of orchestral jazz); a handful of recordings by Cook's colleague James Reese Europe, one of the few blacks to be recorded to any great degree before the phono color line was finally broken down in the late teens; early wax efforts by Broadway performers like Eddie Cantor and Fannie Brice (who often used up-to-date black arrangers and musicians in the recording studio); and, finally, the 1921 discs of bandleader Fletcher Henderson, who took the early arranging and compositional innovations of men like Cook and Europe and used them as the basis for launching the full-scale big band jazz movement, which took hold in the 1920s.[61] All of the above, to one degree or another, intentionally looked toward Cook for direction and ideas or were indirectly inspired by his wide-ranging musical models.

It is possible, however, that Cook's ultimate contribution to the evolution of jazz is something for which he has never been given proper credit: For years, Duke Ellington scholars have contemplated the enigma of how it came to pass that Ellington's music was so thoroughly remindful of composers such as Debussy and Ravel when, in fact, he had never heard this music until relatively later in his career.[62]

"I got most of my instruction riding around Central Park in a taxi," Ellington told the *New Yorker* magazine's Richard O. Boyer in a three-part profile in 1944.[63] His teacher on these occasions was a musician who clearly *was* familiar not only with the French musical impressionists, but with the entire canon of European classical music — Will Marion Cook. Ellington recalled that, driving through the park, "I'd sing a melody and then he'd stop me and say, 'Reverse your figures.' He was a brief but strong influence. His language had to be pretty straight for me to know what he was talking about. Some of the things he used to tell me I never got a chance to use until years later, when I wrote the tone poem, 'Black, Brown and Beige.'"[64]

Nearly thirty years later, Ellington still had Cook on his mind when he wrote his memoirs, *Music Is My Mistress*, published in 1973:

> Will Marion Cook, His Majesty the King of Consonance ... I can see him now with that beautiful mane of white hair flowing in the breeze as he and I rode uptown through Central Park in the summertime in a taxi with an open top. It was always when I was browsing around Broadway, trying to make contacts with my music, that I would run into Dad Cook
> "Going uptown?" I would ask.

"Yes."

Then we would decide to stop in at one of the "friendly" publishers, and Dad would always cause a furor when he walked into one of those places, because everybody downtown in the music world knew that he was "the most" in learning. He knew enough about music to have the occasion to correct several of the masters abroad.[65]

Although Cook ceased to be a major Broadway force after his collaborative efforts with Bert Williams and George Walker, he remained active in the theater in addition to his jazz work: He co-wrote three songs for *The Ziegfeld Follies of 1910*; in 1914 he wrote and arranged music for *In Darkydom*, a Harlem revue starring the popular team of Flournoy Miller and Aubrey Lyles; and the 1927 Ethel Waters revue *Africana* introduced Cook's most famous song "I'm Comin' Virginia" (for which he wrote, atypically, only the lyrics to Donald Heywood's music). Shortly thereafter he conducted the orchestra for Waters' disc of the song in one of the few known (only) instances of Cook in the recording studio.

One of Cook's numbers from the 1910 *Ziegfeld Follies*, "Lovie Joe," was the first song Fannie Brice ever sang in the legendary series of lavish revues. When the future star was signed for the production she was a 19-year-old completely lost in the crush of dozens of Ziegfeld stars and performers, "each fighting for a song, a lyric, anything to help increase their own standing in the show," writes Brice biographer Norman Katkov. "Fanny went to the telephone and called [her mother] Rosie. Then she waited until almost everyone else had left the theater. Approaching [Will Marion's writing partner Joe] Jordan and Cook, Fanny said: 'How would you boys like a real home-cooked meal? My mom is the best cook in New York.' ... Fanny led the pair uptown to Rosie's food."[66]

After polishing off the meal prepared by Fannie's mother, the two men said they would try to help the youngster; in fact, the food was so good and they had eaten so much, Cook and Jordan felt they had no choice. Right then and there the pair began reworking and polishing a pre-existing tune of Jordan's, one that up to then had no lyrics. The next day, the result of their handiwork brought down the house *in rehearsal* (!). A few nights later, "Lovie Joe" had the same effect on a paying audience and went a long way toward establishing her as a star. For many years afterward it was a signature tune of Brice's.[67]

Toward the end of his Broadway days, Cook was named choral director of the 1929 musical *Great Day*, an infamous Vincent Youmans flop which nevertheless introduced three "standards" still widely heard today: the title tune "Hallelujah" and "Without a Song." There were also such ventures as a 1924 musical Cook devised with Abbie Mitchell, *Negro Nuances*, based on the history of blacks in North America, and a musical written with son Mercer, *St. Louis 'Ooman*. Neither, however, received full-scale productions, but were only performed in various concert settings. The problem was that by the late 1920s the landscape of the black musical had begun to change from vaudevilles like Cook's shows to more jazz-oriented productions like *Hot Chocolates*. At the same time, the frivolous Cotton Club was beginning to really flourish. Cook just didn't fit into either picture.[68] The last ten years of his life found things beginning to fade away from him; he dabbled at music publishing and writing *A Helluva Life*, but they were never finished.

In the early 1920s, Cook's re-alliance with the musicians' organization, the Clef Club (of 1912 Carnegie Hall concert fame), afforded him an opportunity to recreate his recent European musical success with the Southern Syncopated Orchestra on U.S. soil. The "Clefties," mainly under Cook's direction, became one of the first musical groups to perform on regular transmissions during the early days of radio. Paul Robeson received an early career break as a result of Cook's hiring him — along with Fletcher Henderson — to be part of a Clef Club vaudeville package that toured the east in the spring of 1923. It is interesting to note that no mention is made of Henderson in a review of the show appearing in the April 7 edition of the *Pittsburgh Courier* for that year, and that Robeson's "bass renderings of folk melodies" are given no precedence by the reviewer over the work of such long-forgotten artists as Miss E. McKinney, Bessie De Sasso and Marie DeVoe. Also on the program was Georgette Harvey, an African American entertainer once popular with members of Czar Nicholas' court who appeared regularly on the Broadway stage from 1930 through 1949. In addition to solo performers, the "Clefties" package also featured twenty-four musicians and a glee club of eight, "all conducted with that Will Marion Cook artistry and efficiency."

The African American performers and musicians Cook aided along the way, in addition to Paul Robeson, are numerous and legend. He brought together Josephine Baker and his son-in-law Lewis Douglas, the producer of the Paris production *Revue Nègre*.[69] Cook also introduced his friend and associate Will Vodery (who had assisted in orchestrating the Williams and Walker shows) to Florenz Ziegfeld when the latter, still in the early stages of his producing career, approached Cook for advice on hiring a musical director. Vodery impressed Ziegfeld, who handed him the prestigious job — a position he held for many years.[70] Cook was also one of the few respected and conservatory-trained black musicians to lend moral support to blues musicians: Perry Bradford ("Crazy Blues," "Lonesome Blues") is only one of the many such vernacular artists who benefitted. Along with Eubie Blake, other young African American musicians who looked to Will Marion Cook for guidance and inspiration were the great Harlem stride pianists Luckey Roberts and James P. Johnson.[71]

At least one major white musical figure also owes a debt of gratitude to Cook. Harold Arlen — later to compose such standards as "Blues in the Night," "Come Rain or Come Shine" and "I Love a Parade" — was 24 years old and had written only a few undistinguished tunes when he was hired as a performer and rehearsal pianist for composer Vincent Youmans' show *Great Day*, on which Cook was serving as choral director. Once during rehearsals, writes Arlen's biographer Edward Jablonski, "a song fragment strayed far enough from the original idea [of Youmans] to take on all the proportions of an original song. Will Marion Cook, a composer himself, recognized a potential song in the one-time vamp, and suggested that Arlen make a song of it."[72] Arlen took Cook's advice and the result, "Get Happy," turned out to be the big hit song from *Cotton Club Revue of 1930* (and also the Broadway show *The 9:15 Revue*) and one of the major tune successes of the year.

But Cook was primarily a booster of black talent as exemplified by his writing in 1938 an original song for a broadcast by Alberta Hunter. In promoting the NBC radio program, he wrote of the singer, "Her art is as great as that of the great French artist, Guilbert, whom all of France recently honored on her sixtieth birthday."[73] It is a testament to Cook's good taste and prescience that, by the late 1970s, octogenarian Hunter was at last experiencing a wave of major popular and critical appreciation when she returned to performing after many years spent working as a practical nurse.

In the NAACP's publication "The Crisis," Mercer Cook writes that he once witnessed his father entering the offices of the Shapiro, Bernstein Music Corporation to get $20 to send an obscure ailing Negro singer — one whom his father scarcely knew — to the country. Mercer Cook added: "I have seen him, after an unprofitable week at the old Lafayette, pay out every cent to his men and go to his furnished room without his own rent. And I have seen him object to a small daily allowance merely because it would not permit him to treat unfortunate chance acquaintances to lunch."[74]

In a retrograde irony, according to Cook's son his father was also instrumental in launching the career of blackface performer Al Jolson by introducing him to the Shubert Brothers producing team.[75]

In a series of articles about the Harlem Renaissance appearing in *The New Yorker* in 1982 (and later published in book form as *This Was Harlem*), author Jervis Anderson depicted Cook in the 1930s as a man who was "brusque, insulting and short-tempered, [resenting] the fact that racial prejudice confined him to the world of Negro music."[76] But the unflattering implications here are counterbalanced and put into perspective by an accompanying quote from Cook's friend James Weldon Johnson who said that for all of his professional life, the composer's philosophy had been "that the Negro in music and on the stage ought to be a Negro, a genuine Negro; he declared that the Negro should eschew 'white' patterns...."[77]

Toward the end of his life, Will Marion Cook was so ill with cancer that he had to be hospitalized while visiting Mercer Cook in Haiti, but he remained ever on the lookout for new talent. Recalls the younger Cook:

On one of my daily visits, not long after he entered the hospital, I was surprised to see him sitting at a table writing frantically. "There's genius down the hall," he explained, "with a voice that surpasses [French actress Sarah] Bernhardt's. I'm writing to Gene Buck, Al Jolson and Abbie [Mitchell]. If only Abbie can come down and train that girl and a few other talented Haitians, we can give Broadway its greatest thrill since Williams and Walker!" "But, Dad," I objected, "your first job is to get yourself well. Then you can start thinking about others." "Damn it!," he thundered, "I've been helping people all my life, and I don't intend to stop now!"[78]

Will Marion Cook died in New York's Harlem Hospital on July 19, 1944.

Throughout the later part of Cook's career he was closely associated with another powerful force in American music, "Father of the Blues" W.C. Handy. Their publishing offices were at one time located in the same building, and in April 1928 the "St. Louis Blues" composer brought the music of Cook back to Carnegie Hall once more when he included "Exhortation" and "Darktown Is Out Tonight" in a concert he conducted there. Sixteen years later, upon hearing of his friend's passing, W.C. Handy said:

"I had emulated our greatest conductors in the use of the baton, but when I saw Cook conducting the Clef Club of a hundred musicians and singers; when I saw him set the tempo with the sway of his body and develop perfect crescendos without a baton by the use of his open and extended palms, he was again my ideal."[79]

*   *   *

In 2000, I was accorded the privilege of acting as a consultant for a segment about Cook on the popular NPR radio program, *Fresh Air*. And in 2008, Marva Griffin Carter, associate professor of music history at the School of Music at Georgia State University, published her long-awaited biography, *Swing Along: The Musical Life of Will Marion Cook*.

A major musical Cook retrospective, something along the lines of the Duke Ellington tribute show *Sophisticated Ladies*, has still not eventuated. In 1988 I made a stab at it with a workshop production of *In Dahomey*, starring such wonderful performers as Olga James and Rif Hutton. Shortly after that, a major regional theatre group attempted a revival similar to mine. Obviously intended for Broadway, it didn't make it. Nevertheless, all of these suggest an (at last) growing public awareness of the immense part played by Cook in the evolution of American secular music, especially its jazz wing.

2

The Queens of Toby Time
The Whitman Sisters

African Americans might have taken Broadway by storm in the first decade of the last century; but west of the Hudson River the status of black entertainers was still a lowly one — as evidenced by the following letter, postmarked Birmingham, Alabama, appearing in a 1910 edition of the *Chicago Defender*:

> My name is Ruth Coleman, formerly of the team of Phil and Ruth. The tickets failed us, so to avoid laying off down here, we decided for Phil to go to Chicago where he could get work and then send for me the next week.... I wrote him ten days ago and received no reply.... Please do me the favor of going there and asking him to please send me my clothes and I will never forget your kindness.[1]

Appeals for help such as this one from an entertainer left by the wayside were common in the theatrical sections of black newspapers of the day. At any one time during the first two decades of the last century, there might have been upwards of a hundred black companies touring the South. Money and health care were deplorable, and in the South food and lodging were sometimes as hard to come by for African American performers as a seat at the front of a bus. Even the establishments that catered to traveling non-white troupers often left something to be desired.

Meals that might have previously been served to the town's people at 50 cents per plate cost the nomads 75 cents and a dollar; and the rooms that were let to locals for $2 a night sometimes went for much more to black show folk. If a performer was smart, he or she played all the angles to avoid getting stranded. Coming into a new town, for example, you'd usually meet up with people from the show that preceded yours just as they were getting ready to leave. You would ask: "How are you doing, are you getting paid?" And even if the answer was "Yes" and there was a suspicion you might not be fairly treated, you would try to get on another show. As a result, performers sometimes ended up switching employers three or four times a month. Unlike the shows' owners, most of whom were black, the theater proprietors were mostly white, which added further tension.

The Whitman Sisters, circa 1915. Left to right, Bert, Alice, Mabel, Essie (courtesy Ernestine Lucas).

According to actor Clarence Muse in his book *Way Down South*, "No matter how careful he was, the actor ... usually ended up at the close of the season as broke as when he started; having left unpaid board, lodging and laundry bills in most of the towns along the route."[2]

The fervor of the audiences, and the support and friendship you got from the other performers, were all that made such a grueling schedule for months on end bearable. It definitely wasn't the wages—except in the case of a few major stars such as Bessie Smith and ex–heavyweight champ Jack Johnson.

The length of any particular show and the number of times it was performed daily depended on the policy of the individual theater; however, three 45–minute shows nightly was not uncommon. Overwhelmingly these productions had catchy, pointedly racial titles such as *Brown Babies, Chocolate Box Revue, Sambo Jones in New York*, and even *Ebony Vampires*, leading one to ponder the question of why such demeaning titles were used on shows directed toward an African American clientele. Whatever the shortcomings of such presentations, inarguably the majority possessed a high degree of musical quality. Rare is the black jazz player who came to prominence in the twenties, thirties or forties who failed to pay his or her dues in black traveling shows in the South and Midwest, either as a musician traveling with a unit, or else in the pit bands of the theaters where traveling units touched down. Their number included Count Basie, Lester Young and his brother Lee (members of a family band run by their father), Fats Waller, Louis Armstrong, Mary Lou Williams, Jelly Roll Morton, Oran "Hot Lips" Page and many others.

All concerned had long realized that the solutions to many of the above-noted problems in the South lay in the formation of some sort of cooperative venture, such as the northern S.H. Dudley organization that went back nearly to the turn of the century, but whose twenty-one theaters were located no farther below the Mason-Dixon Line than Richmond, Virginia. The extension of theatrical routes southward meant that managers of touring companies would be able to book long and profitable seasons without loss of revenue due to downtime and inefficient transportation bills. In turn, this meant some degree of comfort (however mild) might be passed along to the performer. And while there had long been scattered attempts to schematize southern theatrical territory, just when these efforts began to coalesce, the "road" suffered a marked decline due to widespread government appropriation of railroads during World War I. The end of the war in 1918, however, meant the time was finally ripe for a significant organization of black vaudeville into the deep South and westward. Finally, in 1921 the much-needed solution came in the form of the T.O.B.A (Theatre Owners Booking Association, or sometimes just "Toby Time"), a 28-theater chain which grew within a short time to encompass nearly a hundred venues.

Long before the T.O.B.A.'s coming, however, the vaudeville family known as the Whitman Sisters had managed though grit and self-determination to steer clear of most of the pitfalls and problems—both artistic and pedestrian — that befell so many other black troupes. The four singing and dancing sisters were a class act that had a profound effect on raising the consciousness and racial pride of performers and audiences alike. For many years they were one of the most popular acts in the country. The Whitman troupes which in addition to the Sisters usually included a cast of 15 to 20 youthful performers, barnstormed the U.S. for nearly four decades in shows typified by an elegance of execution and attention to production detail that put most other traveling shows to shame. With few exceptions the Whitmans' audiences were strictly African American. No film or phonographic records of their work is known to survive, which is undoubtedly why they have fallen through the cracks of history. Eyewitness accounts of their handiwork, however, suggest that no finer actor-manager ever existed than the act's unquestioned leader, the greatly gifted Mabel Whitman.

The show biz soap opera *The Jazz Singer* has been filmed on three different occasions (1927, 1952 and 1980), each time from a Jewish perspective[3]; one wonders, though, as has been suggested by jazz critic Gary Giddins, whether the secular vs. spiritual conflicts experienced by first generation Jews were finally as severe as these films imply. In real life Al Jolson, the star of the first *Jazz Singer*, began performing professionally at an early age, yet met with little resistance from his cantor father (as was the case with the character he portrayed in the film). Fledgling songwriter Harold Arlen also had a relatively easy time of it with *his* cantor father; in fact, immigrant Jews practically held a monopoly on pop songwriting in the early part of the century. In actuality, the kind of family disapproval portrayed in *The Jazz Singer* was much more typical of the black community. Dinah Washington, Bobby Womack, Lou Rawls, Sam Cooke — the list of black performers who met with disfavor for going "pop" is lengthy. But the ones who truly wrote the book on the subject — three decades in advance of *The Jazz Singer* — were the singing, dancing Whitman Sisters, for many years among the highest paid performers in black vaudeville.[4]

Their father Albery Whitman (claimed by daughter Essie to be a first cousin of Walt Whitman)[5] was born a slave in 1851, the same year *Uncle Tom's Cabin* began serialization in the abolitionist "National Era." Although the young plow shop worker was able to secure only scant formal education — about a year all told — he would go to teach school before becoming (prior to the emergence of Paul Laurence Dunbar in the early part of the century) the most renowned African American poet of his day. Now almost forgotten, he published several books, including *Not a Man and Yet a Man*, the longest poem ever published by an African American up until 1877.[6] This "metrical extravaganza of over 5,000 lines on the loves and adventures of Rodney, an octoroon fugitive slave," as it was described by Joan R. Sherman in her essay "Albery Allson Whitman: Poet of Beauty and Manliness," was written "to publicize the high aims of Wilberforce [University], beneficiary of the book's profits; and to introduce the poet (who would welcome donations) to his public."[7] Writes Sherman, "Albery Whitman's complexion and features made him indistinguishable from white, according to his contemporary, the poet James Corrothers." Whitman married a handsome woman, Caddie, who appears in her portrait to be entirely Caucasian. Thus, their daughters were mistaken for white by theatrical agents who discovered them singing jubilee songs (i.e., spirituals) at a church concert."[8]

Albery Whitman was prominent enough to have been invited in 1893 to write a special lyric, "Freedom's Triumphant Song," for Colored American Day held on August 25 of that year at the Chicago World's Fair (the World Columbian Exhibition). The work itself was read by Caddie Whitman, perhaps indicating that the family's propensity for public expression was not exclusive to the father and his daughters. Curiously, most biographical works on Whitman invariably fail to mention his equally illustrious daughters; likewise, most coverage of the Sisters from a show business angle refers to the father as a minister, failing even to give a first name.

In 1994 Albery's great niece (and the Whitman Sisters' second cousin), Ernestine Lucas, spoke of the frustration she felt over the achievements of her extraordinary relatives having fallen into obscurity in more recent times—

especially Albery: "[Albery] could read when he was three years old and you know good and well that he didn't get the book out of the slave cabin. He is the only black poet who has written in the Spenserian form. He was just *different*. And he was different in writing in the same way that the sisters were different from the [degrading] minstrel shows that came before them."[9]

Whitman was also a minister of the African Methodist Episcopal Church, and almost from the beginning there was something, well, *different* about the way his daughters sang the old jubilee spirituals to the congregations at the Reverend Whitman's various A.M.E. pastorates in Ohio, Kansas, Texas and finally, Georgia, in Savannah and Atlanta. Songwriter Perry Bradford, the writer and producer of Mamie Smith's 1920 trailblazing recording "Crazy Love," saw the sisters before they turned professional. Years later he recalled:

"You could have bought me for a plug dime when the audience sat spellbound to hear May, Essie and Alberta [the youngest Whitman had not yet been born], those three gorgeous 'ofay-gee-gwarks' (meaning in theatrical language 'high yellow') chirping our Negro spirituals, 'In That Great Gettin' Up Mornin' and 'Shout All Over God's Heaven.' Their swinging style was new in spiritual singing."[10]

Clearly this was the unexpected result of Albery Whitman's having taught his three teenage daughters—strictly as a form of exercise to be carried out in private—some of the old dances he'd learned on the Kentucky plantation of his birth. These moves didn't even have names, but would be recognized today as the double shuffle, the time step, etc. Soon the three young girls began incorporating these "worldly" routines into their renditions of the otherwise stately old Negro spirituals and the next thing you knew they had their father's flock rocking in the aisles. This in turn leads to speculation as to whether a very young "Georgia Tom" Dorsey might not have drawn at least some of the inspiration for his jazz + spirituals = gospel experiments ("Peace in the Valley," "Precious Lord, Take My Hand," etc.) of the 1920s from early exposure to the music of the Whitmans. Dorsey, born in the Whitmans' home state in 1899, was certainly in the right time and place to have done so.

Before long, word of the Whitman Sisters' music spread far and wide. While they were on tour in 1898 and singing at New York's Metropolitan Baptist Church, they were "discovered" for vaudeville (as described in a 1954 issue of *Ebony Magazine*) by "some slumming members of British nobility."[11] Accounts as to who was actually responsible for the threesome's secular crossover tend to vary. Sources other than *Ebony* claim it was composer-conductor Will Marion Cook[12]; still others attribute the honor to theatrical impresario Arthur Hammerstein who reportedly, when he first saw them, thought they were white.[13]

According to one biographical sketch, with their mother Caddie acting as chaperone, the Whitman Sisters were soon off touring the (white) Orpheum circuit appearing with big-time acts such as the George M. Cohan family and the equally popular Carter DeHaven. According to the same source, they were an immediate hit billed — perhaps in an attempt to hide their true identities— as "The Daznette Sisters."[14] But, if so, the ruse appears not to have worked. According to actor Clarence Muse, "They started doing tableaux in churches to gain money for 'rallies.' Somewhere along the line they realized the money-making possibilities of what they were doing and branched out into show business. The old man disowned 'em then."[15] (However, the fact that Albery Whitman left his daughters an estate worth a then-princely $60,000 suggests that the rift between them was not as great as Clarence Muse and others have suggested.)[16]

Whether there was a direct causal link between the poet-minister's problems with alcohol and his daughter's "worldly" ways is open to speculation; but around the turn of the century Albery Whitman began drinking to excess, and was removed from his parish. He died in 1901. There is no question, though, that sects like the A.M.E. church frowned upon the mere attendance at theatrical events; however, Whitmans' great niece has her doubts about the rift between father and daughters:

"From everything I've heard about him, he was a very sensitive, inverted person who hid his feelings and I think that even if he had any antagonism toward them [his daughters] that it wouldn't have come out. Maybe just like the Walt Whitman rumor, it was something the sisters made up because it was a good dramatic show business story."

Just like the Walt Whitman rumor?

"Heavens, yes! That was just something of a family joke. When I went to visit them once in 1955 they showed me a set of china that they said originally belonged to Walt Whitman, but they were just trading on the name. They weren't related to Walt Whitman. In show business you do a lot of things to get attention. I have our ancestry traced back to Port Tobacco, Maryland. You'd be amazed to see the amount of genealogical material I have."[17]

In early vaudeville appearances, the Whitmans sang and danced and accompanied themselves on banjo. However, it was the novel way they concluded their act that made them such a hit: They worked in blackface and wigs, but came out for their encore with their natural long blond-ish hair streaming down their back in the finale.[18]

"The audience was always puzzled," Essie recalled years later, "and someone was sure to ask, 'What are those white women doing up there?' Then they would recognize us as the performers [they had just seen] and laugh in amazement."[19]

The threesome also toured Europe as part of various imported "Direct from the U.S." vaudeville packages; they are said to have given Command Performances before European royalty.[20] Then in 1904 they formed their own outfit, the Whitman Sisters' New Orleans Troubadours; a company of twelve which in addition to Bert, Mabel and Essie (Alice was not yet a part of the act) also featured "the Original Comedy of Willie Robinson: The Little Georgia Blossom" and the formidable Storyville pianist and singer Tony Jackson, an "epileptic, homosexual and an alcoholic, with severe tooth decay and not one good feature to speak of" (he was portrayed in the 1978 Louis Malle film *Pretty Baby* by Antonio Fargas).[21] Jackson was also a songwriter whose most famous tune "Pretty Baby" was actually written about "a tall, skinny fellow," according to singer Alberta Hunter.[22] Tony Jackson left the company in the fall of 1904, but joined again in 1910 at just about the time the Whitmans added their step — or half (?) — sister, eight-year-old Alice* (billed as "Baby Alice"), to their assault on the otherwise almost solely white precincts of the Keith and Proctor, Fox, and Pantages vaudeville circuits.

Even though the Sisters' early success was credited to the guidance of their mother Caddie (who died in 1909), it wasn't long before the producing contributions of singer-comedienne Mabel Whitman (sometimes spelled "Maybelle" (or "Mable") also became widely known, as evidenced by this 1904 review: "This is the first time in the history of Birmingham, Alabama, that the colored people have been allowed seats in the dress circle and parquet [of the Jefferson Theater]. Credit is due to the clever management of Mabel Whitman who can safely say that she is the only colored woman managing her own company and booking them continuously in the leading Southern houses."[23]

As for the other sisters: Essie Whitman, a versatile singer-comedienne with a deep contralto voice, was also noted for her comedy drunk act; she also designed the costumes. Her stage personae is said to have been similar to Mae West's; it's difficult to say who got there first.

The specialties of Alberta (Bert) were legomania (just what it sounds like, i.e., the use of extreme and jiggly leg movements) and male impersonation; at the latter, she is reputed to have been every bit the equal of Vesta Tilley, the world-renowned British practitioner of the art. Alice Whitman, billed as "The Queen of Taps," was a superb dancer whose memory is still venerated by tappers. She was once to have participated in a dance contest arranged by Bill Robinson between herself and the greatly overrated (to put it kindly) Ruby Keeler. The fact that she won by default when the latter failed to show still looms large in tap legend.

At the height of their popularity in the 1920s, no matter how late their Saturday night's last show had run, you were certain to find the Whitman Sisters and most of their company of dancers, comedians, singers, chorus

---

*Most historians do not make the distinction that Alice was not actually A.A. Whitman's daughter. Some sources of the day also state that Alice was Mabel Whitman's child. This may or may not have been so; clearly, however, what confused reporters assigned to cover the Whitmans then, as well as more recent writers on the subject, was the use in their billing of the word "Sisters." States family member Ernestine Lucas, "I've never been able to find adoption papers on Alice, but she was definitely a part of the family from age three."

girls and musicians in attendance at the local A.M.E. church. At some point in the service, Mabel Whitman could be depended upon to open up her purse, reach in and, with an entire congregation of prospective theatergoers looking on, take out an impressive fiver or a ten-spot and drop it into the collection basket. The eldest of the sisters didn't exactly hold a gun on *her* flock to force them to attend church services, but such complicity was known to be a sure way of staying on Mabel's good side.[24]

This canny mix of self-promotion and genuine religiosity was a scene the Whitmans repeated over and over again — mostly in a different city every week — from 1900 until 1940 — the period during which, almost without cessation, they barnstormed the U.S. with their act. The Sunday morning "appearances" at church were considered by some to be publicity-mongering; nonetheless, the door swung both ways. During their heyday, the generosity of the Whitmans was directly responsible for at least twelve churches being able to pay off their mortgages. The summer of 1927, for example, found the four of them pitching a 1,000-seat carnival tent at the corner of 46th and Wabash in Chicago where they played a two-week engagement to help raise money for the city's Grant Memorial A.M.E. Church.[25] Much more "presentable" than your ordinary strutting players, Mabel, Alberta, Essie and Alice Whitman while on the road also visited women's clubs, officiated at local ceremonies, and hobnobbed with the town's hoi polloi. But the high point of socializing with the locals happened Sunday mornings.

Ostentatious church displays aside, however, it was the Whitmans' skill as performers that put them over the top, earned them the sobriquet of "The Royalty of Negro Vaudeville" and accounted for their extraordinary longevity.

* * *

With the exception of occasional stopgap forays onto white vaudeville "wheels" (i.e., circuits) such as Gus Sun "Time" in 1925 and the Publix Theatre circuit in 1928, the Whitmans seldom played white vaudeville. Being just about the only very light-skinned black stars on white stages, they eventually came to realize that, as Mabel put it, they were "breaking in where we were not really wanted." However, black audiences gave them, she said, "full appreciation without grudge,"[26] and the Whitmans soon became the most popular exclusive-to-the-black-community act in show business. It was a position they would hold for nearly two decades, even during the post–World War II financial recession which prompted Mabel to split the family "business" in two, with herself and Bert going off on their own in an act billed as "Mabel Whitman and Her Dixie Boys," and Alice and Essie touring in a separate unit. This setup was successfully retained throughout the early 1920s, with Mabel and Bert doing one hundred non-stop weeks on the road beginning in early 1922.

There could, however, be no surer sign that the postwar economy had fully rebounded than an announcement appearing in the June 7, 1924, edition of Chicago's leading black newspaper the *Defender* informing that *all four* of the Whitmans along with a full complement of players would be coming to town to appear for an entire month, performing two shows a night, at the city's premier black vaudeville house, the Grand Theater. Also—just like the good old days—there was to be an entirely new production every week, each with different sets and costumes—which the Whitmans always kept sparkling clean and in top notch condition (rare for traveling shows).

The opening night audience at the sold-out Grand Theater for *Romping Through* (the first of the four productions) found that little if anything had changed during the time the Whitmans had been away: Even the opening production number—featuring a chorus which was, wrote one reviewer, "plainly selected for its youth and beauty as well as for its talent"[27]—stopped the show, as did Albert (Alice's four-year-old dancing prodigy son) with his "I Don't Have to Die to Go to Heaven," Alice with her solo turn, and Bert in male drag backed by a chorus line doing her specialties (one of which went, "When you do the teddy, and you do the bear, but when you do Jack Johnson, kid, you're there"; she then froze in a boxing pose). There were also crowd-pleasing turns by sister Mabel and seventeen other principals, including Dorothy Langston, "The Girl with the Saxophone," and a "special added attraction," the popular comedy team of Harris and Holly ("You pull, my end will follow" was their popular catchphrase).

There was no lessening of enthusiasm for *Stepping Some*, the second week's show, deemed by one reviewer to carry "half a hundred different things for which it might be recommended."[28] The third week at the Grand found them performing their *Going Some* revue; the final week there was yet another entirely new entry, this one featuring, as an extra added attraction, the popular husband-and-wife comedy team of Butterbeans and Susie. Like the Whitmans, they were an almost exclusive-to-black-audiences act who played far, wide and long (for nearly fifty years up until the time of her death in 1963).[29]

It is a measure of the Whitman Sisters' immense popularity around this time, that Mabel, Alice and "Bert," along with another of the act's star attractions, Princess Wee Wee, and several other cast members were invited to the White House to meet President Coolidge and to be given a tour by Mrs. Coolidge. In all likelihood, this was, for its time, not only a rare instance of high-level racial harmonization, but an early example of the intermingling of politics and show biz.[30]

Shortly after her month-long Chicago run, Mabel Whitman sat for a talk with a reporter from Pittsburgh's leading black newspaper, the *Courier*. Reclining on a chaise in her hotel room, she was dressed, he wrote, "in a long rose satin negligee with slender draperies of pastel-shaded georgettes, the morning sun playing upon her smooth complexion." Right off the top she informed him, "I am not eager about interviews—one might be misunderstood. But I like your face, so fire away." But it was Mabel Whitman who did most of the talking: about "pioneers" such as herself who had "paid the price," and of the progress blacks had made on the legitimate stage. "If my art hasn't been an inspiration to some ambitious youth," she vowed, "I would rather give it up today."[31]

The truth was, Mabel Whitman was always "eager" to talk with the press. She was especially known for the lambasting she reserved for white theater managers who—she told a reporter for the *Baltimore Afro-American* in 1929—"feel that any kind of show is good enough for a colored audience, and their only desire is to have a comedian and a few half-naked girls on hand to keep the doors open. They insult the intelligence and prey on Negro patrons."[32]

Mabel didn't reserve her wrath for whites alone: On one occasion the Whitmans were about to play the Regal Theater in Chicago when its black manager reneged on what he'd promised to pay them. "Sister May," as she was known to all, stalked off across the street to the Metropolitan Theater, which really wasn't competition to the Regal at the time because it didn't have a stage. She had one built there, opened with a different show than the one contracted to the Regal, and totally wiped out its business for two weeks.[33] Actions such as this led one anonymous *Pittsburgh Courier* scribe to write of "Ma May": "Managers and theatre-owners all over the country have tales to tell of how the wily 'boss' of the Whitmans pulled a fast one on them — and made them like it. Nothing underhanded, but just shrewd business."[34]

Modern show business' first major female entrepreneur Mabel Whitman's harsh-tempered and highly opinionated ways earned her the sobriquet of the "Tiger Show Woman."[35] She honed her rough-and-ready deal-making skills on the black circuit, the T.O.B.A.* The letters officially stood, as noted earlier, for Theatre Operators' Booking Association, but unofficially and less genteelly for "Tough on Black Actors" or "Tough on Black Asses" (the circuit slowly began to expire with the coming of the Depression).

Many of the T.O.B.A. houses were fallen-down affairs which had long since outgrown their usefulness as places of amusement to the white community and which probably should have been razed instead of being given a second chance as "colored" theaters. Because of the Whitman Sisters' popularity, however, May was able to make strong demands and receive special treatment from the T.O.B.A. theater proprietors and managers, most of whom

---

*At least two recent books on the subject on African Americans and entertainment offer 1909 as the year the T.O.B.A was founded; but this date is incorrect. There was an organization by that name in existence at the time, but the T.O.B.A. that has come to be synonymous with black show business was begun in 1921. See *The Chicago Defender* for January 29 of that year. Under the headline "New Organization," the opening lines of the story noted, "An event of importance has transpired in the vaudeville world. Recently there was formed in Chattanooga, Tenn., the Theater (sic) Owners' Booking Association..."

were white (with the few blacks owners being primarily women). This may not have been quite as difficult as it sounds: Blacks had "product" that whites were unable to deliver — entertainment tailored for the hundreds of segregated black theaters in the country — and with the help of organizations such as the C.V.B.A. (the Colored Actors' Benevolent Association), formed in 1910, and the C.A.U. (the Colored Actors' Union)[36] of a few years later, African American performers and entrepreneurs like Whitman were able to aspire to and attain — for the times — a rare degree of black bargaining clout.

Needless to say, from 1900 to well into the 1930s (mostly on the T.O.B.A. circuit after 1921), May, Alberta, Alice and Essie Whitman — in various touring combinations of duos, trios and quartets — provided jobs for hundreds of talented blacks in the twenty-to-thirty member troupes with which the sisters usually traveled. Innovative jazz singer Leo Watson was part of the Whitman Sisters' troupe for several seasons beginning in 1929; pianist Clarence "Pinetop" Smith also frequently toured with the company. A few of the other well-known alumni include: singer-dancer Jeni Le Gon, who later had substantial roles in such films as *Hooray for Love* in which she was partnered by Bill Robinson; Willie Bryant, who became a popular bandleader in the mid–1930s; Eddie "Rochester" Anderson, Count Basie, comedienne Jackie "Mom" Mabley, composer-pianist Mary Lou Williams, and tap dancer Bunny Briggs who in 1988, more than fifty years after his service with the Whitmans, starred in the Broadway musical success *Black and Blue*.

The Whitman Sisters' penchant for very young performing talent was a big part of their "act." Shamelessly, they would announce from the stage that one or another wunderkind performer the audience was about to see was an orphan or a homeless youth they'd picked up along the way. The truth was that in most instances the sisters were sending salaries home to the minor's parents.[37] That the money was hard-earned was driven home by dancer Briggs in a mid–1960s interview: "You sang one week, danced the next, sold peanuts the next, and if you got caught breaking any of the rules you got shipped home in a hurry."[38]

Dancer Joe Jones, who joined the company at age seven, once confessed that he was "scared to death" of the sisters because they "had deep voices like men and could really spank."[39] Bandleader-dancer Willie Bryant later remarked, "It was the fastest paced show on the road. If you tried to take it easy, you were fired."[40] Frequently in rehearsal, with all the warmth of a drill sergeant, Mabel could be heard ordering her young charges to "Get those feet moving!"[41]

When Bryant was 16, one of his Whitman show specialties was partnering with one of the most fondly remembered entertainers in all of black show business history, yard-high Princess Wee Wee, alternately billed by Mabel — with a touch of P.T. Barnum flair — as "the world's smallest perfect woman"; "the most talented midget in the world"; and "the smallest Racial performer on the American stage." A midget whom the Sisters met up with sometime during the 1920s, the Princess was at first taken into their family, but eventually was put into their show. Six-foot-tall Bryant recalls that Princess Wee Wee "[sang] in a cute, high-pitched voice, and then she danced around and between my legs" in a routine that seems remindful of the one performed in the 1936 film *Captain January* a few years later by Shirley Temple and Buddy Ebsen.[42]

As for the rest of the show: "Sometimes the first scene was a plantation number," Alice Whitman recalled years after she and her sisters retired: "Mammy peeling potatoes and the kids singing and dancing around her; then came the specialty numbers."[43] These usually consisted of a shake dancer, a comedian, a solo singer (perhaps a blues singer), Alice singing with the chorus line followed by her tap solo, a Rockettes-like chorus line, Princess Wee Wee's number, Bert and Alice backed by a chorus line with a boy-and-girl song-and-dance, comedy, *more* music, then, the finale with the entire cast fronted by "Bert" doing her Strut. Little Pops, Alice's son, usually had the encore all to himself.[44]

Like mother, like son: Just as in the early part of the century when "Baby Alice" Whitman had played an integral role in the popularity of the Sisters, so did her son Albert years later. Born in 1921, he was greatly responsible for galvanizing continuing interest in the Whitmans in the mid–1920s and early '30s. "By the time he was four years old," wrote Marshall and Jean Stearns in *Jazz Dance*, "he was performing the Charleston in a miniature tuxedo. [Alice was the same age when she began appearing with her sisters.] Nicknamed 'Pops,' Albert developed into one of the first great acrobatic dancers, a master of cartwheels, spins, flips, and splits—swinging with the rhythm."[45] During his brief life (he died in 1950), Pops teamed with a series of highly talented dancers, the most notable being Louis Williams. At first, Mabel was part of Pops and Louis' act, "to inspire the kids," she said, but soon dropped out to concentrate on managing them.[46]

The May 5, 1934, edition of the *Defender* announced that the Whitmans (who "have always hit the road in the early spring, generally opening in Chicago and proceeding South") for the first time in many years did not have a show. Mabel, who "does all the work"[47] for the sisters' shows, was unable to find a proper chaperone for Pops and Louis and would have to go herself. Eventually there was one more Whitman show, *Swing Revue* (1936), but by and large that was it.

By the mid–1930s, vaudeville as Mabel Whitman had known it was a shadow of its former self due to the Depression and inroads made by talking pictures. But the oldest Whitman sister was undaunted; in 1934 the fifty-ish Mabel told an interviewer: "Some gave the little woman [i.e., Whitman] the ha-ha, but we're still here."[48] In an interview from around the same time she said she planned "to keep the name of Whitman at the top until I am no more. At least another twenty-five years."[49]

It was probably one of the few times the astute show woman was ever wrong about anything: Mabel Whitman died only a few years later, in 1942. And shortly thereafter, thanks to Mabel's successful business investments, Alice and Bert retired comfortably to the family's 15-room mansion on Chicago's South Side (purchased in 1925), content to play the role of beloved local social figure-mentors.

The Whitman Sisters revues were no more, though Alice continued to work occasionally in such shows as *Hot Chocolates* at New York's Connie's Inn in 1935 and, the same year, at the popular Grand Terrace in Chicago; and Essie, after going it alone in 1934 with her own variety show featuring Princess Wee Wee, packed it in to become a full-time travelling evangelist — a career decision gradually reached after her miraculous recovery from a near-fatal car wreck seven years earlier.

The late 1950s found Alice and Essie still living in the family home in Chicago, just around the corner from the Regal Theater; usually it was also occupied by at least one or more of their former protégés who might happen to be working in town. In 1962 they were joined there by Bert, returned to Chicago after living for several years in Arizona (each of the Whitmans were married and divorced several times). The following year, 1963, Essie died of smoke inhalation; Bert's death came shortly thereafter (natural causes). Now only Alice was left.

Pops Whitman's dance partner told Marshall and Jean Stearns in *Jazz Dance*, "The Whitman Sisters stood for something. They were the ones I was going to build a monument for on Broadway — they knew talent when they saw it and gave hundreds of dancers their first big break."[50]

Such a monument was now badly needed: Ironically, while several of their father Albery Whitman's books from the late 19th century were still in print, by the mid–1960s the memory of the artistry of the Whitman Sisters — along with their contributions to racial-sexual parity — had faded. It was around the time of Essie's death in 1963 that Louis Williams made his remarks. Then in 1969 "Baby Alice," age 61, died of a cerebral hemorrhage, thus bringing to a close one of the most remarkable chapters in the history of (extra-racially) modern show business.

In 2000, a full-scale biography, *The Royalty of Negro Vaudeville: The Whitman Sisters and the Negotiation of Race, Gender and Class in African American Theater 1900–1940*, by Nadine George Graves, was published by St. Martin's Press. And if the somewhat astronomical prices the book is now fetching on the Internet are any indication, there is an ongoing degree of interest in the fabulous Whitmans' story.

3

The Color Line
Billy McClain

Despite a growing acceptance of African American producers and song-writers on Broadway at the start of the 20th century—along with the success of their performing counterparts in all-black shows—the color line between blacks and whites on American stages remained the rule well into the first two decades. Some Broadway musicals and revues did manage to go against tradition and feature fully integrated casts, notably 1904's *The Southerners* (with music by Will Marion Cook), but as a rule, shows tended to be either all-white or all-black, particularly in the hinterlands. Who attended these black or white productions depended on the kind of show it was, the location of the theater, and local racial customs. Often in the South, for example, whites and blacks might both attend, but on separate days; other venues relied upon a common form of audience segregation well into the late 1950s—a rope stretched down the middle of the venue (especially in carnivals and dance halls).

By 1910, due to the increasing popularity of such traveling African American revues as the Whitman Sisters' productions, *The Smart Set* and the long-running Black Patti's Troubadours, there were, according to the census, nearly 200 black showmen, owners and managers operating in the U.S., with Mabel Whitman being one of the most prominent among their number.[1] Other well-known black showmen of the period included Clarence Muse (who went on to later fame as a Hollywood character actor), J. Leubrie Hill, and the teams of Miller and Lyles, Cole and Johnson, Tutt and Whitney; and S.H. Dudley.

Parades were a popular form of advertising such shows when they came to town, and in larger cities where the stays could last as long as a week, the company's members tended to dig in and fraternize with the locals. Renting a flatbed truck, throwing some entertainers on the back, and riding over to the local factory or mill was a surefire way to give locals a taste of what was available at the theater. The team of Butterbeans and Susie employed a novel method of drawing attention: They would strew trails of beans through the neighborhood and then put up signs that read, "Follow these beans" ... with the beans, of course, leading straight to the nearest black theatrical emporium.

Theaters were not the only places where these productions appeared. There were often stops in smaller towns for appearances in places like fraternal halls, churches, airdromes, school auditoriums and tents. But by far, the most unusual of venues (for shows that in themselves were rather far-out affairs) were those scouted out by African American producer-performer Billy McClain, of whom a reporter of the day wrote: "Mr. McClain is to the theatrical world what Fred Douglass and Booker T. Washington are to the educational phase of the race today."[2] The life and times of this

Billy McClain, circa 1890.

showman—especially when you factor in the determinant of post–Civil War racism—were high-wide-and-handsomer than can possibly be imagined today. In 1893 he had appeared in and stage-managed the extravaganza *South Before the War*. This was a rare mixed-race experiment, with a cast of 50 and a brass band, which toured the country for several years—including a stay at New York's popular Niblo's Garden. Around this same time, McClain also scored a first when he was the star of the otherwise all-white production *Suwanee River*—another gargantuan affair. But it was when he pulled together the diverse elements for the mega-vaudeville show *Black America* that McClain created a production which for scope, conception and sheer size remains unmatched even today: an outdoor musical event that made *South Before the War* (which McClain had also helped devise) and even the famed Oberammergau Passion Play look positively puny by comparison.

When McClain first came up with the idea for *Black America*, recalls performer-historian Tom Fletcher, "his friends gave him the laugh, pointing out that he had no place to present such a show and furthermore, the cost of the scenery and salaries for the number of people he wanted—even though salaries in those times weren't very large—put the idea way beyond his reach. No one knows what kind of luck McClain carried but, at any rate, he found his man, a Mr. Nate Saulsbury [sic], promoter of large enterprises."[3]

Performed throughout the summer of 1895 at the same spot were *Buffalo Bill's Wild West Show* had been presented the previous year—Brooklyn's Ambrose Park—*Black America* featured an enormous cast of African American entertainers, most of whom were ex-slaves. McClain rounded up, among others, 63 jubilee quartets, many from productions of *Uncle Tom's Cabin*, as well as veterans who had served with the black U.S. Ninth Cavalry. He then had Ambrose Park transformed into a Southern plantation, with cotton bushes blossoming, bales of cotton and a cotton gin. A working farm (with poultry and livestock), which served as living quarters for the performers, was also built. Advertisements for the event trumpeted among other sights to be beheld:

"A Stupendous Aggregation of Actual Field Hands from the Cotton Belt, A veritable Invasion from the Sunny South of 500 Colored Men and Women, Representatives of a Race Famed for Spontaneous Exuberance of Human Humor Who Will Present the Lovable Bright Side of the Negro Character, Living in a Village of Plantation Cabins."

Among other divertissements promised were "Phenomenal Natural Voices," "Buck and Wing Dancing," and in tribute to Abraham Lincoln, "A Great Sociological Exhibit, A Historical Apotheosis—The Man Who Freed the Slaves."[4] The advertisements could have been a lot worse, considering in what little esteem blacks were still held by most of White America—especially when you take into account the fact that the offensive buzz word "coon" never appeared in advertisements for the spectacle.

After *Black America* opened, a regularly scheduled ferry full of predominantly white audiences traveled between the Battery in Manhattan to the Brooklyn park (bounded by Second and Third Avenues and 34th and 38th Streets), bringing crowds that spent the afternoon walking through McClain's environmental set. Upon a signal fifteen minutes before show time, the crowd took its seats in a huge outdoor amphitheater and an elaborate musical spectacle commenced. Since it was summer—usually a slow time for indoor theater in pre-air conditioned America—McClain was able to secure the talents of some of the top black singers, musicians and dancers. The music director for the affair, however, was none other than Victor Herbert, who would soon stake his claim as America's greatest contributor to operetta as composer of such classics as *Babes in Toyland, Naughty Marietta* and *The Red Mill.* At the time, the Irish-born Herbert was in transition from being a member of the Metropolitan Opera orchestra to becoming the conductor of the Pittsburgh Symphony in 1898.[5]

"*Black America,*" wrote the *New York Times* when the extravaganza opened, "is as instructive as it is entertaining.... The old melodies are sung by large choruses of natural voices in the same manner that they have always been sung below the Mason and Dixon line.... The entertainment is a delightful one, as it brings before the spectators the peculiarities of the Southern negro in a manner that most Northern persons have ever been able to observe..."[6]

Admission was 25 cents to tour the grounds, 50 and 75 cents to sit in the grandstand and one dollar for box seats. In the wake of the show's success, white producer Salsbury took credit for much of the production's originality, but based on evidence from McClain's earlier show activities, there's little doubt that the concept for this extraordinary slice of Black Americana was his and his alone. As was explained by his friend Tom Fletcher: "McClain was the type of fellow who did not wait for a manager to look for him; he went out and looked for managers."[7]

Years later McClain told a reporter, "I can handle hundreds with more ease and better results than I can smaller productions of forty or fifty. I can't explain why, but the task appears easier."[8]

That McClain had been performing almost from the time he could walk played a large part in the honing of his DeMille-like skills. Born in Indianapolis in 1866, McClain in 1910 wrote, "I was the first boy to sell the *Indianapolis World* and the first colored page in the Indiana Senate Chambers before the present court house was built ... the first boy cornet player in the old Indianapolis Capital City band ... [and] Dan Palmer and I were the first acrobats and trapeze performers out of Indianapolis."[9]

Having made his professional debut at age seventeen with Lew Johnson's Minstrels (which some claim was the first all-black minstrel troupe),[10] he also worked such popular outfits as Blythe's Georgia Minstrels, Cleveland's Minstrels, and Callender's Consolidated Colored Minstrels. In addition to performing and producing, McClain also wore the hat of songwriter, having composed and copyrighted dozens of titles including "Hand Down de Robe," "Don't You Think So" and in 1897, fifty years in advance of the Joe Turner hit of the same name, a tune prophetically entitled "Shake, Rattle and Roll."

After his Promethean producing successes at home, McClain made his first major journey abroad when, in mid–1899, along with wife Cordelia, he signed on as a star performer with M.B. Curtis' All-star American Minstrels for a tour of Australia. He shared the limelight with the equally famous singer-dancer-comedian Ernest Hogan, fresh from his run in the Will Marion Cook–Paul Laurence Dunbar musical *Clorindy*. It is not known how long this foreign tour was to last or its eventual destination, but it is a matter of record that soon afterward, in a dispute over money, McClain quit Curtis to link up with the also-traveling O.M. McAdoo Georgia Minstrels. But after the McAdoo company returned to America, McClain and Cordelia stayed on Down Under. Continuing to perform in Australia, the venturesome McClain also became involved in professional boxing. In 1892, he had found the time, aside from his show business activities, to train as a boxer. Now, however, his interest was strictly managerial when he hooked up with Australian black boxing hopeful, Peter Felix.[11] The career of heavyweight Jack Johnson was also well underway just then; starting in 1899 he began a run of success—100 bouts over the next ten years with only three losses—that would culminate in his winning the World Heavyweight title in 1908. It was an augury of things to come: By 1950, nearly half the boxers listed in *Ring Magazine* were African American.[12] So it is not surprising that the enterprising McClain would turn his sights in this direction. But he also continued to perform: August 1901 black newspapers made it known that Billy and Cordelia McClain and their Australian-grown company had just closed an eleven-week engagement in Sydney and now were booked for six months in Melbourne and Adelaide.

The U.S. black press regularly wrote about the activities of African American entertainers abroad, McClain among them. September of 1901 found McClain himself reporting in on his activities in the black paper the *Indianapolis Freeman*. In a letter appearing there, he wrote: "I am battling along at the same old rate with the view of something better. I have a very good class of singers and specialists, all white. Great things are expected of us, as Cordelia and myself are the only colored people on the bill, and I don't know that I am colored until I look in the mirror."[13]

In all, McClain worked in Australia for nearly three years. Finally, however, in the spring of 1902 he wrote the *Freeman* that he now felt his client Felix was ready to tackle the States.[14] On the way home, with the boxer in tow, McClain and his wife performed at the Orpheum Theatre in Honolulu (and perhaps other venues in the Hawaiian Isles). What McClain found upon his return, however, was disheartening; Racial discrimination in the field of boxing was still quite strong; fighter Felix couldn't get a fair shake after all and he soon went back home.[15]

By now McClain had, according to one reporter, "made a hundred thousand in the show business and besides healthy bank accounts, owns real estate in New York, Missouri and Indiana. Billy denies this statement, but modestly admits that if a rainy day comes it will find him prepared."[16]

The writer found McClain "in his aerie in the New Zealand Building on Broadway (where the humorous writers would have the public believe him the first of his race to be a factor in theatricals on Broadway)* ... [A]ccording to common report, [he] is waiting an opportunity to swoop down on Broadway and elsewhere; and more fully establish himself into the hearts of the amusement public."

But McClain was not allowed into the mainstream of American entertainment, and in the years to come would practically write the book on the expatriation of black entertainment professionals.

Shortly after McClain gave this interview, he commenced touring with

---

*Apparently the reporter, one Zeke Blossom, was taking umbrage over one or another of his colleagues failing to give proper public recognition of the achievements of entertainers such as Will Marion Cook, Bob Cole and Rosamond Johnson who had already successfully worked on Broadway and in New York City.

his old friend Ernest Hogan in a company known as *The Smart Set*.* But a sour note was soon struck: Pulling into Kansas City, with a private secretary in tow, wearing diamonds worth about $7000 and a gold nugget chain weighing 14 ounces and worth in excess of $523 and with 37 trunks, 13 hat boxes, 24 rugs, 14 brass instruments, three typewriters, nine bird cages, and seven dogs, McClain was arrested. The charge leveled against him by police?: Having in his possession entirely too many possessions for any one black man.[17] He was eventually released after he proved ownership of the items in question to the authorities; but for McClain this undoubtedly was a barometer of the racial climate still prevailing in the U.S.

Before long, McClain turned over the reins of the Smart Set Company to Hogan and was once again bound for foreign soil; he would remain abroad for the rest of the decade.[18]

To his credit, McClain always found time to write letters home to the *Indianapolis Freeman*. Although his communiques sometimes smack of personal braggadocio, clearly they were also intended to be inspiring and instructional to fellow blacks in America who could not realistically dream of the kind of opportunities McClain found awaiting him in Europe and the British Isles.

> October 27, 1905: Just on my way to Paris, the biggest joy I ever took in my life. I have been talking French for a month and my teacher goes with me to say what I forget. The country is bounding with colored acts at the present.... I came to England to try myself out among the wise; to get the technical education in the art I love so well, and I find handling white people the same as colored. You must teach them to understand you and you must know what you are talking about. When you make a rule, live up to it. I fined myself once.... In ten years from now, in every town of five thousand colored inhabitants there should be theatres owned and run by colored people, and if they can't do that they can run stock companies. Williams and Walker are good enough to appear before the King and good enough to play in any first-class theatre in the world.[19] No, it is the few blood suckers in the syndicate that control American theatrical enterprises who say, "We will shut the Negro out. He's alright, but where is he going?" But the time has come when the Negro must wake up and march on. He is a factor and they can't rush him out, thank God.
>
> A white man kicked me on producing and playing a star part in a white cast. John Tiller [one of the top theatrical entrepreneurs in Britain] said to him, "I hire whom I please, do as I like and pay what I owe, and do not want any direction from anyone in that matter. As long as that man does my work, what do I care he is black, green or grey. He is a gentleman and that means something in this country." ... I would come back to America tomorrow and fight for my people if they would only stick together. I have everything that I want, motor car, big fine house, servants, valet, etc., but I am not satisfied. I have a home

*The Smart Set Company ran for many years and became one of the premier black touring troupes in the early part of the century. Among the many famous plays, playlets and routines it offered were *His Honor, the Barber* and *The Black Politician*: It hit its stride in 1904 after being taken over by S.H. Dudley.

in America as well. But above it all, I have a mission on earth to perform. I want to be teaching my own people. I hope the day will come when the Negro will be loyal to each other and until then his progress will be at a standstill. [This was four years before the founding of the NAACP.][20]

October 20, 1906: I sail for Paris tomorrow night, Sat. Oct 20. I am booked solid until Oct. 07 and have some time in 08 and am refusing further time.... There is just as much prejudice as in America and you will find it if you stay long enough, but I have made my own personality win with all my manhood! An Englishman believes in fair play and an American doesn't. I am very busy and am staging a pantomime at the Folies Bergere as I did last year.

An act with which McClain shared the bill at London's Oxford Theatre around this time, Fred Karno's comedy troupe, had as one of its members Charlie Chaplin. Then, the name meant nothing; however, years later McClain, with only the mildest prompting, would proudly display a 1906 advertisement showing himself on the same bill with the future Little Tramp.[21]

November 26, 1906: I have purchased fifteen new [stage] gowns for Madame Cordelia and five each for my girls, making a total of forty dresses and twenty suits for my boys. My people change four times a night, and never wear the same gown the second time during the week's engagement.... My troupe is a big success. Every step I have made has been successful. Now I am turning money away. Here is a clipping about my auto and my work: "Billy McClain, since his return to Paris has become quite an expert chauffeur. On a 40 h.p. De dion, the other day, he created a record between Paris and Monte Carlo for touring cars. His success at the Folies Bergere is assured, while his troupe is gaining rounds of applause at the Casino De Paris."[22]

January 25, 1910: [Black Australian Heavyweight boxing champ] Sam McVey fights Saturday night (tomorrow), and I am his second, as I always have been. His opponent is Al Kubiack.[23] I am the ballet master here (at the Olympia Theatre) and am very busy rehearsing for a big production.... Well, old man, I am representing the race and I am proud to say that I am the only Negro that has risen to such a position in the history of show business and foreign [sic]. It only goes to show you what can be one where prejudice does not exist. But I tell you what. Yankees over here will put a knife in a colored man's back every time they get a chance.[24]

A letter to the *Freeman* from around the same time found the showman in a retrospective frame of mind. He was, he reminded readers, "the first colored man to open a music hall and picture show in St. Louis ... the first Negro to produce, play, sing, dance and talk in French ... the first to write the *Freeman* on theatrical news ... the first to do a sketch of a Chinaman and a Coon...."

To this casual résumé he also added the achievement of having been "the first to put a cakewalk on the stage."[25] This, however, was highly debatable, as a number of others also made the same claim of having introduced the dance sensation, most notable among them the team of Williams and Walker.

Seconding boxers; mastering seven languages; choreographing for the Olympia and the Folies Bergère; auto racing; barnstorming the British Isles appearing with the famed Tiller's Girls; periodically touring with his own opulent revue! Small wonder that the successful McClain stayed away from the problematic U.S. for such a lengthy period.

Such forays were nothing new for American black entertainers. One's imagination can't help but be stimulated by the likes of popular singer and character actress Georgette Harvey (1883–1952) who— after the dissolution in Europe of her group the Creole Belles—"lived in St. Petersburg for over a decade and was popular with members of Czar Nicholas's court."[26]

But such exoticism was not in the cards for McClain's wife Cordelia, who in 1910 finally journeyed back to the U.S. It would be three years before McClain came back for good, at which time he was reduced to operating on a much smaller scale: The year 1915 found him with a twenty-member cast performing a traditional revue in a tent in Kansas City.[27] Apparently, however, McClain was every bit as well fixed financially as had been rumored for years; the tent he was appearing in was on a lot situated next to the city's Yellow Front Café, which McClain owned. And the somewhat notorious Kansas City night club was just a small part of his portfolio, which also included half-ownership of the newspaper the *Tulsa Star* and various real estate investments, including the Crescent Theater Building in Buffalo, which McClain bought in 1923 at a cost in excess of a hundred thousand dollars. The complex contained lodge rooms, dance halls, stores and a building adjoining the theater.[28] For most of the remainder of the teens, McClain traveled around the country, often in a private railroad car, looking after various business interests. Arriving in towns across the country, it was common for McClain to be met by members of the local black press to whom he would dispense wisdom on subjects such as race improvement and bettering the lot of the "colored" entertainer.[29]

In the book *100 Years of the Negro in Show Business,* author Tom Fletcher recounts a chance meeting he had with his old show biz cronie McClain in the early 1930s, in the course of which Billy told him how, a few years earlier, he had effected a rather abrupt career change:

"You know how I used to fool around acrobats and prize fighters? Well, I went to school and took a course in osteopathy. I finished, got my diploma and I am now known in Washington as Dr. McClain."

"Now, Tom, don't laugh," he continued, "but I might as well tell you. I was mixed up with the Klan."

Fletcher asked him, "What Klan?"

"The Ku Klux Klan," he said. "I was the masseur. I attended meetings and had the password and everything for their Washington headquarters. They had a camp on the outskirts of town where nobody but the high-ranking officers would be admitted. Classed as one of the doctors on their staff, I had to be a 'royal something' to get in so they name me the 'Royal Buzzard.'"

Whether McClain engaged in what might be seen by some as "consorting with the enemy" simply because felt he had no Hippocratic choice in the matter; thought he was beating the white man at is own game; or in the wake of the Depression simply needed the money, is unclear.

In 1931, adding to his already rich résumé, Billy McClain moved to Los Angeles where he secured the job of physical trainer for the Pasadena police department. Almost immediately upon his arrival on the West Coast, he made it clear that he also intended to keep his hand in as an entertainer. August of that year found him at the Shrine Auditorium appearing at a benefit, spearheaded by popular African American actor Clarence Muse, for black Boy Scouts. In a scene played by McClain, he held forth for 18 minutes as playing both Uncle Tom *and* Simon Legree, capped by a rendering of faithful slave Tom's deathbed scene. It was, he said, a test of his ability after being off the stage for 21 years.[30]

"Uncle Billy," as he had come to be known, also moonlighted from the police department, appearing in a number of films, including *Dimples* with Shirley Temple; a Melvyn Douglas vehicle, *Nagana*; and *Rhapsody in Black*, a 1934 short subject in which he sang four "southern melodies."[31]

When in the late 1940s old-time showman Tom Fletcher first began writing his *100 Years of the Negro in Show Business*, it was natural that he get in touch once again with the man who had practically written the book on the subject. He wrote to McClain, with whom he had not spoken to since the early '30s when Billy had confided the story of his KKK affiliation. McClain soon answered back; he had a home in Los Angeles but a trailer that he preferred living in; and he would send some material to his old friend as soon as he was able to get to yet a third location in Pasadena where his trunks were stored. But McClain never got the chance.

"One night there was a short circuit of something that caused the trailer in which he was sleeping to catch on fire," wrote Fletcher. "That night, January 19, 1950, Billy McClain died."

"An unsung pioneer"—Fletcher called him—for "it was the result of his untiring efforts to put together the cast for *Black America* that producers began to see and hear colored talent in any great quantities. And it was after the run of that same show, in 1895, that the colored musical shows came into being."[32]

Certainly by today's standards, *Black America* would leave a somewhat unpleasant taste in the mouth; blacks being put on display almost like zoo animals, with only marginal status as human beings ("the Lovable Bright Side of the Negro Character, Living in a Village of Plantation Cabins"). The entire affair also suggests the lengths to which not just McClain but most others of his race — and not just those in show business— had to go in order to survive during those times. But *Black America* also underscores—by virtue of the sheer number and quality of the talent employed — that McClain was also motivated by more noble aims, among them gaining the opportunity to give massive numbers of blacks steady employment; and, once he had "ensnared" his predominantly slumming white audiences, to show them a much more human side of "the Negro Character."

Excellence and relative ease of execution by blacks in show business has been taken for granted almost from their very beginnings in the profession. But when you delve deeper into the life and times of Billy McClain, you begin to sense just how large a price was paid; how much contradiction, bravery, and painful compromise (not to mention talent) was called for from African American entertainers. When, for example, a white producer took nearly all the credit for the success of McClain's *Black America*, it would have been tantamount to (career and perhaps literal) suicide for the show's true creator to publicly suggest otherwise.

Asking "Who were Will Marion Cook or Mabel Whitman?"— performers whose careers next to McClain seem to proceed in an almost straight line by comparison — is far easier than asking, "Who was Billy McClain?" If he wasn't "making it" in show business, he was doing so in boxing. If he wasn't "cutting it" on the stage — because a black man might have been offensive to certain audiences— then he stepped behind the scenes. If America turned inhospitable to his talents, then McClain left the country for sunnier climes.

Whether the story he told his friend Tom Fletcher about working for the Ku Klux Klan was true or a flight of fancy on McClain's part — one hopes it was the latter — is finally beside the point. He *might* have; illustrating the extreme degree to which Billy McClain played by the rules *and* dared to buck the odds. McClain got sidetracked from full-time show business in his early 40s. But unlike others (such as Mabel Whitman who had the "good sense" to stay on the black side of the line), McClain wanted power — and real power was an exclusively white commodity. By his own admission, he wanted to conquer Broadway in much the way that Belasco and Hammerstein had done — wanted something that just wasn't about to happen for an African American back then.

4

Over Here ... Over There
Valaida Snow

African American composer-conductor James Reese Europe made musical history with his "Concert of Negro Music" at Carnegie Hall in 1912. But his real quarter-hour in the public spotlight came not for his musical liberation of the Eurocentric concert hall, nor did it arise from his role as musical director for the sensational white dance team of Vernon and Irene Castle who, in dance critic Arlene Croce's words, "were perhaps the first large expression of modem mass society and its cult of good taste"[1] and who inspired a generation of young women to get rid of their corsets and petticoats and bob their hair. (Cultural conspiracy theorists should take note that more than two decades later, in order to mollify southern exhibitors of the 1939 film musical *The Story of Vernon and Irene Castle*, Europe is depicted as Caucasian.)

Rather it was as a World War I hero that Europe truly caught the fancy of the American public. "It is a sad fact," writes University of Alabama Professor of American Studies Reid Badger in his *A Life in Ragtime: A Biography of James Reese Europe*, "that New York's black infantry could not be trained at home but had to be sent abroad to foreign soil to acquire the skills necessary to fight for their country" (because of racial prejudice in South Carolina where they were initially stationed).[2] Thus it was with French troops, he writes, that James Europe became the first African American officer to lead men into combat in the Great War and "very likely the first American to cross no-man's land and participate in a raid on the German lines." Over 200,000 blacks were sent to France, with more than 30,000 of them engaged in direct combat. The majority of the nation's black leaders (even hardcore realists like W.E.B. Du Bois) felt certain the gesture would have a positive effect on the cause of democracy on home soil after the war was over. Emblematic of the part African Americans eventually played in the routing of "the dreaded Hun" was a remarkable postwar editorial in the *Jewish Daily News*: "These Negroes have helped win the war. Let us hope that their unflinching courage in the face of death will be remembered."[3]

James Reese Europe's participation in battle was in addition to his leadership of the famed all-black 369th U.S. Infantry Hellfighters Band. And on February 17, 1919, the day of their homecoming, when the 369th marched uptown to Harlem, with a crowd of nearly one million lining Fifth Avenue from Madison Square Park to 145th Street, the result was one of great patriotic spectacle. But a rosy conclusion to America's conflict on its own shores was not to be. Observes David Levering Lewis in his *When Harlem Was in Vogue,* "Southern newspapers editorialized ghoulishly about the fate of any African daring to come home uniformed, bemedalled, and striding up Main Street like a white man."[4]

"You niggers are wondering how you are going to be treated after the war," Lewis goes on to quote an unnamed source. "Well, I'll tell you, you are going to be treated exactly like you were before the war."[5] In short, not since the days of John Brown had Americans been so fearful at the thought of black men carrying guns; blacks who had even been extended the *courtesy* of being allowed to kill whites (i.e., Germans). Clearly, a "monster" had, of necessity, been created to help win the war, but now it was time to dismantle the creature. Not since the era of Reconstruction had such bad feelings existed between the races; the summer of 1919 saw an unprecedented twenty-five race riots, with hundreds of blacks killed and lynched by whites in a time known as "Red Summer."

After the war, live entertainment appeared to be back to business as usual. But thanks to a number of virulent anti-black social forces— not the least of which was the Ku Klux Klan newly revived via the success of D.W. Griffith's *The Birth of a Nation*— the conditions under which the black performer continued to labor had never been worse. This was particularly true of the Deep South where "coloreds" were not even allowed out of doors after nine o' clock in most places. Inasmuch as this was impossible for show people to avoid, arrests for curfew violations by blacks were a degrading and common occurrence. But as difficult as conditions were for the black male entertainer, they were even worse for women — especially when you factor in the constant potential for rape. Ethel Waters, a favorite at Atlanta, Georgia's, "81" Theater, was appearing there in 1920 when she and "this Georgia Cracker and a sort of self-appointed czar," as she later described the theater owner, got into an argument over an out-of-tune piano. In what was for the notoriously difficult Waters a rare act of compromise, she told the showman she was willing to pay either to have the piano tuned or for the rental of another one.

"Who do you think you're talking to?" the "81" owner angrily replied.

"If I'm not mistaken, I'm talking to Mr. Charles P. Bailey."

"That's right, and look, you. No nigger bitch is telling me how to run my theater."[6]

An argument of some duration ensued, and were it not for the happenstance appearance the next morning at five A.M. of a horse and buggy which

To my Pal Dean.
your trumpet playing is Wonderful,
your disposition is Wonderful,
naturally that makes you Wonderful.
Sincerely your Pal.
Val = Rhapsody in Black.

Valaida Snow, inscribed to Demas Dean, 1931 (courtesy Chet and Joann Gudger).

carried her off from downtown Atlanta, Waters remained convinced for the rest of her life that she would have died at the hands of henchmen Bailey had hired to kill her.

It is against this post–World War I backdrop of heightened racial tension — a world made safe for democracy, but clearly not the black entertainer — that the multi-talented Valaida Snow first made her way onto the vaudeville stage. Unlike Will Marion Cook, the Whitmans and Billy McClain, Valaida Snow is a figure of *modern* entertainment. Born just a generation later, she benefitted greatly from the sociological and artistic groundwork laid down by her predecessors. Unlike them, however, Snow not only "trod the boards," she also did films, recordings and television. Extra-categorically, she happens to be one of the most extraordinary figures in the annals of show business, black or white. Valaida Snow — a jazz trumpeter who didn't merely "play well for a woman," but was tops in her field; a vagabond entertainer whose life and times were filled with incidents that seem straight out of adventure fiction; an ambassador of American jazz who transported the music to lands where no one had taken it before; and an all-round entertainer who also sang and danced. In short, Snow embodied Showbiz Versatility of the sort later taken to its ultimate logical conclusion by Sammy Davis, Jr.

Perhaps the best place to start with Snow is at the defining moment of her career, Lew Leslie's 1931 Broadway production *Rhapsody in Black* whose ostensible star, Ethel Waters, a refugee from the rough and tumble of regional black vaudeville, was making her most important Broadway appearance yet. Her co-star Snow, while not exactly an unknown quantity, had established more of a reputation abroad than in the U.S. She was now in her late twenties or her early thirties— depending on the conflicting dates she herself supplied over the years.[7] In 1991, Demas Dean, a trumpeter (see Chapter 10) who played in *Rhapsody*'s orchestra, talked with me about what it was like to work in a production with two such headstrong types. We met in his small Los Angeles apartment; one that was overflowing with show business mementoes, including one 8 × 10 glossy inscribed, "To my pal Dean. Your trumpet playing is wonderful, your disposition is wonderful, naturally, that makes you wonderful. Sincerely your pal Val [i.e. Valaida Snow]: *Rhapsody in Black*."

Dean waved toward the photo as he explained why it was unlikely Ethel Waters might have received a similar photo during the ten-week run of *Rhapsody in Black*: At the time she and Snow were engaged in a War of the Colossal Divas; it was, however, a standoff that most other members of the company didn't mind in the least. "People in New York were falling all over themselves giving parties for the cast almost after every performance," Dean recalled, "but no one would dare invite Ethel and Valaida to the same affair, and since they couldn't afford to offend either of them, it was generally understood that you had to throw *two* parties, one which included Ethel but excluded Valaida and vice versa."[8]

The feud was a new development between the two stars who previously had shared a friendship going back to their early days in vaudeville when Snow was being billed as "Valaida Snow," and not just plain "Valaida," as she was in *Rhapsody*,[9] and both women were still putting up with the degrading conditions that tended to prevail in the mostly white-owned black theaters.

The cause of the friction between the temperamental and established Waters and the slightly lesser-known Snow? Apparently it was *Rhapsody* producer Lew Leslie. The showman had just sustained a serious financial loss with the eye-popping 1930 edition of his *Blackbirds* revue series. And even though *Rhapsody in Black* was a relatively plain-wrap affair, throughout pre-production he continued to search for ways to save even more money. Finally, during out-of-town tryouts, Leslie came to the conclusion that the much-less-costly Valaida could probably carry the weight of *Rhapsody in Black* alone, and he set about squaring off Snow against the high-salaried Waters, with hopes that the latter would quit the show in a huff.[10]

Leslie's tactics included giving Valaida most of *Rhapsody*'s choicest material, a tactic which under ordinary circumstances might have worked. Like Al Jolson (who ran water in his dressing room rather than hear other performers receive applause), Waters was known to be fearful of even the least-important of her supporting cast stealing her glory. No one else in a Waters production, for instance, was allowed to do an act even remotely resembling hers.[11] But Ethel was having some financial problems of her own at the time and at first refused to fall prey to the producer's wiles. Eventually, however, she did agree to a $500-a-week salary cut (down from $1,250) in exchange for Leslie's agreeing to hire additional songwriters to pen some decent new material for her.[12]

As for Snow's participation in the show, in addition to the flashy "Rhapsody in Blue," another number in the revue found her positioned atop a huge drum, blasting out a series of her specialty high Cs on the trumpet, then launching into a frenetic dance. Moreover, Snow got *Rhapsody in Black*'s best piece of original material, "Till the Real Thing Comes Along," which, ironically, was written by the new team of writers hired to appease Waters.[13] Snow even managed to toss in a popular routine of hers which involved seven pairs of footwear: soft shoe, adagio shoes, tap shoes, Dutch clogs, Chinese straw sandals, Turkish slippers and Russian boots. All were placed in a row at the front of the stage and she did a different dance to match each pair.[14] It's hard to imagine the always volatile Waters being anything other than apoplectic over all the attention Valaida Snow was receiving; especially after Snow's success in *Rhapsody* which found certain of the press writing of her as being second in popularity only to Ethel Waters.[15]

An interesting sidelight: During rehearsals, producer-director Leslie, a specialist in black-cast revues, was so confident that a choral version of George Gershwin's "Rhapsody in Blue" (arranged by choir master Cecil Mack and conducted by Snow) would set the tone for the rest of the evening that he made it the Act One curtain-raiser. But opening night, not even the spirited efforts of lithe, glamorously attired Snow could get the audience revved up. The unusual choral version of the popular Gershwin work brought everything to a full stop.

"I'm probably the only person still around who remembers how Lew Leslie solved his problem," mused Demas Dean, who had also played in the pit bands of most of the major black Broadway musicals of the late '20s and early '30s. "The second night of *Rhapsody in Black* after the curtain fell, none other than George Gershwin himself showed up dressed in evening clothes on his way to some late night affair, but he took several hours to work with us, changing tempos, and doing some re-harmonizing and so forth. Before he was finished, he had cut our 'Rhapsody in Blue' down to less than half the length we'd played it before."[16]

Several years after *Rhapsody in Black* found Snow performing in Chicago where an adolescent singer-pianist by the name Bobby Short first caught sight of her. In his 1971 autobiography *Black and White Baby*, Short wrote about "Fabled Valaida Snow who traveled in an orchid-colored Mercedes-Benz, dressed in an orchid suit, her pet monkey rigged out in an orchid jacket and cap, with her chauffeur in orchid as well."[17]

An equally intriguing portrait of the artist emerges in an article by author-musician Carman Moore that appeared in *The Village Voice* in 1981 and alluded to problems that would later befall Snow:

"She was black, outspoken in seven languages and good-looking and smart rather than beautiful and dumb, so it's perhaps a tribute to her ingenuity and iron will (lightly veiled behind a panther-taming smile) that she was not chained down and jailed in the U.S."[18]

* * *

The biographical facts concerning Valaida Snow's early years are surprisingly murky, with a clearer picture only coming into focus in the mid–1920s. By most accounts, she was born on June 2 in Chattanooga, Tennessee, in either 1900, 1903, or 1909; jazz archivist Frank Driggs, however, offers yet another date, 1905. But measured against other facts of her life, it is 1903 that seems most plausible. Further throwing would-be biographers off her scent, Snow was known to have claimed as her birthplace both Washington, D.C., and Chattanooga (with the latter being most the likely).[19]

And yet further confusion exists: Valaida's father John V. Snow was said by her to have been involved in show business, but scant records of his performing or producing activities seem to exist. One salient fact about him we do know is that, at least according to Snow in an article in a 1934 issue of London's *Daily Mirror*, he was apparently Caucasian — which may account for some of the confusion and vagueness that hover over much of Valaida's life and times.[20]

With miscegenation, the parties involved tended to distort the truth to stave off social opprobrium or legal complications. What is known about Snow's mother, Etta, is much more concrete, including the fact that she was educated at Washington, D.C.'s Howard University. She is also believed to have been involved with John V. Snow in various show business pursuits in and about the Chattanooga area.[21]

Unlike the Whitman Sisters, who as youngsters slowly evolved into professional entertainers, Valaida along with her younger performing sister and brother, Lavaida and Arvada, may have been more or less shoved onto the stage. One record of the family's early show business activities that has survived finds four-year-old Valaida and an adopted brother, J. Gould Snow, touring in an act billed as "Snow's Gold Dust Twins."[22] It is unclear whether or not Valaida played a musical instrument in the Gold Dust act, but she *was* tutored as a youth by her mother on cello, bass, violin, guitar, banjo, mandolin, harp, accordion, clarinet, and saxophone. It was most likely the era's prevailing prejudices against female jazz players that brought about Snow's later professional concentration on the trumpet at the expense of other instruments which she also played well. A sense of how truly expert a musician Snow was is illustrated by an incident that happened in 1924 when she was on tour with the hit musical *Chocolate Dandies* starring the team of Eubie Blake and Noble Sissle. According to Robert Kimball and William Bolcom in the 1973 book *Reminiscing with Sissle and Blake,*

> Eubie Blake [Sissle's partner] always used an A-440 tuning fork for his orchestral tune-ups. One day on the train Valaida heard him strike the fork and said, "Mr. Blake, your tuning fork's flat." Blake looked at her incredulously — how can a tuning fork be flat? "I say your tuning fork's flat," she insisted.
>
> At the next town Blake grabbed Valaida by the arm and ran off to the nearest music shop. The music dealer listened to the story and got a tuning fork off the shelf, struck the two forks together on his counter, and winced. Then he struck one, then the other. Finally, he took Blake's fork and sighted down its side. "She's right," he said; "it's a tiny hair bent." Evidently Blake's tuning fork, jostling about in his metal trunk, had gotten slightly out of true, but the difference in pitch could only have been extremely slight.[23]

Recalled pianist-bandleader Earl Hines, who was once romantically involved with Snow, in 1931 she not only appeared in but also produced shows at the legendary mob-run Grand Terrace night club in Chicago: "She was so talented. She picked out numbers from the band's book that could be used, memorized them, and hummed or scatted them to the chorus. Then when we came in, the rehearsals were very short, because the girls already knew the band's routines."[24]

Fellow trumpet player Doc Cheatham has speculated that it was this versatility coupled with her ability to entertain that would result in Valaida's life being spared when she later, in widely reported adventures, clashed head-on with the Nazis during World War II.[25]

Along with her many lovers, Snow would eventually take three husbands, the first among them being a dancer who went by the stage name of King Knappy Brown and whom she married in 1919.[26] The year following the dissolution of Valaida's marriage found her father dead — shot to death in an altercation[27] — and Etta Snow and her three young children moving to Washington, D.C., where the mother taught school while Valaida attended Armstrong High and performed with local bands on weekends.

After graduation in 1920, Valaida began to expand the radius of her appearances. In what was Snow's first professional foray out of the U.S. in June of that year found her in Vancouver, British Columbia, appearing on the white Pantages vaudeville circuit under the name of "Valyda" (more than likely her birth name).[28] In the fall of that year she was back in the States working with well-known female entertainer Gonzelle White, who sang and danced in front of a six-piece band which, aside from Valaida and the leader, was all-male. White dabbled on the saxophone, but was far from being the musical equal of Valaida or of the young musician who held down the piano chair in the band: William (soon to be "Count") Basie from Red Bank, New Jersey.

It was while Valaida was working for Gonzelle White in 1920 that songwriter Perry Bradford and singer Mamie Smith were making recording history with the first million seller by an African American, "Crazy Blues." Bradford was becoming increasingly concerned over copyright infringements of his work. Just *how* concerned can be gauged by the way he reacted to Snow's performance on the trumpet, with White, of a musical number at Gibson's Standard Theater in Philadelphia.

"Stop it," he jumped up and shouted, "I've got that tag copyrighted."

It was only an improvisational phrase which Snow had unconsciously expropriated from a trumpet solo on a Smith-Bradford recording and not intentional theft of the song in question that resulted in Bradford's over-the-top reaction. Nevertheless it was Bradford's unrelenting vigilance over his copyrights (rare for a black man of the era) that enabled him to survive long enough to tell the story about Valaida in his memoirs more than forty years later.[29]

After her brief stint with White, Snow began touring *Toby Time* — as the T.O.B.A. vaudeville circuit was also called — and other black vaudeville routes with the Will Mastin troupe (with which, a few years later, a three-year-old Sammy Davis, Jr., would make his entertainment debut). But the Mastin *Holiday in Dixieland* also occasionally played white venues; and in 1922 at the popular Reisenweber's Cabaret on New York's Columbus Circle, Snow stepped out of the chorus, played trumpet, tap danced up a storm and had her first real taste of what it was like to stop a show. The standout turn led to her being hired for several appearances at the popular Harlem spot, Barron Wilkins' Exclusive Club, which despite its way-uptown location at 134th Street and Seventh Avenue catered almost exclusively to a white clientele.[30] Wilkins would soon fall victim to a rubout allegedly engineered by the notoriously touchy Cotton Club owner Owney Madden over a complaint by Wilkins about being shorted on a beer shipment. But by then Snow was long gone, back on the T.O.B.A., Dudley and other black vaudeville circuits. She was in the 1923 revue *Ramblin' Round* (produced by Clarence Muse), which also starred Cab Calloway's talented sister Blanche. Typical of the T.O.B.A. theaters Muse and Snow were booked into was Atlanta's "81" Theater. In addition to its official meaning — Theatre Operators' Book Association — and a couple of more risible ones as well, the T.O.B.A initials were also said to stand for "Take Old Bailey's Advice" — "Old Bailey" being Charles P. Bailey, owner of the "81," and the meanest and most disliked straw boss of them all.[31] Not that most of the other owners exactly had the performers' best interests at heart: Other T.O.B.A. houses included the Douglass Theater in Macon, Georgia, which was so dirty performers didn't even bother to dress in the theater but in their own hotel rooms; the Park Theater in Dallas, more like a barn with no toilets, water or any other accommodations backstage; the particularly grueling Lincoln Theatre in Baltimore, and others which were "poorly constructed wooden and plaster firetraps often located next to railroad tracks. Many had tiny stages, no wings or backstage area and no dressing rooms."[32]

Mercifully (taking into account the condition of many T.O.B.A. Theaters), it was shortly after the Mastin affair abruptly folded on "Toby Time" due to financial problems, that Snow was given the chance to make her Broadway debut; the show was *Chocolate Dandies*, the eagerly awaited Eubie Blake and Noble Sissle follow-up to their early-twenties hit *Shuffle Along*. But when *Chocolate Dandies* opened on September 1, 1924 at New York's Colonial Theater, it turned out to be not quite the success that *Shuffle* had been. Nonetheless Valaida was saluted by one reviewer as "thrilling"[33] and the "Evening World" found that Josephine Baker, whose sensational Paris *La Revue Nègre* appearance was still a year away and whose first major show was *Dandies*, gave "the most unique performance seen in some time."[34]

Valaida and Josephine remained good friends for many years after appearing in the Blake-Sissle show, leading to a persisting belief that Snow's eventual World War II problems might have arisen out of her relationship with Baker, a staunch and outspoken foe of the Nazis who famously dabbled in spying against the Germans. When *Chocolate Dandies* closed, Snow, like Baker, went to Europe where her own experiences would make up for in exoticism, what they lacked in the way of *la* Baker's sheer sensationalism. Then after a short stint understudying Florence Mills in the 1926 edition of *Blackbirds* at the London Palladium, Snow chose not to accept Lew Leslie's offer of replacing the ailing Mills in the show.

In a curious move that would seem to represent a career step backward, Snow took off for Shanghai with a jazz octet — which counted among its members the great New Orleans clarinetist Albert Nicholas — led by Chicago drummer Jack Carter. But the tour (which was supposed to have been for a brief ten weeks) forged onward to Batavia in the Dutch East Indies and then to such far-flung locales as Rangoon, Calcutta and Singapore for dates at top hotels and restaurants patronized by what was then known as the "International Set."[35] With the exception of a brief return to America for the birth of her sister Lavaida's child and an appearance with Louis Armstrong's band at Chicago's Sunset Café, this exotic jazz mission ended up lasting two years.

While there is some general disagreement as to exactly how free and unprejudiced conditions were for blacks away from America at the time, there is little doubt that they were at least better; which was an important factor behind this near-stampede of black American jazz musicians (many of whom never returned). Black players could even draw perverse satisfaction that on foreign soil, *white* jazz musicians were often reduced to an indignity long familiar to African Americans — blacking up in order to secure a job.[36] At the very least, in racially mixed groups, white instrumentalists were often shunted off to play behind potted palms. The presence of genuine African American musicians in their midst was also of benefit to the locals who in many instances had previously only heard jazz on the wireless or Victrolas but now had a chance to listen to the music played first-hand. This was especially true in the ultra-exotic locales where Carter, Snow and their merry band performed.

In a 1934 British newspaper article by Snow entitled, "I've Met No Color Bar in London," she does not come right out and say that diminished racism abroad was a reason for her extended absences, but she does imply that. However, Snow was soon refuted by a British-based American black, A. Ward, in a *Chicago Defender* article counter-headlined "You've Just Been Lucky" in which he spikily advised Valaida, "I would kindly ask you in the future before undertaking to write such misleading articles, you should consult some coloured person who was born and who has lived here and to whom such a subject is of vital importance."

Ward proceeded to tick off a number of men of color "such as the millionaire Abbott of Chicago, business men from the British colonies, students and outstanding Indian politicians [who] have been barred in this country from entering hotels."[37]

How long Snow was prepared to remain abroad is not known; what *is* known is that her return was hastened by a certain Lord and Lady Sassoon who, according to jazz historian Frank Driggs, "heard Valaida and induced her to leave the troupe and come with them to Europe. What follows remains shrouded in mystery, but she did appear in a nightclub in Paris, possibly the Croix du Sud, and was the star in dancer-impresario Louis Douglas' show

Louisiana which toured from Russia to the Balkans playing the European capitals in 1929 and 1930."[38]

For the four years previous and for nearly the next ten, Snow spent more time abroad than in the U.S. via lengthy excursions that amounted to unofficial expatriation. But she remained interested in maintaining her professional reputation in the U.S. and was miraculously able to transcend the show business maxim "Out of sight, out of mind." Her first significant return to the U.S. came in 1930 with an appearance in what became a failed attempt to revive the classic *Shuffle Along* (followed shortly thereafter by the 1931 *Rhapsody in Black* with Ethel Waters).

It was also around this time that Snow took her second husband, 19-year-old dancer Ananias Berry of the dancing Berry Brothers. At the beginning, relations between Snow and her in-laws seem to have been cordial enough, but in 1933 when Nyas, as Ananias was known, left the family act to form a duo with Snow — thus killing off the family's main source of income — the tide suddenly turned. The father, A.J. Berry, began doing everything in his power to bring an end to his son's marriage to a woman at least seven years older than his son. Berry Sr.'s tactics Included dredging up King Knappy Brown aka Sam Lanier, the dancer to whom Snow had been briefly married 14 years earlier, and having him swear out a warrant that he and Snow were never properly divorced.[39]

The messy affair (and attendant headlines splashed across the pages of the nation's black press) dragged on for much of the year with Snow ending up in jail several times charged with bigamy, disorderly conduct and corrupting Nyas Berry's morals. Finally, in November of '33, Snow miraculously managed to produce papers legal enough for a Washington Heights magistrate to acquit her of all charges, and the two remarried before heading west for a series of professional engagements.[40] It is at this point that Lew Leslie once again showed up to play an important part in Snow's life.

Although by this time the kind of black-cast theatrical revues in which the showman specialized had thoroughly run their course on Broadway, they were still received with open arms abroad, especially in Great Britain. When even the participation of Bill Robinson failed to get his *Blackbirds of 1933* off the ground (it got no closer to Broadway than Harlem's Lafayette Theater), Leslie retooled it slightly, added Snow and Berry to its cast (now minus the departed Robinson), and shipped it off to London for an August 1934 opening at the London Coliseum. Predictably, *Blackbirds of 1934* met with much greater success abroad. Snow's numbers consisted of a salute to the late Florence Mills, "I'm a Little Blackbird"; "Porgy"; "I Can't Give You Anything But Love"; and "Heat Wave." As could be expected, reviews for Valaida's contributions to *Blackbirds* were full of praise, especially in the *London Daily Express* of September 14 which breathlessly proclaimed, "She has a big personality, wails your tear ducts dry, blows a mean trumpet, and conducts as Toscanini never could."[41]

Unlike the legendary black diva Florence Mills, of whom no permanent record remains, except for (perhaps) a test side executed for Victor in 1924 shortly before her death, Snow recorded fairly prolifically throughout her career. She made a series of highly praised recordings in London for Parlophone Records around this time. Featuring both her singing and playing, these thirty-two sides are considered by many to be the first real swing recordings executed in England and demonstrate that Snow justly deserved the sobriquet "Little Louis" (Armstrong) accorded her by European jazz critics and her billing as "Queen of the Trumpet."

During this period, Snow's marriage to Berry broke up and she returned to America for a few appearances including dates at Harlem's Apollo and Chicago's Grand Terrace, while Berry rejoined his brothers' act. Back in the U.S., Snow traveled to California for a date at the popular Sebastian's Cotton Club in Los Angeles, during which time she claims to have appeared in the feature films *Irresistible You* and *Take It from Me*; however, no sound films bearing these titles exist. (Snow did appear in two French features and at least two American shorts.) Somewhat curiously, Snow also says she appeared in films starring Cary Grant and Miriam Hopkins, but her name does not appear in filmographies for either performer.[42]

In 1936 Snow toured Shanghai, Hong Kong, Peking, Burma, Rangoon Turkey, Tokyo, Bombay, and Cairo. The sojourn was unexpectedly capped by what was unquestionably the most celebrated misadventure of her already highly colorful career: With the coming of Germany's occupation of Europe, each day it became increasingly important for Americans tourists and others — especially non–Aryans — to remain abreast of Nazi activities. And it was while she was appearing with Maurice Chevalier at a Paris night club in late 1939 that Snow learned about a possible German invasion and the wisdom of a quick departure from French soil. Instead of returning to America immediately, however, Valaida fled in her Mercedes to Holland where she had hastily arranged several bookings. When it became clear in early 1940 that Holland was due to fall to the Nazis *before* France, Snow then moved on to Denmark to work. Paris, which Snow had fled, ironically did not fall to the Germans until the following June. Instead, Denmark where she now found herself, on April 9, 1940, turned out to be the first of the three countries to fall to the Nazis (with Holland succumbing a month later). Snow had called all the shots wrong; her luck had finally run out.

Unable to get a passport, she and many other (mostly) Americans were placed under arrest by the Germans in the Vestre-Faengle prisoner of war camp in Copenhagen where she was the only black to be confined. Two unfounded rumors have long been circulated about Snow's capture: that she was involved in the drug trade, and that she was a spy. What *is* uncontestable is that being a non–Aryan American who trafficked in something even *worse* than drugs (what the Nazis called decadent Negroid music) was more than enough to have resulted in Snow's detention. It lasted for eighteen months, during which time she was constantly subjected to brutalities and punishment that would haunt her for the remainder of her life. On at least one occasion, according to jazz scholar Rosetta Reitz, Snow performed a kindness that resulted in a devastating act of sadistic behavior on the part of the Nazis:

"One day when a child was being beaten almost to death, Valaida fell out of line and covered the little girl with her body. The lashes fell on Valaida and split her head open, causing blood to gush. For the rest of her life, she had a long scar underneath her hair which she tried to comb carefully in order to hide it."[43]

One day Valaida learned that, for reasons that were not at first clear to her and obviously caused her great fear, she was to be taken to Gestapo headquarters in Copenhagen. Arriving there, she saw piled in a heap before her the belongings that had been confiscated upon her capture, including a trunk, expensive gowns, a mink coat, and a gold-plated trumpet given to her by Queen Wilhelmina of the Netherlands at a Command Performance. $5000 in American money and $2000 in Danish currency, along with her Mercedes, had also been taken from her when she was captured. Snow was told she was being exchanged in the first draft of war prisoners for the German manicurist of the S.W.S. *Bremen*, a noted Nazi spy. At first, she assumed that her effects were being returned to her by Nazis whom she scarcely expected could be so generous or honest. She was, in fact, given just enough clothing for a change, including a cheap cloth coat that wasn't even hers, then flown to the airport at Lisbon, Portugal, under guards of the Nazi Gestapo. There she was put aboard the Swedish S.S. *Gripsohlm* bound for New York (the *Gripsohlm*'s journey had commenced near the site of the notorious German concentration camp Bergen-Belsen).[44]

*   *   *

"The life of Valaida Snow is imperfectly known," begins the biographical entry for her in one reference work which goes on to note rumored inconsistencies of her arrest by the Nazis:

"She was arrested in Denmark or Sweden for theft and drug possession and deported to Germany.... Or was she arrested in Sweden and deported to the U.S. Others variants also exist."[45] What is beyond dispute in the entire affair is that Snow arrived aboard the *Gripsohlm* in Jersey City a few weeks after her release in a state of near-total debilitation with only 20 cents in her purse and her body covered with scars and defacements. She weighed only 68 pounds, down from a weight that normally would have been in excess of 100 pounds. Almost immediately she made her way to Harlem to see Jack Carter, the bandleader with whom she had spent so many years touring the Far East, and who was now operating a popular tavern bearing his name on

Seventh Avenue at 115th Harlem. Carter was not able to recognize Snow at first; but he finally did, sprang to her aid and placed her in a private sanitarium where she remained for the next six months.[46]

In an article written by Snow shortly after her return, she recalled her camp experiences in a chilling *memento mori*, "I Came Back from the Dead," which was scarcely hyperbole, for Etta Snow is said to have perished from the grief she suffered over the prevalent rumor that daughter Valaida had actually died in the Nazi prison.[47] Dancer Fayard Nicholas, who as an adolescent performer had drawn inspiration from Snow, remembers seeing her on TV in the early 1950s talking about the nightmarish experiences of more than a decade earlier: "I don't remember what show it was, but she just broke down like a baby and began sobbing and wasn't able to stop."[48]

But self-pity was definitely not Snow's forte; almost immediately upon release from the sanitarium where she'd been sent by Jack Carter, Valaida Snow set about getting her career, as well as her personal life, back in order. Marrying a man by the name of Earle Edwards (who eventually became her personal manager) on April 24, 1943, Snow also made her first stage appearance since her return to America, at Harlem's Apollo Theatre. She played New York City's Alhambra Theatre and Café Society Uptown and in 1945 began recording again. That year she and Edwards moved to Los Angeles, where work was plentiful due to a night life scene fueled by World War II defense plant workers. It was during this period that musician Melba Liston was on a bill with Snow at the Lincoln Theater located on L.A.'s popular black entertainment strip, Central Avenue. The Valaida that the twenty-year-old trombonist saw appears to have been more healed in body than in mind:

"There was something about her, the way she acted, that saddened me and that I never forgot.... She was so talented, so beautiful and so sweet. But she was so unhappy. She was like hurt at the time. In my youth I didn't understand. But I felt the pain from her all the time.... There was the confusion there that I couldn't understand in my youth..."[49]

If behind the scenes, Valaida was perhaps still showing the wear and tear inflicted on her by the Nazis, on-stage she was still in good form. Clora Bryant, the foremost female trumpet player of a later generation, recalls catching Snow's act around the same time as Liston:

When I first saw Valaida Snow she was playing the Orpheum Theater [in Los Angeles]. She came out in this beautiful white bouffant dress with big pockets on each side and sang "My Heart Belong to Daddy." And *then* ... she reached into her pocket and pulled out her trumpet and I fell on the floor. I'd *never* seen anything like that! The way she hid that trumpet in her dress which was like a coronation outfit and the way the dress was lighted — they knew how to light everyone. And her hair was shining and her makeup was good. Great paste diamonds. Beautiful! I never met her though. I was too shy, too overwhelmed. Reached in her pocket and pulled out a trumpet!"[50]

The end of the decade found the Edwardses living back in New York, with Snow now limiting her performances mostly to the eastern seaboard and Canada. A May 20, 1949, date at New York's Town Hall (where she was backed by an all-male choir and sang a program of Arlen, Gershwin, and spirituals) would seem to indicate that Snow was still in demand. But if so, it was not to last much longer: The '50s found her in working at hotel clubs in the Catskills for room and board and a low weekly salary. Conductor Maurice Peress, who would go on to be the musical director for the premiere of Leonard Bernstein's *Mass* in 1971 and oversee the 1989 recreation of the Clef Club Concert at Carnegie Hall, was still in his teens when he was employed as a musician in this Jewish vacation region known as the "Borscht Belt." It was there that he first encountered Valaida Snow:

"I was playing trumpet in a Catskills hotel. These places kept full time bands. We played for social dancing six nights a week and on the weekends we also played for vaudeville shows. I was starting to arrange music for a few acts at the time and Valaida somehow found out.... I'm sure I sent a signal in rehearsal some way, fixing up parts on the spot and so forth, and she asked me to write something for her."

At this point, Peress was unfamiliar with Valaida's reputation and previous accomplishments, and her performing skills came as a surprise: "I recall her *presence* above all. She overpowered any 'creative' ideas I had with her own. On stage she was energy and motion and the loudest trumpet player you could imagine. I was quite intimidated by her sexuality as well ... she oozed womanliness." Peress went on to say that as he grew into his twenties, "my American music curiosity moved from conducting anything that reconnected me to my jazz roots at every opportunity, into the serious research stage." But he had not thought of Snow again much after that summer "until around 1983. Valaida's name came up in association with black shows like 1924's *Chocolate Dandies*. It was only then that I realized she had to have been in her mid-forties when I worked with her." Peress also had another realization: "If Valaida is representative of the depth of talent of the 1920s 'dumb showgirl' who was supposedly hired for her looks not her talent ... and I think she is [representative], then we have to conclude, albeit from this one example, that *Shuffle Along* and other such [black shows] were chock-a-block with enormously skilled and disciplined artists."[51]

Snow was a dancing, singing, trumpeting Catskills headliner when she and Peress' paths crossed. He was on his way up, she was on the way down to playing the "Belt" (and, Peress recalls, *lesser* Borscht Belt hotels at that). Thus, on the increasingly rarer occasions when she could still find work at some of her old stomping grounds a few hundred miles south in New York City, the money she received was far less than before.[52]

We can never know the kind of trajectory Snow's career would have taken had she not been captured by the Nazis. Even though she was gone for only a relatively brief period, in a business that, as Mort Sahl once remarked, "eats its young," two years away from the spotlight is an eternity. Snow never regained the career momentum that was hers before the war. Race was only part of the problem. Gender was likewise crucial in that Snow wasn't just a singer or dancer (traditional female showbiz occupations), but a trumpet player as well (a male pursuit if there ever was one). This in turn leads to the problem created by Snow's triple-threat skills. While her talents in all areas were genuine, they are nonetheless remindful of the ersatz "multi-talent" tradition of classic vaudeville — the last gasp of which is embodied by cornball performer Wayne Newton.

World War II America was quite hospitable to women who played "as well as a man," *vide* such successful musical "takes" on Rosie the Riveter as the International Sweethearts of Rhythm, and Ina Ray Hutton and Her Melodears. But when Johnny came marching home, the gals were expected to pack away their axes and don their aprons once more. In Snow's case, this would have meant trimming her sails to concentrate on one of her several other talents; singing, or dancing, or even acting would have been more acceptable. But less so, trumpet playing. Having shown remarkable skill on her instrument of choice for more than thirty years, it's hard to imagine that Snow would have put down her horn without a fight.

In the end, Valaida Snow went out with the sort of quasi-mythological flair befitting a star of her caliber: In May of 1956 she secured a high-profile booking at the Valhalla of vaudeville, New York's Palace Theater; and it was upon completion of her well-received week-long engagement at the historic showplace that she suffered a cerebral hemorrhage and was taken to Kings County Hospital where she died 21 days later, on May 30.[53] It was a passing foreshadowing that of her friend Josephine Baker who died in 1975 on the day after her triumphal return to the stage at Paris' Bobino theater. Snow's death, though, was far less swift and merciful than that of Baker, who went peacefully in her sleep.

Valaida Snow and Josephine Baker were both black women born in the early 20th century into humble circumstances in the interior of an America that had little regard for their existences. After a modicum of early stateside success, they were daring pioneers in an expatriation movement that found American blacks moving in large numbers to climes that held out least some slim potential for a kind of achievement and self-respect not available in the land of their birth. In the process, both became international stars. Likewise both also had their problems with the Nazis, although, obviously, Snow's were much worse than Baker's.

Snow and Baker, however, differ greatly in at least one regard: While the latter's life is an open book, having spawned a cottage industry's worth of books, biopics and documentaries, Snow seems to have taken many secrets to her grave, leading to the likelihood that her curious and colorful existence might never be perfectly known.

*   *   *

Postscript to first edition: Not long ago, as a result of this book, I gave interviews on the subject of Snow to the NPR radio show *Jazz Rhythm*, and a few weeks later I taped a segment for a new TV "magazine" show hosted by Tim Reid of *Once Upon a Time When We Were Colored*, *WKRP*, and *Frank's Place* fame.

I'd appeared on TV before and was never too happy with the way I looked, but Reid took some pains to light me and when the show finally aired I could actually look at myself and not flinch. He worked like a veritable von Sternberg achieving those modest results, and while he shifted light stands and moved about, he also told me a bit about the making of *Once Upon a Time*.

The film was actually one of the first black ensemble cast films ever to turn a profit by playing almost exclusively theaters in African American neighborhoods. And what a cast! If you had dropped a bomb on the film, you risked wiping out black show business: Al Freeman, Jr., Phylicia Rashad, Paula Kelly, Leon, Richard Roundtree, Isaac Hayes, Taj Mahal, Bernie Casey, Ossie Davis, Ruby Dee, Anna Maria Horsford, with the one significant white role played by singer-actress Polly Bergen. *Once Upon a Time When We Were Colored* cost less than three million dollars to produce for a film that appeared to have a budget many times that amount. "Not to sound like a braggart at all and not to diminish Steven Spielberg's talent," Reid confided to me, "but I'd like to see him make the same film for anywhere near that small an amount."

His cast and crew worked way above and beyond the call of duty to make the film possible. The 1940s-period film had more than 200 costumed extras and speaking parts with the entire budget allotted to dressing them amounting to a little over a measly $20,000. The costumer had to work so diligently bringing the miracle off, Reid informed me, that she suffered a stroke during the film's making and had to be hospitalized.

And there was yet another calamity. The gas lines of the '40s antique cars were forever getting clogged. Whenever this happened, filming would cease long enough for a production assistant to suck gas from the line and expectorate it. Finally, the act became such a common occurrence that one day when the p.a. did this, either because he acted too reflexively or perhaps coughed during the process, he accidentally swallowed gasoline and went into cardiac arrest. Reid recalled that he ran and began to apply CPR to the man who was out cold. After a minute or two, the p.a.'s eyes fluttered open and he looked up at a relieved Reid. Almost soundlessly he muttered the same words over and again to his rescuer. At first, Reid could not quite hear what was being said and bent closer. Then very faintly he could make out the words:

"I don't want to come back."

Said Reid to the man, "Well, damn it [perhaps with visions of the notorious *Twilight Zone* movie set catastrophe suddenly swimming in his head], you *are* going to come back whether you like it or not."

"And," Reid told me, "I continued pounding on his chest with all my might."

"And did you manage to save him?" I asked.

"Yes."

"And was the man grateful?"

"I suppose. Later I went to see him in the hospital and asked him, 'And so ... was it warm and peaceful with beautiful bright white light everywhere?'"

"Y-y-y-yes. And I just didn't want to come back."

When I finished laughing, Reid then returned to quadruple duty as producer-director-lighting man-camera man. And I began to talk, on camera, about the fabulous Valaida Snow.

Over the past several decades there have been several failed attempts, including one by Diana Ross, to develop a movie based on Snow's extraordinary life and career. But to the best of my knowledge Reid, with the segment on his TV "magazine" show, is the first to have widely disseminated Valaida's amazing story.

Around this time a novel, *Valaida*, by African American writer Candace Allen, also appeared. However, the impressive work only uses elements of Snow's life in an impressionistic and a-temporal manner, and cannot be considered a substitute for a long-overdue biography of its subject.

5

Renaissance Woman
Nora Holt

Researching the life of a certain much-storied figure of the famed 1920s Harlem Renaissance cultural movement, one might reach the understandable conclusion that, while sharing the same historical space and legal name, there were several women who went by the name of Nora Holt. But there was, in fact, only one educator-classical composer-blues singer-cabaret star-radio personality-courtesan-public school teacher-magazine editor-beauty salon proprietor-social activist by the name of Nora Lena Douglas James Scroggins Jones Ray Holt.

A headline-grabbing *femme fatale* who threw caution to the wind in a manner otherwise unthinkable in the 1920s, Nora Holt, not unlike certain well-known white "playgirls" of the era — the name most readily springing to mind being would-be actress Peggy Hopkins Joyce — was much-married. By her late '20s she had been to the altar five times and was accorded the dubious honor of inclusion in a 1949 *Ebony* article entitled "Most Married Negroes."[1] Like playgirl Joyce, it was from her marital adventures that Holt's initial notoriety sprang. But, unlike Joyce and her ilk, Holt was genuinely talented: Among her several talents and skills, she could sing, *really* sing — accompanying herself on piano on all manner of songs, ranging from light opera to lowdown dirty blues.

Born Lena Douglas in Kansas City, Kansas, to an A.M.E. minister, Reverend Calvin N. Douglas, and his wife Grace in either 1885 or 1890 (given birth dates vary), from the very beginning she was marked as being *different,* as was evidenced by her starting to take piano lessons at the age of four, and entering, at age five, private primary school. She was ahead of the game in college as well, graduating as valedictorian of her class in 1915 at Western University, an A.M.E. church school in Quindaro, Kansas. After this, she enrolled at Chicago Music College.

Similarly, her marital dossier began remarkably early; at age 15, already a slender and stunning red-haired beauty, she took husband number one, a musician by the name of Sky James. By age 17, having divorced him, she wed husband number two, politician Philip Scroggins; in short order Holt then divorced him and married her third mate, unaccountably (given Holt's propensity for "marrying well") a barber by the name of Bruce Jones. Early on in Chicago, Nora Douglas, as she was known then, also began to cover the waterfront professionally as well as maritally. Years later she recalled helping to pay her college tuition by "singing light songs ... melodies, and spirituals at elegant dinner parties" given at the Gold Coast homes of Chicago's meat packing and farm machinery barons, the ones with names like Armour, Swift and McCormick.[2]

Nora Holt, circa 1938 (photograph by Carl Van Vechten, from the collection of the Library of Congress).

But these *soirées intimes* did not constitute Holt's only paid appearances; she also sang and played piano at the expensive and lavish Chicago brothel operated by the city's infamous Everleigh Sisters, located on the so-called *Line*, the Windy City's notorious red-light district. At the Everleigh Club, "Prices began at fifty dollars, and champagne was twenty dollars a bottle.... Even the grand piano was leafed with gold, and the cuspidors, discreetly hidden by long velvet draperies that framed exotic murals, were gold-plated. Upstairs were gold, silver and copper rooms.... There were also a Persian room, a college room, a Pullman room fitted as a private railroad car, a mirrored room covered from floor to ceiling and wall to wall with silvered glass."[3] Understandably, here Nora's repertoire tended to eschew "Un Bel Di" in favor of songs like "Some Black Snake's Been Sucking My Rider's Tongue" and "My Daddy Rocks Me with One Steady Roll" with its more-than-generous assertions about her man's sexual prowess. It was a number that went far beyond the realm of the mere *double entendre*:

"My Daddy rocks me with one steady roll, there's no slippin' when he once takes hold; I looked at the clock and the clock struck one, daddy ain't we got fun," and on around the clock for a number of verses until ... well, you get the picture.

Several decades later, in 1954, the ditty had a rebirth in the form of the song generally considered to have launched the rock 'n' roll era; as the record's producer, Milt Gabler, pointed out, "'Rock Around the Clock' is an old blues, 'My Daddy Rocks Me With One Steady Roll' ... it's just a re-write of it with a change of tune."[4]

At the time Holt first sang it, the melody was being played and recorded by almost everyone working in Chicago; so much so that, for a time, it became a kind of jazz anthem for the town. As for Holt, she sang it so much then and later, in some of the swellest watering holes on the Continent, that it became more or less a signature tune for her. All the while, she continued working her way through college. By night she entertained high and not-so-high society, and by day, in 1917, she began a four-year stint as music critic for the influential black daily, the *Chicago Defender*. Newspapers like the *Defender* and the *Pittsburgh Courier* were read faithfully, not just locally, but nationally by hundreds of thousands of black Americans. In the long history of such journals, Holt is (arguably) said to have been the first African American to write regularly about music for a black daily. In an early display of her lifelong talent for unifying the vernacular with the academic, she instituted a column simply called "Music" in which she wrote freely not just about the activities of African American classicists like violinist Clarence Cameron White and tenor Roland Hayes, but also composers of spirituals and jazz; musicians such as Harry T. Burleigh and Wilbur Sweatman. Here, for example, is what she had to say about master spiritual arranger Burleigh in a typical column — this one for the week of March 27, 1920:

"It was during this second year at the conservatory that he had the great privilege to meet and sing to the late Dr. Antonin Dvorak, and while he never actually enrolled as a pupil in the great musician's class he was frequently with him. He copied some of his manuscripts and the old plantation songs for him at his home. Dvorak was so interested that he was ever ready to help Burleigh in his earlier compositions."

Her columns also carried news of musical goings-on at auditoriums, churches and schools in the Chicago area.

Shortly after joining up with the *Defender*, Holt received her B. A. from Chicago Music College in 1917, and the following year, her Masters, her thesis being a symphonic piece entitled "Rhapsody on Negro Themes," based on the spiritual "You May Bury Me in the East." As such, she became — it is believed — the first Negro in the U.S. to receive an M.A. in music.[5]

It was while Holt was with the *Defender* and attending Chicago Music College that her public image as a major league vamp playing for big stakes began to truly take hold. She took her fourth husband, hotel owner George W. Holt, forty years her senior, who upon dying two years later left her an extremely wealthy woman. Among other inherited assets, she became the largest single stockholder in the thriving black Liberty Life Insurance Company (which when it merged with another such outfit in 1929 claimed assets of $1.5 million).[6] Rather than sit back and clip coupons, however, Holt continued writing for the *Defender* and editing and publishing a magazine, *Music and Poetry*. She also kept on composing music, with her activities in a relatively brief time amounting to some 200 works for piano, voice — several of which, especially "A Florida Night" (her setting of a Paul Laurence Dunbar poem) — were featured by black tenor Roland Hayes.

However, almost none of Holt's work remains, having disappeared from Chicago storage during one of her many trips to Europe commencing in 1926. Only by dint of its appearance in *Music and Poetry*, the magazine published and edited by her starting in 1921, does one of Holt's four "Negro Dances" for piano survive. Seemingly almost as an afterthought during this time, in the Midwest (in 1919) she helped found the National Association of Negro Musicians. Other original members included the important composer and spiritual arranger Nathaniel Dett and violinist Clarence Cameron White.

Upon announcement of her engagement to a man even richer than the recently deceased George Holt, Nora became page one news in nearly every black newspaper in the U.S. In fact, her intended, Joseph Ray, a food concessionaire and right hand man of steel magnate Charles Schwab, was described in one report as being "one of the wealthiest men of the Race."[7] Interestingly, considering her later penchant for white café society, all of her five husbands and many known dalliances were black.

Nora's July 29, 1923, wedding to Ray was, according to the *Chicago Defender*, "one of the most brilliant weddings in many a season." Music was provided by the distinguished African American violinist Clarence Cameron White, with the services performed by her father, the Rev. Douglas. Holt herself was "a picture of loveliness gowned in a gorgeous creation of crepe Elizabeth, beaded on masses with pearls ... and a tulle veil [which] fell gracefully to the floor, caught here and there with orange blossoms."[8] Understandably what the *Defender* left out was that Nora's tulle veil concealed a black eye that was given to her by a certain Dr. Jackson whom she had been seriously dating before suddenly switching her attentions to Ray.[9]

Immediately the couple headed off on a two-month honeymoon in Europe; they returned to the steel town of Bethlehem, Pennsylvania, where Ray had furnished a luxurious home for his new wife and himself. But In divorce papers filed against Nora the following year, Ray claimed that she had managed to spend a total of only thirty-two days in Bethlehem during the entirety of their stormy eighteen-month marriage. Or as one gossipy news account put it, "Mrs. Ray soon tired of the lonesomeness of the steel city and made frequent trips to New York." Nora (now Holt-Ray) defended herself in interviews: Ray showed signs of jealousy of her prominence, she said, and was resentful of being introduced as "Mr. Holt." Also, she charged, he had reneged on a pledge to settle certain of his real estate holdings on her as a wedding gift.[10] Somewhere in the midst of all this, during one of Nora's many alleged forays to Manhattan from Bethlehem, she met at a Harlem speakeasy the person who would remain her closest friend and confidante for the rest of her life: writer Carl Van Vechten.

"I was out last night with the Sheka of Harlem," Van Vechten wrote to H.L. Mencken shortly after meeting Holt in 1925. "She looks like [opera singer] Mary Garden & her trail is strewn with bones, many of them no longer hard."[11] In the same letter, Van Vechten offered up yet another reason — blunt and to the point — for the split between the Holts: "She began to operate on so extensive a scale that [president of Bethlehem Steel president and Joseph Ray's boss] Mr. Charlie Schwab became alarmed and demanded that her husband divorce her so that she could be removed from Bethlehem."[12]

But the real corker in the divorce court proceedings were certain of her actions during one of her excursions to late-night Manhattan from the nine o'clock town of Bethlehem: "It is reported that Mr. Ray charges his wife with adultery, naming one Leroy Wilkins, brother of the late [Harlem café proprietor] Barron Wilkins," screamed a front page story in the July 25, 1925 *Chicago Defender*. Ray used the testimony of a maid of Wilkins who said that she "served them breakfast in bed together every morning from May 17 until May 24." The paper, which opined that the divorce suit would "stir fashionable society East and West," was right on target.[13] (After several years of legal wrangling played out on the front pages of most major African American newspapers, Holt won her battle to retain most of the approximately $42,000 that had been promised to her by Ray prior to their marriage.)

By now Nora Holt-Ray was all the rage. *Heebie Jeebies*, a black weekly, ran an August 1, 1925, story about Holt, "(Little Lena) The Mamma Who Can't Behave."[14] During this period, news of her exploits also filled the pages of the *Inter-State Tattler*, a popular black gossip periodical. And, more importantly, with her provocative reputation and a sizable legacy in tow, this great beauty had arrived just in time to become one of the most dazzling figures of that period in American arts and letters known variously as the "Black Renaissance," the "Negro Renaissance," and the "Negro Movement," the "Negro Awakening"[15] but, ultimately, as the Harlem Renaissance. This "burst of creativity in the 'high arts' eventually produced," according to academic John S. Wright, "a circle of some three dozen leading artists who generated more than two dozen novels, ten volumes of poetry, five Broadway plays, reams of essays and tales, three performed ballets, and a huge expanse of canvas and sculpture."[16]

It was an artistic movement that also had its lighter side consisting of night club hopping in popular mixed race cabarets such as Connie's Inn and Happy Rhone's. This sidelight of the Renaissance represented a new era in black and white relationships, for as journalist Chandler Owen pointed out in his 1925 essay "The Black and Tan Cabaret—America's Most Democratic

Institution,"* this relatively new wrinkle in race[17] was not a case of blacks push-ing themselves on the white people. Just the reverse; it was the white people push-ing themselves among the colored. "[T]hey all get along. There is no fighting, no hostility, no suspicion, no discrimination. All pay alike and receive alike."[18]

Van Vechten was not only Nora's new best friend, he also was the Harlem art movement's colorful and controversial *eminence grise* and hovering guru. He also happened to be white! He was born in Cedar Rapids, Iowa, in 1880 into a prominent progressive family; in 1906 this somewhat shambling and ungainly figure journeyed to New York where he joined the staff of *The New York Times* as a music critic, then before long became (although mostly for-gotten as such today) one of the country's most popular novelists. The actions for which he is now most remembered, however, were the support, financial aid, social comfort and guidance he offered to the many gifted painters, musi-cians and writers (Langston Hughes, Countee Cullen, Aaron Douglas et al.) who made up the vanguard of the Harlem Renaissance movement.

By the time Holt and Van Vechten met, his stewardship and mentoring of blacks had already earned him a fair degree of scorn and derision from many African Americans (his was a familiar name to them nationwide) who were deeply suspicious of his motives. The title of his most famous novel *Nig-ger Heaven* (the vernacular for the seats where blacks sat in segregated the-aters) earned him massive opprobrium. But he was also the recipient of much credit and approval: The highly *un*suspect author and NAACP leader James Weldon Johnson and Langston Hughes were part of his intimate circle and long sang his praises, as well as did Holt who, years later, wrote to "Carlo," "It will be decades before America and the Negro in general realizes that you have done more to engender social equality and human rights behavior between the races than any other individual or organization in the country."[19]

These arguable sentiments notwithstanding, it is safe to conclude that in most quarters Van Vechten's reputation (and motives) is probably more secure today than it was more than half a century ago. He was an equally con-troversial figure with whites because of his free, unfettered social relations with blacks; practically unheard of during those times, he openly socialized with them, dined with them in his homes and, generally, as Nora later wrote, brought about "social equality ... through the good old American tradition of the family — in the parlour and the dining room."[20]

Soon after meeting Nora, Van Vechten immortalized her as Lasca Sar-toris, the sexual predator of his classic and notorious *roman à clef* of the Harlem Renaissance, *Nigger Heaven*.† "She's just naturally full of pep and she

---

*The phrase "black and tan" is incorrectly thought by some to refer to clubs frequented by blacks only. In fact, it strictly applies to mixed race establishments.

†She was also the basis for a character in Countee Cullen's only novel, the lesser known *One Way to Heaven*.

bounces the papas off their rails," he wrote of Holt's fictional counterpart in his book, which was set in New York in the mid–'20s.[21] Though his fictional portrait of her might have differed from reality in some areas— in *Heaven* the male protagonist Byron succumbs to the charms of Sartoris, "a legend in Harlem ... who had married a rich African in Paris and had eventually deserted him to fulfill her amorous destiny with a trap drummer"— still it was clearly recognizable as Nora, a fact she later acknowledged.[22] "The affair between Lasca and Byron," writes Van Vechten biographer Bruce Kellner, "eats through the pages of two or three chapters with an erotic sensibility, in spite of the lawyer's pre-publication deletions...."[23] Of Lasca Sartoris (and presumably Holt herself), Van Vechten wrote in *Nigger Heaven*, "[T]hose who knew her apparently liked her [because of] her money, her beauty, her wit and her charm."[24] ... "To know her is to forgive her [because] you know what usually happens when you've been brought up in a minister's family: when you get the chance you cut loose and go to the devil ... Lasca knows what she wants and goes after it, more than most of us do."[25] And ... "She was rich and successful and happy. She had won. Problems didn't bother her. She had found what she had wanted by wanting what she could get, and then always demanding more, more, until now the world poured its gifts into her bewitching lap."[26]

All of which rang a bell with real-life Harlem where, shortly after Nora blew into town for the first time, apparently every woman who had a vested interest in the male of the species was up in arms. Typical of the impact Holt must have made is felt in a June 1925 diary entry of Paul Robeson's wife Essie, who wrote that Nora was "a red hot mama" whom she "couldn't bear" and that "if she went after Paul I'd eat her alive, and I meant it, and they know I did."[27] (At least where Essie Robeson was concerned, contrary to Van Vechten's sentiments, to know Lasca/Nora was not enough to bring about forgiveness.)

In May 1926 — in the wake of nearly a year's worth of screaming tabloid headlines— Holt felt the need for a change in environment and set sail for Europe.[28] Shortly after arriving in London armed with introductions to royalty from her white New York friends, Nora's performing career took off like a rocket; she quickly became one of the top café society draws on the Continent and throughout the Near and Far East. As such, she was following in the footsteps of many dozens of other African American entertainers like Alberta Hunter, Bricktop, Valaida Snow and the popular piano-vocal team of Layton and Johnstone, all of whom were drawn to foreign locales where the money was good and the social atmosphere generally less oppressive than in the U.S.

In London, Nora first secured a booking at the chic Coventry Street Restaurant where her appearance brought about the following rave (though by today's standards somewhat offensive) remarks from the critic for the *London Daily Express*:

Creole femininity has often exercised a strong fascination over the most iron-willed of men, the most celebrated of all was no less than Napoleon's Josephine.... [S]omething of this attraction may be felt in the singing of Mrs. Nora Holt, a blond Creole whose first London appearance I've witnessed at a Coventry Street restaurant early yesterday morning. She has a presence and manner similar to Sophie Tucker. Same mop of golden curly hair, the same perky good-natured lift of the head and the same appealing smile ... but her voice is even more astonishing. She can produce sounds not comparable to orthodox singing, ranging from deepest low voice to shrilling high, often unaccompanied by words.[29]

Clearly, in a manner not unlike the men in Holt's private life, the critic had lost his head over Nora. Apparently no commercial recordings of Holt were ever made, for Van Vechten biographer Bruce Kellner (himself a latter member of the author's circle of friends) can only guess at the sound of her singing voice, surmising that her style might have resembled that of "the currently popular Cleo Laine."

In Paris, Holt appeared at a small dinner club located in the Empire Theatre — "very much," she said, "like 21 or the Stork Club"[30] — where an exclusive French clientele gathered after the opera for late supper and music. In Paris, she studied conversational French with Madame Jocelyn, a member of the *Comédie-Française,* and supplemented her income appearing at private parties. Every winter for four years, beginning in 1926, she also entertained at a night club in Monte Carlo.[31] During her first trip abroad she also found time to inform Van Vechten of the shock waves felt all the way to Europe after his *Nigger Heaven* had been published in America: In August of 1926 she wrote him: "The cries of Harlemites reach me even in Paris.... Strange that in such a short time you caught the attitude of the Negro toward the Negro and not one in a thousand will admit it."[32] She also kept Van Vechten abreast of her own activities: In December of '26 she wrote to him: "I went to tea at Gertrude Stein's and adored her. She is a great person."[33]

In years to come in London she performed in the private homes of royalty and the elite like the Armstrong-Joneses and the Guinesses, where she "played little songs and melodies from the current musicals, such as 'The Man I Love,'" she later recalled, adding proudly, "I knew Mr. Gershwin."[34] Holt was also booked into the swank Café de Paris in London at exactly the time the Prince of Wales and Wallis Simpson were carrying on their not-so-*soto voce* affair. One night the couple came to the café; afterward, the prince made the gesture of coming forward to congratulate her on her performance there.[35]

Not confined just to England and France, Holt also worked in Rome and for several years on and off in Shanghai where she was employed at a "smart [and] typically British" club run by an Englishman, Sir Victor Sassoon. "*Everybody* passed through Shanghai," she later recalled.[36] For the next twelve years she lived a bi-continental existence with many trips back home not just to see friends, but also for work. On one occasion in New York in 1929, Holt came to the liner the *Mauretania* to see Van Vechten off to Europe. A *bon voyage* party came to life in the writer's stateroom and she was entreated to play the piano and sing. She gave out with the usual, "My Daddy Rocks Me with One Steady Roll"; afterwards a dowager from the Deep South complimented her: "How well you sing spirituals, my dear."[37]

Nineteen thirty-four was a particularly active year for her in the States. In St. Louis she headed up a regional defense fund show for the NAACP (an announcement for the event called her "the toast of four continents") where she sang J.C. Johnson's "Little Black Boy," the theme of the campaign, and also "Lift Every Voice and Sing." The evening also featured such stars as Chicago singer-dancer Mae Alix (Al Capone's favorite), dancer U.S. "Slow Kid" Thompson and Velma Middleton, future singing sidekick of Louis Armstrong.

At a similar benefit in Chicago earlier the same year, she had appeared wearing a gown of golden sequins singing "The Physician" from Cole Porter's *Nymph Errant*. In the fall of '34, Holt starred in an ill-fated New York revue entitled *Rhythm Bound,* but elsewhere demonstrated that, even heading into her fifth decade, she still retained much of her old "party girl" edge. Extrapolating from the private papers of Langston Hughes, author Arnold Rampersad writes in his biography of the author, "May also brought lively visitors to 'Ennesfree' [the Carmel, California, estate of Hughes' friend Noel Sullivan], including the quixotic black cabaret star Nora Holt, a fleshy favorite in New York and Los Angeles, who swept into Carmel for a week and left the white village in shambles. Having arrived in a humble Ford, Hughes noted gleefully, Holt had departed in a Cadillac — most likely driven by Noel Sullivan, who had hustled down from San Francisco to meet her; Edward Weston photographed her about forty times, Langston counted."[38]

When Japan took Shanghai, it was finally all over for Holt abroad: War in Europe and elsewhere found her reevaluating her priorities and options. And so in a life overflowing with sudden, abrupt and unexpected transformations, both professional and private, she pulled off, unquestionably, the biggest one yet. Langston Hughes reported in a summer 1937 letter to Van Vechten that, as Van Vechten in turn reported in a letter to his wife, "Nora Holt intended to go back to China but she has just passed the school examination in Los Angeles so brilliantly (for teaching music in the high schools— she has been doing this part time) that she is going to stay in L.A."[39] How Holt managed to secure such a position given the notoriety that had followed her most of her adult life must qualify as one of the great mysteries of modern education. What is known is that she had now reverted to her maiden name of Douglas, so perhaps that helped. She remained in Los Angeles for several years, teaching successfully and also obtaining a position on the school board. In 1941 she opened up a beauty parlor in the city.

For the many years still remaining to her, Holt continued to successfully cast herself more and more in the role of prim and proper middle-aged woman and less in the part of *femme fatale.* In the final analysis, it was perhaps common sense that drove her on in this direction, for the years had prematurely begun to take their toll. A 1937 photo of her by Van Vechten shows the aging process already in high gear; and a 1950s one finds her looking ten years older than she was. As Van Vechten once wrote of his anti-heroine Lasca Sartoris, she "certainly cut loose, but in the old days she never quite went to the devil. She always kept a certain dignity."[40]

Nora, like Lasca, apparently knew when enough was enough ... when it was time to quit the game of glamour girl and move on. In 1943 she relocated back to New York City to assume the position of music critic for the *Amsterdam News* (and later the *New York Courier*). Under sponsorship of composer Virgil Thomson, she became the first black member of the New York Music Critics Circle, and also she was the first African American to work as a music critic and editor under a CIO (American Newspaper Guild) contract. In addition, from 1953 to 1964 she ran a popular weekly radio show, *Concert Showcase,* heard on local station WLIB which featured such up-and-coming concert stars as Betty Allen and Margaret Tynes. As well, she became a friend and mentor to other young stars like Leontyne Price, William Warfield, Martina Arroyo and Adele Addison.

"Think of It! Nora and Ethel [Waters] are now highly respected women on the top of the heap," Van Vechten wrote to a friend in the summer of 1950 on the occasion of a testimonial dinner for Nora, "while Paul Robeson and Walter White, great men in the twenties, are in the dog house."[41]

In April 1966 she was appointed a member of Communications Committee at the First World Festival of Negro Arts, which was to be held in Dakar, Senegal. And so, Nora's amazing transformation into "dowager music critic" was now — as noted by Van Vechten biographer Bruce Kellner — complete.[42] Shortly thereafter she retired to Los Angeles, at age 81 (or 86?) a highly respected community elder.

In a brief "portrait" of Holt written by Van Vechten in 1942, he was of the opinion that his old friend and literary inspiration model "deserves a biography of her own."[43]

A paradigm of paradox, she was a gifted exponent of vernacular music who still managed to give over a large part of her time to supporting academic music. In her sexual deportment, she transgressed gender mores, but was able to sidestep the usual ostracizing associated with doing so. Holt also helped "write the book" on both American café society *and* black expatriation. A deeply resourceful woman with a taste for the finer things in life, in her pursuit of adventure she also played a significant role in expanding the constrictive boundaries imposed on African Americans and on women. Nora Holt died in Los Angeles on January 25, 1974, and no complete book of her life is yet on the horizon. But — considering the amazing life she led — who could argue with Van Vechten's conclusions?

* * *

Postscript to first edition: In Spring 2006 I received the following email: "Dear Mr. Reed: I am working on a segment for the PBS series *History Detectives* re: composer, Nora Holt. I hope to speak with you about your research into her life and work. If there are other experts you feel I should also contact, I would really appreciate this information as well, as I am attempting to conduct an exhaustive research on her. I know this might be a long shot, but thought I would inquire, as I am familiar with your book containing a chapter on Holt."

It was signed "Gwendolyn Dixon, Associate Producer, *History Detectives.*" On its website, *History Detectives* is described as a series devoted to "exploring the complexities of historical mysteries, searching out the facts, myths and conundrums that connect local folklore, family legends and interesting objects."

Naturally, I was curious about how Holt fit into the program's formula and responded at once, asking Dixon for more details regarding the Holt segment. She wrote back:

> The object that we are researching is an autograph book that belonged to Nora Holt — it is a small autograph book and the autographs in it are mostly of politicians including: Calvin Coolidge's signature: May 1921, Warren G. Harding's signature 192, and for the date: May 10, 1921, several Harding cabinet members signed the book. Herbert Hoover also signed the book, when he was Sec. of Commerce I believe — but for this entry we only see his signature and it is undated; there is also a signature for someone named Richard B. Gilbert (the signature signed verbatim is "Henry Waterson for Richard B. Gilbert." Also Carl Van Vechten, June 1928. I am trying to determine how these men and Nora Holt would have gotten in contact with each other, if there was an event on May 10th that would have put them or someone that Nora Holt knew in the same space, so that her autograph book could have been signed. I am also wondering if this was common practice ... did cabinet members and presidential figures sign autograph books. Just really wanting to see if there is a way to solve this mystery through documentation of some sort.
>
> Any thoughts on this would be appreciated!

I was happy to assist in any way I could, and emails began to flow back and forth between Dixon and myself prior to the production of the segment.

I later learned from the episode when it was finally broadcast that the autograph book also contained the signatures of such men as novelist Theodore Dreiser and financier Andrew Mellon. "What an incongruous group," the show's narrator Gwenn Wright correctly enthuses. Then, subjecting several of the signatures to various scientific analyses, it is determined that they are indeed authentic. But as for how Holt could have come to collect such a diverse lot of autographs — and all white personages, at that — this was a mystery never quite solved by *History Detectives*. But if nothing else, the segment managed to shine a brief but bright light on the undeservedly forgotten life and times of the fabulous Nora Holt.

6

All That Jazz
Billy Strayhorn

"The fast dance mania and new jazz music were shaped by Afro-American culture, a fact completely disregarded by those who capitalized on their union," write Russell and David Sanjek in *American Popular Music Business in the 20th Century*.[1] The "mania" to which the Sanjeks refer was the national upsurge in jazz interest that began in 1917 with the release of the Original Dixieland Jazz Band's recording "Livery Stable Blues," b/w "The Original Dixieland One-Step." As for the "disregard" to which the writer refers, it arises from the fact that the ODJB was a five-man white group — the first to make a recording of something that passed for genuine New Orleans–style jazz. And in fact, so inhospitable was the phonograph world to the more genuine jazz of blacks, the music's true innovators, that African Americans did not begin to become represented on disc playing jazz until well into the third decade of recorded music. Ironically, even the first million-selling recording by an African American, "Crazy Blues" by Mamie Smith, was originally slated to be recorded by white Sophie Tucker. Given the enormous struggles that African Americans faced in other realms of the entertainment world, it should come as no surprise that the radio and recording industries did not exactly welcome them with open arms.

After Smith's triumph, it was an altogether different story. In an act of racial redress, for reasons no more idealistic than there was money to be made, whites began recording black blues and jazz musicians in large numbers. Before long, African Americans also got into the act in the recording booth when the black-owned Pace Phonograph Corporation was founded in 1921 in New York (an early success was Ethel Waters' "Down Home Blues"). The following year on the West Coast, African American–owned Sunshine Records was the first to commit a small black jazz combo, Kid Ory's group, to disc. Sunshine also cut the inaugural sides of the great jazz innovator Jelly Roll Morton, but these recordings have never surfaced. Sunshine was owned by brothers John and Benjamin "Reb" Spikes, both born in Dallas (John in 1882, Reb in 1888); the Spikes were business and music partners and the co-authors of two of the most recorded jazz tunes of all time, "Someday Sweetheart" and (with Jelly Roll Morton) "Wolverine Blues."

It is safe to say that up until the start of widespread civil rights victories in the 1950s, the jazz phonograph record offered the broadest forum available to African Americans. And while it should in no way be taken by the reader as a derogation of jazz to say so, the sad fact of the matter is that many of its greatest African American players and innovators only turned to it as a form of expression upon discovering that the world of the classical concert hall was almost entirely closed to them. This was true of both instrumentalists and singers, although a few in the latter category, most notably Marian Anderson, Roland Hayes and Paul Robeson, were able

Billy Strayhorn, circa 1958 (photograph by Carl Van Vechten, from the collection of the Library of Congress).

to squeak through. This was an unfortunate state of affairs that has continued to obtain until only very recently. And while it should not be construed as lending approval to this lockout, it is an unavoidable fact that some of jazz's finest practitioners came to artistic fruition because of (and in spite of) these racist career limitations. "If I can't get fame [as a violinist], I'd like to make money," said Will Marion Cook after having been allowed only limited chances to concertize.[2] He then went on to become a pioneer in the evolution of big band jazz. And a large number of other early- and middle-period jazz instrumentalists only fully realized the wonders of jazz expression upon being faced with a loaded economic gun at their heads. Aside from Cook, the African American jazz musicians who found their way to jazz via this circuitous route included Hazel Scott (see Chapter Seven), Bud Powell, and Duke Ellington associate Billy Strayhorn.

"Billy looked into colleges but was discouraged because of his race and could not get the necessary financial aid," recalled his high school friend, Harry Herforth, years later. "The very idea of a black concert pianist was considered unthinkable. It had nothing to do with Billy's considerable talent."[3] Thus Strayhorn, who apparently never played a jazz lick until he was well into his teens, went on, almost by default, to become one of the most important figures in jazz — a fact only belatedly coming to be understood.

In the summers of 1932 and '33, occasions of major cultural significance took place that would forever alter the way the world viewed the abilities of African American artists: Louis Armstrong's tour of the British Isles, followed a year later by a first visit there by Duke Ellington. Thanks to the serious critical attention accorded Armstrong and Ellington — word of which quickly spread back across the Atlantic — jazz, once thought of at home as something Dionysian and vernacular, was now considered in terms more Apollonian and academic. As a result, the minstrel image of the terrified Sambo and fat and sassy earth mammy that many still equated with African American art was dealt a significant blow.[4] Duke Ellington, especially, thrived and prospered on this elevation to "serious" musician. Now it was seemly, affordable and even necessary for him to acquire the services of a full-time musical collaborator. In 1939 he found one; one who was not, Ellington would explain later, "my alter ego. He was more than that. Billy Strayhorn was my right arm, my left arm, all the eyes in the back of my head, the brainwaves in his head and mine."[5] It was an exalted position and — given the social changes of the 1930s— Strayhorn's life as an African American artist was much less chaotic and more "respectable" than it would have been in previous times.

* * *

When it comes to having a case of the "mean reds," not even Billie Holiday's signature tune "Gloomy Sunday" can touch Strayhorn's late-blooming standard, "Lush Life," with its depiction of demi-monde pub-crawling and urban ennui. But "Lush Life" (when it was written in 1935) with its blasé, world-weary sentiments, was about as far from the realities of Billy Strayhorn's life as it was possible to get back then. Sounding like something that might have been written by Cole Porter, it was in fact composed by a black teenager living in obscurity in Depression America. Then in his late teens,* Duke Ellington's future musical amanuenses had just finished high school, was studying piano and found himself employed at Pittsburgh's Pennfield Drug Store delivering packages and slinging sodas. He'd not even reached legal drinking age; yet he evoked with a fair degree of accuracy a boozy milieu

---

*Estimates as to when Strayhorn wrote "Lush Life" vary. He was 15 according to critic Leonard Feather; but author Will Friedwald puts his age as 22. I have chosen a "guestimate" somewhere between the extremes.

of which he had (presumably) never been a part. We are left then with the image of a young man, his imagination working overtime in a manner remindful of the adolescent Truman Capote, roaming to places far wittier, sophisticated and soigné than a Depression-ridden factory town in Appalachia. In fact, Capote wrote his first novel, *Other Voices, Other Rooms*, when he was roughly the same age as Strayhorn was when he wrote "Lush Life." Perhaps the explanation for their mutual precocity is supplied by the tendency of homosexual adolescents to project themselves into sophisticated circumstances as an exercise in wish fulfillment.[6]

*   *   *

When Billy was born in Dayton, Ohio, in 1915, his mother was only fifteen. A short time later, Billy's father, a plasterer by trade, left his wife and son behind, ostensibly in search of work; but later, Billy contended that there was a touch of "plain old wanderlust"[7] to his father's peregrinations. When he was five, the boy was bundled off to live with an aunt in Montclair, New Jersey, beginning what Strayhorn would later call his "see-sawing"[8] years: As a result of his father's nomadism, the youngster moved back and forth between several family members throughout his childhood. Mostly he found himself in North Carolina in the care of his fraternal grandmother Lizzie Strayhorn. It was she who bought Billy his first piano. His great-grandmother on his mother's side had been a cook for Robert E. Lee during the Civil War (his father's grandparents had also been slaves).[9]

By the time the boy had reached early adolescence, his family's situation had stabilized enough for mother, father and five siblings to settle under the roof of a modest four-room dwelling in Pittsburgh. The black Hill and Homewood districts of the "Iron City" were home to many future jazz stars; over the years they also yielded up the likes of Mary Lou Williams, Ahmad Jamal, Earl Hines, Erroll Garner, Roy Eldridge, Art Blakey and Billy Eckstine. The Homewood section of the city where Billy lived has been written about by novelist Jerome Wideman in books such as *Hiding Place* and *Damballah*. In his short story "Hazel," one of the major characters in fact bears the last name of Strayhorn.[10]

At first, Billy wasn't caught up in jazz. When he began formal music studies around 1925 after moving to Pittsburgh, his repertoire was made up strictly of traditional keyboard works like Chopin waltzes and Edvard Grieg's "A Minor Concerto." He also began to compose, and played his own classical "Concerto for Piano and Percussion" at his Westinghouse House High School graduation exercises. But by then he had begun to expand his musical interests. "Each year in school, each class would get together and present sketches," Billy later reminisced. "I wrote the music and lyrics for our sketches and played too. It was successful enough so that one of the boys suggested doing a whole show, *Fantastic Rhythm*. We made $55."[11] Variations on the production, whose cast at one time featured a very young Billy Eckstine, continued to be performed around southwestern Pennsylvania for the next five years.

After graduation, Strayhorn continued working at the Pennfield Drug Store. He started out as a delivery boy; when he would deliver packages, people would ask him to "sit down and play us one of your songs." "It's funny," he later remarked. "I never really thought about a musical career. I sort of drifted along in music."[12]

Friends continued to tell Strayhorn he should do something about becoming a professional, but he was wary. He did, however, continue to study theory and classical technique, and for a while attended the Pittsburgh Musical Institute. He also (unsuccessfully) continued to look for a musical mentor, and by the time he was in his late teens, the teachers he'd gone through also numbered in the upper teens. Then in 1934 came the unforgettable experience for Billy Strayhorn of seeing Duke Ellington perform in person for the first time: "Nothing before or since has ever affected my life so much," he later said.[13] "Yes, I was *shook up*," he told Ellington historian Stanley Dance in 1966. "I got over my fears and went backstage to see him. I didn't have anything to say and I just stood there with my mouth open."[14] It was doubly perplexing for him; until then he'd not been that much of a fan of the Duke. Then a few years later, in late 1938, he made his first personal contact with Ellington during one of the band's semi-annual swings through the area. The introduction between the two, which took place backstage at the Pittsburgh Stanley Theater, was set up by new friend George Greenlee.

Ellington asked Billy what he did: "I play piano." Duke in typical wry fashion replied, "But we already have a piano player."[15] When Strayhorn added that he also wrote songs, Duke gave him a shot at displaying his wares, liked what he heard and asked the 23-year-old to leave some of them behind. "Maybe we can do something with them," he said.[16] But Billy hadn't even bothered to write them down. This further captured Ellington's interest, because the songs were too good *not* to be committed to paper. Right there on the spot he invited Strayhorn to arrange one of the songs for the band and paid him $20.

"I was so thrilled," he later told one jazz journalist, "I didn't know what to say. Duke was very nice to me and let me stay in the theatre all the next day working on the number; and he said he'd like to take me to New York."[17] Strayhorn couldn't go just then, but Ellington told him to keep in touch; the remark, tossed off lightly, nevertheless made an impression. The years of friends and family nagging him to turn pro had finally begun to sink in. Two weeks later — without even bothering to find out whether Ellington was actually in New York at the time — with his songs now in written form and six dollars in his pocket, Billy took off via train for Manhattan. But by happenstance Billy met up with Ellington in Philadelphia. The band was then on the road and would not be returning to its home base of New York for a few weeks to Manhattan with Billy, catching up with Ellington and company just a few hours before they were to set sail for a European tour. "See that he's taken care of until I get back," Duke told son Mercer Ellington[18]; and in some versions of the meeting is said to have told Billy, "You are with me for life."[19] Whichever it was, in essence, he was asking Billy to become a permanent fixture of the Ellington organization shortly after the point in Ducal history when Ellington's first European tour (1944) had elevated him to world stardom. Mercer Ellington oversaw the band's departure for Europe and then took on the responsibility of looking after the new band member. In his surprisingly candid memoir of his relationship with his father, *Duke Ellington in Person* (a kind of jazz *Mommie Dearest*), the younger Ellington recalls that initially he'd moved Billy into the only accommodations he could afford — the "Y":

"But he used to come by the apartment and stay so often and so long, often for several days, that I finally said, 'Well, Billy forget it. Come on and make it this way at the house, and like later for the YMCA!,' so by the time Pop got back from Europe, Billy, Ruth [Duke's sister] and I were like one family."[20]

It was at this early stage in his friendship with Strayhorn that Mercer began to realize that Billy's skills extended beyond lyric writing:

"Strayhorn had a good solid foundation in the facts and theories of music. He was capable of playing good piano — not great piano, but good piano. He had enough training in composition to be able to appreciate Pop's work, and it was just a matter of having the instrumentation [of the Ellington band] shown to him for him to grasp the general principles."[21]

By the time Ellington returned from Europe a few weeks later, Billy's full musical worth was already becoming apparent; and in 1938 his first arrangement for the band, the lovely "Like a Ship in the Night," was recorded (the session was released under Ellington sideman Johnny Hodges' name). This arranging debut a success, his assignments increased along with his confidence and the quality of his writing. Among his early arrangements for the band were "Savoy Strut," "You Can Depend on Me," and a specialty number for clarinetist Barney Bigard, "Minuet in Blues." Strayhorn became especially involved with working on material for various small-band units drawn from the Ellington band — such numbers as "Dream Blues," "Watch the Birdie," "The Rabbit's Jump" and "I Know What You Do." His own favorite among his small unit work was "Black Beauty,"[22] with its stunning Cootie Williams solo. Full Ellington band arrangements by Strayhorn during this period include "Flamingo," "After All," "Chloe," and parts of "I Got It Bad and That Ain't Good" and "Sepia Panorama."

Not too long after Billy became an official Ellingtonian, Duke and the band travelled to Europe once more. Again Billy remained behind. With time to himself for experimentation and reflection, he composed the beautiful, languorous "Daydream," a classic which is even more widely performed and recorded today than when first written. (Ellington put the finishing touches to the song when he returned from Europe, and a short time later, lyrics were added by John LaTouche.[23]) But it wasn't talent alone that accounted for his rapid rise within the Ellington ranks. Shortly after he came on board, a strike by the songwriters' representative organization ASCAP (the American Society of Composers and Publisher), of which Ellington was a member, resulted in Billy's being handed important assignments at a swifter rate than might have otherwise been the case (Strayhorn was a member of the competing BMI group). The strike raged on until the latter part of 1941, during which time virtually no ASCAP compositions were heard on the radio; but anything Strayhorn wrote was permissible. To some degree Billy might have acted as a "front" for Duke, i.e., a vessel through which Ellington could funnel his own writings, but this is clearly not the reason he was hired originally.

Around the time Strayhorn wrote "Daydream" in 1940, he also began appearing as a pianist, without credit, on some of the band's recordings. Similarities between Ellington and Strayhorn's piano playing were apparent almost from the beginning, but it wasn't just a case of protective coloration on Strayhorn's part; it also worked the other way around. Wrote jazz critic Barry Ulanov in 1945, "Billy picked up Duke's florid arpeggios, Duke picked up his [Strayhorn's] bright skipping notes...."[24] Not only were their playing styles beginning to merge, their arranging styles were also become more and more similar.

Songwriter Don George's book on Ellington points to the total indispensability of Strayhorn to Ellington, asserting that the self-effacing Billy "was Duke's musical equal, with all the musicality and all the great classical knowledge he brought to Duke. For example, on many pieces that appear with Duke's name, occasionally Sweetpea [Strayhorn] got the credit, but so many others were written with Duke doing part, then handing it to Sweetpea, saying, 'Here, man, you finish it.'" Conversely, George notes, "Duke seeing some of the things Sweetpea started, would take them from him in the middle, saying, 'Hey, man, I'll finish that thing.' They had gotten into each other's minds and musical areas so completely that when it came to anybody's being able to discern who wrote what, very often they themselves didn't know what part each had written. They were incredibly close musically."[25]

Sometimes the two even worked via long distance phone, often with uncanny results. Strayhorn was hospitalized in New York when Ellington was writing his first "Sacred Concert" in California. The Duke phoned up and told Billy he wanted him to write something: "Introduction, ending, quick transitions," he said. "The title is the first four words of the Bible — 'In the Beginning God.'"[26] Strayhorn had not heard the Duke's theme, but what he

sent to California started on the same note as Ellington's. Duke wrote in his
Music Is My Mistress, "Out of six notes representing the six syllables of the
four words, only two notes were different."[27]

In 1962 Strayhorn told *Down Beat* magazine that the musical mind meld
existing between the two was "an uncanny feeling, like witchcraft, like looking into someone else's mind."[28] Whatever the ultimate creative ratio actually was, what is clear is that the dynamic between the two of them resulted
in healthy rivalry and mutually beneficial competitiveness:

"Billy was inspired by Ellington and wanted to do things for him," wrote
Mercer Ellington. "And then, like flexing your muscles, just to show off, to
show Billy what he was capable of, Ellington began to write more himself."[29]

The professional jazz world through which Billy began to move in 1938
was just as ill-disposed to homosexuals as mainstream society ... if not more
so. In a 1995 interview, vibist Gary Burton said he believed that "of all forms
of music, jazz is the least tolerant of homosexuality." He deemed the jazz
milieu "macho in the extreme."[30]

Typical of the times, Billy's social life was not exclusively gay, but instead
consisted of a shifting "set" made up of black and white straight, gay, male
and female (mostly) artists and entertainers, one of whom was dancer Tal-
ley Beatty, who was gay. The former star of the Katherine Dunham troupe
recalls that there was never talk of sex, no matter what the their free-float-
ing salon's gender makeup of the moment might have been: "We weren't
guarded, but we came from families where conversation and manners were
so puritanical."[31]

"Oblique jokes about homosexuality were permitted," writes Jay Weiser
of a '40s scene such as this, "but in some salons, breaking the taboo could
mean expulsion."[32]

Initially, world-class womanizer Ellington probably wasn't aware that
Billy was homosexual. And the likelihood is that by the time the Duke finally
knew—Billy would eventually become more open about his sexual orienta-
tion—he was too indispensable for Ellington to put his prejudices into operation. It was very daring to be "out" in the jazz world; and it has been
suggested that dwelling in the semi-anonymity of Ellington's shadow was the
price Strayhorn paid for his gayness.[33] In the long run, Ellington increasingly
picked and chose from the useful palette of Strayhorn's colorful life in such
a way that he was able to assume the marketable demeanor of an urban sophis-
ticate. British jazz journalist Derek Jewell quoted a friend of his as noting
that "Duke was a much simpler character before he met Strays [Strayhorn].
You could even say he was sweeter. But he was so much more interesting once
Strays happened along. Duke picked up some of his language from the elegant sentences Billy used. He had an ear for sentences. Peculiar words fasci-
nated him.... Duke Ellington didn't even go to the Taj Mahal. He let Billy
Strayhorn cover it for him."[34]

*   *   *

One day in 1940 Billy was riding the Eighth Avenue Express (i.e., the "A" train) when he pulled out pen and paper and began working on an instrumental designed to appease the appetite of the ever-hungry Ellington big band machine. Given the circumstances, it was only natural the song eventually be titled "Take the A Train," the lyrics for which, when they were added a few months later by Billy, transformed the number into an attempt at solving a New York City transportation problem (one that continues to some degree to this day). "They were building the Sixth Avenue Subway at the time," he recalled to writer Stanley Dance, "and they added new trains, including the 'D' Train, and it would go to Harlem and 145th Street, and then turned off and went to the Bronx, but the 'A' Train kept on up to 299-and-something Street. People got confused. They'd take the 'D' Train, and it would go to Harlem and 145th Street, but then the next stop would be Eighth Avenue under the Polo Grounds, and the one after that would be in the Bronx. So I was writing directions—take the 'A' Train to Sugar Hill. The 'D' Train was really messing up everybody. I heard so many times about housewives who ended up in the Bronx and had to turn around and come back."[35] Ironically, "Take the 'A' Train," one of the most famous of New York City songs, was first recorded in Los Angeles when the band was appearing in the memorable stage production *Jump for Joy*.[36] Unquestionably the most well-known of Strayhorn's songs, it is one seldom properly credited to him; instead being generally attributed to Ellington, even though the latter almost always referred to it as "Billy Strayhorn's 'Take the A Train'"—which, in the early 1950s, replaced "East St. Louis Toodle-Oo" as the Ellington theme song.

For Ellington, Strayhorn wrote suites, jump numbers (with and without lyrics), riff tunes and programmatic material, but it was his ballads, many inspired by Billy's interest in French impressionist composers like Debussy and Ravel, that have had the most lasting impact. "Chelsea Bridge," a 1942 instrumental, happens to closely resemble Ravel's "Valses nobles et sentimentales."[37] Curiously, when the similarity was brought to Strayhorn's attention, he insisted he'd never even heard the Ravel work. Billy's "Passion Flower," which in turn was thematically similar to "Chelsea Bridge," was the inspiration for one of Strayhorn's several nicknames—"P.F." He was also known as "Weely" (i.e., Willy) and "Strays," but the one which finally took hold was given him some time during the early 1940s when the band was en route to a date via train.

"Your new name is 'Swee' Pea,'" band member Toby Hardwicke told him.

"Why?"

"Because you look like him."

"Who?"

"'Swee' Pea.'"

"Who?" asked Strayhorn, whose tastes tended to run to French literature rather than comic strips.

"'Popeye's baby."

"Oh," Billy reflected for a moment. "Oh," he repeated, then laughed. "Popeye in the comic strip of the same name. Oh."[38]

Aside from his duties as an alto and baritone sax player in the band, part of Hardwicke's job seems to have been handing out nicknames: Among the other Ellingtonians who were renamed by him were Joe Nanton who became "Tricky Sam" and Roy Eldridge, re-monickered "Little Jazz." Befitting his elfin yet dignified bearing, almost always after that, Billy was known as Swee' Pea. (Songwriter Don George described Strayhorn as looking like "a small, slightly burned, whole wheat toast owl."[39])

The account of how Billy became "Swee' Pea" is from Barry Ulanov's 1946 book *Duke Ellington*, the first major work devoted to the bandleader. Ulanov also writes about Strayhorn's long friendship with Lena Horne. But it is not possible to gauge from Ulanov's prose that Lena and Billy were just good friends.

Typical of the times, Ellington felt that all Strayhorn needed to set himself "straight" was the love of a good woman.[40] And so, long before Billy and Lena ever met, would-be matchmaker Ellington began dropping hints to both of them. The meeting finally took place in Los Angeles in 1941 at the premiere of Ellington's *Jump for Joy*. "At intermission," Horne later recalled, "a pixie, brown color horn-rimmed glasses, beautifully cut suit, beautifully modulated speaking voice, appeared as if by magic and said, 'I'm Billy Strayhorn — Swee' Pea.'

"We became one another's alter egos. We were both at that time necessary to other people, me as a provider, Billy as Duke's collaborator. But when we were together we were free of all that. We seemed almost like siblings. We knew what each other was thinking, the same things were funny, the same food was good. We seemed wrapped in a web of good will that people spun around us. It was Lena and Billy. Billy and Lena. Everything we thought and said to each other made sense — and I began to talk and it poured out of me. I had a friend."[41]

In 1993 Lena Horne came out of several years of retirement to take part in a tribute to Strayhorn at the JVC Jazz Festival in New York City. Undimmed by time, if possible even improved, Horne scored a memorable triumph singing a half-dozen songs by her "soulmate" who, she informed the audience, comes to her in dreams three or four days before any "musical crisis in my life." Avoiding the "hits" like "A Train" and "Lush Life," she instead concentrated on lesser-known songs such as "Maybe," "Love Like This Can't Last" and "You're the One," written especially for Horne, but not recorded by her until 1993 in an album that followed shortly on the heels of the JVC evening. The lion's share of the material on the release, *We'll Be Together Again*, was by Strayhorn.[42] Essentially the recording operated as a tribute album to her friend.

Because of Horne's strict upbringing, she didn't force the sexual issue during the few months the couple "dated," and Strayhorn had no sexual interest in women. Horne later said that Billy had never once discussed his homosexuality with her.[43]

Son Mercer recalls that his father "once surprised the hell out of a late party in his suite at the Shamrock Hotel in Houston by airing his belief in a Faggot Mafia. Stanley Dance [jazz journalist and Ducal confidante] was there and he found the idea amusing until he realized how serious Pop was."[44] But even though he never could quite make peace with homosexuality itself, Ellington apparently became resigned to Strayhorn's—in the parlance of the times—*differentness*.[45]

"Swee' Pea never worked the neighborhoods, never cruised. Most homosexuals I've known cruise," wrote songwriter Don George in his Ellington biography *Sweet Man*. "If they don't cruise they keep their eyes open for someone to make it with. Swee' Pea wasn't like that. Swee' Pea was faithful, sincere with his friend.[46] He never cruised or rampaged around, not even when he had a few drinks. He was always the gentlemanly fellow in the group. Homosexuality was as normal for Swee' Pea as any other area of life, heterosexuality or whatever, was for anybody else."[47]

Despite his general discretion, Strayhorn (whose watch cry was "Ever onward and upward")[48] had his moments. He liked to drink and party, and he tended to act as a lightning rod for the free-form social set which seemed to spring to life wherever he touched down. Talk at such gatherings—liberally oiled by alcohol—tended to run the gamut from music to books to clothing and Billy's favorite hobby—French. He often lapsed into self-taught French: "*Quel drole. It est fou a lier, un hurlerberlu.* Ooh. I've been waiting for a chance to use that idiom. Mmmm."[49]

One of Billy's extracurricular activities when he was not on the road or working with the Duke was acting as president of the legendary tap dancers' social club, the Copasetics. He spent much time socializing with its members whose roster included Cholly Atkins and Honi Coles as well as "civilians" such as B. B. King and Dizzy Gillespie. Among its activities, the organization staged shows to aid various charities; Strayhorn was a regular contributor, sometimes composing complete revues such as *Welcome Aboard* which, like the others, was never recorded or filmed and today is presumed to be lost.[50]

Sometimes Billy would play too long and too hard and drop with exhaustion. He was proud of his ability to fall asleep without spilling so much as a drop of liquor; he also boasted that he could smoke a cigarette down to the last quarter-inch without losing the ash.[51] Strayhorn was accompanied on many of these nocturnal revels by his longtime companion and roommate

Arnold Bridgers, a non–pro musician who acquired thoroughly professional pianistic skills through the coaching of Art Tatum and Billy. On the subject of piano, Strayhorn often took pains to defuse the mystique surrounding the similarity between his and Ellington's approach to the keyboard:

"Although my style of playing away from Duke is quite different, when I play with the band I play like the leader. I know what Duke would do in a particular section of a composition, and I know what the band expects to happen."[52]

Strayhorn not only recorded prolifically with the Ellington band, he also often took charge in live performances, playing the piano and leading until Ellington arrived on the stand after a strenuous round of table-hopping and backstage socializing. In addition to his many credited and unbilled appearances as an Ellingtonian, he was a sideman on other musicians' studio sessions (Clark Terry, Johnny Hodges, et al.), as well as recording a handful of albums under his own name. One of the most memorable Strayhorn discs is a release on which he duets with Ellington throughout; *Great Times*, recorded in 1950, is the only collection of their playing in tandem.[53] When Billy first heard the finished product, he was uncertain as to who was playing what: "I really have to sit down at the keyboard and play it out to know who is playing."[54]

There is disagreement among Strayhorn's friends and associates as to whether he was bothered by being overshadowed by Ellington all his professional life. Ellingtonian Toby Hardwicke insisted, "Neither money nor business was an issue between them ever. Billy just wanted to be with Duke, that was all. It was love — a beautiful thing."[55] Lena Horne, on the other hand, found the relationship loving, protective, but somewhat destructive. "It wasn't physical at all," she told writer David Hajdu. "But it was very, very sexual. Billy loved Duke. Duke loved Billy. The problem is, Duke treated Billy exactly like he treated women, with all that old-fashioned chauvinism."[56] Ultimately, as Horne saw it, her friend was unequipped to deal with the vicissitudes not only of his profession but of daily life (Strayhorn's family experienced great difficulty with the IRS after his death).[57] The tradeoff that Strayhorn made allowed him rare social freedom as a homosexual in a highly competitive, macho-driven profession. But the price he paid was near-total invisibility as an artist.

In a variation on Ellington's relation with his former manager Irving Mills who took writing credit on songs he had nothing to do with, Ellington is known to have placed his name as co-writer on at least two songs penned by Strayhorn before he ever met the bandleader: "Something to Live For" and "Your Love Has Faded." Ascertaining the extent of Billy's uncredited contributions to numerous other projects is now the basis of a still-expanding cottage industry of musicological research and scholarship, On at least one occasion, however, Ellington must have insisted Billy share the spotlight, for both appear on the cover of their fondly remembered reworking of "The Nut-cracker Suite." But Strayhorn appears more than a little self-effacing, smiling, eyes cast down, while Ellington stares straight at the camera.

Socially the two might have been worlds apart, but music made the situation "all right,"[58] Billy once remarked; Ellington described the symbiosis that transpired between the pair as a "covetous collaboration between flower and beast."[59] Ellington deferred to Strayhorn on nearly all musical matters. He seldom went into a recording session without having him on hand in the engineer's booth, and Billy generally had the final say-so on which takes were to be issued. Sexual preference was undoubtedly on Strayhorn's mind when he said — somewhat in code — the following: "What it comes down to is that, although we feel very differently about *life* [italics mine], we really understand what each of us wants in a composition."[60]

Billy Strayhorn was responsible for writing, arranging or shaping hundreds of songs and extended works in the Ellington repertoire including, in addition to those already mentioned, "Just a Sittin' and a Rockin'," "Satin Doll," "Rain Check," "Grievin'," and the lovely but overlooked ballad "My Little Brown Book" (from Billy's high school revue *Fantastic Rhythm*), and such longer works (mostly co-written with Ellington) as "A Drum Is a Woman," "Such Sweet Thunder," and "Suite Thursday." There are numerous instances of Strayhorn rolling up his sleeves and acting as an equal collaborator, but receiving no credit at all, with the most widely discussed examples of his self-effacement being two of the Duke's stage musicals, *Jump for Joy* and *Beggar's Holiday*.[61]

Ironically, the Ellington band played little or no part in popularizing the composition with which Strayhorn is most often associated, "Lush Life." In 1949, long before it had become a standard, Strayhorn told writer Stanley Dance in *Down Beat* that it was "a song most persons have to listen to twice before they understand it."[62] Perhaps this was because "Lush Life," in the vein of other songs by homosexuals like Cole Porter, John LaTouche and Noël Coward, was not exactly reminiscent of hard-core heterosexual sentiment. He told Dance, "The only ones who knew the old tunes were my friends in Pittsburgh. One night I remembered it and played it for Duke. He liked it and we've been using it occasionally, with Kay Davis singing, and myself on piano. I made a record of it once for an album of modern arrangers' works Norman Granz [owner of the Norgran and Verve jazz labels] was putting together, but it wasn't used. I was calling it 'Life Is Lonely,' but when anyone wanted me to play it, they asked for 'that thing about lush life.'"[63]

It is probable that Strayhorn somewhat overstated Ellington's fondness for the song. While the Duke perhaps appreciated the number from a strictly technical standpoint, in all likelihood he found its outlook far too decadent. Curiously (or not so), Ellington himself never got around to commercially recording "Lush Life"; perhaps it unconsciously pressed several of his homophobic buttons.[64] And were it not for the intercession of Nat "King" Cole, "Lush Life" might never have been widely heard. In early 1949, Cole happened to be cutting some instrumentals at Capitol the day Billy was recording "Lush Life." Cole hung out at the session and when he heard the tune he immediately asked Billy for a copy of the music. Cole cut his record of the composition a few weeks later, in April. Although the undistinguished novelty number on the other side of the recording was projected to be the "A" side, finally it was Strayhorn's song that captured all the attention, setting it off on its course toward eventual standardhood. "Lush Life" has now been recorded commercially by nearly every respected jazz instrumentalist and singer, with the glaring and notable exception of Frank Sinatra who did, in fact, once try to give it a whirl. A bootleg recording exists which captures him attempting to come to grips with the song, intended for his album *Only the Lonely*. But after several false starts and stops, he can be heard slamming a door and storming out of the studio—the closest that the unarguable final arbiter of American Popular Song came to recording this late-blooming classic, one of the few to have eluded his imprimatur.[65]

A few months before his death in the spring of 1967, Strayhorn sat for an extended interview with Ellington historian Stanley Dance, who wrote that his subject "was recuperating from his first serious operation [for cancer of the esophagus], but he was apologetic about getting anyone up so early in the day. He felt at his most alert then, the medicines he was obliged to take making him drowsy in the afternoons." Although his last few months were physically painful, he maintained a moderately active life as well as his sense of humor: Even though he could no longer eat most of his personal chef's cooking, he retained his services, telling Dance, "I can still smell, can't I?"[66]

The final days of Strayhorn's life were spent in the care of Lena Horne. She took him with her to California for a final visit and then returned with him to New York City where she remained with him at his home until May 31, 1967, when between three and four A.M. he died in her arms. He was 51. Word of Strayhorn's death reached Ellington in Reno, Nevada, where he was performing. The reaction of the normally unflappable Duke was to lock himself in his hotel suite where he went into a state of profound and inconsolable rage. Outside in the hotel corridor he could be heard sobbing and banging his head against the wall. When he had sufficiently recovered, his first act was to pen a eulogy.[67]

Services for Billy Strayhorn were held at New York's St. Peter's Church. In attendance were friends from diverse worlds, such as ballplayer Jackie Robinson, filmmaker Otto Preminger, record producer John Hammond, many of his hoofer friends (after Strayhorn's death, his title of president of the Copasetics dancers' fraternity was permanently retired), as well as hundreds of other civic leaders, politicians, artists from every field and past and present Ellingtonians. Pianist Billy Taylor played "Chelsea Bridge" and "Passion Flower" and Ellington vocalist (and trumpeter-violinist) Ray Nance's sorrowful and funereal rendering of "Take the A Train" is still vividly remembered by many who were there that day. Ellington's eulogy went, in part:

> Poor little Swee' Pea, Billy Strayhorn, William Thomas Strayhorn, the biggest little human being who ever lived, a man with the greatest courage, the most majestic artistic stature, a highly skilled musician whose impeccable taste commanded the respect of all musicians and the admiration of all listeners.... He spoke English and French very well. He demanded freedom of expression and lived in what we consider the most important of moral freedoms: freedom from hate, unconditionally; freedom from self-pity (even through all the pain and bad news); freedom from fear of possibly doing something that might help another more than it might help himself; and freedom from any kind of pride that could make a man feel he was better than his brother or neighbor.... His patience was incomparable and unlimited. He had no aspirations to enter into any kind of competition, yet the legacy he leaves, his *oeuvre*, will never be less than the ultimate on the highest plateau of culture (whether by comparison or not).[68]

All that was left to be said (and the normally profoundly egocentric Duke would have been the first to admit it) was that without the contributions of Billy Strayhorn, there probably would never have been the Ellington Legend and Mystique as we have come to know it today. A few years later, Ellington recalled these Four Freedoms at a White House celebration of his 70th birthday; film of the occasion shows a Richard Nixon made decidedly uncomfortable, in sharp contrast to the Duke's confidently rendered reading.

After Strayhorn died, whenever performing in public, Ellington opened up with a haunting and painstakingly slow piano treatment, performed in the dark before the spotlight came up, of one of Billy's loveliest compositions, "Lotus Blossom." An unorthodox beginning to an evening of big band jazz, it was mediation upon the memory of Billy Strayhorn, of whom Ellington until his death in 1974 would always speak of in the present tense.

Shortly after Billy's passing there came the first strong wave of interest in his music with an identity *apart* from Duke Ellington; it was triggered by the album *And His Mother Called Him Bill*, a superb collection of Strayhorn's music cut by the Duke shortly after his collaborator's death. This growing awareness of the latter reached a pinnacle of sorts in 1991 with the best-selling *Lush Life: The Music of Billy Strayhorn* by saxophonist Joe Henderson. The Grammy-winning album not only helped solidify its subject's reputation, but also worked to put Henderson back on the map. It was a mutual renaissance that saw the saxophonist pouring out the notes and tones of Swee' Pea's work on global TV as well as in "live" milieu on several continents.

This musician's life — from when he was taken up by Duke Ellington until his death — was unprecedented. Up to that time, no black artist had ever been so unhampered in the creative act, so devoid of the surround of racial strife — thanks to the protection and freedom afforded by the association with Ellington. As such, Billy Strayhorn suggests a model of something that still has not completely come to pass: African American artists functioning to their full potential minus the obstacle of racism.

*   *   *

Postscript to first edition: David Hajdu's superb *Lush Life: A Biography of Billy Strayhorn*, appearing two years before the initial 1998 publication of this book, launched a cottage industry of Strayhorniana in the form of TV documentaries, CD anthologies, and wide critical coverage of the book itself. Movie rights for *Lush Life* were quickly snapped up by producer Irwin Winkler (*Rocky, GoodFellas*), with Jay Cocks (*The Age of Innocence, Gangs of New York*) set as screenwriter. Will Smith and Denzel Washington were announced as Winkler's leading men of choice. But as of this writing, realization of the project has not occurred. Perhaps it still languishes in Hollywood "turnaround" hell.

A review by Joel Roberts in the publication *All About Jazz* nicely sums up the excitement generated by Hajdu's bio, which was a major best-seller (rare for a jazz book):

> Hajdu follows Strayhorn from Harlem to Hollywood to Paris, as he lives out the "lush life" of his fantasies. We are presented with vivid and memorable portraits of Strayhorn's friends and associates from various walks of life, including Lena Horne, Rachel and Jackie Robinson, Dr. Martin Luther King, Jr., and Medgar Evers, as well as Ellingtonians like Ben Webster, Jimmy Blanton, Johnny Hodges, Harry Carney, and most of the major figures in the jazz world. All of them, it seems, held Strayhorn in extraordinarily high regard, as a uniquely talented musician and as a man of rare intelligence and grace. By the end of this extremely personal account of Strayhorn's life, we have come to know him quite well and the tragic details of his final months are extremely distressing. David Hajdu has done an outstanding job of elucidating the complicated life of this enormously talented and too often overlooked artist. *This is surely one of the best books ever written about jazz.* (italics mine)

More than any other subject covered in the first edition of this book — the *sui generis* Sammy Davis, Jr., and Dinah Washington aside — Billy Strayhorn has been fortunate to have finally received cultural retrospection commensurate with his major artistic contributions.

7

The Movies
Hazel Scott

The relatively new medium of film began to seriously entrench itself in mass consciousness in the late teens, causing already movie-struck white Americans to commence a mass migration to Hollywood. The talent that most of these would-be film players possessed was nearly non-existent, but it was enough to only *want* to be a star. Even for those who failed to make it all the way up the ladder of achievement, employment turned out to be plentiful as extras, bit players, etc., For African Americans, though, such opportunities were in short supply, and blacks were even portrayed by Caucasians in the earliest silents. The first true black star, Stepin Fetchit (Lincoln Perry), did not arrive on the scene until the late 1920s. Upon the occasion of the first all-black Hollywood talkie, 1929's *Hearts in Dixie*, in which Fetchit appeared, white critic Robert Benchley wrote the following in *Opportunity*, the magazine of the National Urban League: "With the opening of *Hearts in Dixie* ... the future of the talking movie has taken on a rosier hue.... It may be that the talking-movies must be participated in exclusively by Negroes, but, if so, then so be it. In the Negro the soundpicture has found its ideal protagonist."[1]

The writer was especially impressed with the way blacks' voices sounded on film — generally deeper and more mellifluous.

Benchley's *apologia* notwithstanding, the future for blacks in the movies was not rosy; and for the next three decades they continued to be cast almost exclusively in stereotypical servile roles. The only antidote to such imagery was a steady series of independent low-budget black cast films turned out on a regular basis, circa the '20s and '30s, and aimed at the 600 or so U.S. theaters devoted to the showing of such films to African American audiences. These movies, with nary a demeaning mammy or buck in sight, included director Oscar Micheaux's melodramas on the subject of "passing," along with all-black detective tales, comedies, westerns, musicals, horror films, and in the instance of *The Spirit of Youth*, biography. Even though the character that boxer Joe Louis played in this independent production was named "Joe

97

Thomas," in nearly every significant detail it was the story of the champ's life, down to a scene of the youthful Louis cutting his violin lessons in order to box.

But it wasn't until the beginning of World War II that social and economic conditions were favorable enough for significant numbers of gifted blacks to begin migrating en masse to the film capital. However, even as late as 1951 things had not changed sociologically all that much as evidenced by the panic that set in during the daily screening of rushes for the film *Show Boat*, when it was discovered that, during a crucial scene, a black character actor had helped a white actress out of a boat by reflexively reaching out and taking her hand. The gesture was almost invisible, but nervous MGM executives, concerned about film exhibitors in the South, had the entire scene re-shot.[2] One can just imagine, then, the shock waves sent through the industry more than a decade earlier when African American actress-musician Hazel Scott — who did not suffer fools gladly — arrived in Hollywood.

As famous, arguably, as Lena Horne was in the 1940s, singer-pianist Scott is chiefly remembered today as the onetime wife of controversial politician Adam Clayton Powell, Jr. Like Horne, Scott was a cool, sophisticated performer; displayed in motion pictures as a distant and non-threatening black sex symbol. Off screen, it was another matter. Working without the safety net of any civil rights organization, she lashed out against the U.S. racial situation nearly every chance she had during the 1940s and early '50s. Marking her actions as doubly daring was her gender, for as Scott remarked years later: "Any woman who has a great deal to offer the world is in trouble, and if the woman is black, she is in deep trouble."[3]

Hazel Scott was born in Port-of-Spain, Trinidad, in 1920. Her mother, Alma, bore five children, but only Hazel lived past infancy. Scott's father, Thomas R. Scott, was a teacher and a scholar who, among his other accomplishments, could speak 17 different Chinese dialects. Originally from Scotland and of African ancestry, he had come to Trinidad to teach at St. Mary's College. Alma Scott, a debutante and a talented pianist, was from an upper-class island family.

"I remember the instant I realized I could play," Hazel Scott recalled years later. "I was two and a half. My grandmother finally got tired and fell asleep. I managed to climb on to the piano bench and start picking out a tune with one hand. I kept doing it until it came more easily. Then my grandmother woke up and asked, 'Who's there?' She thought it was one of the students who had come. I said, 'It's me,' and she said, 'Yes, but who?' I said, 'Me, Hazel.' She jumped up and called in the neighbors to hear the prodigy."[4] It was soon discovered that Hazel had perfect pitch. She began studying music with her mother Alma and shortly thereafter began appearing publicly in Port-of-Spain. When Hazel was four, the Scotts left Trinidad for New York City. On the boat trip, while her mother was laid up in her cabin suffering

Hazel Scott, 1947

from seasickness, Hazel spent most of the voyage performing at the piano for the other passengers.

The family's first home in New York was a brownstone in Harlem on 118th Street. Two years after arriving in the city, Hazel gave a classical performance at Town Hall (her jazz playing was still a few years away). At the age of eight, although still too young for formal admission to Juilliard, Scott was allowed to begin studying at the school on an informal basis after one of the teachers heard her play and pronounced her a genius.

In 1934 when Scott was 14, her father died from pneumonia, and Alma Scott, who would have preferred a career as a classical pianist, but suffered from weak wrists, turned to pop music as a means of supporting the family. Quickly learning the saxophone, she got a job playing in the band of Louis Armstrong's second wife, Lil Hardin Armstrong. To Alma's surprise, one night when they were backing the acts at Harlem's Apollo Theatre's boisterous amateur night, 12-year-old Hazel, who she thought was home asleep, came out on the stage to compete. The same year she was heard downtown at sedate Carnegie Hall performing Tchaikovsky's "Concerto No. 1 for Piano and Orchestra." "I was a prodigy," she said years later, "but nobody expected anything to come of it. No matter how good I was, it wasn't going to happen" [at a time when the idea of blacks playing classical music was still considered a tasteless and pretentious notion by most whites].[5]

Alma worked with Lil Hardin for only a short time before deciding to start her own band, Alma Long Scott's All-Woman Orchestra: The American Creolians. Hazel's mother also moonlighted in Chick Webb's band, which — since she was the only woman in the popular outfit — brought her a lot of attention. Hazel recalled later that one time a man came up to Alma after a performance and said to her, "Lady, you play that thing just like a man." To which Alma responded, "Mister, you carry your children just like a lady."[6]

Hazel's mother worked very hard at sheltering her daughter and turning her into what she considered to be a proper young lady, but teenaged Hazel had her mind set on becoming a music professional. "I cannot stay home with people who aren't in the business," she told Alma. "If you won't let me play in your orchestra, I'll become a juvenile delinquent."[7] Thus at age 12 she began touring with the American Creolians; she also formed her own band, 14 Men and a Girl. When she was 15, Scott and her musicians were working at a bar in Port Chester, New York, when, according to a story appearing in *Time* a few years later, the musician's union tried to have Scott fired for being underage. This marked the early appearance of a brand of rhetoric that would serve Scott well in the years to come: "I *am* over eighteen!" Hazel lied to the union. "And I'll outplay, outswing and outsing anybody who says different."[8]

In 1936 Scott got her own three-times-a-week radio show on the Mutual network, which chose her for the slot from among 1500 hopefuls. The same year, at Roseland, she made her first major downtown club appearance on a bill headlined by Count Basie. She was, she recalled in 1970, "scared to death. I had three footprints on my back — those of Lester Young, Jo Jones and Count Basie."[9] In 1938, at age 18, Scott made her theatrical debut in the Broadway revue *Sing Out the News*. Even though she was only part of the ensemble that sang the show's hit "Franklin D. Roosevelt Jones," her appearance was favorably singled out in several reviews.[10]

It was around this time that Scott also began refining the unique piano style with which she made her mark — swinging the classics. Hired as an intermission player in support of star Frances Faye at New York's popular Yacht Club, Hazel soon began receiving notes on stage via the busboy that she was no longer to play the song she had just sung because Faye was using it in her act. "Let's see if Frances Faye can do this!" she grumbled, and tore into a Bach invention played boogie-woogie style. "Needless to say," she later recalled, "Miss Faye didn't do *that* in the show, so I was able to get through a complete show without being interrupted by the busboy."[11] Scott was by no means the inventor of the gimmick,[12] but at the Yacht Club she sensed immediately that she'd stumbled onto a good thing, mined it for all its worth, and soon was one of the hottest club attractions in town. In his *Brown Sugar*, author Donald Bogle describes Hazel's act during this period: "She began her classical numbers in a conventional way, gradually changed the rhythm, letting the boogie-woogie notes creep in until, finally, Hazel Scott gave in to the sounds within her and pounded the keyboard as if each minute might be her last."[13] (Scott also sang occasionally, but with only marginally interesting results.)

A Carnegie Hall appearance in 1945 where she swingingly deconstructed Liszt's "Second Hungarian Rhapsody" was typical, and at least one reviewer was ecstatic: Scott's performance, he wrote (with tongue tucked slightly in cheek), constituted a form of musical analysis. The evening was, he said, "the most impudent musical criticism since George Bernard Shaw stopped writing on the subject. It was witty, daring, modern, but never irreverent. I think Liszt would have been delighted."[14] One of the writer's colleagues from another paper felt very differently about Scott, however; he stomped out in the middle of her performance and in print deemed it akin to sacrilege.[15]

While jazz aficionados generally found that Scott's straight-ahead playing possessed merit, they too tended to reject Scott's attempt to wed the classics with jazz, finding it mainly corny: "Very very hepcats writhe in agony at her antics and point bitterly to the relatively unsung genius of one Mary Lou Williams at the Café Society Downtown in New York City," reported *Newsweek* in its November 29, 1943 issue. But long after Scott discontinued purveying such harmless hoke, the memory of it continued to haunt her. Writing about Hazel in 1963 in his widely read book *Blues People*, Leroi Jones

(Amiri Baraka) dwells upon "the shabbiness, even embarrassment of Scott's playing 'concert boogie-woogie' before thousands of middle-class white music lovers."[16] But there is no mention made of the many middle-class *black* music lovers Scott also counted among her fans, nor of the excellent jazz sides she cut in the early 1950s with Charles Mingus and Max Roach.

Scott first became familiar with jazz due to the steady stream of musicians who frequented Alma Scott's Harlem apartment. Art Tatum was an early friend of Hazel's, tutoring her extensively at the keyboard. Lester Young would often stop by to pay his respects to Hazel's mother, and usually end up taking out his sax and instigating a jam session. Fats Waller was like a beloved uncle to her. And then, there was Billie Holiday. "I would put a nickel in the local jukebox and hear Lady Day sing," Scott told *Essence Magazine* in 1978, "and then come home and find her sitting in the kitchen with my mother." One night a 15-year-old Scott sneaked out of her apartment to play with a swing band on New York's jumping 52nd Street. In the middle of the action, she suddenly heard what she described as a "scream that was absolutely primeval." It was the sound of a dutiful and angry Billie Holiday accidentally encountering the underage Hazel in what she considered less-than-ideal circumstances. She chased her off the stage and out of the club.[17] It was this protective attitude that led Scott to forever think of Holiday as a big sister.

Scott's more-or-less "discoverer," Barney Josephson, was the owner of two New York night spots, Café Society Uptown and Downtown, famous not only for the superb and eclectic mix of performers who could be heard there, but also for their progressive policy of total racial integration. "We believe in democracy," Josephson said, "and are willing to practice it even if hurts our business."[18] The talent policy at both clubs was equally interracial, with a typical evening of entertainment consisting of Billie Holiday, the boogie-woogie piano team of Albert Ammons and Pete Johnson, comedy relief from Zero Mostel, and the Golden Gate Quartet. The pool of singers, instrumentalists and comics who regularly shuttled back and forth between Josephson's Greenwich Village and Park Avenue locations also included Lena Horne, Imogene Coca, Teddy Wilson, Eddie Heywood and theater comics Jack Gilford and Jimmy Savo; all of this now-legendary talent was presented within the confines of two sensibly priced bulwarks against racial bigotry. "Despite the potentially explosive mix of customers," writes James Gavin in *Intimate Nights: The Golden Age of New York Cabaret*, "Josephson created an atmosphere of tolerance; white customers who complained — 'What have you got here, a nigger joint?' — received a check and were asked to leave."[19]

The first audition of Scott by the club owner resulted in a legendary amalgamation of talent and locale, much like that of Bobby Short and the Café Carlyle of more recent times. Josephson told her, "You have a home here for life," and she soon became the reigning queen of his little empire.[20] Primarily appearing at the uptown operation, she began in 1938, earning $65 a week; seven years later she was pulling down $2000 weekly. At this point Scott was being offered far greater sums to switch alliances, but refused: "Why should I work for any other night club in town? I'd be a jerk."[21]

Describing the spell she cast over the intimate night spot, Scott's eventual husband, New York congressman Adam Clayton Powell, wrote:

> Café Society was then *the* supper club of New York and Hazel Scott was its *grande vedette*. No one came to challenge her in her domain. There was nothing like Café Society and there has been nothing like it since. Way at the end of the long room was the black concert grand piano sticking its nose up out of the audience. All the lights would go out, Hazel would make her way to the piano and then suddenly a spotlight would catch her. For a moment the audience would gasp, because it looked as if she were seated there nude — the height of the piano, the bare-shouldered dress, nothing by the golden-brown shoulder and arms, super-talented fingers.[22]

There were, of course, problems: One night, Josephson later recalled, he was sitting at the bar when Scott "arrived for her early show, radiant in a new gown and a new hairstyle, and obviously in an 'up' mood. I gave her a nice compliment and a fatherly good-luck kiss on the cheek as she left to do the show. A well-dressed woman farther down the bar left her stool, glared at me, and spat out, 'Nigger lover! Only a Jew could kiss a nigger!'

"I ignored her and turned to the bartender, telling him to give her a check and get her out. The bartender made me promise to hide the incident from Hazel, but some employee must have leaked the news, because as she left the club later she very dramatically planted a kiss on me and at the door turned and said, 'Only a nigger would kiss a Jew!'"[23]

The early years of World War II found Hazel's career taking off with a velocity rare for an African American. One New York department store reported that it had sold 3,000 copies of her "Swinging the Classics" album in just two weeks[24]; in addition to features about her in *Time* ("Hot Classicist")[25] and *Newsweek* ("Hep Hazel"),[26] she was the subject of an in-depth profile in the popular *Collier's* magazine in which she announced she would be co-starring with Louis Armstrong in an upcoming Orson Welles project, *It's All True*. As to exactly *when* the project might commence shooting was problematic: "He's [Welles] such a vague character," Hazel told *Collier's*.[27]

It wasn't vagueness, though, that finally did the venture in: RKO Pictures was automatically expecting a light, frothy jazz musical from Welles; but what they were getting, they soon realized based on early footage sent back from Brazil, was a film *specifically* about the plight of the black laboring class south of the border and the universality of African culture. Needless to say, the plug was soon pulled by front office Hollywood on a project which has since become legend.[28]

Shortly thereafter came a film opportunity that seemed to represent a step down from starring for the Magnificent Orson: a bit part in the not-quite-

"A" musical, *Something to Shout About*, to be directed by Gregory Ratoff. In fact, so minimal was her participation, Hazel didn't even need to be flown to Hollywood; instead, she was filmed in New York. Columbia executives saw the footage of Scott who, by comparison, made "most sweater girls look underfed"— Broadway columnist Earl Wilson once wrote — and they were so impressed that they signed her to a four-picture deal. Hazel was put on a plane for California to shoot her now beefed-up part in *Something to Shout About*.

There is little doubt that what the studio had in mind for twenty-year-old Hazel Scott — a first-rank night club and concert hall attraction and now about to making her film debut in a movie with a Cole Porter score — was their own version of competing MGM's "exotic" black diva Lena Horne. As such, she would be glamorously clad and used primarily in big musical production numbers which Columbia could conveniently snip out in the South or wherever else scenes featuring African Americans might bring offense (a standard practice in the motion picture industry at the time).[29] Scott later admitted that she was troubled by abetting such racist schemes, but just about the only dramatic roles available to her as a black woman were domestics or quasi-prostitutes; in a rare occasion of compromise for her, she chose to take the route of the musical.[30] After wrapping up work on *Something to Shout About*, which went without a hitch, Scott was loaned out to MGM for two similar all-musical inserts; one of them, *I Dood It*, featured Lena Horne as well. Then Scott returned to Columbia for *The Heat's On* and, she assumed, more gowns, glitz, and glamour lighting. But a clash Scott would soon have with the notoriously domineering and vindictive Columbia studio chief Harry Cohn over her part in the Mae West movie paints a picture of Scott — some might say — working against her own best interests.

The film, made at the height of World War II, like many other musicals of the period, was to contain the perfunctory production number featuring women singing, dancing and rallying their men onward into battle. Then Scott found out how the females in the all-black ensemble were to be depicted:

"My costume was fitted, and the guys were all fitted, too; then they started bringing the costumes for the girls. They were wearing aprons, and [choreographer] David Lichine said they looked too new. He told the makeup men to spray them with oil and I blew sky-high. I honestly did. I said, 'I don't understand you. How can you think that young women are going to see their sweethearts off to war wearing dirty aprons?'"[31]

The racist implications seemed perfectly clear to Hazel: Black women had so little self-esteem that they didn't care what they were wearing when sending their loved ones into battle. She refused to do the number unless the costumes were cleaned up. Such non-self-serving behavior was as unheard-of in Hollywood then as it is now and studio officials were puzzled. After all, Scott, in a WAC outfit, wasn't called to wear one of the maid outfits herself.

Production on the number was held up for three days and several thousand dollars were lost. "So," she later crowed to jazz drummer-author Art Taylor in his *Notes and Tones*, "I had hit the man where it hurts most — in his pocketbook." Hazel finally got her way (she usually did); but in the long run she suffered consequences far more severe than those she'd levied on Columbia: It seems that, in retaliation, Cohn effectively blackballed her from films. (Two Scott films were released after *The Heat's On*, but one was shot before the costume incident, and a contract for the other had already been signed.[32])

But the powerful Cohn's influence only reached *so far*. Fifteen years later she was able to secure a role in a film ... in France. It was *Le Désordre et la nuit* (*Night Affair*) starring Jean Gabin and Danielle Darrieux. An underworld melodrama, typical of the vehicles Gabin was turning out at that time, the film gave Scott some brief acting chores, but chiefly used her in a nightclub scene, singing and playing the piano. The French, it appears, were no better at utilizing her talents than the Americans.

Scott reported one interesting sidelight to the shooting: "I came home from the studio and picked up the *Herald-Tribune* from my door. When I looked at the paper, I started shaking all over. I had just finished my first day of shooting, and Harry Cohn had said I'd never make another picture as long as he lived. Well, I read in the paper that he dropped dead the previous night. Isn't that strange? You see why I don't fool with God."[33]

* * *

"What Congressman has been stage-door johnnying what boogie-woogie pianist? And don't think his wife doesn't know," read a wildly transparent "blind" item in the November 1944 issue of *Ebony Magazine*. Everyone knew to whom the squib referred; the pair was undoubtedly Hazel and charismatic black politician Adam Clayton Powell, Jr. Although married, Powell was the possessor of a reckless playboy image totally out of keeping with his dual roles as a Congressman and pastor of the largest Christian congregation in North America, Harlem's Abyssinian Baptist Church (Powell had inherited the pastorship from his father).

The first big brush with public notoriety came in 1933 when Powell committed the outrageous (for the son a prominent minister) act of announcing his intentions of marrying a Cotton Club dancer, Isabele Washington, sister of popular actress Fredi Washington. Adam's father and church deacons were strongly opposed, but Powell stood his ground, publicly lashing out against "the unreasonable formalism" of the church, and threatening to leave it altogether if his father refused to confer his blessings.[34] Eventually Powell Sr. gave in and even performed the Powell-Washington nuptials.

By the time "Mr. Jesus," as Powell was known to his congregation, met and rapidly fell in love with Hazel ten years later, he was one of the most well-known African Americans in the country. Powell later claimed that by then his first marriage had hit the skids because of his wife's failure to grow along with him.[35]

Long before Powell met Scott, the black press was regularly full of innuendo regarding his extra-marital affairs. In the prevailing manner of the day, long-suffering Isabele Washington put up with her husband's philandering. But she did not give up her husband to Hazel without a fight. When Powell shocked her with his request for a divorce so that he could marry Scott, she refused. The case was dragged through the gossip columns, with Washington bitterly charging that Powell had talked her into giving up a promising career to become a housewife, and then dumped her.[36]

Finally a settlement was reached and the first Mrs. Adam Clayton Powell went to Reno. A little more than a month after the Powells' quickie divorce, Hazel and Adam were married in Connecticut. This was followed by a reception later in the day at Café Society Uptown where 3000 showed up (only a third of them invited); most of them were turned away and mounted police had to be called out to keep order among this strange amalgamation of bedfellows from the worlds of politics, show business and the church. The crush was so great at one point that Scott fainted dead away while shaking hands with well-wishers.[37]

Rather than turning into a serious vocational and political liability — especially when it came to Powell — the marriage was a veritable public relations coup. Both Scott and Powell, individually, were regarded as being, in the unfortunate parlance of the times, "a credit to their race." Thus, in the mirror world of black society, their marriage was considered a "storybook marriage," somewhat along the lines of the alliance between the great houses of Mary Pickford and Douglas Fairbanks of a slightly earlier era. *Life Magazine* printed a two-page spread of the wedding and reception showing a radiant looking Powell and Scott, calling him "a rabble rousing champion of Negro rights." Had they been white, the Powells would probably have received no more royal treatment.[38]

Almost immediately, the couple was faced with an incident of the sort that cut across all class barriers wherever blacks were involved. Powell had leased a lakeside chalet as a honeymoon resort, then received a call from the Chief Justice of the Supreme Court of Vermont who owned and had rented the property to them. Homeowners in the vicinity of the Vermont hideaway had held a meeting and voted down the possibility of blacks living in the exclusive compound. Powell was encouraged by the justice to force the issue. "Come ahead," he advised Powell, "and I will support you."[39] But the Powells decided that that was not how they wanted to start married life and instead checked into the Waldorf-Astoria. It was one of the few instances where either of them ever backed down from a racial confrontation; in the years to come,

Powell and especially Scott would become involved in fighting dozens of similar situations.

A few months after her marriage, Scott got into a clash similar to the heavily profiled 1939 standoff between the Daughters of the American Revolution and black contralto Marian Anderson. In that incident, Anderson lost her battle to book the D.A.R. Constitution Hall for a recital and instead had to *settle* for a concert on the steps of the Lincoln Memorial and an apology from Eleanor Roosevelt, who quit the D.A.R. in protest. The resulting Anderson outdoor appearance with 75,000 in attendance got front page newspaper and newsreel coverage around the world. Now, in 1945, Scott was attempting to book the hall — not that it was likely she entertained any serious belief she could bring it off. Instead, Scott and Powell were perhaps trying to gauge how much the racial climate had changed in the six years since the Anderson case. A tête-à-tête was set up between Scott and the D.A.R. president, Mrs. Julius Talmadge. "It was a nice harmonious meeting," Talmadge told the press afterward, as reported in the October 22, 1945, issue of *Time*. One wonders, though, exactly how harmonious it was. Scott didn't get the hall.

Immediately Powell fired off a letter complaining of the incident to President Truman, asking him to intervene. Truman wrote back, comparing the actions of the D.A.R. to those of the Nazis, but added that he did not want to interfere with "private enterprise."[40] A few minutes later the Powells received a backup letter from the first lady Bess Truman in which she stated that she too "deplored" the D.A.R.'s stand — all of which *might* have temporarily mollified the Powells. But on the very day of these transmitted sentiments, Powell was marching up New York's Fifth Avenue during a Columbus Day parade when a newsman stopped him and showed him the headline, "Bess Truman Goes to Grace the D.A.R. Tea." Powell, brashly for a black of that era, remarked, "From now on there is only one first lady, Mrs. Roosevelt."[41]

At first, Bess Truman seemed to be trying to mollify the Powells (for Adam Powell was surely a powerful political ally) when she told the press she'd accepted the invitation to high tea before the Powells' troubles with the D.A.R. But she put her foot back in it deeper than ever when she impolitically answered, "Why not?" when a reporter asked if she ever again attend a function given by the organization.[42] The Congressman now went even further in his castigation of Bess Truman, declaring her not the first, but "the last lady,"[43] commenting elsewhere that he immediately intended to press for legislation to strip the antediluvian women's organization of its tax-free status. The war was on.

Immediately, a commissioner of the District of Columbia pronounced Scott's move "a Communist-inspired plot."[44] Such rhetoric surrounding the uproar was typical, as volleys were lobbed back and forth for nearly two months, sometimes with page one results. Powell wasn't the only one who was angered. The *Philadelphia Record* commented on the Scott–D.A.R. contretemps, "Doesn't the D.A.R. know the Civil War is over?"[45]; the *San Francisco Chronicle* editorialized with similar sentiments a few days later[46]; the *Christian Science Monitor* said that "this entire affair gives us cause for regret"[47]; and the *Washington Post* deemed the right-wing women's social club "misguided and unreasonable."[48]

An ad hoc group formed in support of Scott also called itself the D.A.R., the Drive Against Reaction, and booked the singer-pianist for a concert at Carnegie Hall; while Powell said the first D.A.R.'s initials stood for "Daughters of Asinine Reaction." The *New York Times* reminded its readers that descendents of Crispus Attucks, a black man and the first victim of the Boston Massacre in 1770, had the door slammed in their face by the Daughters.[49] Wherever D.A.R. president Mrs. Julius Talmadge appeared, pickets sprang up.

Between October 1 when the story broke in *The New York Times* and early December, by which time it had played itself out, 26 items on the affair appeared there, including several concerning the possibility of the House Un-American Activities investigating to find out if "subversive elements" might be behind Scott's actions. But the D.A.R. stood firm against Scott: The Powells learned that little had changed in the intervening years since Marian Anderson had tried to bring a little class to Constitution Hall.

Almost from the beginning of her career, Scott had written into all of her contracts an anti-segregation clause (she was one of the first black performers to make such demands).[50] The proviso stated that promoters would be legally obligated to forfeit half of her minimum guarantee and she would not be expected to perform if she arrived for an appearance to discover that an audience was racially segregated. "What justification can anyone who comes to hear me and then who objects to sitting next to another Negro?"[51] Scott reasoned, defending her position. She also refused to perform in any town where unsegregated hotel facilities weren't available: "If I'm not good enough to stay in a hotel in certain towns, I figure those people are not good enough to hear me play."[52]

Still, there were slip-ups: In 1946 Hazel arrived for a performance at the University of Texas and, looking around the auditorium, spotted a bright red carpet running down the middle of the 7500-seat hall. Immediately sensing that it was nothing more than a tonier version of the notorious *rope*, which had been used for many years to separate black audiences from white in the South, she dared the university to sue her by refusing to perform. (The school declined to sue.)[53] The same year, Scott and a friend were both refused service at a restaurant in the Seattle suburb of Pasco. She later incredulously remarked, "If we'd been any farther north we'd have been in Canada." Deciding to report the incident, Scott marched to police headquarters where, she later recalled, she looked into "the coldest green eyes I'd ever seen in my life." When she finished stating her complaint, the police officer's response was, "Are you going to get out of here or am I going to run you in for disturbing the peace?"[54] Scott and Powell sued the owners of the spot, Harry and Blanche Utz, for $50,000, claiming the couple had violated a 1909 Washington law banning such discrimination. The following year the Powells won $250, a point was made, and the Utzes went out of business.[55]

Whatever scandal had clouded the marriage had mostly evaporated and the couple's activities and increasing fortunes were written about constantly, not only in black newspapers but also *Life*-like black periodicals such as *Ebony* and *Jet*. As portrayed in their pages, the Powells' was a model marriage for all of striving young black America to emulate. The May 1946 *Ebony* announced in headlines, "Happily Married, Famous N.Y. Couple Anxiously Await an Heir."

Four years later the same publication ran a story appearing under Adam Clayton Powell's name (but probably ghosted) entitled "My Life with Hazel Scott" which also contained photos of the couple engaged in full-tilt domestic bliss with their 2½-year-old son Skipper (Adam Clayton Powell III). Powell went into detail about Hazel the cook whipping up a "gorgeous supper topped with cream filling and coconut"; Hazel the perfect mother to little Skipper; and Hazel the pastor's wife dutifully going over Powell's sermons in advance each week.

Powell wrote in *Ebony* of Scott sometimes saying to him before a night on the town, "Kiss me, daddy, and forget we're late. I wasn't dressing for a first-night audience. This is all for you. I'd just as soon stay home now.'

"And we did," he wrote.[56] Thus, if the press was to be believed, the first few years of the Scott-Powell marriage were idyllic; at the very least, to judge from the *Ebony* article, the pair seem to have agreed on the public image they wished to convey. Alongside dippy stories such as these, the press—both black and white — also continued to carry news of the couple's continuing political activism, such as their successful attempt to bring about the integration of Veteran's Administration hospitals.[57]

* * *

The incident that triggered Hazel Scott's eventual listing in the notorious right-wing smear sheet *Red Channels*, which printed the names of artists and performers suspected of being fellow travelers, was her performance at a 1943 rally for Benjamin Davis, an avowed Communist running for New York City Council. Although Scott's support was not without incriminating overtones, clearly her backing of Davis had more to do with the fact he was black rather than his politics. "One such benefit," she later recalled to *Essence Magazine*, "was for the Russian War Relief at Madison Square Garden. Everyone did it. My manager booked me. Who are they kidding? Russia was our ally then."[58]

Scott was typical of others eventually victimized by McCarthyism who took part in wartime activities and causes which for the most part could have been construed as "communistic" only by the wildest stretches of the imagination. In 1949 Adam Powell gave an interview to *Ebony* in which he naively dropped the bomb that Hazel had been to a party recently where she had played a piano-flute duet "with America's number 1 Communist [Earl Browder, president of the U.S. Communist Party]."[59]

In 1950 Scott defended herself before the House Un-American Activities Committee (HUAC) after her name was placed in *Red Channels*. Unlike most witnesses who appeared before HUAC, Scott was not subpoenaed but *requested* to appear. Prior to taking the stand, she was addressed directly by Congressman Woods of Georgia (who also happened to be a Ku Klux Klan member) who said, "We have agreed to hear you because you are the wife of a colleague [Powell]." Hazel responded, "Well, what about the 400 others [i.e., names appearing in *Red Channels*] who are not?" She went on to lash out against *Channels*, deeming it "vile and un–American," and to lambast HUAC itself as being "un–American."[60]

These were strong, courageous words long before newsman Ed Murrow's tide-turning anti–HUAC TV editorial in 1954. Other celebrities who came before the Committee during the 81st Congress were Edward G. Robinson and Jackie Robinson. But while the former spoke out against Paul Robeson's contention that blacks should not fight in a war against Russia, Jackie Robinson was more forthright: "The fact that it was a Communist who denounces injustice in the courts, police brutality and lynching when it happens doesn't change the truth of his charges."[61] One commentator on the era later remarked, "It was particularly troubling that persons whose livelihood was imperiled, as Hazel Scott's was, could find no better forum from which to reply."[62]

Shortly after Hazel's HUAC appearance, she proposed that musicians and performers should boycott all radio and TV networks suspending those performers listed in *Red Channels*.[63]

In 1950, Scott was earning $100,000 annually for about five months of work a year.[64] But overall public sentiment against her, which had been building for some time because of her politics, reached critical mass with her HUAC appearance. Shortly afterward, Scott's TV show on the Dumont network, one of the first such ventures for an African American on coast-to-coast TV, was yanked from the air. Its cancellation was a harbinger of the descending arc her career would take as the 1950s wore on. Still, some of the deceleration had nothing to do with blacklisting. "I had to give up clubs," she told a writer in 1978. "What? A minister's wife appearing where whiskey is sold?"[65]

By the mid–1950s much of the luster of Scott's career began to dim; and the Powells' marriage was similarly in decline. Scott says her husband was increasingly jealous of her success as a performer.[66] Moreover, Powell had begun to return to his old womanizing ways. At first, the pair tried an open marriage arrangement. But whenever *she* got involved with someone, Scott later claimed, Powell would do his best to try and make her feel guilty.[67] Finally in 1956 they legally separated, then divorced. The end of her marriage also marked a beginning for Scott: She went to Paris for three weeks to rest and play an engagement. But Powell, with whom Hazel was still on friendly terms, advised her, "If you're not happy here [the U.S.] why don't you stay over there for a little while and work." "A little while" would end up lasting more than three years.[68]

Scott played clubs all over the continent, North Africa and the Near East. She also appeared in two films in France and was slated to appear in a French stage production of *Anna Lucasta* which never came off. But there were long stretches where Scott did little but rest and relax. Even though she thrived on the liberated (by U.S. standards) Parisian racial attitudes, a desire to return to the U.S. eventually began to set in.

"While I was there [Paris], some of my dearest friends died and some were murdered. I lost Lester Young and Billie Holiday. I went to the door of death myself after a serious operation. Lester, who is— not *was*— such a beautiful individual, came to see me every day during my recuperation and we listened for hours on end to Frank Sinatra's album, 'Only the Lonely.' It pains me that he went from my apartment to an airplane which took him to America to death."[69]

When Scott finally returned to the U.S. in 1960, it was a country where the increasingly prevalent attitude among young militant blacks was to publicly attack certain entertainment figures for their failure to take an active, in-your-face part in the rapidly escalating attack of the racial status quo. No matter what their past activities might have been, it was the present that mattered. Scott did not escape this trend. "Since my return to America," she told one writer then, "I have been attacked by some misinformed people who say I have been away from the problem. In one New York hotel where I was staying, the room service waiter said, 'I since thought you were the greatest, but you have fallen in my estimation because you left America where the fight is.'"[70] Rather than defend herself by invoking her past Civil Rights activities, she tended to slough off such attacks, remarking that racism was not confined to America, but was worldwide.[71] She observed: "It is difficult for a woman alone in this industry. Everyone wants to sleep with you. If you don't, you've got problems." She added that she'd long been rumored to have been a lesbian because of her refusal to heed the call of the casting couch.[72]

Scott had arrived back in America just when Adam Clayton Powell's various legal entanglements— including a lawsuit brought by a Harlem grandmother whom he'd characterized as a criminal — resulted in his becoming front page news throughout the U.S.[73] Scott later said that she felt that her refusal to side with certain opposing forces against her ex-husband was another reason she was frozen out when she came back from Paris.[74] She remained loyal to Powell throughout the latter part of his life until his death in 1972; she could not imagine being otherwise:

"If I had my way, I would have pictures of anyone who talked badly about someone they had been intimate with shown on a large screen — in the most intimate position — reminding them that they once cared. So I would never attack my son's father, even if I hated him, which I do not."[75]

Scott's return to America didn't last much longer than it took for her to gauge the political and occupational climate and then leave once more. By the end of the year she was again in Paris where the colony of American jazz musicians living there, along with visiting players and sundry others, were glad to have her back. "I'd have a dozen musicians maybe out of the Ellington band in the living room," she told jazz chronicler Leonard Feather (who in 1937 had produced her first recordings). "You'd go in the next room and there stretched out on a couch because he hurt his back at the studio that day is Anthony Quinn. You keep going and there in the kitchen is Quincy Jones testing what I have in the pot."[76]

Upon her return, she married Enzio Bedin, an Italian-Swiss 15 years her junior. But the union was short-lived: When the marriage broke up after only 22 months, Bedin told a friend, "Hazel is a Maserati and I can only handle a Fiat."[77]

It was around this time that Scott's life began to become increasingly complicated by drinking, leading a Catholic priest whom Scott had consulted about her problem to term her — in a subtle Jesuitical distinction — a hardcore drunk rather than an alcoholic. Ex-husband Powell later simply described her in this period as "drinking heavily." But then there occurred in Hazel's life one of the greatest acts of faith he had ever seen:

> She was living on the Left Bank in Paris, with Skipper's godmother and our lifelong friend Mabel Howard. They lived just across the Seine from Notre Dame, whose spire they could see shimmering in the dawn. One morning, accompanied by Mabel, Hazel went to Notre Dame, got down on her knees in front of the altar, and vowed she would not move until God gave her strength. She stayed until her knees actually became bloody. When she finally did rise to her feet, she had the power, strength and faith never to again touch or desire a drop of alcohol.[78]

It was during this second stay in Paris that Hazel could also be seen one morning — on the same day as the event in the U.S. — leading a band of disparate artists, including James Baldwin, Richard Avedon and Anthony Quinn, from the American Church to the door of the U.S. Embassy to deliver a petition in support of Martin Luther King's 1963 march on Washington, D.C. Scott's familiarity with black pride went all the way back to her early childhood when she could recall accompanying her father to a Marcus Garvey lecture in which Garvey intoned over and over again that he was a "man." Years later Scott said she had been puzzled; it was evident beyond a shadow of a doubt that the magnificent person in the black uniform with the gold epaulets standing before her was the male of the species. Why did Garvey keep saying it over and over? "That's just it," her father replied. "I'm afraid there are people who cannot see that he is a man."[79]

Coming back to the U.S. in 1966 (this time for good), Scott began more forcefully to defend herself against the kind of personal attacks first leveled against her a few years earlier. In drummer Art Taylor's book *Notes and Tones*, she is quoted, "People would say to me, 'You went away from the fight,' and I'd say, 'Come on, you're looking for a fat lip! When you were sitting very comfortable in your Jim Crow quarters or your all-white quarters or in the North in Harlem or on the south side of Chicago, I was down South desegregating audiences in town after town getting one jump ahead of the sheriff. So don't be telling me I ran away from the fight.'"[80]

Scott came home because of her son; she was now living in the U.S., alone due to Adam Powell's fleeing the country to escape his legal problems. She sought out dramatic roles in TV and films, but after landing only a handful of parts on shows such as *Julia* and *The Bold Ones*, Scott refocused her energies on music. The jobs she was able to land, however, were a far cry from her Café Society glory years. Many of the dates were at East Coast Holiday Inns where, instead of typically staring the audience down to achieve silence, she pragmatically made no attempt at all to quash the inevitably noisy patrons.

In the fall of 1981, Scott had known for several months that she was dying of cancer, but continued performing for her small but devoted New York following at New York's Milford Plaza Hotel. By then she'd long since given up jazzing the classics; and it was a rare occasion when she'd give in and revert to the gimmicky Hazel Scott style of the 1940s. Remembering back to her struggling formative Yacht Club days, she told a reporter shortly before her death on October 2 of that year, "It was something I wish I'd never done." It was an act carried out, she added, "strictly for self-preservation."[81]

During the era of World War II, Scott was a household name to most of the nation's African Americans, and to a large part of sophisticated white America. She was also among the first entertainers of any race to combine political activism with professional undertakings. Ironically, by the 1960s, Scott, who accomplished so much in the area of civil rights throughout her career, had disappeared from the screen of public consciousness. In 1968 an obviously hurt and bitter Scott told *Ebony Magazine*:

> I have a deep and abiding resentment of the "new Negro" because I think he has been a little late in arriving, number one. Number two: I'd like to know where they — and they're going to say they weren't born, but their parents were — 25 years ago when I put myself out of work, when I was called among

some of the other kind of things, a black Joan of Arc, a Communist and a radical professional black lady and an apologist for my race. I was told I waved my color like a banner. I am not about to sit still now and let anybody tell me that nothing was done until these "new Negroes" started letting their hair grow long.[82]

She was absolutely right; Hazel Scott had nothing to apologize for.

*   *   *

Although at least one news story reported that, toward the end of her life, Scott had completed writing her memoirs, no such publication ever appeared. However, in 2008, a long overdue and well-received biography, *Hazel Scott: The Pioneering Journey of a Jazz Pianist, from Café Society to Hollywood to HUAC* by New York–based writer and actor Karen Chilton was published by the University of Michigan Press.

8

Forcing the Issue
Dinah Washington

When Ella Fitzgerald died in 1995, eulogists paid deserved attention to Ella, the Singer, almost to the total exclusion of Fitzgerald, the Civil Rights Crusader. Ella Fitzgerald, a political activist?, you might well wonder. But the facts are that in 1954, Fitzgerald and a party of several other blacks were bumped from first class reservations on a Pan American Airways flight in deference to another group of travelers whose only overreaching claim to the accommodations was that they happened to be white. The First Lady of Song missed her flight, but instead of letting the matter slide, she sued the airline and won her case. Afterwards, she saw Fitzgerald vs. Pan American Airways, fought in the courts a year before the Birmingham bus boycott, become a landmark legal brief in the area of African Americans and air travel.[1] In 1948, entertainer Nat "King" Cole forced the issue of segregationist housing covenants when he bought a residence in L.A.'s "old money" enclave, Hancock Park. Almost immediately the equity hit the fan. Picket lines were thrown up around the house by the all-white neighborhood association in an attempt to stop Cole and his family from moving in. They told the singer that he shouldn't take it personally, that they simply did not want any undesirables moving in.

"Neither do I," said Cole, who actually tried to sit down and reason with the racists. "And if I see anybody undesirable coming in here, I'll be the first to complain."[2]

The singer continued to stand his ground and shortly thereafter Hancock Park residents were headed off at the pass by a U.S. Supreme Court ruling against restrictive real estate covenants. Cole kept his house.

In a less procedural fashion, Lena Horne also struck a blow for freedom one night at a Hollywood night club in 1960 when, upon being called by another patron the most unpleasant of all racial epithets, she recalls in her autobiography, *Lena*: "I began throwing things. The lamp, glasses, an ashtray.... He had a cut over his eye and he was bleeding, as they say, profusely."[3] The incident made national headlines for weeks.

Dinah Washington, late 1950s.

Less rambunctiously, Horne was also responsible for desegregating several major entertainment spots in the 1950s—most notably Hollywood's Cocoanut Grove—by refusing to perform unless blacks were seated (these were locales where even as the main attraction she was forced to enter through the side door). And yet, when Horne became a forthright civil rights activist in the mid–1960s, some in the black community opined that her turn to militancy was only a fashionable face-saving career move. "Where was she when we needed her most?" seemed to be the crux of the criticism. But, of course, Horne had been there all along, as had been Fitzgerald, Cole, Hazel Scott and any number of other African American entertainers who for years had been responsible for redrawing and redefining the racial line in the sand.

The problem of perception in many cases seems to have lain not with the entertainers' lack of social commitment, but with the short memory of their critics. Not that the performers necessarily deserve any special medals for their actions; in the final analysis Cole, Horne and the others were only trying to save face and to retain what little amount of respect that they had, as blacks, managed to accrue for themselves over the years. But such gestures as Fitzgerald suing Pan Am didn't exactly hurt the cause of social justice for African Americans. However, given the No-Actors-or-Dogs-Allowed stigma that until very recently associated with show business, the general tendency has been to discount the significance of any political gesture—no matter how great or small—executed by a mere entertainer. Thus, it is also often overlooked that when Lena Horne arrived in Hollywood for the first time in 1942, she came with a list of demands as long as your arm regarding how she, as a black woman, was to be used in films. In turn, the dignified manner in which Horne was allowed to deport herself on the big screen helped change the way African Americans would eventually come to be portrayed on film.

For Dinah Washington, according to the 1995 musical *Dinah Was*, the defining moment in her fight against racism happened when she was chosen as the first African American to play the "big room" (not the lounge) at Vegas' Sahara Hotel. Like just about every other black performer who had appeared in the gambling capital before her, the blues great acceded to the customs of the country and accepted substandard accommodations. Come opening night, however, she caused jaws to drop when, after her first number, she forsook her accommodationist ways and blew the whistle on the dichotomy of star-billed black performers compelled to come in through the back door. In fact, Oliver Goldstick's play is a semi-fictionalized gloss on the singer's life and the incident never happened. But knowing Dinah, it could have; for her life not only invites larger-than-life dramaturgy but suggests the heroic component that was a part of almost every African American performer who trod the boards in the first half of the 20th century.

"Her range as a stylist was as wide as the range of her voice," jazz critic Dan Morgenstern once remarked of singer Dinah Washington. "There are all kinds of girl singers. Somehow Dinah made most of the others sound like little girls."[4] But it wasn't just a sound that separated Washington from the rest of the pack, it was personality. Everyone who ever worked with her has at least one larger-than-life tale to tell. A *monstre sacrée* of the first order, hers is no garden variety show biz saga but a complex tale of near-mythic proportions. She sang hard-as-nails blues, lushly orchestrated ballads, and straight-ahead jazz with equal dexterity. Add to that a reputation for personal extravagance, volcanic temperament, warming generosity, and a rock-bottom insistence on having things done "her way," and you've got a personality you don't so much talk about, but dream of. Consider the following headlines: *Dinah Washington Quizzed About Gun*; *Blues Queen Sheds Sixth*; *Dinah Washington Will Be Tried in Third Degree Assault*; *Hearing Soon on Dinah's Insult Rap*; *Blues Singer Escapes Death By Gift of Glass Candy.*[5]

She was born in Tuscaloosa, Alabama; the actual date of her birth is something of a mystery because of poor records kept on blacks back then. The date generally agreed upon is August 29, 1924.* But the veracity of much else that happened to Dinah Washington is less important than the way it was remembered by those who lived it with her.

Three scenes from *Unforgettable*, an imaginary movie based on the life of Dinah Washington:

Scene One

"Any minute now that son of a bitch is going to come through that door," Dinah Washington shouts. She thrusts out her hand — a drink tightly clutched in it — in the door's direction, and holds it there for several seconds. Then she pulls it back, mutters something inaudible, and takes a swig of her drink. The dressing room is very quiet, very intense. This isn't just another date. This is the "downhome" and popular Roberts' Show Lounge† in Chicago, a club Dinah has played many times before. Ordinarily she'd be laughing and joking with the musicians, holding court backstage as friends and admirers dropped by to pay their respects between sets. She'd be cooking too, passing around plates of some special dish or other to whoever wanted it. And above all there would be Dinah's furs. She loves nothing better than taking out her many minks and sables to comb and pet them. She loves showing them off to others. She loves looking at herself before a full-length mirror. Tonight, though, Dinah isn't in the mood, and she isn't making her upset a secret.

"That son of a bitch from Mercury Records," she barks to her band leader, Danny Young. "Jacking me around for months, and *now* he's coming over." She tells Young how her contract is coming up for renewal with the record company, and how they aren't rushing to have her re-sign. "They're trying to bluff me, those motherfuckers — trying to get my price down." Then comes a knock

---

*The facts concerning her matrimonial career are similarly fuzzy. Officially, she was wed seven times, but an additional three men claim to have married her, with one alleged ceremony having taken place on a boat off the coast of Sweden.

†In 1961 Washington bought the Show Lounge, but the same year defaulted on payments to Herman Roberts, who then took the club back.

at the dressing room door. "Well, who the hell is it?" Dinah yells, knowing perfectly well who is there.

The record executive, a typically middle-aged, business-suited individual, comes through the door. Dinah sits with her back to him. "Can we talk a minute?" he asks. "Go ahead and talk," she says, not moving around to look at him. "I'm not going anywhere."

"Well, it's private," he says, pointing at Danny Young.

"Shit!" hisses Dinah. "You can say anything in front of him you want to, but you won't change my mind. I've spoken to three other companies already. You fucked up." The man puts a large box on the dressing room table before her.

Mr. Mercury Records then leans over the box and opens it slowly. It is a mink coat. White. Full-length. Tens of thousands of dollars. Dinah stops talking; Dinah starts smiling. A great big lusty smile obliterates the gloom that had come before.

"Well, why the hell didn't you say you wanted me to sign the godamned contract?" she says, picking up the mink coat and wrapping it around her in a continuous motion.

Everything is going to be all right.[6]

Scene Two

The occasion is a Royal Command Performance in Great Britain in the late 1950s. Orchestra leader Val Parnell strikes up the first few bars of "Unforgettable." Out strides Washington onto the stage of London's Palladium. She looks up approximately in the direction of the Royal Box. A mischievous look passes over her face. "There is one heaven, one hell, one queen and your Elizabeth is an imposter," she outrageously remarks, then launches into her opening number.[7] Cut to a shot of HRH Elizabeth II, queen of Great Britain, not knowing quite what has hit her.

Scene Three

A montage of Dinah's 1963 funeral. At a Chicago mortuary, 25,000 mourners come to view the body, 6,000 attend her funeral, and 30,000 attempt to attend memorial services at the Detroit church of Aretha Franklin's father, the Reverend C. L. Franklin, which is inundated with 400 floral sprays. The casket is solid bronze, she wears a glittering tiara, one of Dinah's many beloved mink coats is draped across her and expensive rhinestone shoes twinkle up at the endless procession of those that have come to pay tribute. The cortege consists of twenty-five Cadillac limousines and over a hundred cars, resulting in a thirty-block traffic jam.

* * *

Seven times married ("I change my husbands before they change me"[8]), wildly temperamental and a prodigious advocate of the high life, Dinah Washington at first glance brings to mind other music figures who flamed out tragically. But there is only a superficial resemblance. She died at the early age of 39; nevertheless, Washington was nobody's classic show business "victim." Despite her often reckless lifestyle, she was at the time of her death still a highly sought-after performer and a relatively wealthy woman, not at all like Judy Garland, Edith Piaf and other troubled divas one could mention.

"I kind of think he'll be the one I grow old with," Washington said in 1963 on the occasion of her latest marriage, this time to football player "Night Train" Lane.[9] But only a few months later, on December 13, she passed away in her sleep after mixing too large a quantity of sleeping pills and alcohol. Having become casually addicted to both uppers and downers over the past decade, partly because of a weight problem, by this time she'd gotten so nonchalant about pills that there's little question that the overdose was accidental: Dinah's two sons were home from private school for the Christmas holidays, she had spent the day before she died shopping for presents, and stayed up long into the night wrapping them.

Like Garland and Nat "King" Cole, Washington's popularity and influence are nearly as great now as when she was alive. Songs like "What a Difference a Day Makes" and "Unforgettable" are as synonymous with her as "One for My Baby" with Frank Sinatra or "People" with Barbra Streisand, and many of the more than two dozen albums Washington cut are still in print. Aretha Franklin, Etta James and Nancy Wilson are just some of the influential standard bearers of the Washington tradition. Still, no matter how many singers have followed in her footsteps, there's no mistaking her precisely enunciated, soulful style for that of anyone else.

* * *

Born Ruth Jones, Dinah's earliest years from her birth in 1924 up until 1926 were spent in Alabama, after which time her parents Ollie and Alice Jones, Dinah and brother Harold moved to Chicago. The Joneses were among the nearly 200,000 African Americans who migrated there during the period from 1910 to 1930. At an early age Dinah became deeply involved with music at the city's St. Luke's Baptist Church where her mother was the choir director, and by age eleven she was playing piano and leading the choir herself. Soon she and her mother joined up with the Sallie Martin Singers, one of the most important forces in gospel music at that time, and began touring the South and Midwest. Their gospel group was in great demand and Dinah and her mother remained with the outfit for several years participating in all-night gospel "sings," campground meetings and concerts as they ceaselessly roamed from one town to another.

In 1938, Washington went behind her mother's back and won second place at an amateur singing contest at Chicago's Regal Theater where she performed the pop song "I Can't Face the Music." This "shocking" break with gospel was not an isolated incident; it marked the flowering of the rebel spirit that was characteristic of Dinah for the rest of her life. And while not immediately leaving the gospel world behind her, the die was also cast: She slowly began to make her move from the world of sanctified religion into early rhythm and blues performance and the Chicago nightlife of the early 1940s;

she started with a job as a women's room attendant at a night club. Before long she was singing at the popular Dave's Café, and even got an invitation to share the opening bill with Fats Waller at the new Down Beat Room of the Hotel Sherman.

Dinah's first important job in secular music, with bandleader Lionel Hampton, lasted from 1943 to 1946. It was a great break for her after a half-dozen years of professional uncertainty which found her bouncing back and forth between gospel music and rhythm and blues, working as an intermission pianist in clubs and as rest room attendant. But the initial enchantment of signing on with Hampton began to quickly pall. Life on the road during those segregated times was a near-nightmare and played a big part in the formation of Washington's bulletproof exterior. One-nighters caused her a good deal of hurt. She was subjected to a lot of things most people would cave in under: Girl band singers suffered as badly, if not more so, than the musicians. Because they were black, in the South, as likely as not the Hamptonians would pull into a town to discover that there was no place to eat or sleep due to segregation laws. Often the "boys" in the band had to crash on the bus, with Dinah doubling up with them. And it was nothing for her to get down on her hands and knees backstage, playing the game of tonk and cussing up a storm just like the guys.

Because Hampton would generally only let her do funky, bluesy material and not the songs she wanted to sing — standards and current hit parade tunes, etc. — Washington quickly became disillusioned. Another blow she withstood during her Hampton years was being featured on only one recording of the many the band cut during the nearly three years she was with the outfit. "I knew I was going to be the best singer in the business," she said years later, "but I wasn't going anywhere with Hampton."[10] In his book *Jazz Anecdotes*, bassist Bill Crow describes what happened next:

> After one broken promise, Dinah partially drowned her anger with a fifth of gin and went to work that night carrying quite a load, as well as an old pistol with no firing pin that someone had sold her. She laughed all the way through "The Man I Love," because the musicians kept whispering, "Sing it, Miss Gin." When Hampton called her on the carpet after the show, Dinah lit into him for breaking his promise. [Saxophonist] Arnett Cobb described the scene:
> "Hamp told her, 'Kiss my ass.' She went upstairs and got her pistol and came back down, and said, 'You told me to kiss your ass,' and put that gun right over the top of his nose, and Hamp's hair turned green. I ain't never seen anybody's hair turn green. I'm right there."

Five minutes later, Hampton's wife Gladys terminated Dinah's ten-year, $75-a-week contract on the spot. Cobb added, "She didn't know it could have been broken, but she broke it for herself right there. She broke it with a pistol and it wouldn't even fire!"[11]

Such behavior verged on the heroic: Back then, for a woman (read "girl singer") to try and gain control of her career was an unusual occurrence. And although her situation did not initially improve much after her departure from Hampton, still the money she made as a free agent was better and she was able to upgrade her repertoire. Dinah continued, however, to be booked almost exclusively into black clubs and auditoriums.

It was a long trek upward from Washington's gospel beginnings to the big showrooms of Vegas with, along the way, Dinah being called upon to constantly re-adapt herself to a number of ever-shifting personal and professional requirements. It wasn't until the 1950s that she was allowed the chance to regularly perform at more lucrative and prestigious locations, which, as custom had it, catered to a white clientele.

When Dinah left the gospel world for secular music, the move was more scandalous—more problematic—than when, in the 1950s, performers the likes of Sam Cooke, Bobby Womack and Lou Rawls did the same thing: When singers of the late '40s and the 1950s such as these turned away from gospel, the move was made with realistic hopes of establishing a broad mainstream career base. But during Washington's formative era, such an outcome wasn't in the cards. The most she could have expected was a modest payoff, for the sales barrier between black and whites was severely drawn. The end result was a career marked by several distinct musical identities.

First there was the Dinah who, by necessity, worked the segregated "chittlin circuit" (as it was called then) throughout the 1940s. Playing these black clubs and revues, artists were expected to place as much emphasis on bawdy carryings-on and just plain old letting the good times roll as they put upon music for music's sake. Then there was the Dinah of the recording studio who successfully walked the line between artistic invention and turning out numbers aimed at the rhythm and blues sales charts. One session might find her trying to make the most of some dreary commercial material, the next working out with first-rate jazz players under the direction of Quincy Jones. And then there was the Dinah Washington who in later years played those top rooms in Las Vegas, New York and Hollywood—where she was generally expected to present the best of all her musical faces to the public. No other performer before or since has had trailing along behind them such a diverse and fragmented audience. For Dinah it was both a curse and a blessing. It kept her on her toes as an artist, but finally it hemmed her in and held major stardom at bay due to her lack of a fixed "image." Not until the more socially enlightened 1960s was she able to begin consolidating and integrating her several musical selves—and this, just before her death.

At the beginning of her recording career, Dinah Washington was limited to basically two kinds of material: blues, either idiomatic or risqué and giddy like "TV Is the Thing This Year" (and the risqué consequences that ensue each time the channel selector of the narrator's TV set is turned), and duplicate "cover" versions of current hits by white recording stars (songs like

"Cold, Cold Heart" and "Wheel of Fortune"), none of which were intended to break through to the large mainstream market. Washington was usually able, however, to bring most of them to life. Along the way, too, she began to experiment with songs and arrangements. And it is the far more credible jazz sides she began recording in the 1950s, directed at the white "college elite" jazz festival crowds, for which Washington is probably best remembered today. Those and, of course, her first major crossover hit of 1959, "What a Difference a Day Makes."

Despite all this versatility, there still exists the tendency in some quarters to label Washington a blues (not jazz) singer, first, last and always. Her billing as "Queen of the Blues," which Dinah finally grew to dislike intensely, helped this misconception along. Granted, her first recording work tended to favor songs like "Blowtop Blues" and "Salty Papa Blues," but Washington soon began broadening her range, with her songbook beginning to include material by the cream of American popular composers. At a club date it was not unusual for her to rip into feisty and double entendre numbers like "Fat Daddy" and then to turn around and sensitively render Harburg and Lane's "Look to the Rainbow" from *Finian's Rainbow*.

Categorically inclined critics and music fans of the 1950s considered the question of Washington's correct stylistic niche a subject of major importance: Was she a jazz, blues or pop singer? And the debate still flares up from time to time. In retrospect, the answer now seems to be that she was any and all of these things at once: While the gospel influence is always unmistakable, just like Mahalia Jackson (even though she sang gospel exclusively), everything Dinah touched bore the jazz idiom's most important trace marks. She toyed with the melodies of even the most banal pop tunes and on ballads she tended to rush the beat in a fashion that lent them a heady lilt. Her stylistic calling card, however, was the way in which she usually attacked the notes of a lyric line in a pitch-perfect staccato fashion capped by closure (on the final note of a line) effected by an upwardly gliding vibrato one could almost drive a truck through, i.e., repetitive attraction alternated with release ... much like the blues form itself. And as for her blues credentials: Early blues great Alberta Hunter seems to have put that question to rest when she told writers Nat Shapiro and Nat Hentoff, "They don't have blues singers now like they had then, except maybe Dinah Washington."[12] So, while it is true that Washington wasn't the last authentic blues singer or even the last very good one, she remains the final star to link up with the golden era of the idiom (1915–1925) in so many behavioral and artistic ways.

Nowadays, the first female blues stars like Trixie Smith, Clara Smith and Mamie Smith (no relation to one another) are remembered nearly as much for their excesses and colorful lifestyles as they are for their artistic achievements. Mamie Smith wore $2,000 beaded gowns and Ma Rainey, sometimes openly referred to as "the ugliest woman in show business," offset an ungainly physical appearance by decking herself out in elaborate, expensive jewelry made from gold coins, leading her also to be called (somewhat more kindly) "The Gold Necklace Lady of the Blues."[13] When it came to matters of flash, though, none of them outdid the "Empress of the Blues" Bessie Smith. During her relatively short lifetime Smith went through today's equivalent of several million dollars. Much of her earnings went to maintain a highly extravagant way of life; what was left was largely embezzled by associates. Bessie also had a hair-trigger temper, was highly mistrustful (bordering on paranoiac) and was greatly addicted to gin.

And so it was—for the most part—with Dinah Washington. It is a testament to her talent that the colorful and outrageous life she led (the clothes, the furs, the men, the booze) failed to overshadow her greatness as an interpreter of song. Typical of the kind of outré circumstances she often found herself in was in 1950 when husband number three, Walter Buchanan, sued *her* for alimony. "Just think, he wanted me to pay him money for only eight months of his time," Washington dryly remarked to the press about this novel (for the times) legal move.[14]

Of the singer's seven mates, several were well known in their own right: actor Rafael Campos, jazz musician Eddie Chamblee and Detroit Lions star halfback Dick "Night Train" Lane. As recently as 1983, Chamblee was being introduced from the stage as a former husband of Dinah's. And while this isn't as radical as a former singing husband of Lady Soul billing himself in advertisements as "Mr. Aretha Franklin," nevertheless it indicates that identification as a former spouse of Washington's dies hard. Divorced from Washington in 1955, Chamblee's relationship with his ex-wife was sufficiently amicable to allow him to continue as her musical director for several years. Following the singer's death, Chamblee reflected upon the paradoxical nature of Washington's personality:

> People fell in love with that voice. And she had womanly wiles. She was warm and kind to me. I respected her musicianship. I had nobody. I was just divorced at the time. She evinced an interest in me. Under certain circumstances she was a beautiful woman. On stage she could tear your heart out. Dinah was deeper than most people could see. At first you saw only the harsh side. She had a shell around her.... She was a split personality. There was a medical problem involved. Like Bridey Murphy.[15] That will explain exactly what I mean. There was another person there. You could see the change, it was visible. As I was looking at her, her expression, even her choice of words, would change. Dinah Washington would call you all kinds of names, and Ruth Jones [Dinah's real name] would apologize.[16]

"She was both vain and insecure. She wanted to be the creator of everything she did," said club owner Herman Roberts.[17] Several, including Chamblee, have observed that Washington felt that nobody liked her—which apparently wasn't the case at all. After her death, all these sources spoke of the great love they had for her, despite Dinah's being—the word most used to describe her — "difficult." Hot-tempered she clearly was, but — most contend — basically a nice person who became nasty only when others got that way with her.

When a very young and inexperienced Linda Hopkins made her maiden appearance in the late 1950s at Harlem's landmark Apollo theater, nothing matched. She came on stage and looked more like she was dressed to go shopping. Afterwards Washington, the headliner on the bill, went backstage, talked to her, told her what a wonderful job she had done, then added, "Please, I don't want you to be offended, but I've been in the business a long time and in my basement I've got trunks full of gowns and jewelry and shoes as well. You're welcome to take any of it. You're just starting out in the business and you can use some of these."[18] This was the same Dinah Washington who with some had a reputation for being evil and a bitch. Backstage, Washington also usually had on hand enough furs to stock a small salon. Singer Anita O'Day remembers, "One night she showed up with eight or ten fur coats which she hung up in her dressing room. She sold some wholesale and gave more to friends. She said somebody had given them to her.... I wanted one badly, but I couldn't risk receiving stolen goods."[19]

Throughout most of her years of high visibility, Washington was one of the most widely traveled acts in show business. Foster's Rainbow Room in New Orleans, L.A.'s Tiffany Club, Club Tijuana in Baltimore and Roberts' Show Room in Chicago were but a few of the regular stops Washington hit as she barnstormed the country, seldom stopping even to take a break at the opulent homes she maintained in Chicago and New York. "To hear her at her very best," wrote jazz critic Dan Morgenstern, "you had to catch her at Birdland where the instant and total communication with the cream of show business and the ladies and gentlemen of the night was something to behold, or at the Apollo, where she went all the way down home, eliciting those unique responses from the audience that have so much in common with what goes on in black sanctified churches."[20] As jazz critic Gary Giddins wrote in an appreciation of Washington in the *Village Voice* in 1988: "Few performers have ever taken a stage or stormed off one with quite the noblesse oblige of the Queen."[21]

The backstage scenes that went down at the clubs where Dinah worked were often as memorable as what took place out front. Describing a memorable night at Birdland, jazz writer-record producer Ross Russell claims, "The combination of Dinah Washington and Charlie Parker on the same bill was a booking oversight that [agent] Billy Shaw would never repeat. Dinah ordered booze by the caseload. [She] held open house in her dressing room, hosting non-stop parties from which artists reluctantly took time to perform their sets."[22]

Pianist Dorothy Donegan recalls, "Dinah had a reputation as being an excellent cook. She could really put on some pots."[23] Washington would set

up shop backstage at theaters where the two women might find themselves
billed together and end up inviting everybody *but* Donegan, with whom the
singer carried on a long rivalry bearing overtones of the social warfare between
the Lucia and Mapp characters in the 1920s comic novels-of-manners of
British writer E. F. Benson. Thus, once when Dinah was working at a club
and Donegan walked in wearing a full-length chinchilla, Washington went
apoplectic, stopped singing and said, "Sit down, bitch, we've all seen it."
Dinah's then-husband "Night Train" Lane later told Donegan he had to give
his wife some smelling salts when she got back to the dressing room: "She
knew that with me wearing that full-length chinchilla, she could only top it
with sable."[24] Apparently Dinah never quite got over Donegan coming in first
place and beating her out once on the talent contest at the Chicago's Regal
Theater back in '38. A second-place occasion, but one responsible for setting
Washington off on her journey down the pop music trail. "In the end," Donegan bluntly stated, "I don't believe she liked herself."[25]

At the Village Vanguard in New York, where Washington often performed, she began toying with an affectation that eventually became a kind
of trademark. To those unfamiliar with the racial climate of the times it must
seem unbelievable that in the 1950s an innocuous gesture like a black woman
donning a platinum wig for a nightclub appearance could cause a flap.[26] But
even the club's ultra-unflappable owner Max Gordon lost his cool one night
when a blonde Dinah Washington strode on stage. He immediately got on
the phone to the performer's long-time manager Joe Glaser, who had been
through a lot with the singer. He too was taken aback.

"A blond wig!?" Glaser shouted back at Gordon over the phone.

"Yes, a blond wig! Here's a handsome black woman, a great singer, a
star, and she comes out—I don't believe my eyes—with a blond wig sitting
on top of her head."

"These *schwarzes* [crude Yiddish slang for blacks] are nuts," Glaser shot
back. "She's got herself a new guy, that's what it is. Otherwise why should
she put a blond wig on her head? She's got a new guy taking her money. Don't
pay it any attention. Make believe you don't see it. I know Dinah."[27]

But Glaser was wrong; Washington continued to top off her basically
stylish look with the controversial wig for some time to come. And no matter what happened in the way of extra-musical *contrétemps*, Washington's fans
remained loyal and supportive: Jazz musician Donald Byrd recalled to a
reporter an incident later written up in *The Soul and Jazz Record* magazine:
"[Byrd] and his musicians were on the same set with Dinah. The stage was
slightly raised at one point. She was quite drunk, and during the course of
her show, tripped and fell on her ample backside. She didn't even hesitate or
break the rhythm of her song. The audience never laughed, murmured a word
or interrupted."[28]

Despite Dinah's wild stage deportment, she was usually on time and seldom cancelled engagements. And so, one time in the late 1950s, the manager of the Apollo Theater, Jack Schiffman, constructed an elaborate set to be lavished on the presentation of Dinah's currently popular number "This Bitter Earth." "We had the stage carpenter build a huge sphere that looked like the Earth. It was a damned big thing," he recalls, "and Dinah was supposed to be discovered seated in the middle of it. Holding a hand mike, she would sing her hit song." The construction was suspended on wires and hung several feet off the floor. When the smoke machines were hit and multicolored floods were turned on, the overall effect, the theater manager remembers, was "just like the cover of a Gothic novel. It looked like all the world was coming to an end." Even major stars like Washington weren't generally used to this kind of fancy treatment at the Apollo. Proud of his handiwork, he did a test run for Dinah the night before she opened. "Well, what do you think?" he asked her as he pulled the switch and the Bosch-like affair began to smoke and rumble. Turning to Schiffman in wide-eyed disbelief, she groaned, "Sheeeeit," and without another word turned on her heels and strode out of the theater.[29] But come opening night, she was her usual semi-cooperative self. Washington always did her show, and usually didn't have to be called twice to come on stage. She was dedicated to her profession. At the Apollo, for example, many big stars refused to stay around for the finale of the show, but not Washington. She took her bows with everybody else.[30]

In the 1950s, African Americans tended to view entertainers as a barometer of the general racial climate in the land. And when someone like Dinah managed to beat the odds, especially without losing control of her destiny, fans tended to take great personal pride in the victory. In 1960 she made the unprecedented move of urging a boycott of purchases of her recordings in states which tacitly approved of segregation policies. Washington was also known for standing her ground against the predominantly white entrepreneurs who controlled the world of black show business down to the tiniest detail. And her followers loved her for it. To African Americans back then, there was no such thing as a pyrrhic racial victory. A victory for Dinah was a victory for everyone: Today, this refusal to lie down, play dead and assume the role of victim is remembered with nearly as much respect and affection as Washington's extraordinary artistry. As jazz musician Donald Byrd says of Washington, "She was baaad and she knew it!"[31]

In September of 1957, in the wake of the federal government's refusal to help enforce school desegregation in Little Rock, Arkansas, Louis Armstrong went on record to a Grand Forks, South Dakota, reporter to the effect that President Eisenhower had "no guts" and "that the way they are treating my people in the South, the government can go to hell."[32] Whether there was any connection or not, a few days later Ike did send in troops.

Dinah Washington may have been no racial crusader in the style of Hazel

Scott or Paul Robeson; nevertheless, her boycott of record distributors is indicative of the turning tide of U.S. racial affairs beginning in the 1950s. It's at this point in history that, for the first time, black entertainers as a group — aided by the safety net of the Civil Rights Movement and the Supreme Court — begin to openly speak out against racism.

9

On Broadway

Sammy Davis, Jr.

Come the 1950s, white America was finally ready for *the* big African American crossover star, if for no other reason than all the legal and social barriers which had helped maintain the mirror worlds of black and white show business were now beginning to topple. Hard on the heels of the Supreme Court's Shelly v. Kraemer decision that prohibited restrictive housing covenants (see Chapter Ten) came its 1954 Brown v. the Board of Education ruling, which struck down the concept of separate but equal education. Extra-legally, other events of the early 1950s lent strong symbolic credence to the fact that the old ways were now dying: In 1950, Ralph Bunche became the first African American to receive the Nobel Peace Prize; the following year the University of North Carolina admitted the first black student in its history: and the year after that, 1952, the University of Tennessee followed suit. Looking back upon popular performance from its beginnings in minstrelsy up through the 1950s, based upon the ways in which racial tensions softened and attitudes became increasingly enlightened as a result of the show biz interplay between the races, one might have predicted this. The permanently integrated 1937 Benny Goodman Quartet (the first of its kind) can be seen as a milestone in the stride toward racial equality. The unprecedented mainstream acceptance of Louis Armstrong, beginning in the 1930s, and Nat "King" Cole's ascendancy to popularity in the mid–1940s can also be viewed, in retrospect, as an augury of things to come.

* * *

If Sammy Davis, Jr., had not existed, he would have to have been invented. For it is this singer, dancer, actor, comedian, page-one sensation who finally wrote the book on erasure of the line between black show biz and social issues. Davis was an entertainer whose life reflects not only a vital entertainment era, but also a crucial juncture in the history of American race relations.

There has never been anyone quite like Sammy Davis, Jr., every aspect

Sammy Davis, Jr., 1945.

of whose existence seems to have been lived out in full public view. From the obscurity of segregation era vaudeville, to the heights of worldwide "crossover" fame in nightclubs, television, film and the Broadway stage, his life was shot through with paradox and contradiction. This slight, black, one-eyed entertainer dazzled audiences on five continents with his energy, show biz savvy, and magnetic appeal. His generosity and personal warmth were legendary. Yet for three full years he required round-the-clock security for fear that a racist assassin would bring his life to an end.[1] In the 1950s, Davis almost singlehandedly broke through the "Jim Crow" barriers that had kept blacks out of white-run show business.[2] On the other hand he was criticized by many African Americans as an "Uncle Tom" for seeking the favors of the white world as epitomized to blacks by his friendship with Frank Sinatra and his embrace of Richard Nixon. Yet in spite of four decades of non-stop press coverage up until the time of Davis' death in 1990, one salient aspect of his life and times seems to have eluded most who chose to write about him: the idea of Sammy the genial, untemperamental pro who (even at the lowest points in his life) managed to keep on ticking even when all those around him were dropping in their tracks. It is this Davis whose unflagging energies managed to salvage a seemingly doomed Broadway musical in the face of overwhelming odds.

"Sammy Davis in *Golden Boy,*" blazed the marquee of New York's Majestic Theatre. Just plain Sammy Davis. The "Jr." that had been a part of his billing for more than thirty years was suddenly no more. Eight years earlier, when he made his Broadway debut in *Mr. Wonderful,* the ads had read "The Will Mastin Trio Starring Sammy Davis Jr." But the concept of the Trio, by then, was largely a fiction. The act had been together since the mid–30s; however, by 1956 Sammy Sr. and Will Mastin had been relegated to the status of background effect — whistling, handclapping and a doing few dance turns. Anybody buying a ticket to the show was doing so for one reason only: to see the singing-dancing dynamo known as Sammy Davis, Jr.

Part of the Trio's night club act in its final days consisted of the song-and-dance routine "My Daddy, My Uncle and Me," in which the young Sammy proudly pointed to the two old-timers who had "taught me everything I know." It was even included, for a time, in the encore of *Mr. Wonderful,* where Davis would break character and go into his night club act. Will Mastin was not a blood relative of Davis,' but Davis Sr. and Sammy and Mastin had been together as an act for so many years that the youngest member of the trio referred to Mastin in familial terms. The latter was an African American show business veteran who oversaw touring companies of black players as early as 1916, with the show *Holiday in Dixieland.* Three-year-old Sammy joined his company of *Struttin' Hannah from Savannah* in Columbus, Ohio, in 1929; by the end of his first year he had travelled to more than 50 cities. One gets the feeling, though, that if Davis had listened only to his father and "uncle's" advice, he probably would have not gone very far in show business. In a 1985 television interview he recalled:

> When I got out of the army, the first night we were working at a place called Shepp's Playhouse [in L.A.]. The opening night I step up to the microphone and say, "Thank you very much. It's nice to be out of the army. I've got something that my dad and uncle don't know that I can do. We talked about it, but

204½ East First Street

LEONARD REED PRESENTS

The Three Cuban Diamonds
From Havana, Cuba

SAMMY MONTGOMERY
TAP DANCER

WILLIE LEWIS
COMEDIAN

BING WILLIAMS
THE EBONY BING CROSBY

Music by
Gerald Wilson and His Orchestra

New Show Starts Monday, December 4

● Continuous entertainment in Lounge with Red Callander and his trio. In the Ballroom music by Gerald Wilson and his 15 piece band. Leonard Reed, producer.

G. H. Sheppard, Proprietor   Ben C. Waller, Manager

I never got a chance to do it for them. But I'm gonna do it for you nice folks tonight. How about *Jimmy Stewart?*" People went "aggggh!" We got off the stage and people were standing! But my dad said, "If you ever do that again, I'm going to kill you."[3]

In his own small way, Sammy had just made show business history: No black man had ever *dared* to imitate a white man on stage before. The fact that he brought it off was testimony to his talent; that he had defied his senior partners was a clear sign that it was no longer going to be business-as-usual with the act. Frances Nealy, an actress-dancer who worked with Davis periodically from 1952 onward, recalled:

> When I did the *Colgate Comedy Hour* with him from the Hollywood Palace — this was in the early 1950s— Sammy Sr. and Will Mastin were old men even then. I think he wanted to keep them busy for sentimental reasons. They didn't want to hang up their shoes: Why let go of a good thing? But when the producers were getting ready to make up the billing, they said, "The Will Mastin Trio featuring Sammy Davis Jr." That's the only time I saw him stand up for his rights, because he said, "No! I want that 'starring.' I've earned this, paid my dues."[4]

Singer Olga James, who appeared opposite Davis in *Mr. Wonderful*, remembered an even sharper Trio clash:

> The Sammy who went into rehearsals for *Mr. Wonderful* was very different from the Sammy who came out at the end of the run of that show. He wasn't all that sure of himself at first — even when we got to Broadway. Will Mastin was very much in control, initially. I remember Mr. Mastin getting angry with Sammy over something during rehearsal, shortly before we opened, and saying "Boy, remember who I am!" Sammy ran back to his dressing room and was very upset about that. I think the deciding moment that created a change in his character — and a change in that relationship —came about when Sammy got sick. We were about three months into the run of the show when he suddenly became really ill and had to stay out. They tried to put in his understudy, but in the end they just had to refund people's money. I think Sammy discovered his power then, because when he came back you could see that he was no longer subservient to Will Mastin. It was like, "Wait a minute. This show can't go on without me!" So shortly after that, the Trio was no longer part of the act that had been incorporated into the show. They were either sitting on the sidelines or off-stage altogether. And in the encore, it was just Sammy doing his act.[5]

With *Golden Boy*, Will and Sammy Sr. were entirely out of the picture — Mastin off to play around with Harlem real estate and the elder Davis making a sad attempt to start all over again at age 63 as a single. But the three-way financial split that had existed between the troupers for more than twenty years was still in effect.[6] Arthur Penn, who directed the show, felt Davis' process of self-liberation was still ongoing in 1964: "It was never discussed,

Opposite: Shepp's Playhouse advertisement, 1946.

but I think dropping the Jr. was a signal that he was looking for a new sort of legitimacy. I think the Jr. hung on because it was some sort of acknowledgment. Getting rid of it was really shucking that *wunderkind* aspect and saying, 'Here I am. I'm a man in the middle of his life, and I'm nobody's Jr.'"[7]

Mr. Wonderful was a vehicle for presenting on the Broadway stage the Sammy Davis, Jr., that everyone knew from night clubs, TV and vaudeville; laughing, dancing, telling jokes and doing impressions. *Golden Boy* was something else entirely. It wasn't a musical comedy at all, but a serious dramatic play — Clifford Odets' 1937 study of the rise and fall of a young boxer — *set* to music. Doing this show meant for Davis that he would be forced to jettison performing techniques on which he'd relied for years: eye contact with the audience, rapid-fire delivery, freedom of movement, and cabaret-style singing. The production required him to play it straight: in character; in tandem with other dramatic performers; on his mark.

Golden Boy offered an unprecedented opportunity for Sammy. If he brought it off, he'd be making the same sort of impact Robert Preston had with *The Music Man*, and Rex Harrison with *My Fair Lady*; not mere star turns, but substantial roles that overhauled the public images of these well-established performers. Certainly no one from the Vegas-vaudeville milieu from which Davis came had ever attempted such an ambitious career leap — least of all the man who so strongly advised him against doing *Golden Boy* in the first place, Frank Sinatra. "Chicky baby, you don't need New York critics," he told him. "Why expose yourself to the critics?"[8]

On the one hand this was perfectly sound advice. Starring in a Broadway musical is one of the most difficult things any performer can do, no matter how much experience they've had in front of live audiences. On the other hand, why should Davis listen to a singer who, for all his fame and talent, had never ventured any closer to a Broadway musical than a $9.90 orchestra seat? Back in 1947 when the Will Mastin Trio had opened for Sinatra at the Capitol Theatre, advice from "The Voice" had been welcome. He'd gotten them the job, and made a point of telling the audience to "watch the kid in the middle, he's going to be a star."[9] By 1964, however, things had changed considerably. Davis was practically the equal of Sinatra as a draw. But thanks to the Rat Pack — a private consortium of Sinatra cronies gone public in 1960 as part of the publicity for the film *Ocean's Eleven* — Davis' celebrity was inextricably linked to Sinatra. In the public mind this linkage was so strong as to make it almost inconceivable that Sammy would do anything without Frank's blessing. But there was no room on the stage of the Majestic for the likes of Joey Bishop, Peter Lawford, Dean Martin or Sinatra to run up and make with the sort of hipster schtick that they'd done so successfully in Vegas.

In the past, Sammy had been a prisoner of the Will Mastin Trio; now if he listened to Frank's warning and passed up the show, he'd be a prisoner of the Rat Pack. Going ahead and doing *Golden Boy* when Sinatra said "no" was in many ways an act of defiance. Though the public would be largely unaware of it, relations between Frank and Sammy cooled for a time as a result of Sammy not taking his old friend's advice.

But *Golden Boy* wasn't the first time that tensions surfaced between the two performers. In 1957, on Chicago radio personality Jack Eigen's interview show, Davis complained, "Talent is not an excuse for bad manners.... I don't care if you are the most talented person in the world. It does not give you the right to step on people and treat them rotten. This is what he [Sinatra] does occasionally."[10] It was far from the harshest thing one could have said of Frank Sinatra, but Davis' candor effectively banished him from the singer's circle for over a year — losing him a featured role in the Sinatra-produced film *Never So Few* in the process. Just prior to *Golden Boy*, and unbeknownst to Frank, Davis went further than he did on the Eigen show when he ran into Nevada Gaming Commission head Ed Olsen in a Las Vegas casino.

"That little son of a bitch, he's needed this for years," Davis told the man in charge of investigating Sinatra's ties to organized crime. "I've been working with him for sixteen years and nobody's ever had the guts to stand up to him!"[11]

Olsen's gutsy stand — his threat to revoke Sinatra's gaming license — resulted in one of the few times the Show Business Caesar ever blinked. Utilizing his involvement in a new deal with Warner Bros. for cover, Sinatra withdrew his interests in Nevada gambling.[12] It was a virtual Waterloo in Sinatra's life, and here was Davis speaking of it as a comeuppance. Yet in 1969 when interviewed for *Playboy* by Alex Haley, Davis claimed, "I can say, honest to God, I've never seen him say or do anything rude to anybody."[13] Whether second thoughts, forgetfulness, or naked fear prompted this response is anybody's guess, but it does underscore the fact that Davis' feelings about Sinatra were, to put it mildly, ambivalent. Their relationship was in many ways a lifetime of mixed signals and confused feelings. In the 1989 "Ultimate Event Tour" with Frank and Liza Minnelli — which was a personal triumph for Davis— he sang a chorus of one of his signature songs, "I Gotta Be Me," changing the lyrics to "I Wanna Be Him," directed at Sinatra. In the videotaped version of this performance it's impossible to ignore the dark look Sinatra shoots Davis during this number.

Outside of his desire to effect an image makeover, Davis had another reason for signing on with *Golden Boy*: He needed the money. Debts and back taxes had left him strapped for cash. The new show offered him a salary that completely overshadowed the previous Broadway high — $5000 weekly — that Jackie Gleason had received for appearing in the 1959 musical *Take Me Along*. Davis was to get $10,000 weekly *plus* 10 percent of the weekly gross, 15 percent of eventual profits and an expense account, all of which could add up to an enormous (even by today's standards) $20,000 per week.[14] Theoretically this was small potatoes compared to what he was capable of pulling down doing concert tours, Vegas, TV and films. But that would have meant submitting himself to a grueling, non-stop series of dates. He had, in fact, gone through such periods of work in the past. But the chance to settle down and work in one city was extremely attractive to him at this point in his career. Moreover the prestige of doing a show on Broadway was too tempting to pass up.

Davis couldn't have picked a better year to do a Broadway show than 1964. *Fiddler on the Roof*, *Hello Dolly*, and *Funny Girl*, three of the greatest musicals ever produced, opened that watershed year. But they weren't the only indication that the musical comedy form was in solid shape. Two of 1964's most notable flops were *110 in the Shade* and *Anyone Can Whistle*, both experimental, ahead-of-their-time musicals, have since been successfully revived. Consequently a downbeat, socially conscious libretto like *Golden Boy* (even more common today with such shows as *Miss Saigon* and *Kiss of the Spider Woman*) wasn't out of character for the period.

Ever since *Show Boat*, the Broadway musical had shown a propensity toward the larger statement. Even 1956, the year of the lightweight *Mr. Wonderful*, saw the premiere of Frank Loesser's bittersweet quasi-opera *The Most Happy Fella*. This tendency towards seriousness perhaps reached its apotheosis in 1957 with *West Side Story*. The Bernstein-Sondheim-Robbins classic was clearly the prototype for the kind of show *Golden Boy* wanted to be — balletic, socially significant, 180 degrees away from the "tired businessman's" musical. (Ironically its music and lyrics were by Lee Adams and Charles Strouse, composers of the all-time happy-go-lucky hit *Bye Bye Birdie*.) Still, because of Sammy's fame, the show had the sort of box office appeal that would attract theatergoers who would otherwise have given deep-dish musicals a wide berth.

The original of the Clifford Odets drama was a product of the Great Depression, more specifically of the Group Theater — a federation of left-wing writers, directors and actors (John Garfield, Irwin Shaw, Elia Kazan, Harold Clurman, and Lee Strasberg among them) formed in 1931. Like many of its productions, such as *Men in White* and *The House of Connelly*, *Golden Boy* dealt with class conflict and the struggle for social betterment. Unlike previous Group efforts, however, it opened on Broadway. Starring Luther Adler, this story of an Italian youth who puts aside a promising career as a violinist for the fame and fortune of the boxing ring wasn't as hard-hitting as such earlier Odets works as *Waiting for Lefty* and *Awake and Sing*— a fact many critics commented on at the time.[15] But fashionable Broadway theatergoers had never quite seen anything to match the play's realism and naturalistic acting style, and *Golden Boy* went on to become a popular success. In 1939 William Holden starred in the motion picture version; in 1952 it was successfully revived on stage with John Garfield, who had played a small role in the 1937 production, having been considered too lightweight, then, to essay the lead.

The idea for casting Sammy Davis in a musicalized *Golden Boy* belonged to successful talent agent-turned-producer Hillard Elkins. But with an African American as its star, the only way to make Odets' play valid, twenty-seven years after its original production, was to reframe it in light of the Civil Rights movement. The original version's Italian-American youth fighting his way out of the slums may have been a big deal in 1937, but not in 1964, the year when President Lyndon Johnson signed the long-struggled-for Civil Rights bill into law; when the bodies of three murdered "Freedom Riders" (Michael Schwerner, Andrew Goodman, and James Chaney) were discovered in a swamp near Philadelphia, Mississippi; when Martin Luther King won the Nobel Peace Prize for his activist efforts; and when Sidney Poitier garnered the Best Actor Oscar for *Lilies of the Field.*

Working from his California home, Odets drafted the libretto for a new musical version of his play — with a black boxer, Joe Wellington, rather than an Italian boxer, Joe Napoleon — at its center. But no sooner had this first draft of the show opened in Philadelphia, the initial stop of its pre-Broadway try-out tour, than Odets died. Someone would have to be found to do the rewrites needed to get the show into final shape.

Meanwhile, the production struggled on to Boston with a book producer Elkins described as "a scissors-and-paste job put together by a committee of non-writers,"[16] i.e., himself, Davis and the show's original director, Peter Coe. It was in Boston that playwright William Gibson (*Two for the Seesaw, The Miracle Worker*), an old friend of Odets,' was asked to come aboard to try and make something coherent out of this piecemeal libretto. "Sammy's biggest difficulty was a lack of material," Gibson later recalled. "He was trying to establish the whole entertainment value of the show in the songs. He knew there was nothing else *except* the songs and he was overacting."[17]

"I was not prepared to find the book gutted of content, no writer present at all, the audience yawning, the director in the third week of a holiday at home in Merrie England, and, with its Broadway unveiling a month and a half off, the star in an impotent wrath that the production was saying nothing of what he knew it must say — if only for verisimilitude — on the most divisive social issue of our time."[18]

The "vacationing director," Peter Coe, had over the course of his career successfully staged everything from *Macbeth* to *The Skin of Our Teeth.* But he had never done a show involving African Americans. It was no secret that Coe and Davis had nearly come to blows during rehearsal.[19] Consequently, as much as it needed a librettist, *Golden Boy* also required a new director. And to fill that slot, Gibson turned to the man who had so successfully shepherded his plays in the past, Arthur Penn. "Bill Gibson said he wouldn't do the show if I wouldn't want to do it," Penn recalled. "I was prepared to work with him on *anything*"[20]:

> As it stood then, the show was heading in the direction of being a really quite frivolous comic musical — with a sad ending. I remember the first time we got together to talk about it we were in this hotel room with Hilly Elkins, on a gurney because his back went out, being massaged by someone as he and Sammy and Bill and I talked about the show. We wanted to reach deeper down both into the black experience and the Clifford Odets play. For example, there was an opening scene at a gym. We changed it into a number where someone was punching a bag to one rhythm, someone else was shadow-boxing to another rhythm, someone else was skipping rope, and so on. Originally it was a number with a bunch of boxers that ended with all of them jumping up on bars and screaming, "Ooh a mouse!" It was just plain silly.[21]

But the restaging of this number was a minor detail compared to the problems presented by *Golden Boy's* love story which, thanks to the casting of Davis and the libretto's resultant re-conception, had become interracial. In the original play, Odets' boxer hero falls for Lorna Moon (played in 1937 by the beautiful Frances Farmer), the embittered, alcoholic ex-girlfriend of his manager. In the musical her cynical/sentimental character (played by Paula Wayne) is just as it was in the original. The libretto even retains the line where she explains her drinking: "There's a lump I drink to dissolve, baby, do you mind?" But thanks to the racial alteration, instead of a downtrodden woman making a last-ditch attempt at happiness, Lorna had become a downtrodden woman risking the little she had by crossing the color line. According to Penn, this wasn't at all clear in the Coe-directed version of the show, where the interracial nature of the love story was "simply glossed over."[22] Penn was determined to bring it into sharper focus. And the best way to do so, he felt, was through a scene in which the lovers kiss.

The kiss between Davis and Wayne in the show was an earth-shattering event in 1964 prompting walkouts in all the cities on the show's tryout tour. Even supposedly sophisticated New York was troubled. Not since actress Mary Blair (the wife of critic Edmund Wilson) kissed the *hand* of Paul Robeson in the 1924 Provincetown Playhouse production of Eugene O'Neill's *All God's Chillun Got Wings* had any interaction between the two races on a New York stage caused this kind of an upset.[23] When Penn took over the staging of the show in Detroit, the kiss was one of the first contributions he made. He discovered, however, during one rehearsal run-through that the love scene he'd created was back to the way it had been in Boston — nonexistent. Penn stopped the action and questioned Davis, who freely admitted that he was frightened for both himself and Wayne to do the scene as Penn had blocked it. But Penn convinced the actors that, because the love story was the heart of the tale, it couldn't be invisible to the audience. "I've never seen a love scene in my life in which people don't kiss. Hold hands, do something, otherwise there's no declaration of love...."[24] The kiss was back in the show for good.

Golden Boy wasn't the only interracial romance to open on Broadway in 1964. Lorraine Hansberry's *The Sign in Sidney Brustein's Window* offered a fairly discreet one during its brief run. Then there was the long-running comedy *The Owl and the Pussycat,* with Alan Alda and Diana Sands entwined in a lighthearted romantic tussle. However the most controversial interracial pairing New York saw that season was Off Broadway in Leroi Jones' *Dutchman.* This scathing chamber drama in which a buttoned-down, middle-class black man stands up to the taunts of a white temptress during a subway ride was by no means a love story. But the image it offered of abiding racial hatred set aflame by sexual attraction kept fashionable cocktail party tongues wagging for many an evening. Still, *Dutchman* was an Off Broadway art piece — a plaything of the cognoscenti: *Golden Boy* was a mainstream show with a major star. Moreover, that star's offstage life had a direct bearing on his onstage one — particularly in relation to that pivotal kiss.

"I've never gone by rules set by other people," Davis told Italian journalist Oriana Fallaci in an interview done at the time of his work in the musical. "I've always felt they don't count for anything, rules; don't tell me I can't have that Rolls-Royce because it's against the rules, don't tell me I can't marry a white woman because it's against the rules. If I love her, the white woman, if she loves me, if I can be a good husband to her and give her what she desires, why can't I marry her?"[25]

Sammy Davis wasn't merely making conversation. He had gone against the rules all his life, particularly where white women were concerned. In 1957, Hollywood reeled when rumors of Davis' dalliance with actress Kim Novak began to leak out. What happened next — which quickly became the stuff of show business legend — was best summarized by Truman Capote in the infamous "La Côte Basque" chapter of his unfinished "non-fiction novel" *Answered Prayers.* As the celebrated writer and full-time café society gossip relates, Novak's boss, Columbia Pictures president Harry Cohn, "ordered a hit man to call Davis and tell him: 'Listen, Sambo, you're already missing one eye. How'd you like to try for none?' The next day Davis married a Las Vegas chorus girl—colored."[26] What the otherwise well-informed Capote doesn't note is that no sooner had Davis' marriage to dancer Loray White run its two-month, seventeen-day course, than the singer announced that he was engaged to Joan Stuart — a white Canadian dancer who was a dead ringer for Novak. Because of the opposition of her family, those marriage plans quickly fizzled. But in 1960, when Davis met Swedish actress May Britt, he refused to let any force stand in his way.

A rising starlet in the Italian cinema whom 20th Century–Fox planned to make a major star through such films as *The Young Lions* and *The Blue Angel,* Britt stunned the industry by putting her career aside for marriage to Davis. Even before vows were exchanged — with Sinatra as best man and Peter Lawford and his wife Pat Kennedy as witnesses— the pair became the target of death threats; so many they were forced to hire round-the-clock security guards. Things had settled down somewhat by the time of *Golden Boy* (Davis had dismissed the bodyguards, having won legal permission to carry a concealed weapon), but the entertainer and the former actress were still, in journalist Fallaci's by no means hyperbolic words, "the most talked about couple in America."[27] The Davis-Britt marriage was so much a part of the zeitgeist of the 1960s that two decades later in *GoodFellas*, Martin Scorsese used it to evoke the period: "I can see how a white girl could go for a guy like that," claims a mobster's moll in a scene at the Copa — much to her paramour's distress.

There was no way that anyone, regardless of their level of racial enlightenment, could watch Davis kiss Wayne in the musical and not think of May Britt — particularly in the touching scene where the couple sing and vow to maintain their romance despite any and all obstacles in their path. Ironically, the musical wasn't the first interracial pairing project that came Davis' way at this time. Just prior to *Golden Boy* he had been asked by Elizabeth Taylor (with whom he'd long had a purely platonic friendship) to play a part in *The Sandpiper*, the much-ballyhooed romantic drama she was set to star in with husband-to-be Richard Burton. The part was of a beatnik artist friend of the Taylor character with whom, it was clearly implied, she was having a casual sexual affair — much to the Burton character's annoyance. Taylor thought Davis would provide the film with a major casting coup. Producer Martin Ransohoff, however, saw Davis' casting as providing nothing but trouble. The part was given to a white actor, Charles Bronson, without the alteration of a single line.[28] Had Davis been able to go through with it as planned, the film would surely have been grist for controversy. But its fanciful vision of race-busting bohemians is a world away from the serious interracial love story of the Odets drama, and Davis was keenly aware of this. "*Golden Boy* is me in a way," he remarked to Oriana Fallacci. "I know exactly what it means to be involved in a love story of that kind, to feel yourself stared at when you walk down the street, to feel humiliated knowing that, however things go, you're going to get very hurt."[29]

The marriage to Britt was far from the show's only touchstone to Davis' life. There were also references to his squashed nose and overall facial ugliness, his propensity for wearing tight pants and, in one of the show's biggest numbers, "Don't Forget 127th Street," the oft-leveled charge that he'd turned his back on the black community in his quest for acceptance by whites. But the most striking parallel of all was the finale, in which the hero dies in an automobile accident. In the Odets play, both Joe the boxer and his girl Lorna are in the death car. In the musical, Joe dies alone. It was strikingly reminiscent of the 1954 automobile crash in which Davis lost his eye and nearly his life.[30] What it all added up to was that six nights a week plus two matinees, Sammy had the leading role in a veritable Passion Play of his own life.

The connections between the real Davis and the character he was playing in the musical were in no way coincidental. From the moment he signed to star in the show, Davis was involved in every aspect of its creation. He was determined that *Golden Boy* reflect something of the African American experience as he knew it: "Write colored!" he would often say to Gibson. "He would talk about what it was like to be black and live in Harlem and stand in Central Park to see the lights downtown sparkling and seemingly forever out of reach," recalled the playwright, who was more than willing to take character and dialogue suggestions from his star. "My boy wouldn't say that. I know. I've lived his life," Davis told Gibson when he came across a line he didn't like.[31]

Prior to Gibson and Penn's alterations, the production was kept afloat on the road mostly on the strength of Davis' personal appeal — but only just barely. In Philadelphia its makeshift libretto was panned, but the score, the supporting cast (which included veteran singer Billy Daniels and an up-and-coming singer-dancer named Lola Falana), the Tony Walton sets, and, most important of all, Davis himself were praised. The Philadelphia audience gave him a five-minute standing ovation on opening night. Boston, however, was less embracing. Critic Elliot Norton, who at the time carried almost as much clout as Broadway reviewers, scored the show as a "soap opera," and panned Davis as well. Sammy cut out the review and kept it pasted on his dressing room mirror for the length of the Boston run.[32]

The original plan after Boston was to head straight to Broadway, but a newspaper strike in Detroit inspired a re-routing. Since there were no theater critics to cover the show (and accord it what probably would have been negative notices), the company could gain valuable time to keep improving the show with full houses assured. It was in Detroit that the major Gibson-Penn changes were instituted. New songs, sets and costumes were created, and choreographer-director Herbert Ross (*House of Flowers, On a Clear Day You Can See Forever*) was brought in — unbilled — to "integrate" dances into the action, supplementing official choreographer Donald McKayle's work.[33]

Making adjustments in these areas was fairly standard procedure for musicals on the road to Broadway. But *Golden Boy* wasn't getting a simple tune-up; it was being reconceived from top to bottom. The changes were so drastic that in order to bring them about, for four days the company played the "old" show at night while rehearsing an almost entirely new one during the day. The production was, in effect, going back to square one. Elkins called it "Operation Transfer": "[We] closed the old show on Saturday night, rehearsed around the clock and opened up a brand new show on Monday night."[34] Still the project wasn't out of the woods. When it finally reached New York, after a nearly unheard-of twenty-two weeks on the road, its two weeks of previews prior to the official opening were immediately stretched to four. Clearly *Golden Boy* was a show in trouble, but it was of a kind quite different from the sort faced by other musicals.

With most shows, gauging audience response is a fairly easy matter;

jokes that work get laughs; winning numbers get applause. But even though the show featured elements of sardonic humor, it had no jokes to speak of; and while there were many effective numbers, they weren't the sort designed to lift audiences out of their seats like the title number from *Hello Dolly* or "Get Me to the Church on Time" from *My Fair Lady*. Gibson's book was likewise subtle for a musical; striving for quiet intimate effects over dramatic flash. The most moving scenes in the show, the interchanges between Davis and Wayne, couldn't hope to elicit anything from a theatergoer other than hushed attentiveness.

For Sammy Davis the problems presented by *Golden Boy's* singularity couldn't be more frustrating. As a performer with more than 35 years of experience, he was keenly aware of what made an audience tick, but none of his standard show business instincts applied here. A scene that would get applause one night would be met with stony silence the next, and there was no simple explanation as to why this was happening. In night clubs Davis was a master at projecting his voice to the farthest corner of the room; for short periods of time he could even produce the sort of volume normally associated with opera singers. But a half-year of pre–Broadway tryouts in massive auditoriums, unequipped with the elaborate "sound design" systems of today, had left their mark. Davis' voice was beginning to deteriorate, and he wasn't the only member of the cast experiencing sound production problems. The show's unusual mixture of loud musical scenes and soft dramatic ones had preview audiences at the Majestic yelling, "Louder, louder, we can't hear you."[35] To counter this situation, Elkins had an elaborate and expensive sound system installed. Still, sound was only one problem among many as script and song changes continued to mount. The breaking point came on the Saturday afternoon preview before opening night. Sammy didn't show. After holding the curtain for twenty minutes, Elkins was forced to cancel. The evening performance went on with Sammy's understudy, Lamont Washington, but three-quarters of the audience got in line at the exchange window.[36]

The history of Broadway is filled with hair-raising tales of big-star "temperament" and "unprofessional conduct," but to hear it from those who worked with Davis it wouldn't be fair to list his absence from those two performances among them. According to Arthur Penn, the cumulative force of the pressures placed on Davis had become evident in the last days of rehearsal.

"He couldn't absorb what I was saying. He had worked himself to the end of his resources and could do no more. He was trying to play a character, not just be the Sammy Davis you saw in night clubs, and he took all the show's problems on himself. I think he thought that if *Golden Boy* failed, all was lost for him — that he couldn't count on simply being able to go back and do what he did before.[37]

> Sammy was a very naturally gifted person. I remember one day, early on in the rehearsals of a scene with him and Paula Wayne, I said, "We've got to find a

dramatic level for this scene to be played. What I want you to do is go offstage and do a preparation." So they both went offstage. Ten minutes later Sammy came back and said "What's a preparation?" I had to explain to him that it was an acting technique; remembering a prior circumstance that related to the scene you were doing and putting yourself in touch with the feelings that you had. As soon as I told him that, he knew exactly what to do. But pulling a show out of a hat the way we were doing is extremely hard, and it was hardest on Sammy most of all. What it came down to in the end was he was afraid of losing his voice. That can happen when you're emotionally tense. He was panicked."[38]

Panic apparently subsided enough for Davis to call producer Elkins at four A.M. the morning after his disappearance. He told him that he had never in his professional life, done anything like this before, and would make it up to him. Elkins suggested that perhaps more time was called for "to freeze the show." Davis objected to further delay, offering to write a $600,000 check to cover the show's cost, and close it. "But we're not postponing, baby," Davis said, "we're gonna do it."[39]

On Tuesday evening, October 21, 1964, Sammy Davis hit the stage of the Majestic Theatre in a manner the *Saturday Evening Post* characterized as being less than assured — at first: "Davis' voice was harsh and gravelly. His first number was disappointing. He was spitting out his lines. An uneasy feeling swept over the audience. Suddenly during the middle of act one he recovered."[40]

It was this recovered Sammy that the critics remembered in their reviews; favorable — if not completely enthusiastic — about the show, but strongly supportive of Davis. One radio scribe went out of his way to fault *Golden Boy* for dealing with the "race issue"; to which Davis at a post-premiere party responded, "The race issue! With me in it, what do they expect, the Chinese issue?"[41] But the majority of the press reacted in a manner similar to Howard Taubman of the *New York Times*. To Taubman, the evening proved that "Mr. Davis is a lot more than a night club performer. He can act as well as sing and dance." As for the show itself, "one can have nothing but admiration for the snap, speed, and professionalism of this kind of musical.... [It's] a knockout, not only for the whirling excitement of its action but also for the powerful punch in its comment." The *Times* man did have some reservations: "The central story does not ring true," he felt.[42] But it was the Odets story itself that was responsible for this shortcoming, rather than the current production, in Taubman's view. It was an assessment remarkably similar to the one Odets' play had originally received from the critics in 1937. And just as before, critical misgivings failed to deter public support. History was, in effect, repeating itself.

Davis was ecstatic about the *Times* review. At the party he began jumping up and down and shouting, "I'm ten feet tall. I'm a Broadway star! We've got a hit, we've very definitely got a hit."[43] But his spirits dimmed momentarily when someone asked him how he felt about Sinatra's failure to send congratulations. Sammy remarked to a *Life* magazine reporter that he'd never been more hurt in his life, but then brightened, adding, "Who needs Sinatra?"[44] He later denied in Hank Grant's column in *The Hollywood Reporter* that such a remark had ever been made.[45]

Ironically, it was Sinatra who needed Davis, at least in the short run: Just nineteen days after the opening of *Golden Boy*, Sammy was summoned to testify on the singer's behalf at a federal grand jury appearance in Kansas City, Missouri.[46] He made it back to New York just in time to be roasted by the Friar's Club at the Hotel Astor that same evening. Per his current preferred billing, the Friars honors were accorded to just plain Sammy Davis—no Jr.

In the long run, though, the musical was unable to bring about the kind of career metamorphosis Sammy expected. Just a little over a year later, despite his Broadway success, things were back to business-as-usual with the premiere of his new weekly NBC-TV series *The Sammy Davis Jr. Show*. He would remain Sammy Davis, Jr., for the rest of his life.

During the early part of *Golden Boy*'s year-and-a-half run, Sammy embarked on a promotional blitz for his new autobiography *Yes I Can*. Around this time, he also took part in the historic March on Selma, Alabama, with Martin Luther King. And as if to demonstrate just how accurate was the title of his memoirs, Davis also undertook shooting a film, *A Man Called Adam*, during the day, as well as taping the first installments of his new TV series. It was probably the first time that anyone had starred simultaneously in all three media at once.

Soon afterward Davis and May Britt would unofficially separate, and the film and the TV ventures would prove to be resounding flops. After more than twenty years at the peak of his profession, Davis' career was starting down the first big drop in a rollercoaster ride — of old show biz, new drug culture, radical chic, traditional politics, and even a brush with satanism.[47] In 1966, through actress Jean Seberg, whom he briefly dated, Davis even formed a loose alliance with members of the Black Panther Party. Not long after, first Martin Luther King and then Robert Kennedy, both personal friends of Davis, were assassinated.

In 1972 Davis, a lifelong Democrat, was the featured entertainer at a Republican fund-raising event. As startling as this sudden right turn was in and of itself, it was nothing compared to the tumult created at this same fundraiser when in a seemingly spontaneous gesture of affection, Sammy gave a bear hug to Richard Nixon. A picture of this embrace proved to be the photographic equivalent of a shot heard round the world. The black community, intermittently critical of Davis, was now firmly united against him. He was loudly booed at an appearance for Jesse Jackson's "Operation Push" later that year where he struggled through the song "I Gotta Be Me." The Nixon-Sammy photo would haunt him for the rest of his life. He would also be haunted by the success of "Candyman;" the treacly novelty number that he recorded at this time; it ironically became his greatest commercial success.

In 1975, writer Bruce Jay Friedman penned the short story "Let's Hear It For a Beautiful Guy" for *The New Yorker* magazine; it was a devastating parody of Davis' personal style and the show business unctuousness he'd come to stand for in the minds of many. At one point, Friedman's protagonist, the ultimate Sammy fan, says:

> It must have been a terrific blow to him when he switched his allegiance to Agnew and Nixon, only to have the whole thing blow up in his face. I was angry at him, incidentally, along with a lot of other fans of his, all of us feeling he had sold us down the river. But after I had thought it over and let my temper cool a bit, I changed my mind and actually found myself standing up for him, saying I bet anything that Agnew and Nixon had made some secret promises to Sammy about easing the situation of blacks — ones that the public still doesn't know about.[48]

Health problems, exacerbated by cocaine use and alcohol abuse, began to mount for Davis. Once again he returned to Broadway, but this time the kind of magic sparked by *Golden Boy* failed to ignite. His 1978 revival of *Stop the World, I Want to Get Off*, later filmed as *Sammy Stops the World*, was unable to gain for him the kind of acclaim he'd received in the past.

In 1987, at what must stand as the artistic low point of his career, Davis was nonetheless feted at the Kennedy Center Honors in Washington D.C. It marked the beginning of a major objective reassessment of Davis the Performer — above and beyond the enormous amount of political and sociological baggage he'd increasingly come to shoulder. The following year Sammy appeared as a legendary hoofer in the Gregory Hines–starring film *Tap*. Though not a commercial hit, the occasion of the film continued the newfound media interest in the performer, creating a sense of respect he hadn't been accorded since the early '60s. He successfully toured with Jerry Lewis, and later with Sinatra and Liza Minnelli in a show called *The Ultimate Event* in which his participation earned him as good a set of reviews as he'd received in years.

And then at the height of it all — August '89, when he was in Florida undergoing a routine physical — came the diagnosis of throat cancer. A benefit for the United Negro College Fund on November 21, in the form of a salute to Davis' 60th anniversary in show business at the Shrine Auditorium — which began planning long before Sammy learned he had cancer — took on the unfortunate and eerie aspect of a wake with the deceased in attendance. As a parade of entertainment industry notables (Bob Hope, Bill Cosby, Clint Eastwood and Eddie Murphy among them) took turns singing his praises, Davis, who could no longer sing, and barely even speak, his neck reddened and raw from chemotherapy, sat smiling. The 5000 in attendance heard Frank Sinatra say at the event (which was later televised), "My little friend, the best friend I ever had. Sixty years! That's a lot of bourbon under the bridge ... I knew you would amount to something, but I didn't feel that you would amount to everything.... You're my brother."

In archival footage shown at the tribute, Davis was seen saying that when he first heard it, he hated what had in more recent times become his signature song, "Mr. Bojangles":

> That's my fear. That I'd end up like Bojangles [a song not in reference to the great dancer Bill Robinson who bears that nickname]. When I do that number some nights, I get so hung up in it. One night in Vegas I said, that's me. I was projecting. That's how I'll be when I'm seventy years old. I'll be working little joints, I'll talk about what I used to be and that'll be the end of it.... That man, that culmination of different black performers, minstrels that I've known, performers who got hooked on junk, who got wiped out by alcohol, who got wiped out by changing times, I've seen them disappear, great dancers.

A little more than six months later, on May 16, 1990, Sammy Davis, Jr., was dead. Non-denominational funeral services were held two days later at Los Angeles' Forest Lawn Cemetery. Several eulogies were given, including one by Jesse Jackson. Inside on the p.a. system Davis' recording of "Mr. Bojangles" played; and outside people sang "We Shall Overcome." Freeway onramps and transition roads were closed to accommodate the 1,000-car motorcade that then wended it way to Glendale's Gardens of Honor where Sammy was buried next to his father, Sammy Davis, Sr., who had also died recently. Most area TV stations cut into their regular programming to carry various portions of the proceedings, lending the events the overall feeling of a state funeral.

But only a few months later, Sammy Davis proved in death to be as vulnerable to the kind of hard knocks which he had weathered in life. Davis had at one time wanted to bequeath his personal effects (which reflected not only his own life history but the span on 20th Century African American show business as well) to Wilberforce University. Somehow that didn't happen. On September 23, 1990, the saddest estate sale in Hollywood history was held at the auction house of Butterfield and Butterfield. Attempts to keep Sammy's collection of personal effects intact had failed after several of his celebrity friends declined to pick up the tab. The entertainer's estate was auctioned off at a fraction of its actual worth to cover $5.3 million in federal taxes, mortgage payments, grocery charges and debts he left behind. Eight hundred fans were on hand, including Jason Priestley of TV's *Beverly Hills 90210*, who bought a pair of Sammy's cuff links.

Sammy Davis, Jr.'s career is in many ways the culmination of the dreams and aspirations of most of the figures dealt with in this book. In 1931 when Mabel Whitman of the Whitman Sisters spoke of passing up opportunities for "breaking in where we were not really wanted," in white theaters, preferring the "full appreciation without grudge" received from black audiences, she was speaking of a situation that persisted right up to the moment of Davis' emergence on the entertainment scene in the late 1940s. Until that moment there wasn't an African American performer alive who didn't understand the fact that black and white were separate — unequal — show business spheres. Even when a black artist's work "crossed over," gaining the support of whites, as was the case with Louis Armstrong, Nat "King" Cole, Duke Ellington and other performers, the culturally understood proviso remained that their efforts were to be considered exceptions to a white-run rule. Sammy Davis, Jr., changed all that.

Once he "broke through" from years of struggling on the black vaudeville circuit onto the nightclub stages of New York, Los Angeles, and Las Vegas, he never went back. Regarded as the artistic equal of top-flight white performers, he insisted on being their personal equal as well. He demanded to be housed at the Las Vegas hotels where he performed, rather than retreat to substandard accommodations on the "black side" of town. He likewise demanded — and received — entry into New York night spots that previously turned a cold shoulder to black customers. Davis took these bold steps with full knowledge of the fact that he was doing so not only for himself, but for the sake of the black performers who would follow him.

Yet as fearless and forthright as Davis was, these and other actions caused controversy. His friendship with Frank Sinatra, and the formation of the Rat Pack, was, by his likes, a species of interracial triumph: Here were white artists who not only respected him as a performer but cherished him as a friend. Still, the Pack's frequent jokes about Davis' race didn't sit well with many African Americans. Likewise his marriage to May Britt caused almost as much of an uproar in some areas of the black community as it did with whites. Sammy's conversion to Judaism dumbfounded black and white alike. But it was his conversion to Nixonism that really rankled.

As a man who had spent his entire life not only fighting racism but contributing financially to numerous civil rights organizations, Davis obviously felt he had nothing to answer for when he suddenly shifted party affiliation. But the fact that he spent the rest of his life defending that move testifies to the problematic situation that's created when art and politics collide. Davis wanted to speak for African Americans; he wanted to speak for himself; yet his failure to do so without ensuing complication is hardly surprising. Sammy Davis is inextricably tied to the late 20th century America cult of celebrity in which he stands as a seminal figure; it's safe to say that no one ever used the base of power of show biz to more useful and noble ends.

PART TWO

Zeroing In

10

Full-Service Showfolk
Leonard Reed, Demas Dean,
Frances Williams

I am fortunate in having met and known showman Leonard Reed (no relation), musician Demas Dean and actress-activist Frances Williams (all now deceased). All of them played a significant role in expanding my awareness of the extraordinary world of African American entertainment, which, in turn, culminated in the writing of this book.

What Reed, Dean and Williams had in common with each other was a rare awareness of the important role that entertainment played in keeping things on track in the African American community; if for no other reason than the thesis stated in the introduction to this book to the effect that, even the earliest of black comedians had seldom failed to touch, if only lightly, on the subject of racism, and that two-timing lovers weren't the only source of most blues singers' woes.

It seems only fitting that I devote a chapter to these three knowledgeable and highly articulate African Americans entertainers whose lives circled back almost to the very beginnings of modem show business.

Leonard Reed

I met Reed in 1985 as the result of a book about singer Dinah Washington (see Chapter 8) I wanted to write (a project that finally never came about). I was searching for people who knew the singer personally when Fayard Nicholas, of the tap dancing Nicholas Brothers, suggested, "Call Leonard Reed." Frankly, I'd never even heard of Reed, but Nicholas said, "I think he worked with Dinah early in her career and he might be able to help you." He also told me that Reed had been a performer since 1915 but, by the late 1950s, had begun increasingly to work behind the scenes.

The Hollywood Boulevard address in L.A. that Nicholas gave me for

Leonard Reed and Willie Bryant, 1930.

Reed was a ten-story office building owned by Scientologists and occupied mostly by fringe entertainment industry types, including two-bit talent agencies, scuffling record promoters and exploitation movie producers — all just a scream away from downtown *Day of the Locust*. As a result, my preconceptions of Reed were of some wily over-the-hill promoter, straight out of Mel Brooks' *The Producers*.

But I was pleasantly surprised a few days later when I went to his office for an interview I'd set up: The phone was ringing off the hook, business associates were shuttling in and out, and Reed, a man nearly eighty, but looking many years younger, was in the process of coaching a talented young performer on how to "put it across." After he was finished with this last student of the day, Reed took me into an office adjacent to the studio, closed the door, and began to talk about how he had given Dinah Washington one of her first professional jobs at Chicago's Regal Theatre in the late 1930s. "I was the first one to teach her," he said, "the first one to say, 'Here's what you do. How to walk on stage, here's how to walk off.'"[1]

The rest of what I learned during an interview that lasted much longer than I originally planned had mostly to do with Reed himself; he seemed almost aching to inform me about his own past accomplishments. This is scarcely unusual in show business where rampant egomania is the order of the day; but in Reed's case, I sensed something else was going on. There was an urgency in his voice. He also wanted to set the record straight about the history of African American entertainment. Before meeting Reed, I had heard of the black theatre circuit, the T.O.B.A. However, that plus my awareness of the handful of early African American performers who managed the transition to Broadway and the movies was just about all I knew of black show business history. And when Reed told me that his uncle was the obscure, but nonetheless major African American entertainment figure Will Marion Cook (see Chapter One), it was almost as if I had fallen into a science fiction time warp. He said, "I never thought I would ever live long enough to see the day when my once-famous uncle had been totally forgotten."

Reed began his show business career when he was barely in his teens, working as a candy butcher (a.k.a. barker) in carnivals and a spieler (a.k.a. pitch man) in medicine shows. He moved on to the show business "big time" as a dancer and comedian in vaudeville and later as a producer, director, choreographer and songwriter. In fact, Reed's first job on stage was in 1918 in Kansas City with the man who practically invented modern show business, Billy McClain (see Chapter Three).

Possessing only ⅛ black blood, the light-skinned Reed was able to pass as white, enabling him to work both sides of the show business street during one of the most highly segregated eras of American history. But there was no special advantage to Reed's position, for passing as white in high-profile situations brought with it danger. But as a black performer, he faced the invisible ceiling that cut him off from the highest reaches of show business that were available only to whites. Reed had to deal with racial prejudice on two separate fronts: He was forced not only to cope with white intolerance, but black intolerance as well. He was sometimes turned away from pre–civil rights "blacks only" hotels because he was "too white" and posed the danger of getting hotel owners in trouble with the (white) law. One story Reed told me illustrated (if you will) the *lighter* side of such dichotomies.

In the 1950s Reed toured with Joe Louis as a partner in the standup act of the boxer's later years. One example of just how far Louis would go to get a laugh, Reed told me, requires a little background. Until somewhat recently, there were hardly any hotels below the Mason-Dixon Line that catered to other than whites. When black performers toured the South, they were forced to make do with whatever lodgings they could muster up. This was the situation in 1953 when Reed and Louis were touring their standup comedy act as part of a package called *The Big Rhythm and Blues Show*. Ninety cities in nearly the same number of nights! Louis was the headliner, but the others on the bill were fairly big stars in their own right: Ruth Brown; Buddy Johnson and Ella Johnson and a sixteen-piece band; comic Dusty Fletcher; singers Wynonie Harris, and the Clovers.

Inasmuch as he looked too white to stay in most places that catered to blacks anyhow, he usually stayed in white establishments. Most rooming houses in the South were willing to allow a white manager traveling with an all-black show to stay with his cast, but still things could get messy. Many more times than he cared to recall, during the first two decades of his show business career he'd been routed by the local constabulary in the middle of the night and thrown out of his lodgings, bag and baggage. On one occasion he was even arrested. The charge? Being a white man cohabiting with coloreds! Naturally, the housing problem proved especially great for a traveling unit as large as this one, with its two busloads of nearly fifty blacks. Or, a "problem" to everyone in the troupe but Reed.The bus would pull into a town, he'd get off at a white hotel, and the rest of the cast and crew would head off to the black side of town to scuffle.

"Not everyone in the company accepted my excuse that I was checking into the white hotels to avoid trouble with the law," recalled Reed, "and others were annoyed by the fact that many of the places I stayed just happened to be located conveniently near the nice whites-only golf course in town. A few just thought I was being 'uppity.' But mostly there were no strong, hard feelings and things went smoothly. Except once in Houston. I got off the bus at the swank Shamrock Hotel, waved goodbye to the others, and after checking in at the desk I went to my room and was just getting comfortable when there was a knock at the door. I got up, opened it, and it was the manager of the hotel.

"'I'm sorry, sir, but you can't stay here,'" he said in this very starchy voice.

"'Why, what's the problem? I paid in advance and everything,'" I said.

"'We'll refund your money. I think you'll be happier elsewhere.'"

Reed began to catch this "draft" (back then when blacks sensed white prejudice, they called it feeling a "draft," and this was a positive hurricane). Knowing that there was no use in bothering to protest, he told the manager he'd leave, and packed up to go.

"When I reached the lobby," Reed continued, "the reason for the manager's attitude was obvious. Actually, three reasons. There stood one of our show's star attractions, Ruth Brown, and pulling up the rear were two of the most pathetic, little, wide-eyed black waifs you ever laid eyes on playing the part of her children. She strode angrily across the lobby, and when she reached me, shook her finger in my face, grabbed me, and as she dragged me toward the hotel entrance, shouted back over her shoulder at her two supporting players: 'Come along, children, we've found your daddy.'"

In 1929, as part of the now-forgotten Norman Thomas quintet, Reed opened for Ethel Barrymore at the Valhalla of vaudeville, New York's Palace Theatre. With his partner Willie Bryant, Reed once supported great Yiddish star Molly Picon on a bill at the Bowery's Grand Theatre. In fact, for several years Reed and the equally light-skinned Bryant were presumed to be a white act. The eventual disclosure of their black heritage spelled the death knell for an act that possessed, in all other respects, all the necessary ingredients for stardom. In short, Reed had "done it all" in a career spanning seven decades of vaudeville, night clubs, the Broadway stage, television, and the recording industry; and for a half-dozen years in Harlem he was a jack of all trades for 125th Street's famed Apollo Theatre.

Starting in 1952, he worked as emcee of the legendary Wednesday Amateur Nights (a recording of a typical one of these shows was released on Vanguard Records, *Night at the Apollo*, with liner notes by Langston Hughes). After a year, in addition to rehearsing the productions and acting as emcee and comic for many of the shows, he went on to co-manage the showplace. Just as impressively, he had produced and dance-directed the 1937 show at the Cotton Club, *Tall, Tan and Terrific*. After this initial exposure to Reed, whose beginnings in "the business" went all the way back to the era of horse-drawn medicine shows, I wanted to know more. He clearly sensed this; when I left his office that first afternoon, as I got into the elevator, he called after me:

"Do you have a place to hang out?" (He might as well have added "kid.")

"No," I said. "Well, you do now," he told me just as the elevator doors sprang shut.

And so, the next time I went to Reed's office, it wasn't just to talk of Dinah Washington, but of this *other* show business. Through Reed, I also began meeting a number of other survivors of that long-gone mirror world of African American entertainment, including: the great tap dancer Willie Covan, Sunshine Sammy Morrison (of the first wave of "Our Gang" players), Ellington vocalist Herb Jeffries, chorine Frances Nealy, black movie leading man Babe Wallace, vocalist Sonny Craver (who though somewhat younger than the others still managed to have worked as a straight man for the wonderful black comic Dewey "Pigmeat" Markham), and many more.

In 1992 I co-curated an exhibit at the California Afro-American Museum about Black Hollywood in the 1940s. Part of the exhibit was devoted to Reed's activities as a producer-choreographer on Central Avenue, Los Angeles' fabled entertainment strip. In the course of working on "Hollywood Days/Harlem Nights," I interviewed a number of old-timers—African American entertainment professionals and "civilians" alike. Invariably I was told that Reed was a "very famous man in his time" who had performed "everywhere." But he was thought by many I spoke with to be no longer among the living. Not so surprising when you consider he had managed to outlive nearly every one of his contemporaries. He passed on more than a decade later, in 2004, at age 97.

Demas Dean

The potential for film, theatre and night club employment — and the chance to put an end to the misery of life "on the road"—caused hundreds of African American entertainers to settle in Los Angeles during the decade of World War II. For some, the relocation meant a new lease on professional life. For others— especially those who miscalculated the amount of "live" performance work available in the movie capital — the move spelled the beginning of the end of their show business careers. There was a limit as to how many people jump 'n' jivin' Central Avenue could employ, and much of the remaining L.A. theatre and club work was still closed to African Americans.

Musician Demas Dean was one such individual; after moving to Los Angeles in the early 1940s he would soon became professionally inactive and remain so for nearly the next half-century. In his time, though, he played trumpet and cornet with many of the best singers, bands and musicians during the '20s and '30s; and as a result was a walking history book of black show business.

When I met him in the mid–1980s, Demas lived in a pleasant, neat, well-kept studio apartment in L.A.'s mid–Wilshire area. Despite its size, the apartment still managed to contain a library consisting of most of the key books about jazz and black entertainment (along with a copy of the Bible and an omnibus of Longfellow, his favorite poet). The walls were an arresting photographic who's who of black entertainment at the time — with many of the photos having been personally inscribed to Dean when he was professionally associated with them during the 1920s and '30s— including: Maxine Sullivan, Duke Ellington, Louis Armstrong, Lena Horne, Paul Robeson, Adelaide Hall, Billie Holiday, Valaida Snow, Elisabeth Welch, et al. I asked him once about the photos, which most people might have lost or thrown away over the years: "I can't take credit for it," he said. "I just sent them home, and

instead of sticking them in a garage, my mother or my wife took care of them.
I don't know why, they just did."

That sort of low-key candor was typical of Dean (as most of his friends
called him), as well as lack of complaints about his cramped but comfortable
surroundings. Harkening back to the "gentleman farmer" surroundings of
his early years (he was born October 30, 1903), his small back yard had a rock
garden that he tended with regularity up until a few months before I first knew
him. One might even go so far as to call his early years "Gatsbyesque": His
father had been a caretaker on the swank Sag Harbor Long Island estate of
wealthy doctor Charles Napier, and as a result, most of the year — off season — Demas, his brother and sisters had the run of the estate: stables, library,
the works, in a highly beneficial but nonetheless — for an African American
of the time — anomalous environment.

"My father was also named Demas. It's from the Bible, Timothy II: 'For
Demas having forsaken me [Jesus], having loved better the things of this
world.'" He laughed, then added, "I haven't forsaken Him, but I *do* love the
finer things of this world." Why both he and his father should have been
named after one of the more wanton characters in the Bible, in addition as

**Demas Dean (second from left) with Noble Sissle and His Orchestra, Paris, 1929 (cour-
tesy Chet and Joann Gudger).**

to why Dean Sr.'s second-born and not first son should have inherited the name, was a mystery to Dean even in his eighties.

The early years in Sag Harbor, a pastoral little village (a hundred miles or so from Manhattan) that originally had been a whaling port, afforded lots of opportunities for boating, swimming, fishing and horseback riding. In addition, Demas Sr. bought musical instruments for all his children — violins, drums, trombone — and hired some of the best Sag Harbor music instructors to tutor them. "The only thing we heard in the house when we lived in Sag Harbor was church music, hymns; but my parents loved music, especially my mother who lived long enough to see me play in the bands of two Broadway shows."

Dean's curiously privileged childhood was further aided by the Russell Sage Foundation which, taking into account the enormous number of African Americans living on Long Island (like Dean's father, most were caretakers and servants), funded a school and library for blacks that was the envy of even the better white schools in the area.

In 1921 Dean entered the Music Conservatory at Washington D.C.'s Howard University. While there, he played professionally with Russell Wooding's Orchestra, and during the summer break of 1923 toured and recorded with blues singer Lucille Hegamin as one of her Blue Flame Syncopators. Then in 1922 he attended a performance of the legendary Sissle-Blake musical *Shuffle Along*:

"When I heard that pit band for *Shuffle Along*, the way the brass played together under the direction of Eubie Blake, I had never heard such fantastic music. I said in my mind, 'I've got to play on Broadway with an orchestra like that.'" Shortly thereafter, he left Howard University to try his luck at it. "My parents were quite upset at first," he told a writer for *Storyville Magazine* in 1977, "but finally decided that maybe that was the best for me. Then, too, my brother and older sisters were in New York. That's how I happened to be in New York, the Big Apple, during the Roaring Twenties.[2]

"It was something else!! Unbelievable!! Live music and jazz musicians everywhere!! It was the beginning of a fantastic era for me. Harlem in 1924 was really something else, a musician's paradise. Night clubs, ballrooms, and speakeasies were everywhere. It was the age of live music."[3]

Dean's first New York City engagements were in 1924 — the same year he quit Howard University — at Harlem's Nest Club and Bamboo Inn. In the fall of the following year, he journeyed to Florida with Ford Dabney's Show and Dance Band (with Will Vodery as conductor) to play at a swank Palm Beach night club owned by Florenz Ziegfeld. It was a professional interlude that turned out to be not nearly as much fun for the blacks involved as it was for the whites, as he later explained to Peter Carr in *Storyville Magazine*:

"Ziegfeld reserved the entire train to take the band and his show to Palm

Beach. We did have to keep our shades down whenever we stopped after leaving Washington. When we arrived in Palm Beach we had to wait until the trains pulled into the yards before getting off. A black band coming into the Deep South to play a white show was enough to make us more than a little apprehensive."[4]

Returning to New York at the end of the winter season, Dean joined the Bearcats, the first band to play at the newly opened Savoy Ballroom. Then in May of 1927, he was off on a six-month tour of South America with Leon Abbey's jazz orchestra. Somewhere along the line he had picked up a few Charleston steps and his dancing was incorporated into the Abbey revue as it barnstormed Buenos Aries and Brazil — the Empire and Maipu theaters, the Sportsman's Polo and Florida clubs. "Can you imagine that?" he said of his brief turn as a dancer. "It was fun for a couple of weeks."[5]

In the fall of that same year, after returning from South America, Dean finally landed his dream job of playing in the jazzy pit band of a black Broadway show, one which would turn out to be arguably the most famous of the era, *Blackbirds of 1928*, starring Bill "Bojangles" Robinson. Several similar shows then followed in rapid order, including *Hot Chocolates* with Fats Waller and *Rhapsody in Black* starring Ethel Waters and Valaida Snow. It was during the run of the latter that the following happened:

> ...Ethel Waters had this routine she did about a dance hall girl. The production was more like a stage show than a revue and so the band was on stage when she did it. For her monologue we were to play "St. Louis Blues" softly behind a curtain. Anyway, I improvised a chorus of "Nobody Knows the Trouble I've Seen" against the melody of "St. Louis Blues." It fit and it seemed appropriate to the character and situation, but when Miss Waters came off the stage right after the number, she was furious. She summoned the bandleader Pike Davis into her dressing room even before the show was over and really let him have it for playing that spiritual. After the show was over I went back to her dressing room and confessed that I was the culprit. She took a good long look at me and just said, "Don't you ever do that again." And I didn't. Years later she became a very religious person, one of Billy Graham's followers, but I guess the sincere spark was there even way back when.

Of all his professional accomplishments, the ones he liked to talk about most and of which he was clearly most proud were the two recordings sessions he did with Bessie Smith, the first on February 9, 1928, and the second on February 21, for a total of six sides: "Thinking Blues," "Pickpocket Blues," "I Used to Be Your Sweet Mama," "Standin' in the Rain Blues," "It Won't Be You" and "I'm a Cheater." Here is a little of what he had to say about the experience:

> I had never heard Bessie Smith, I'd only heard *of* her up until the time I recorded with her. I was so surprised when I finally heard her in the studio. She was so far above all the other blues singers I'd heard up till then — and that includes Lucille Hegamin whose band I was in at one time and who probably was just as well known as Bessie in those days.

You just couldn't stop listening to Bessie and looking at her too when she sang. She was a large, attractive brown-skinned woman, very good legs. Later on I heard a lot of stories about how difficult she was, but I found her very relaxed, very sedate. As long as you were no problem to her, she was no problem to you. I was a little nervous about playing with her because she was expecting her favorite trumpet player, Joe Smith, and instead she was going to get me.

When my friend the trombonist Charlie Green asked me to come down and record with Bessie, I said, "Where's Joe?" He said he couldn't find him for this recording, so I was lucky enough to be in the right place at the right time. Ten days later they still couldn't find Joe, he must have been on the road with Fletcher Henderson, so I recorded with Bessie a second time. There was no written music at all except for a lead sheet that her piano player Fred Longshaw had. We didn't have microphones, but horns we played into, like megaphones. These were what they called acoustical recordings. How it ever got into the booth I'll never know. These were very, very primitive recordings ... so primitive that you couldn't even record drums because it threw everything out of whack

After meeting Bessie, we went right to work. She turned us over to her pianist, Fred Longshaw. The only thing that was interesting to him as far as any rehearsal we might have done was the introduction. We played an eight-bar introduction, then Bessie sang. We'd never heard these numbers before, no music, but you're supposed to know the blues. If you didn't know the blues, you were like a lost ball in the tall grass.

Every number she sang told a story. One was "Pickpocket Blues." When she sang it, you knew right away what she was talking about — she was a pickpocket, her friends were trying to tell her to stop it. But she ended up in the jailhouse anyhow." It was a short story.

The first number recorded by Demas with Bessie found him with Longshaw and Green playing a four-bar opening and then trading off two-bar obligatos with Green throughout the remainder of the cut, ending with a brief trumpet smear played over Green's end notes. It sounds a little rough at first, but by the end of the last song on the date, "I Used to Be Your Sweet Mama," Dean has things under control, sounding similar in style and attack, intentionally or otherwise, to Joe Smith, Bessie's trumpet player of choice. In fact, before the art of jazz discography was as advanced as it is now, Smith was presumed to be the player on both the first and second Bessie Smith sessions on which, in actuality, Dean held down the trumpet chair.

"I didn't hear those records that we made those two days until almost forty years later," Demas told me. "I was in California when the record producer Chris Albertson called me and he asked if I had ever heard them and I said no. He sent me copies and I was pleasantly surprised. You couldn't listen to playbacks back in the days we first recorded them, because test pressings took a couple of days to get back. Musically, you were flying by the seat of your pants. But we only had to do one take on each of the songs to be satisfied." Dean's discography would grow to include recordings with such other stars as Lena Horne and Sidney Bechet.

In May of 1929, Dean began the lengthiest association of his career when he became a part of the orchestra of Noble Sissle, the musician who inspired him, a few years earlier, to turn pro when Demas had seen him spiritedly conduct the pit band for *Shuffle Along*. Soon he found himself in Paris with Sissle and company for an extended engagement at the Ambassadeur's Club "where Cole Porter liked us and really pushed us." Dean always took pains to stress that, even though its roster of musicians over the years included the likes of Sidney Bechet and Buster Bailey, Sissle's wasn't really a jazz band. I asked him one time, might it have been a good solid meat-and-potatoes outfit like Paul Whiteman's?

"Not up to that standard really, but on that order. We were more a commercial society band that played a lot for the Rockefellers and Wanamakers, the Nunns and the Stokesburys."

In 1930, after coming back to America and a brief return to Broadway, Dean rejoined the Sissle Orchestra for a stay that lasted the rest of his professional career. He performed thousands of engagements throughout the U.S.—"Somehow in the entire fourteen years, the only major city we managed to miss, of all places, was New Orleans"—and Europe with the band from 1933 to 1942. Then after the band's engagement at Billy Rose's Diamond Horseshoe in New York, Dean stopped playing music to become the band's road manager until Sissle split up his group in 1944, at which time Dean and his wife moved to Los Angeles. And like so many other show business types who in the 1940s moved to Los Angeles thinking that it was a land of golden opportunity for "live" as well as movie show folk, Dean got fooled. It wasn't. There were employment opportunities all right, but they weren't in show business. Demas took a job with the U.S. Postal Service in '44 and never picked up his horn again. He kept the job until 1965 when he retired. During his last 25 years, Dean mainly relaxed and shared memories of his extraordinary career with many journalists and historians. These recollections appear in several books devoted to jazz, including John Chilton's *Sidney Bechet: The Wizard of Jazz* and Chris Albertson's *Bessie*.

Just a few of the other musicians and performers with whom Dean was professionally associated include Benny Carter, Adelaide Hall, Elisabeth Welch, Juan Tizol and Dexter Gordon. One afternoon I took a VCR to Dean's house to show him *Symphony in Riffs*, a new documentary about jazz man Benny Carter. His reaction was one of elation that African American musicians had "come such a long way from my time" and latterly were accorded the kind of general respect shown Carter in the film. Even though he was classically trained, Dean had great respect for the music he was playing in the 1920s:

"We were one of the first bands to play the Savoy Ballroom and nearly all of our arrangements were by Fletcher Henderson and Don Redman, and a lot of it was new to me — the stomps, like 'Stampede' and so forth. But I knew it was music for the ages even then."

*   *   *

At a certain point during the taping of a (still-unfinished) documentary that I was making about Demas in late 1989, he took from his closet his fifty-year-old Conn trumpet, an instrument he had not touched in nearly as many years, and soon had the three-person crew and even myself more or less convinced — his shot embouchure notwithstanding — that he was going to play for us. He continuously fondled the horn and from time to time, with a devilish look in his eyes, would bring it near his lips only to find that "the valves are stuck." Still, several more times, he asked the crew, "What would you like to hear?" And so on.

One of the many things hard to forget about Demas is his sense memory for events that happened more than a half-century ago: When I told him my home town was Charleston, West Virginia, he was able to describe in detail where he and the Sissle band had played on at least one occasion in the late 1930s; what the building was like, where it was situated, its size, etc. It sounded to me like a ringer for the Ferguson Hotel complex, an *avant* mall — restaurant, barbershop, haberdashery, ballroom, movie theatre, record store, smoke shop and hostelry — that served many of the needs of African Americans in the community for more than forty years until its demise in 1966. (It was known as "The Block.")

Dean forthwith proceeded to check a meticulous diary he had kept while on the road with Sissle, and sure enough that's where the band had played. The ancient-looking notebook book also contained notation such as "Drive to [such and such an address] in Kansas City. Pick up new union man, Charles Parker." Dean was the band's road manager, in addition to playing trumpet, and was deputized in April of 1942 to make sure that new Sissle recruit Charles (soon to be "Bird") Parker made it to his first date with the band in Chicago.

So too did some of Dean's compatriots from earlier times possess remarkable memories: One day Dean told me that both Lena Horne and Benny Carter had recognized him on separate occasions in the early 1980s after not having seen him for several decades. That made him happy. Horne was with the Sissle band for slightly less than a year in 1936, and at one point even led the band and helped keep it together after its leader was sidelined by injuries from a car wreck. When Horne eventually left to get married, "our band was a sad bunch of musicians for a long time," Dean told *Storyville Magazine* in 1977."[6]

Until only a few weeks before his death, Demas continued to maintain extensive friendships and correspondences with many individuals (professional and otherwise) throughout the U.S., Europe, and elsewhere. One day I came to visit and found Demas reading a letter he'd just received from Kansas from dancer U.S. "Slow Kid" Thompson, a major black figure of Broadway in the '20s and the husband of the great singing and dancing star Florence Mills. (Somehow I'd assumed Thompson was dead.) Although Dean was very much grounded in the here and now, sometimes being with him was almost like drifting into a time warp. The letter he received from Thompson is a good example of this; "Slow Kid" (who got his name from the strobe-like, slow motion dance he did) was known to have worked medicine shows at the turn of the century before gaining fame on Broadway in such productions as *Shuffle Along* (1921) and the *Plantation Revue* (1922). Thus, it simply did not seem possible that he was still alive; but he was, and in his hands Dean held the proof.[7]

Looking back now to the spring of 1990, there's little doubt that Demas knew he was dying and not just sick, as his weight began to plummet. Finally he entered Kaiser Permanente for an extensive checkup, and my suspicions (as well as his, one supposes) were confirmed. I later learned it was cancer. One day I received an emergency call from his nurse asking me to drive him from his home to the hospital. The Demas I saw then was alarmingly thin, but still chipper. After a few hours at the facility, I brought him home, and that was the last time I ever saw him.

I later learned that that night, instead of his new near-pabulum diet, Demas had ordered a fried chicken meal from a takeout restaurant. The next night, unquestionably still in his right mind, he upped the ante even more by demanding and eating the best barbecue dinner that money could have delivered to your home: Dean went to bed and a few hours later, on May 30, 1990, he was found dead — having experienced an apparently peaceful passing — in his memento-filled quarters. When people get very old, they sometimes become strangely unafraid of death. I would suppose that such fearlessness must have always been the case with Demas Dean. As evidenced by his final dietary daring, it was truer of him than ever in his last days.

Whenever I was with Demas I never failed to be moved by the fact he was fully aware of the import and cultural significance of everything he had done in the field of theatre and music. Unfortunately, this was not always the case with some I spoke to during the course of writing this book; for one reason or another, it was a part of their life they would just as soon forget. Others simply *could not* remember. In some instances, those with whom I was dealing were musicians, comedians, dancers whose activities dated back almost to the very beginnings of African American show business. Fortunately, Dean was aware of the important role African Americans had played in the cultural life of the U.S.; for the nearly fifty years of his life after show business, he waged a quiet crusade to make sure everyone else understood as well.

Frances Williams

Actress Frances Williams, who died in 1995, links up with events and persons described in the very earliest parts of this book. Born in 1905, two years after Will Marion Cook's *In Dahomey* premiered on Broadway, Williams, with just a few exceptions, knew and/or was professionally associated with nearly every one of the biographical subjects contained herein. She recalls, as a small girl, seeing the legendary James Reese Europe conducting an orchestra in an outdoor space adjacent to the Cleveland apartment house in which she lived. She also clearly remembers her mother taking her to a performance of the historically significant Cole and Johnson black musical, *The Red Moon*, when it toured prior to its 1909 Broadway opening. With a career spanning more than seven decades on the stage and in film, Williams was an important transitional figure between the era of racial segregation — which levied a heavy toll on both the private and professional lives of African American entertainers — and today's ideologically volatile times.

After arriving on the West Coast in 1941, Williams couldn't find a job in her chosen profession for nearly five years because she refused to give in to racial stereotyping. But she had never been at a loss for some worthwhile social cause or activity to which she could devote her energies. Eventually Williams' career did shift into a comfortable gear, yet she only became widely recognized by the general public as an original member of the ensemble cast of TV's *Frank's Place*, the highly-praised series of the late 1980s, in which she created the character of Miss Marie, the venerated elder-waitress of the series' black-owned restaurant in New Orleans. When *Frank's Place* was cancelled, it was a deep disappointment for all concerned, Williams included. "But when life is full," she later told one news writer, "and you keep it full, you go on."[8]

Williams lived in a small, comfortable clapboard bungalow located in the Exposition Park area of Los Angeles, a district directly north of the city's densely black-populated South

Frances Williams in the 1990s (courtesy Frances Williams).

Central section. Adjacent to her house was the three-car garage to which, in the early 1960s, she added lights and theater seats, thus converting it into a little jewel box of a performance space and community meeting and learning center, the Frances E. Williams Corner Theatre. I first visited this thriving little compound in August of 1992 when I went to interview Williams about an upcoming exhibition about black Hollywood in the 1940s that I was co-curating at Los Angeles' California Afro-American Museum; the general consensus being that until I'd talked to Williams, I really hadn't done my homework on the subject.

Going up the path to Williams' house and noticing the door to the theater slightly ajar, I looked in. The cool dark blue interior of the space, in contrast to harsh bright California daylight I'd just stepped out of, was so inviting that I went in and sat for a few minutes. I found my gaze drawn to a turn-of-the-century Steinway upright which I later found out had been played on, since the time Williams had acquired it in the mid–1940s, by everyone from Art Tatum to André Previn.

Meeting Williams a few minutes later, I was immediately struck by her mass of beautiful white hair and pleasant smile. I later learned that when the smile is not there, serious debate or argument was generally on the horizon, for she allowed little with which she took issue to slide by unremarked-upon. Williams was always seated on the TV series *Frank's Place* because, in reality, she suffered from severe arthritis. She had a housekeeper, Betty, and a general aide-de-camp, Spencer; but she still personally booked all the acts at her theater and conducted its writing and acting workshops; the wheelchair to which she was confined was clearly her one major concession to age.

Having some familiarity with Williams' extraordinary life and times beforehand, I found it difficult, during my initial visit, to stay on my subject of black Hollywood in the 1940s and not veer off into other areas of discussion such as the two years in the mid–1930s that Williams spent in Russia where she learned Russian, taught Sergei Eisenstein's wife English, and worked at the Meyerhold Theater and at Natalie Satz's children's theater; or her long friendships with such figures as Langston Hughes, W.E.B. Du Bois and Paul Robeson. (In Williams' copy of his autobiography *Here I Stand*, he inscribed the following to her: "All of us are indebted to you for your complete artistic contributions and integrity.") The initial interview, during which I more or less remained focused on immediately relevant matters, lasted about an hour and eventually ended up as an audio installation at the Museum exhibit which came to be called "Hollywood Days, Harlem Nights."

After my first visit, I attended a number of music and drama events at Frances' Corner Theatre. A number of times I also stopped by to talk with Frances, whose mind was still razor-sharp and capable of recalling in minute detail events of more than a half-century ago: Her remembrances of Ethel

Waters shed new and compassionate light on the emotional landscape of the complex and controversial African American star.

Here is some of what I found out about the *rest* of Williams' life during my talks with her, including several in mid–June 1994, which constituted more formal interviews: As usual, Williams was always seated in her wheelchair in a recently remodeled kitchen full of new appliances and gadgets. In fact, aside from the interior of the theater, this is the only place I ever saw her in the house. And just like life imitating the art (*à la Frank's Place* and Williams' solicitous, nurturing character of Miss Marie), a pot of one thing or another was usually bubbling on the stove in anticipation of guests— expected and otherwise. I came to realize in many more ways than this, that the line between her private and public lives was remarkably blurred, if not in fact non-existent. The first afternoon Williams sat with me to talk on the record, she told of a conversation she'd recently overheard between two neighborhood men standing in her driveway: "One man turned, pointed to the theater and asked the other one, 'What is that?' And the other one answered, 'Are you kidding? That's culture!'"[9]

This vest pocket settlement house began many years ago as an extension of drama classes being taught by Williams at L.A.'s Dorsey High:

> I didn't like what the entertainment industry was doing to my people, stereotyping and all, and I finally figured out that the only way to make things happen was to do it myself. At first it was mainly my kids from Dorsey and people in the neighborhood, but eventually my professional friends also got involved: Tony Quinn, Lloyd Bridges, Roscoe Lee Browne, Maya Angelou ... just oh so many. I bought this property not too long after my husband and I first moved here in 1941. Then, the house was under what was called restrictive covenant. That meant that no Jews or blacks were allowed to own property in certain neighborhoods. But there were sometimes ways of getting around that. This house which was not much more than a shack back then had previously been occupied by a black couple who had whites buy it for them to get around the covenant, and then we obtained it. My husband was a ceramicist and one other time we tried to rent a place for him right at the corner of Arlington and Jefferson that was not even a house but a garage and we could not rent it. We ended up getting a white friend of ours in Hollywood to rent it for us. We paid her the rent and then she'd give it to the landlord.
>
> I never had any serious trouble here, but later when people began moving into [Los Angeles' nearby] Leimert Park it got pretty nasty. Whites were tossing in dead rats, flooding the basements, all kinds of terrible things. I got involved and helped form a patrol group to turn off the water, check the property and things like that ... around the clock. Every week agents, producers and others I worked with back in the '40s were forever asking me to move closer to Hollywood. But just like Langston, I always wanted to live in the neighborhoods where my people were.

"Langston" was author Langston Hughes, who Williams first met in 1920 at Cleveland's Karamu House, a settlement house founded in 1915. The Karamu Players, based there, placed a heavy emphasis on plays written by and starring African Americans, and it is still in operation; "In fact," Williams said, "there was recent talk about starting a West Coast branch of Karamu in San Diego." Some of the most important black writers and actors of the 20th century have been involved with Cleveland's Karamu Players—now the oldest continuing black drama group in the country—with Karamu House proper having long since taken on the same kind of historic luster associated with the likes of Hull House in Chicago and Henry Street Settlement in New York.

Williams, who was born in East Orange, New Jersey, but moved to the Ohio city at a young age, came to Karamu in 1920 when she was fifteen and remained there as a teacher, worker and all-round theatre utility person (actor, director, etc.) until 1934. During her 14 years there she was involved in 85 productions, including premiere performances of works by Arna Bontemps, Langston Hughes and Zora Neale Hurston.

It was in '34 that a two-week stay, funded by Karamu, at a worker's camp, coupled with the encouragement of Hughes and the inspiration of well-known dramatist Friedrich Wolff, inspired in Williams the desire to journey to the Soviet Union. After selling nearly everything she owned, she had only enough for a round trip ticket to what was then widely viewed as "the Workers' Paradise," with seventy dollars left over—not nearly enough for her journey.

"Langston had come back from there the previous year and even though the failure of trying to get his film *Black and White* made there was a disappointment, he remained very pro–Soviet. So much so that when I phoned him in Chicago to tell of my decision to go there, he caught the next train back to Cleveland and personally handed me his Soviet bank book so that I could use the money he still had in accounts there but, of course, could not take out of the country."

Williams sailed to the Soviet Union in the fall of 1934 on the Cunard Line. She remained there for two extremely active years and found the experience gratifying. But like so many other black (and white) intellectuals and artists of the 1930s who undertook the same journey, unquestionably the most famed of whom was Paul Robeson, the Soviet visit would eventually come back to haunt her politically once the McCarthy era rolled around. While living in Russia, Frances played a small role in a 1936 film called *The Circus*, directed by Grigori Alexandrov, former assistant to Alexandrov. In it she sang a lullaby to James Patterson—the son of an African American expatriate and a Russian woman—who was then two years old (he grew up to become one of Russia's leading poets).

In 1936 Williams returned to the U.S. with $3 in her pocket and an expired passport. Almost at once she secured what would prove to be the most lucrative employment of her career up until the time of *Frank's Place*: Right off the boat, she was hired to replace Ruth Attaway in the original New York production of *You Can't Take It with You* and subsequently toured with the road company of the Pulitzer Prize–winning comedy for nearly two years. Around the same time, Williams appeared in two screen melodramas by the pioneer African American filmmaker Oscar Micheaux, *Lying Lips* (1939) and *The Notorious Elinor Lee* (1940). The director's films were notoriously low-budgeted affairs. Langston Hughes viewed *Lying Lips* at a theater with Williams one day and noted that in the movie she smoked non-filtered Camels all the way down to the end; he turned to her and whispered, "What was your budget, Frank? Couldn't they even afford to buy you any cigarettes?" (In fact, Williams was only indulging herself in a real-life habit.) It wasn't long after completing her second film for Micheaux in 1940 that Tony Hill, Williams' husband, whom she'd met and married while on tour with *You Can't Take It with You*, made her an offer that was more in the form of an ultimatum:

> One day Tony told me out of the blue, "Fran, if you want to go to the West Coast, you'd better save your money." I really didn't know much about Hollywood, but I decided that I wanted to go. But when I got here, all I saw were all these bandanas on all these black women in films and I decided this was not for me. I was here five years before I took a film job. I moved to Palm Springs where I helped operate a hotel with my cousin who was also named Frances Williams. Then, finally one day I realized that the only way to change things was to get in the middle of it. I swallowed my pride, came back to Hollywood and took the part of a maid in the movie about Dolly Madison, *Magnificent Doll*. That was in 1946 and it starred Ginger Rogers and David Niven. But when I got the script mailed to me, my part was nowhere to be seen. I soon learned that very often they didn't even bother to write the lines for the black actors; you were expected to improvise. It was as simple as that. During one scene I was standing next to Ginger Rogers out of camera range during a scene where all these plague victims were being carried about on stretchers and I turned to her and said, "Can you imagine that! No blacks caught the plague. We sure must be a healthy bunch of people." I came back after lunch and the shooting was held up until the director got his wishes for black plague victims. I must have said something to the right person. That's what I meant by changing things from within. David Niven was a wonderful person, a thoughtful man, but not everyone was that way. Crew people would sometimes tell off-color stories to a black woman that they wouldn't think of repeating to a white woman. Or you would go on the set and they'd say, "Could you get me a cook?"; or, "Do you know where I might find a good laundress?" or "a chauffeur?" They just looked at you and *assumed*. And you'd look at them and think, "Why should I know any better than anyone else?" but you wouldn't say anything.
>
> I also played a maid in *The Reckless Moment* with Joan Bennett where I had to convince the filmmakers that Joan's character wouldn't be driving her car, in which a big part of the film took place, but that Sybil, her maid, would. The initial assumption was that she wouldn't entrust her maid to do so, or that Sybil couldn't possibly know how to drive. Finally, I got to drive. Again, change from within.

In 1982 she told a TV interviewer what happened next on the set of *Reckless*: "[Director Max] Ophuls said [to Joan Bennett], 'Now, start your speech.'

So Joan started, he interrupted. He said, '*Frahn-ces*, do you know Joan's speech?' I said, 'Of course.' He said, 'You do Joan's speech and let her *re-ahkt* to it.' 'Fine.' I got the whole damn thing! *This is what you have to do!* You have to think ahead. You have to go to bed and figure out what it was. What's going to happen, and make it happen!'"[10]

In 1951 Frances was a maid in MGM's *Show Boat*. "Queenie [was] a nice big part, but they wanted me to wear a bandana in that one too. In every stage and film production of *Show Boat*, the black women had always worn bandanas — that was the reason I'd turned down roles for five years — I just couldn't bring myself to do it. Finally I was able to convince them that [here she adopts a tone like a mother talking to a child] *I worked in the house ... inside. I was not out in the cotton field. And so I didn't have to worry about cotton getting in my hair, so it didn't make sense for me to be wearing a bandana.* And they'd seem to go along with it, but all the way through the filming at intervals during the shoot, which lasted somewhere around 15 or 20 weeks, they kept coming back to me [*she laughs*] and dangle a colorful bandana in front of me in all seriousness and say, 'Isn't this pretty? Wouldn't you like to wear this?' And I'd say no. I counted, and I actually refused seventeen bandanas before the filming was over. I'm fairly certain that I was the first person to play that part without wearing one. And I also refused to speak in [black] dialect."

By the time of *Show Boat*, not only was Williams' acting career in full swing, so too was the spirit of social activism first nurtured at Karamu House some thirty years earlier:

"They had jazz jam sessions in Hollywood around '43 or '44, but no blacks could go to them. So Norman Granz and I started a series of jam sessions at the old Reb Spike's studio at Jefferson and Normandie. All kinds of people attended, especially the USC college kids. People had never seen such fully integrated audiences out here that SC art students would come over and sketch them."

So special were the jam sessions that they served as the springboard for Granz's soon-to-be world-wide touring and recording jazz empire, "Jazz at the Philharmonic."

Soon after my husband and I first came out to L.A., we brought out the first art exhibits by famous black artists. For instance, the first one that we did was with Jacob Lawrence and his Migration series at Reb Spikes' where I had done the jam sessions with Norman Granz. All my life I've just been the kind of person who wanted to do useful and meaningful things. The blacks that came from the South and emigrated into the northern cities as part of the Great Migration in the teens became Republicans; but in Cleveland the Republicans treated us so badly that we worked hard to get the Democratic party established. I helped with that. I also helped set up what should also be done now. We called it the Future Outlook League. First we tried to set blacks up in business, but it didn't work. Then what we did was to have them apprenticed in the banks, in produce, all around Cleveland. After they'd gotten their feet wet, we'd secure the money to set them up in businesses of their own.

That was in Cleveland when she was in her early teens. Years later in Hollywood found Williams still socially and politically involved. She served 20 years on the board of the theater union, Actors' Equity; she was similarly involved with the Screen Actors Guild where she played a major role in the formation of a Minority Actors Committee. But almost before it got started, Ronald Reagan, president of SAG at the time, "dissolved it without our even being consulted," said Williams.

These and many commitments to the cause of labor on Williams' part were enacted mostly from the mid–'40s to the mid–'50s, a period of American history during which anti–Red hysteria was at its zenith, with Williams one of the many performers and artists whose lives were profoundly affected by the "witchhunting" activities of McCarthyism and the House Un-American Activities Committee (HUAC). This is the one subject that I discovered could cause Williams' usually jovial demeanor to turn morose.

"It's long and involved. But around the time when I was on the board of Actor's Equity when we started the Theater of Television Authority, this was also when actors were starting to have to sign loyalty oaths saying ... they didn't say whether or not you were a communist ... just a loyalty oath ... and I refused to sign it. I'd been to New York and happened to come back on the same train and became friendly with the then chairman of Actors Equity on the West Coast, Chris O'Brien. He told me his favorite relative was his grandfather, who had apparently been very militant during his time. Then when I was asked to write a loyalty oath, Chris said, 'That's all right Frances, I'll write a letter for you'; and I let him. Then the night before I was to go before the board, I woke up in the middle of the night and said, 'I don't need anyone to write for me, and I certainly don't want a white man to write it.' So I got up and wrote and wrote until it was almost time for the regular Monday morning Equity meeting. It was a very good letter. All the whites were in positions, heads of this, leads in that. I wasn't." At the TV authority executive board, Frances, the only African American member, responded to the dreaded question of the era: "Are you now or have ever been a member of the communist party?" She read:

> Many of my good friends and advisors on this board have begged me not to take this act of unwillingness to sign an affidavit because my career as an actress will be wrecked. Fellow board members, it is now June 20th, 1952. I have not been employed since the first of June 1951. So I have not much career to wreck. I have worked for thirty years studying and working and built three theaters in this country. I cannot help but say that the recently blacklisted people, difficult as their position is, have no real concept of the blacklist. I am not afraid.[11]

Frances was removed from her seat on the TV authority board. Anti-communist hysteria sentiment was in full swing, but failed to deter Williams from aligning herself with social causes which were targeted as subversive and un–American by a lunatic fringe which had come to occupy center stage in American political life. In 1953 she was assistant director on the controversial film *Salt of the Earth*, described by Leonard Maltin in his popular *Movie and Video Guide* as a "[t]aut drama about striking New Mexico mineworkers, with a refreshing pro-feminist viewpoint." As further evidence as to how radically things have changed in the five decades since the making of this well-intentioned work, Maltin goes on to note, "Director [Herbert] Biberman, actor [Will] Geer, producer Paul Jarrico, and screenwriter Michael Wilson were all blacklisted when the film was made."[12]

A phenomenon that seems to have come into play as a result of post–World War II anti-communist hysteria found film studios wary of hiring black actors, for the very reason that doing so was identified with the idea of progressivism. Thus, parts usually given to blacks— maids, chauffeurs, etc.— were often reshaped for white performers; see, for one example, the Caucasian actress who plays Joan Crawford's maid in 1949's *Flamingo Road* who appears to be a graduate of the Butterfly McQueen School of the Dramatic Arts. Songwriter-actor Hoagy Carmichael also seems to have taken up a good deal of this slack, most notably in a 1945 George Raft film, *Johnny Angel*. When Williams was asked about it, she first shook her head "no" tentatively, but then slowly began to reconsider a bit. "Perhaps," she admitted, agreeing with me that her lack of awareness might constitute a classic case of being too close to the trees to see the forest.

One afternoon during our interview sessions, Williams told me she was thinking about showing a Paul Robeson film as a Corner Theater event; but that it was not easy to find one to exhibit because, of the eleven movies the larger-than-life African American actor-singer-political figure had made both here and abroad, nearly all contained major racial flaws. The last film that Robeson made, *Tales of Manhattan* (1942), was an especially sordid effort and was typical of the way filmmakers sometimes fooled Robeson, Williams said, by changing scripts to a more stereotyped mode after he had signed on to appear in it.[13] The one Williams finally settled on was Robeson's next-to-last film, the British *The Proud Valley* (1939), which tended to rise above the level of movie hokum with which Robeson usually became involved. Here he is the key figure in the consolidation of Welsh miners against mine owners who are not so much exploitative as they are simply uncaring.

But, said Williams, Hollywood wasn't the only culprit when it came to Robeson. "One time [NAACP president] Walter White came to town and [Robeson's wife] Essie Robeson was in town too, around the time when Paul was about to start shooting another one of those films that many blacks, myself included, didn't like him doing, especially that horrible *Sanders of the River*. Katherine Dunham had a dinner and we invited Walter and Essie, but nothing came of it. Essie took the attitude that if they had money they would have power. She was not interested in *not* doing it. And Walter didn't fight for it either; he thought she was right. But you *know* what I thought."

Williams first met Robeson in Cleveland at the Cleveland Playhouse and, was in Moscow at the time of his visit there in 1934. She later recalled in an oral history project how impressed the singer had seemed by what he saw there. The same source also contains the following poignant recollection: Hearing that, broken in spirit by right wing political forces, Robeson was experiencing severe financial problems, she told him, "'Paul, I don't want you to worry about that because, damn it, if we all have to stand on street corners with cups, we'll get enough money so you can keep going.' He sat there and cried. I can see the tears coming down his face. He said, 'Oh, baby you don't have to worry about me and money....' This great man crying. Can you see me standing on the corner with a cup? I loved him. He was a great, great man."[14]

In the mid–1940s Williams was involved with several adventuresome little theater groups, including The Cosmo, Actors Lab and The Circle; the board of directors of the latter included Charles Chaplin. "I remember *Variety* saying something like 'Frances is on her bicycle again going from the first act of this to the second act of that.' I was doing a play at the Actor's Lab, then a movie in the day, and radio."

It was around this period of heavy activity that Williams renewed her friendship with Ethel Waters, whom she had first met in New York a few years earlier:

> Ethel was getting ready to do a tour of the play *Mamba's Daughter* out here. We went down to see them rehearse and at one point she said to me, "I don't have anything decent to wear in the way of costumes. Look in that wardrobe and see if you help me." I helped her piece together something halfway decent, at any rate, from this disastrous grab bag of shrunken, wadded-up costumes, and she was so grateful that she said, "Why don't you go up the coast up with me and be my understudy?" I did and we got to become good friends fairly quickly, but even then I'd look up and see her looking at me in this funny way, like she was still trying to figure out if I might really be an enemy. She'd been really roughed up coming up in show business, and she just couldn't bring herself to trust people very much. But she was really very kind, generous and loyal ... and perceptive. I loved her dearly.

By the way her face lit up when she talked about him, I got the sense that none of her many friendships had ever given her more pleasure than the one she shared with W.E.B. Du Bois (1868–1963), the first African American to earn a Ph.D. from Harvard, who then went on to become the most beloved and admired black activist of his time.

"I met Du Bois when I was going to Swarthmore in 1924. W.E.B. had been going around the country with the Nigerian who was the head of the YMCA in South Africa. And he [the YMCA executive] had two sons who he wanted to be educated in the United States. And he asked Du Bois to go around the

U.S. to help him find a school that would take them, but everywhere they went, they wouldn't take them. Then someone said, 'Ah! We know where you should go, you should go to a Quaker school. The Quakers are the best people around.' So they did and the Quakers ended up treating them just like everyone else had been treating them [*laughs ironically*]. They were both very disappointed and W.E.B. came after that to give a lecture at Swarthmore, and I happened to be there, and he spoke about this thing that had happened, and he said, 'And the Quakers just wouldn't do anything.' People suddenly got very angry because he had just insulted his hosts." Insult his hosts? By that, did Williams mean that by excoriating one group of white people that Du Bois had by extension insulted all?

"Exactly. And when I heard these people acting like this, I went up on stage at intermission, introduced myself...." Again Williams laughed; this time at the temerity of a young African American college freshman introducing herself to the man who was perhaps the era's most prominent African American leader, and telling him:

"'I have a little jitney and I'm going up town and get some beer. Would you like to go with me?' He was this gourmet in every phase of living. I never thought he would go, but we went to town and that's how our friendship started. Years later my husband bought me a custom-made Jaguar. This was wayyy before people had Jags. When the light changed, you were already at the next light. Anyway, a friend of mine went to New York and was at a dinner party with W.E.B. and his wife Shirley and my friend said, 'By the way, Frances now has a Jaguar.' Everyone went on and ate dinner and when they got ready to go home they were in the lobby and W.E.B turned and said, 'By the way, how does Frances handle that Jaguar? On a leash?'" Williams said it made her supremely happy that Du Bois thought her capable of trotting around Hollywood with a jaguar on a leash, signifying that she had Gone Hollywood. "I always told myself that if I don't make it here I'm going to get me a horse and buggy, and preach. Can't you just see me doing that? ... The Rev Williams," she chuckled.

Williams made it, though, and not just by the skin of her teeth; but that still wasn't enough for her: "I'm an actor-*activist*. I think every artist has to be. Like Langston Hughes used to say, "The moon and stars and trees are beautiful, but at this point in our history we must say a little more."[15]

*   *   *

In late 1994 Frances told me in a frank but by no means maudlin way that she was tired and wished she could "just go through a door and never have to come back through it." Lately she had begun to tire more easily, had sometimes begun to nod off at inopportune times, and had recently been hospitalized for a spill she'd taken. Nevertheless, in September 1994 she threw a birthday bash for herself, one that was more typical of the sort associated with round numbers, to celebrate her 89th year. And when her longtime friend Libby Clark asked her why she didn't wait until she'd rounded off nine decades to hold such an affair, Frances replied: "My darling, I just might not be here when I'm ninety."[16]

As usual, she was right; a few days later Frances suffered a serious stroke; and on the following January 2, she died. At the close of its session on January 9, 1995, the California Assembly adjourned in her memory and a few weeks later her friends held a celebration of Frances' life at L.A.'s Southwest College Little Theater that easily passed for the 90th birthday of a head of state. Among the hundreds there to celebrate here were Rosa Parks, L.A. city councilman Mark Ridley-Thomas, state senator Diane Watson, and friends from the performing arts, Tim Reid and Daphne Maxwell-Reid (of TV's *Frank's Place*), actors Brock Peters and Beah Richards and three-fifths of the singing group the Fifth Dimension who Frances had coached in acting and theatre movement in the early 1970s.

C. Bernard Jackson, the founder of L.A.'s Inner City Cultural Center, told about his first encounter with Williams: It was on the telephone and Frances had called up to plant the bug of just such a place as the cultural center in his ear:

> FRANCES: "Is this C. Bernard Jackson?"
> JACKSON: "Yes, but my friends call me Jack."
> FRANCES: "This is Frances Williams. My friends call me Frances."[17]

The exchange brought down the house, with the laughter led by those familiar with Frances' extra-dry sense of humor. On and on the tributes continued for more than three hours: Buddy Collette, the grand old man of modern jazz, played; a West African drum ensemble performed; and singer Marilyn McCoo read a poem written in honor of Frances by her godson, James Patterson, about the Russian film *The Circus* in which Frances had appeared. And then a videotape of Maya Angelou speaking — shot in L.A. a few days before the memorial — was shown; one with all the impact of anything "live" that came before or after. Visibly shaken and tearful, Angelou spoke from the heart:

"Wisdom when it is matched with kindness — the two make for an unbeatable team. And all of us who love Frances are wiser and kinder because of her. She encouraged me once to paint my house. I had been living in West Africa and returned to the United States in the '60s. And I had been living the life of luxury in West Africa. Lots of things, material things. And I had to leave Ghana with $500 which of course didn't go very far. I came down to Los Angles and Frances offered me one side of the front house, the duplex, there's a very rich name for what it was. I think it was $50 a month." But Angelou found herself missing the good life of Ghana and becoming depressed. When she went to Williams with her problems, Frances told her to buy some wall paint: She said, "What you need to do is paint your house." Angelou followed Williams' advice and began painting—first the living room, then its floor and ceiling, then the bathroom, the kitchen, the porch, the lamps. "Everything the brush touched," Angelou painted. "I almost painted myself," she laughed, adding: "Then, my house was shining and the depression was gone, gone, forever gone. I have noticed since then, since 1966, everywhere in the world I have lived if I find myself slipping into a storm of depression I don't paint the house, but I wash walls. I get a pan, a pail, some 409, some soap and water and I wash the walls. I wash all the negative thoughts away. I know that's what Frances was telling me."[18]

Next came a videotape in which Frances spoke to TV interviewer Robert Price: "When you live *now* it's very difficult to remember the past because each day is very full ... it's an ongoing struggle. It never stops. And if you stop, then you're putting down the wrong things. We've got to keep struggling. It's the only way you're going to succeed. And you have to get together and do it."[19]

Heeding her own advice, Williams joined the picket lines of the Progressive Party in the early 1940s to "Stop World War Two"; she helped found L.A.'s first Equity theater and served on the board of Actor's Equity for twenty years; she was also instrumental in starting: L.A.'s first black theatre company, the Negro Arts Theatre, the American Indian Theatre, and the East-West Players. Frances was also the first black woman to run for the Los Angeles City Council and for the California State Assembly. Small wonder then that she preferred to be called an "actor-activist."

In 1991 Frances was to fly to Detroit to speak before the National Negro Labor Council to help celebrate its fortieth anniversary. She astonished me, saying she was traveling unassisted out of curiosity to see if she could handle the changing of planes at the hub stop in Denver in her wheelchair, etc. It was this assertiveness and general daily lack of fear—typical of Frances—plus the fact that her life arced back to the first truly important stages of black entertainment, i.e., Cook; Williams and Walker; Cole and Johnson; James Reese Europe, et al., that caused me to feel such Twilight of the Gods pangs at her passing. Typical of Frances, too, was how passionately she wanted to make sure that others understood—as she did—the importance of African Americans to the overall cultural scheme of things. Without her wisdom and encouragement, this book could never have been written.

11

Stops Along the Way
Three Cities

New York

In the show business scheme of things—because of differing regional laws and traditions—the sense of place held special meaning for black entertainers during this era. There were many performers, for example, who absolutely refused to stick so much as even one toe south of the Mason-Dixon Line. In his memoirs, *Music on My Mind*, pianist Willie "The Lion" Smith avers that he turned down the chance to play the black vaudeville circuit "Toby Time" because in most theaters, "you had to make up in the toilet."[1] For Smith and other black performers like him, New York—with its city-within-a-city, Harlem—was "where it was at." One can imagine the sort of excitement that must have been felt by bush leaguers of black vaudeville, hearing for the first time those magical words: "Ladies and gentlemen, get your coats and hats. In five minutes we'll be arriving at Grand Central Station." *This* was the Big Time.

*   *   *

In 1936 the Cotton Club—founded by gangster elements in 1923 at the corner of 142nd Street and Lenox Avenues—moved downtown to the Broadway-Times Square area. Everything else, though, remained pretty much unchanged; including the feathers and fans, and legs flying non-stop to great music by Ellington and Calloway. Another tradition that remained was the painful reality of the Club's whites-only policy. In the case of the dancing Nicholas Brothers, they may have been moving too fast—and been too young—to notice the glaring irony of it all. They were a sensation almost from the moment they turned professional in 1930; by 1937 when they starred in *Tall, Tan and Terrific* at the Cotton Club—at the respective ages of 18 and 14—Fayard and Harold were already old hands at the glamorous night spot, having first taken the place by storm uptown in Harlem five years earlier.

"When we did *Tall, Tan and Terrific* at the Cotton Club in 1937, Harold and I were doubling. We were in *Babes in Arms and* the Cotton Club show as well," Fayard (who died in 2006) recalled to me. "We only had a few days to rehearse for the Cotton Club, but during that time George Ballanchine, who choreographed *Babes in Arms*, came to the club to watch us work, I seem to recall. It was really something doing both shows at the same time. After we finished *Babes in Arms* at the Shubert, we went to the Cotton Club to do the midnight show. We had a tutor and went to school every day. We would get home so late that we'd sleep until early afternoon. The tutor would come at three o'clock in the afternoon and after we finished we went back to bed."[2]

Fayard recalled that — because of their youth — he and Harold might have been among the few of her fellow performers at the Cotton Club to have ever seen a sweeter side to Ethel Waters. One of the handful of American entertainers unquestionably deserving of the term "legendary," Waters behind the scenes was equally as noted for her dark moods and unpredictable temperament as she was for her stunning interpretations of songs. Nicholas speculated:

> She liked us because we were kids and didn't represent the same kind of threat that adults did. She called us her boys. She didn't mind us getting a lot of applause. At least, not *too* much. But anybody else ... oh, man! I remember one night at the Cotton Club they were doing a tribute to Bill Robinson and she was there, all the Broadway and movie stars were there to greet Bill Robinson. I was sitting in the box with her and Bill was on the stage. He said, "I would like to say a word about my good friend Ethel Waters. Ethel, who would have believed that you and I would be the leaders of our race?" She lit up, stood up and said, "Oh, thank you, thank you." And people applauded. I said to myself, "This is great, this is great, they're finally friends." And then she went back stage. I stayed in the box. A little while after that, Bill came over to my table and said to me, "Can you imagine that?" I said, "What?" And he said, "After I praised her, she came backstage and *still* called me a son of a bitch."[3]

Fayard Nicholas thought he even knew the reason behind the enmity between Waters and Ellington that finally erupted full force during their tandem appearance in *Cotton Club Express*:

> So the story goes, it was Ellington's idea to have her to come in and do the Cotton Club when she first appeared there, and yet ... she demanded billing over him. Nobody *ever* got billing over Ethel Waters. And she got it. I think that was the thing that started the feud. I remember in the Cotton Club when she would do her act, the spotlight was tight on her face. She was a great actress. Certain songs she would sing, tears would come to her eyes. Even Ethel Barrymore recognized her greatness.[4]

You couldn't get much more powerful than Ethel Waters was at the Cotton Club, as she proved one night in 1937. Duke Ellington wasn't playing her

Opposite: Cotton Club program, 1937.

music the way Waters wanted and she walked off the stage the opening night of *Cotton Club Express*. The next night found Waters back in the show, but with an outfit of her own led by her fiancé, trumpet player Eddie Mallory. That she could get away with it demonstrates just how big — and complicated — Waters was.

The original Cotton Club uptown in Harlem began operation on the second floor site of a nightclub, the Club Deluxe, that had previously been owned by black heavyweight champ Jack Johnson. "Decorated in jungle decor, with a proscenium stage, dance floor, and seating capacity of 700 and renamed the Cotton Club," writes Desmond Arthur In *The Harlem Renaissance*, "the club opened in the fall of 1923.... [T]he chorus girls [one of whom was Lena Horne] were uniformly 'high yaller,' tall, and under twenty-one. All of the performers were black, but the club enforced a whites-only policy for customers and a $2.50 cover charge to keep out the undeserving poor."[5]

If anything *did* change with the relocation to the Times Square area, it was the caliber of the entertainers, which became greater than ever. Louis Armstrong had never appeared at the Cotton Club when it was in Harlem, but at the Broadway and 48th Street location he became a regular along with Waters, Ellington, Cab Calloway and Bill "Bojangles" Robinson. For *Tall, Tan and Terrific*, the Club's show for the Fall of '37 (an engagement he eventually had to postpone), Robinson was to receive $3,500 a week, more money than anyone had ever been paid before for a night club appearance, regardless of race.[6] As for the mobsters — led by the notorious Owney Madden — involved in the running of the Cotton Club: "Yes, it's true they were gangsters," said Fayard Nicholas, who laughingly added, "BUT they were *nice* gangsters."[7]

*   *   *

Prior to the coming of the Apollo Theatre in 1934, the Lincoln Theater, on 135th Street between Lenox and Seventh Avenue, along with the larger Lafayette, were the two big-time black theaters in Harlem. Built in 1908, the Lincoln was the longest operating theater in the community specializing in staging shows for black audiences. The Lafayette Theater, located at 132nd Street and Seventh Avenue (now Adam Clayton Powell Boulevard), was, during the teens and '20s, another important hub of African American theatrical and social activity (about 200,000 blacks were shoehorned into the few square blocks surrounding the theater). This 2,000-seat showplace, where all the biggest black-oriented shows played, was built in 1911 and was also the home of the Lafayette Players. During their seasons, the Players opened a new play every Monday afternoon — a total of some 250 plays from 1915 to 1928 during their residency at the theater. Not only were original plays, musicals and classics performed, but recently shuttered successes from Broadway were also staged utilizing scenery from the original productions: works such as *Within the Law, Third Degree* and *The Wolf*, with the all-white casts being replaced by Harlem troupers. The Players are remembered today for the significant role they played in the art and literary movement which has since come to known as the Harlem Renaissance.[8]

In front of the Lafayette (now a church, and unrecognizable due to the ravages of "renovation") grew the theatrical good luck charm, the Tree of Hope. Unemployed black entertainers, both known and unknown, made daily pilgrimages there to touch its bark with hopes of getting a job. Talent agents who were casting shows also came by the talismanic tree to check out the people congregated there. So even if you didn't happen to be especially superstitious, just hanging out at the Tree of Hope might land you an engagement *somewhere*.[9]

Around the corner from the Lafayette on 132nd Street was Big John's, a restaurant and bar (with a piano in the back) that featured good cheap food. It was run by a man who was a soft touch for performers down on their luck. In a basement, also just around the corner from the Lafayette, was the Rhythm Club. There you could almost always find piano players like James P. Johnson, Fats Waller or Willie "The Lion" Smith engaged in "cutting" contests, i.e., trying to outplay one another.

During the Roaring '20s and equally speedy early '30s, along with the theaters there were also hundreds of night clubs of every configuration and legal permutation imaginable in Harlem. Many were not designed to meet the needs of African Americans living in Harlem, most of whom were working class and couldn't have afforded them even if the entrance policy hadn't been so racist; but of whites from other parts of New York and the country. Most of them possessed either a decided *nostalgie de la boue* (i.e., slumming) or a strong interest in intimate race mixing.[10] Or both. In 1932 the noted African American illustrator E. Simms Campbell created what has since become a famous *Nightclub Map of Harlem* which "indicates the places that are open all night.... [T]he only important omission is the location of the various speakeasies but since there are about 500 of them you won't have much trouble." Among the more colorfully named of the spots are the Radium Club which featured a "big breakfast every Sunday morning 4 or 5 am"; the Yeah Man; and the Club Hot-Cha ("ask for Clarence").[11]

*   *   *

The theater was known as Hurtig and Seamon's Burlesque before its name change in 1934 to the Apollo; but owner Frank Schiffman, after purchasing it in 1936 and recognizing the community's need for such, turned it into not just the flagship of black entertainment, but a symbol to progressive young white entertainers as well. Legend persists that it was the first stop for Elvis Presley on his initial visit to New York in 1955. The same held true for the Beatles ten years later.[12] It was also at the Apollo in 1943 that singer-musician Valaida Snow (see Chapter 4) took up her career once again after being released by the Nazis.

In 1939, the *New York World Telegram* described to its predominantly white readership, in tones more befitting an excursion to Mars, a visit to this citadel of great African American entertainment (still standing and operative today)[13]:

> The Apollo is a sort of uptown Met dedicated to furious jazz, coffee-colored chorus girls and grinning drawling comedians ... the first stand and last jump-off for the large caravanserai of Harlem entertainers.... The theater stands behind a gaudy neon sign on West 125th Street, between a haberdasher and a leather-goods store. The sidewalk outside is a favored location for old men lugging sandwich signs and pitchmen unloading razor blades and patent medicines. You buy your ticket at a sidewalk booth (from fifteen cents mornings to a fifty-cent top Wednesday and Saturday nights) and enter through a narrow lobby lines with bathroom tiles, glistening mirrors and photographs of such Harlem idols as Ethel Waters and Louis Armstrong, all affectionately inscribed to the Apollo. At the candy counter you can buy chocolate bars and peanuts but no gum. That is to protect the seats. In the lobby, three or four colored boys generally waiting for their dates to show up.[14]

There was hardly a single black act exemplifying the new teen sound that didn't play the Apollo during the formative years of rock music: Motown Revues, James Brown, Little Richard, along with many white performers, including Buddy Holly, Bobby Darin and Jerry Lee Lewis. In the film *The Buddy Holly Story* the notion is advanced that Holly and his Chirpin' Crickets were booked at the theater under the mistaken notion that they were black. This may have been merely a case of dramatic license, for the theater's astute Frank Schiffman probably never booked anyone without knowing who they were.

The linchpin of the Apollo's programming was its Wednesday amateur night contest which had its beginnings as "Harlem Amateur Hour " at yet another theater — the Lafayette — in 1933. By 1954 it is estimated that some 15,000 people had come from all over the country just to *audition* for a chance at the first prize — a week-long engagement after four first-place wins. Getting their start on the Amateur Night were such performers as Ella Fitzgerald, Sarah Vaughan, Dionne Warwick and Frankie Lymon. Since 1933, the job of emceeing the rambunctious parade of show business hopefuls — often the evening took on the character of something more akin to a demolition derby — had been handled mostly by Willie Bryant (of Whitman Sisters fame) and singer-dancer Ralph Cooper. Cooper, something of an institution himself, was on the opening night bill at the Apollo on January 26, 1934, and before that had emceed the original "Harlem Amateur Hour" at the Lafayette. He remained associated with the Apollo on and off, emceeing shows there and acting as an unofficial spokesman for the New York landmark until his death in the summer of 1992.[15]

By the 1950s, the theater was one of the last in the country to present a film and stage-show package on a regular basis. It was a wild audience at the Apollo. If they liked you, you were probably capable of pleasing any audience in the world. It was also one of the hippest of crowds, one whose savage and wicked sense of humor could prove daunting to the most well-schooled of performers. Even the film portion of the show was not always safe. The author of this book visited the Apollo many times during the early 1960s. One occasion especially stands out not so much for the stage show, headed by Dizzy Gillespie, but the screen presentation, *Angel Baby*, an especially ripe piece of *cinema à clef* about evangelist Aimee Semple McPherson. The film was playing downtown as well, where audiences undoubtedly sat on their hands, taking in all of its camp awfulness without so much as a whimper. But the audience at the Apollo hooted and howled at the unintentionally funny film in all the right spots, killing time until Dizzy Gillespie. Movie studios would seldom rent to the Apollo anything but the very worst of its current product, but it wasn't these Hollywood hand-me-downs the crowd came to see; it was the stage shows. And while these were in progress, the crowd could become both vocal and abusive toward both professionals and non-pro ... especially the latter. "Sometimes," wrote Langston Hughes, "an Apollo amateur hour can be almost as moving and exciting as a Spanish bull fight — except that in a bull fight not always does a matador get killed. But every amateur night at the Apollo, some one or more of the participants are 'done away with' in plain sight, 'killed'— literally shot — but fortunately with a blank cartridge."[16]

During its nearly forty-year heyday, almost every great black star played the Apollo, with many doing so at the peak of their earning power out of a feeling of obligation to "the community." But you had to go prepared; according to Sammy Davis, Jr.: "You didn't go into the Copa lightweight; they'd break your legs. But at the Apollo they'd break your heart."[17]

The portrait of the Apollo that appeared in the 1939 *New York World-Telegram* (an "uptown Met dedicated to furious jazz, coffee-colored chorus girls and grinning, drawling comedians") was typical for the times.[18] And this two-dimensional *naïf-primitif* depiction by whites was the rule when it came to African American show business in general. Given the social and geographical barriers of the era, there was simply no way that white writers— even those with an inside track —could get beneath the surface of African American entertainment and know about the years of struggle most blacks endured in their passage from provincial obscurity to the mainstream fame of the Apollo and the Cotton Club. Phenomena such as the T.O.B.A. and the hard times endured by the likes of Ethel Waters, Bill Robinson and others in their climb to the top were simply beyond the pale of white comprehension. Just as unfathomable would have been the route taken by African American singer-actress Georgette Harvey in her circumlocutive journey from the steppes of Russia to a role in the original *Porgy and Bess* on Broadway[19]; or

by onetime bordello pianist Nora Holt (see Chapter 5) in her splashy arrival
on the scene of the Harlem Renaissance.

Chicago

While the Harlem Renaissance may have secured more lasting recognition, Chicago also had an African American renaissance on its South Side.
An eight-mile long, mile-and-a-half wide section of the city, Bronzeville (as
the area was affectionately known in its heyday) at one time held 90 percent
of Chicago's black population and was not only the crucible for three generations of great blues players—from Muddy Waters and Sonny Boy Williamson
right on up to the present time — it was also: where Richard Wright wrote
Native Son; the home of the influential black newspaper, the *Chicago Defender*;
and the place where, starting in 1912 with filmmaker William Foster and his
The Railroad Porter, the very first films by blacks for blacks were made.
Given this fertile Midwestern soil, it is not so surprising that a large number
of those represented in this book — including the Whitman Sisters, Nora Holt,
and Dinah Washington — all operated out of Chicago at one time or another.

Black Chicago along with its citizens, activities and achievements, from the
city's 1920s heyday through the 1940s, was covered widely in such mainstream
publications as the *Saturday Evening Post*, *American Monthly* and *Holiday* magazine. In fact, because of the city's U.S. centrality and its much more proletar-
ian disposition ("Hog Butcher to the World"), its black artistic renaissance was
just beginning to shift into high gear at the point in time when the Harlem
Renaissance, deeply affected by the Great Depression, was grinding to a halt.

*   *   *

On April 29, 1933, the switch was thrown in Chicago opening the two-
year World's Fair–like Century of Progress Exhibition whose attractions
included, according to one report, "a partial reconstruction of a walled city
in China, a golden-roofed lama from Jehol, a picturesque nunnery of UxMal
representing the Zenith of Mayan culture and a teahouse from Japan." Singer
Herb Jeffries (still active as of the second edition of this book) remembers:

> I went to from Detroit to Chicago to check out the World's Fair there. Back in
> Detroit I'd been singing in dime-a-dance joints and that was pretty much it for
> me. Chicago was like the beginning of the world for me. I've been to a few
> fairs—Seattle, New York — but nothing ever like that. There was a wide outer
> drive for cars, four and five lanes wide. Everyone was working. It was alive like
> I've never ever seen a city ... not even Paris, where I lived for ten years, was as
> alive as Chicago during the 1933 World's Fair. Before too long I got a job singing
> with the Earl Hines band, and I remember the Dillinger slaying on Indiana
> Avenue in 1934, engineered by the Feds. We all got word of it ten minutes after
> it happened; it was all over the place — on the telephones, the radio. We were

all living at the nearby Trenier Hotel where a lot of black entertainers stayed, and I jumped on the running board of a car and went around there to where it happened to take a look. The blood was still splattered all over the movie theater, all over the sidewalk because, boy, they just mowed that guy Dillinger down. I can still see in my mind the tear sheets of the picture that was playing there — *Manhattan Melodrama* — and the glass over them shot all out. They had obviously planned this whole thing very meticulously because otherwise they would have killed the woman in the box-office. I'll never forget that as long as I live.[20]

It was against this backdrop a Chicago still operating in the early 1930s up to Roaring Twenties speed, that Dave's Café became one of the most popular of all the Chicago "black and tans" — clubs that encouraged a racially mixed clientele. This was by no means as new — nor as socially progressive — as it sounds, for black and tans entailed more than a touch of exploitation, and had been around since at least the turn of the century.* Stage shows at clubs such as Dave's featured black performers, just as did New York's Cotton Club. But while the Cotton Club's audience was lily white, Dave's was integrated. So, when carloads of café society "swells" pulled up in front of the club, they were there to see the "show" in the audience as much as the one on stage. Dave's was located on Garfield Boulevard, on the city's South Side, which had become, as a result of the great migration of 200,000 blacks from the South between 1910 and 1930,[21] one of the largest concentrations of African Americans in the country. The area was alive with bars, lounges and neighborhood taverns, most of which operated 24 hours a day. At night, the quarter was aglow with the neon of these establishments, which ran the gamut from holes in the wall to showplaces offering big-name entertainment. Dave's, the most swinging of the lot, was operated for owner Dave Hieligh by his sons Mike and Johnny; and by one Sam "Golf Bag" Hunt. The mob's gambling boss for the entire South Side, Hunt had acquired his nickname from the habit of carrying around a shotgun concealed in a golf bag. He could usually be found in the building next door to the café overseeing gambling operations which, though illegal, were never disturbed by the (well paid-off) authorities.[22] Since, for all practical purposes, gambling was taking place on the same premises as the entertainment, Dave's possessed an atmosphere that was distinctly Las Vegas–like. It was also the only night spot in Chicago with a balcony — a feature used to full effect in the staging of pocket-sized extravaganzas. Here is part of the *Chicago Defender*'s review of the all-black-cast show that patrons at Dave's Café viewed during one week in 1935:

> [Leonard Reed's] latest vehicle brings us back to the days of the dreaded World War. The climax is the presentation of the American flag in tableau. Dainty Marcella Wilson was in male attire and gave Earl Tucker a few lessons in the

*In his novel *The Autobiography of an Ex-Colored Man*, written in 1912, James Weldon Johnson makes it clear that in New York City, such operations were already in existence in the early 1900s.

art of Snake Hip dancing. Carie Marrero, the little Cuban beauty, shook her pretty head as she told us "She Never Had a Chance"; now that's too bad, we'll see she gets one. Chicago's own Mae Alix told of "After All These Years" she learned to love, we wonder who is the lucky fellow. The Three Tan Tippers are a trio of dance boys that really click. Pedro Lane, the beau brummell of dancers, is the heart throb of the female set as he does his strut. As a dramatic reader, Clarence Weems the M.C. has few equals.[23]

The shows at Dave's, which ran slightly over an hour, changed every four weeks, with each being the equivalent of producing a Broadway musical once a month. What *really* put these productions over, according to Herb Jeffries, was the impact made by the chorus line:

"Leonard Reed [the choreographer] had this long line of gorgeous brown skin girls laying heavy taps down — actually *hoofing*. I'd seen chorus girls at the Regal Theater doing their kicks and stuff, but at Dave's they were *laying down iron*. It was the damnedest thing you ever saw. It was the talk of Chicago."[24]

Outstripping the production at Dave's Café, however, was the show both inside and *outside* of the Grand Terrace, Chicago's answer to the Cotton Club. Jeffries worked at the Terrace with pianist-bandleader Earl Hines. "I can remember the pageantry of the wealthy pimps driving up to the front of the Grand Terrace in their Rolls-Royces and European cars," says Jeffries. "Chicago was a wide-open town, but if you didn't play ball with the mob you could end up in a cement suit in the river."[25]

The Terrace ostensibly belonged to entrepreneur Ed Fox, but in reality the elaborate show place had been taken over shortly after it opened by the Al Capone gang, and handed over to the care of Capone's brother Ralph (aka Mimi). Fox stayed on as a front and manager for the operations, but Capone began taking a large chunk of the profits from him in exchange for "protection."

The Capone gang had a stranglehold on bootlegging activities in Chicago, but chose not to push the law too far by running the club as a speakeasy. Besides, nearly all the bring-your-own-booze that was eventually quaffed in the club was of Capone manufacture. Unlike most places, they didn't sell whiskey under the table at the Grand Terrace. You came in with your own bottle (of Al Capone–bootlegged hooch), and they'd serve you a cup of tea and you poured it in. Capone used to come in the Terrace and always would sit in the same seat down front dead center. He had two men sitting on either side of him with guns and anyone who approached his table knew what was going to happen if they got too close, too fast.[26] Of course, gangsterism and bathtub gin were not exclusive to Chicago, with the New York Owney Madden mob (which ran Harlem's Cotton Club) being almost a mirror image of Capone's Midwestern "franchise."

Just like at the Cotton Club, all the entertainers at the Terrace were black, with one of the most popular being comic Billy Mitchell, who specialized in risqué material and was well-liked by the mob. One of Mitchell's routines was supposedly about an automobile: "I can't get her started. She won't turn over for me...." But the audience at the Grand Terrace knew what it was *really* about and they loved it. Another started out, "Two old maids in a folding bed...."

But his most popular routine was the "The Bed Bug Song." He sang: "The bed bugs were marching. I turned on the light, and one took a bite. And they kept marching on."[27] Then he'd hop around the stage on one leg like a cripple. On paper seventy years later it may not sound like much, but the crowd at the Terrace loved it, especially Al Capone and his henchmen.

Opening in 1928 at the corner of Oakwood Boulevard and South Side Parkway, the Terrace occupied the site of a former movie theater and was the grandest of the many popular entertainment spots in the city. Chicago, during the 1920s and the 1930s, was nearly the equal of New York City when it came to the quality and quantity of its night life. Such now-fabled night spots as the Sunset Café, the Savoy Ballroom and the Plantation Club all exclusively featured African American entertainers. The caliber of the talent at the Grand Terrace was the near-equal of the Cotton Club and included such stars as Bill Robinson, Buck and Bubbles, and Ethel Waters. Stairs bookended both sides of the Terrace bandstand and down them "parade girls" trouped, while sixteen chorus girls strutted their stuff on the raised platform in front of the band. Mirrors and blue lights formed the main motif of the decorating scheme, and patrons sat on different terrace-like levels, where once the theater balcony had been.

On February 4 of 1928 — the same year the Grand Terrace opened — *the* theater serving the African American community, the million dollar Moorish showplace, the Regal, went into operation. As the Grand Terrace was to New York's Cotton Club, so was the Regal to Harlem's Apollo Theatre. Located at 147th Street and South Parkway, the 3,500-seat house was in the grand movie palace tradition; the stage could hold four hundred; the lobby could accommodate 1,500.

The premiere featured Cab Calloway and bandleader Fess Williams, among others; opening night found a portion of the theater's ceiling caving in, but it was scarcely a harbinger of things to come. Much like New York's Apollo, the Regal operated nearly around the clock, seven days a week, 52 weeks a years, meeting the entertainment needs of the African American community in Chicago, and serving as performing home to nearly every great black star on the scene for nearly the next four decades.

When it came to African American entertainment, Chicago was second to no other city in America. The first films made for, with and by African Americans, were shot here, beginning in 1912, under the supervision of *Chicago Defender* theatrical columnist William Foster.[28] Historically, Chicago is considered to have been the first stop of jazz when it first made its fabled way up the river from New Orleans. Upon arrival there, the new music was welcomed by the first wave of African Americans who had also recently made their way to Chicago as part of the Great Migration, fleeing oppressive conditions in the South. (The city's black population jumped 148 percent from 44,000 to 109,000 in the years between 1910 and 1920). As a result, Chicago would end up with a far greater number of theaters and other types of entertainment venues catering to blacks than even New York (unquestionably a much greater number of theaters there were owned by African Americans than in any other city in the U.S.).[29] And Chicago was generally where acts either started out or ended up on their tours of the black theatrical booking circuit, the T.O.B.A. That is unquestionably why Chicago became home base to such a large number of African American entertainment professionals from the teens onward through the 1950s. The list included (at one time or another) the Whitman Sisters, Nora Ray Holt, Louis Armstrong, Earl Hines, Will Marion Cook (when he was, for a time during the early part of the century, the musical director of the popular Pekin Theatre) and hundreds more, famous and not so famous. *And* it was where singer Dinah Washington first staked her claim as the once and future queen of the blues.

Los Angeles

"You're going out a youngster but you've got to come back a star," Warner Baxter shouts at a frazzled Ruby Keeler in the classic 1933 "backstage musical," *42nd Street*. Ten minutes of screen time later, that is precisely what happens to Keeler's character, the dubiously gifted chorine "Peggy Sawyer"; she becomes an overnight sensation. But real life can occasionally be found imitating cinematic artifice; witness one spring evening in 1951 at Ciro's, located on Hollywood's Sunset Strip. It was the night of the Academy Awards and the popular spot was chockablock with hipsters and power players. The star attraction was Janis Paige, just peaking in Hollywood musicals as a kind of flip, singing-dancing version of Rosalind Russell. But it's doubtful there were more than a handful in attendance who had ever so much as heard of (much less come to view) the opening act — the Will Mastin Trio featuring Sammy Davis, Jr. Thirty-five years later Davis — echoing his "Bojangles" speech of a previous chapter — reminisced about that opening night at Ciro's on the TV magazine show *Entertainment Tonight*:

"I knew it that night, this is my last chance to do it. Do it now if you're ever gonna do it. Or it's small time the rest of your life. You'll be workin' little joints around and never get that big opportunity 'cause this is as close as you're gonna get. At the end of 40 minutes the whole club was cheering, we walked off and the first persons that we ran into ... right behind us came Jerry Lewis and Dean [Martin]. [Lewis] hugged me and said, 'Hey! It happened for us and I'm so glad it happened for you.'"[30]

So successful was this opening night that the next evening found head-liner Paige demoted to second place on the bill. The Trio now being touted all over town as an overnight sensation was, in fact, an act in which Davis had spent more than two decades knocking about mostly all-black venues— bookended by his father and Mastin — honing his performance skills. In fact, they had made many of their Los Angeles appearances in just the kind of "lit-tle joints" Davis was beginning to increasingly fear; located on and around the city's Central Avenue only a handful of miles, but, measured otherwise, light years away from Ciro's.

By day, Central Avenue was a four-mile-long artery—comprised of fur-niture stores, five-and-dimes, doctor and dentist offices, hardwares, restau-rants, barbecue joints, etc.—just like any other busy commercial street (as it still tends to be).[31] But when the sun set over Central, the avenue metamor-phosized into a jumping thoroughfare that made even the white, mainstream Sunset Strip look positively Victorian by comparison.

Up until the 1920s, Los Angeles— including Central —fairly rolled up its sidewalks when the sun went down. Granted there were perfectly opulent night spots such as Sebastian's Cotton Club in Culver City (where Louis Arm-strong made headlines when he was busted for pot one November night in 1930),[32] the Cocoanut Grove and the Hotel Roosevelt Grill. By and large, though, such locales were few and far between. Part of the problem had to do with L.A.'s being a city without a center. Also, one suspects that many of the hundreds of thousands of migrants who arrived there in the first two decades of the century had other things on their mind than making night time whoopee. In the 1930s, however, the population grew denser, the geograph-ical black holes fewer; and by the early 1940s with the coming of the Second World War, people of all nationalities, races, and backgrounds began stream-ing into the area seeking work in defense plants and other war-related indus-tries.[33] By the same token, entertainment professionals were also arriving by the trainload to meet the needs of night club and other entertainment ven-ues that were opening up by the hundreds. For African American entertain-ment professionals, part of the lure also was the booming wartime film industry which held out abundant on-screen work — albeit mostly in stereo-typed roles.

The city's transformation into a wide-awake round-the-clock metrop-olis was now more or less complete, and no part of the city was more alive than Central Avenue. It stretched from downtown area streets numbered in the teens all the way past Watts and into the low hundreds. The heart of the action was the block of Central between 42nd and 43rd Streets. There one could find jazz musicians strolling shoulder to shoulder with slumming movie stars, and gangsters rubbing elbows with cops walking the beat (one of whose number was future L.A. mayor Tom Bradley).

All up one side and down this main stem (and nearby on such crisscrossing thoroughfares as Washington and Vernon Boulevard) mile after mile during the 1940s and into the early '50s, there flourished countless theaters and night spots bearing such evocative names as the Brownskin Café, the Club Zombie, the Crystal Tea Room, the Jungle Room, and Dynamite Jackson's— owned by the former California heavyweight boxing champion. There were also Lovejoy's (advertised as the home of Big Leg Chicken), Ivy's Chicken Shack (owned by Duke Ellington vocalist Ivy Anderson) and the more prosaically named, but just as popular — if not more so— Down Beat, Last Word, and Memo clubs.[34]

There were also at least a half-dozen ballrooms such as the Egyptian and Elk's Halls that rocked their upwards of a thousand-plus patrons with the music of Lionel Hampton, Erskine Hawkins and other frenzied purveyors of swing-turned-big band bop. Elk's Hall, near the intersection of Santa Barbara (now Martin Luther King Boulevard), was also the site of virtuoso tenor-sax battles between Dexter Gordon and Wardell Gray preserved for posterity by the famed two-sided 78 rpm release "The Hunt," and immortalized by Jack Kerouac in *On the Road* ("blowing their tops before a screaming audience that gave the record fantastic frenzied volume").[35]

Remembering it well was dancer-singer-actress Frances Nealy, a woman who, before she died in 1997, had been steadily employed in show business for more than six decades. Starting out as a chorine in the San Francisco–Oakland area at an early age, Nealy could be seen throughout the 1940s in theatrical and vaudeville productions on the West Coast and throughout the U.S.:

> I came to Los Angeles, I think, in 1939 because I was working in Sacramento at Charlie Derrick's [a popular black club], and a fellow I was going with came by one night and said, "I'm going to Los Angeles, do you want to go with me?" And I said "yes," I quit my job, and that's how I came to Los Angeles. And I've been here ever since. I drive past so many places today and say to the person I'm with that "I used to work there." Now, of course, they're all laundromats and vacant lots, but then there were all kinds of little clubs nestled around everywhere and they all had shows and bands and kept you working all the time.[36]

In the summer of 1942, Nealy found herself dancing at Central Avenue's Club Alabam by night, and by day doing movie "atmosphere" work at Universal Studios, then as now located in North Hollywood. She was paid a handsome eighty dollars a day, and *earned* it.

> It was *Arabian Nights* with Maria Montez and Jon Hall. All I had to do was stand there as the slave girl next to this fur-lined pool. That was the big thing ... this *fur-lined* swimming pool at an oasis in the desert. I had to stand there for three weeks by this tiger and I remember the trainer saying, "Don't turn your back to him because we used to do an act in the circus where she jumps on my back and when she sees a back she may jump on you." That's why in the picture I'm kind of hanging onto the pole and looking around like ... watching him so he wouldn't jump on my back.[37]

And if you look closely at Nealy in the background in the freeze frame mode of the video of *Arabian Nights*, almost 70 years later you can *still* sense her fear from her body language.

Central to the Central Avenue scene were the Club Alabam and the Lincoln Theater — analogous to New York's Cotton Club-Apollo Theatre and Chicago's Grand Terrace-Regal Theatre entertainment axes. Owned since the late 1920s by bandleader and drummer Curtis Mosby, the Alabam had been a focal point of Los Angeles' black nightclub and jazz scene from the late '20s on. Located next door to the Dunbar Hotel at 41st and Central, the combination package of the popular Dunbar and the Alabam, in addition to the numerous surrounding smaller clubs and bars, resulted in the intersection becoming *the* hub of African American social activities — especially during the 1940s. Unlike New York's Cotton Club and other Harlem spots, the appeal and entrance policies of the Alabam and many of the other clubs were trans-racial and cross-cultural, and cut across many class and social barriers of the period. Recalled Nat "King" Cole's former drummer and future Motown executive Lee Young:

> The Club Alabam had had many names. When I came out here as a kid, you know, I used to be a singer and dancer, and it was one of the first places I worked. It was called the Apex. That was in the '30s, when all the movie stars used to frequent the club, so it was really a big business. And the same man who owned the Apex wound up owning the Club Alabam.... They had tables all around the dance floor, maybe three deep, and they had a balcony. And right on the railing they had tables all the way around. I think you could get nine hundred people in. There was a long bar, maybe eighty, ninety feet, and all the hustlers and pimps, they stayed at the bar to fire their shots.... Most of the black people would be there on weekends, and all during the week the clientele was white.[38]

Movie stars were a mainstay of the Alabam clientele; it was not unusual for a headliner like Billy Eckstine to come on stage and spot the ringside likes of Lana Turner (said to have been carrying a heavy torch for this "Sepia Sinatra" at one time),[39] Sinatra, Rita Hayworth, Ava Gardner and Alan Ladd. In addition to featured acts like Eckstine, Josephine Baker and Billie Holiday, the Alabam offered a 16-piece band (usually led by Johnny Otis or Lee Young), twelve or so chorus girls, tap dancers, a comedian, and maybe a practitioner of the now long-lost art of shake dancing. The Alabam was a huge space with silk draperies covering the walls, and mirrored balls reflecting a myriad of colors.

The Lincoln Theater, the other of the Avenue's entertainment linchpins, was located on Central at 23rd Street. It was the largest venue for black entertainment west of the Mississippi when it opened in 1927; the next year the Lincoln began serving as the West Coast home of the long-running Lafayette Players from New York City's Harlem. In the 1930s most of the major swing bands of the era could be seen there, along with a film for the price of 75 cents. Frances Nealy recalled:

The Lincoln [in the 1940s] was trying to do what was happening in New York at the Apollo. The backbone of the show was the chorus girls. We always did the opening, a middle number, and a finale and in between were the other acts. They always had a male vocalist, a female vocalist, an exotic dancer. That's why when I went to New York in 1990 and saw the Broadway show *Black and Blue,* I was surprised at the way everybody kept returning from the east raving about it: "Oh, *Black and Blue* this, and *Black and Blue* that," "It's the greatest thing in the world," and so on. I said, "Shoot, we had entirely new shows week in and week out at the Lincoln that were the equal of *Black and Blue.* Maybe not as lavish, because of the scenery, but just as good."[40]

Even though the clientele of the clubs and ballrooms ran the gamut from solid black to racially mixed black-and-tan, still it should not be assumed that Los Angeles in the 1940s represented any kind of mecca when it came to race. As noted in the previous chapter, actress-activist Frances E. Williams and (then) fledgling jazz promoter Norman Granz's popular racially mixed Sunday jazz concerts were an anomaly for their time.[41]

Inasmuch as Los Angeles was finally no more progressive than most of the rest of the country, the city also abounded with standard issue night clubs whose entertainment might alternately consist of black *or* white performers, but whose door policy was Whites Only. In the 1940s there were a few remaining places in town that were throwbacks to the Cotton and Plantation clubs of a slightly earlier day, where all the faces on stage, *all* the time, belonged to black entertainers who found themselves staring out into a sea of white faces. One of them was the Hollywood Casino: The club (it is now a recording studio) was located at the corner of Sunset Boulevard and Gower Street, an intersection that was close by several major movie studios: Paramount, RKO, Columbia, and a few smaller ones as well.

Ultimately, Central as a vital nighttime scene was too good to last. Owners of white clubs like the Hollywood Casino, the Mocambo and Ciro's—the very club that helped launch Sammy Davis for the ages—became aware that they were losing business with all the customers going down to Central. And so they turned to City Hall and the notoriously racist police chief Ed Parker to help stem the tide of business heading south. The initial battle plan called for—somewhat surprisingly—the hassling not of blacks on Central, but the whites who came there.

Mixed-race couples soon became wise to the fact they would be bothered less by the police if they took busses to where the action was—instead of cars—but still the harassing continued. And by the early 1950s the combination of police jamming, the advent of TV, and the milder postwar economy all combined to ring the death knell for the more recreational aspects of Central Avenue.[42]

In early 1995 I interviewed jazz "trumpetist" (as she prefers to be called) Clora Bryant—the only female musician to ever play with Charlie Parker—about the "scene" on Central Avenue in the 1940s; she was there as a young woman when it all went down and in recent times has become a fervent advocate for getting the strip's story told. She rhetorically asked:

> Why should you know about Central Avenue? Why do I think it's important? I think there's a Central Avenue wherever you go. New York's Central Avenue is in Harlem on 125th Street; in Kansas City it's 18th and Vine; Bourbon Street in New Orleans; Beale Street in Memphis. In order for the whole *thing* to gel, if you don't include Central Avenue in the context of this jazz continuum, you've left out one of the important branches. In 1944 I was living in New York in a hotel room above Minton's [a famous spot for bop experimentation] and that part of jazz has been documented and documented, but it's like they kept … I don't know why they tried to smother Los Angeles, because when I came out here in 1945 I was overwhelmed. You've got to explain to people what it was like sitting in those clubs like the Club Alabam — when I wasn't playing there myself — and sit and watch the shows and I could never get over the fact that "I'm here. Me! With all these great people." I could never be blasé about it. It was always "Dang! I'm here. This is me. Clora Bryant from little old Dennison, Texas." Downtown Main Street was two blocks long and when I was back there recently they had the *nerve* to make it one way.[43]

The list of West Coast jazz musicians who appeared regularly in the clubs on Central constitute a mini-who's who of jazz: Dexter Gordon, Charlie Mingus, Lucky Thompson, Buddy Collette, Howard McGhee, Wardell Gray, Art Pepper and dozens more — in addition to visiting journeymen from the east like Charlie Parker and Dizzy Gillespie. But until recent times, Los Angeles' and especially Central Avenue's contribution to music has been given short shrift. Part of the problem was (and continues to be) ingrained societal apathy to black culture; but, according to oral historian Stephen Isoardi, there's another reason behind the rebuff, one that has nothing to do with race. The compiler of 1998's *Central Avenue Sounds*, a massive UCLA project designed to help set the record straight, says:

> There's very little mention of L.A. jazz in jazz histories until the last couple of years because L.A and the West has always been seen as a kind of backwater. If anyone wanted to get attention they had to go to the East Coast. Plus Central Avenue never produced a sharply defined style like New Orleans and New York — maybe that hurt it in terms of getting recognition — although it produced absolutely fabulous musicians who went on to shape the music.[44]

The music that was heard wafting out of Central clubs as the end of the war was approaching was the new sound of bop, primarily propagated on the East Coast by the likes of Parker and Gillespie, but whose shock waves were being picked up with increasing acuity by young L.A. players like Collette and Mingus.

The general postwar downsizing of nightlife throughout the country had a great deal to do with the eventual demise of Central Avenue in the early 1950s, but as much as anything it was a case of blacks having to give up something in order to gain larger rewards. In 1948 the Supreme Court struck down the legality of the racist "Housing Covenants" in Los Angeles which had been responsible for keeping blacks—in the sad parlance of the times—"in their place" for so many years. The upshot, according to Frances Nealy: "Around the early 1950s blacks started moving to the west side which was around Western Avenue and that was the beginning of the end of Central. They never had the clubs there that they had on Central Avenue. Before my time, in the '30s, that's when Central Avenue was *really* booming. Honey, I got there on the tail end of things, just in time for its last hurrah."[45]

But it was not her last hurrah: She still made numerous appearances all over the U.S. and among her more memorable appearances in film, as the self-described "Queen of the One-Liners," was her screaming hotel maid in *Ghostbusters,* and the school-crossing guard in *Colors* who exhorts Sean Penn to "Get out of my face!"

Frances Nealy was proud of the fact that — although not exactly a household name — she never had to work outside of the entertainment field in order to support herself. When Central folded up its tents, she just kept moving forward. When Sammy Davis consciously opted for crossover success with his smash opening at Ciro's, he must have seen the writing on the wall not just for Central but for nearly all the other such African American areas that had afforded him work over the years. And as for Clora Bryant, looking back on Central nearly a half-century later, she had no regrets. Central had served her well: A short while after she touched down on Central for the first time, she began playing in the band in the Club Alabam, continuing to do so on and off for the next decade until, in the mid–1950s, the club closed for good, after a twenty-five run that almost exactly paralleled the glory years of Central.[46]

"I'd been to a lot of places since I left Denison, Texas—traveling with all-girl bands and such — but I'd never been anyplace like Central Avenue before," a pensive Bryant recalled in 1995. "I stepped off the 'Q' streetcar onto Central for the first time to apply at the musician's union to get my card at the black local. I started walking up to this building and it was like *somebody* was walking me. It wasn't an out-of-body experience, but it was, how would you put it?, somebody was just leading me and I was following like a sheep. And when I got to the building and I walked up to the union and just the thought that I was going to be a part of all of this ... all these emotions were going through my body. It was a thing where I just *knew* this was a place I was supposed to be at that point in time."[47]

12

Some Subjects
for Further Research

Gladys Bentley: "She was a man!" actress-activist Frances Williams insisted when the subject of Bentley, the ostensibly female cabaret singer-pianist and court jester to the Harlem Renaissance, was raised.[1] When confronted with *Sisters of the Harlem Renaissance*,[2] a publication containing information to the contrary, Williams stuck to her guns: She shot a look that signaled case closed, end of discussion. Certainly Bentley gave good cause for Williams to suspect she might be *all* man: She worked entirely in male drag and sang double-entendre songs and parodies that often as not alluded to or celebrated the joys and perils of gay romance. But that was later on; here is Langston Hughes' description, in his *The Big Sea*, of Bentley in action "before she got famous, acquired an accompanist, specially written material, and conscious vulgarity":

"Miss Bentley sat, and played a big piano all night long, literally all night without stopping — singing songs like 'The St. James Infirmary,' from ten in the evening until dawn, with scarcely a break in between the notes, sliding from one song to another, with a powerful and continuous underbeat of jungle rhythm." He goes on to describe the ample, ebony, and deeply butch performer as "a perfect piece of African sculpture."[3] Novelist Carl Van Vechten was similarly taken with her; in his *Parties* he writes of an unnamed character who is clearly Bentley: "There is a girl up there now you oughta hear. She does her hair so her head looks like a wet seal and when she pounds the piano the dawn comes up like thunder."[4]

In her *Black Pearls: Blues Queens of the 1920s*, Daphne Duval Harrison suggests that it wasn't only Frances Williams who felt that this woman imitating a man might have, in fact, been — shades of *Victor/Victoria* — a man (gay, at that) imitating a lesbian pretending to be a man. She describes Bentley as a "tough-talking, singing piano player who some believed to be a male transvestite and others a lesbian."[5] In *Gay New York*, George Chauncey recalls Bentley as an entertainer "who performed in a tuxedo and married her lover in a much discussed ceremony."[6]

If, in fact, Bentley was a lesbian, she recanted her sapphic ways for good in 1952 in a magazine article entitled "I Am a Woman Again."[7] She then married a sailor in San Diego and spent the remainder of her years writing her (yet to be published) memoirs. If ever there was a subject who cried out for further research it is Bentley, who may have singlehandedly engineered the gender-bending-est hoax ever perpetrated on café society. With the growth of gender studies over the last few years, particularly as reflected in the writings of Judith Butler,[8] *someone* must get to the bottom of this before it is too late. Whoever that might be, however, has their work cut out for them. The relative lack of contemporary accounts in black newspapers and other journals of the day, along with often missing germane arcana such as birth, education, and medical records (a much more common occurrence), presents a major problem for researchers: Even if the overall number of newspapers reporting on the activities of black artists and entertainers hadn't been so relatively few in comparison to white papers, the fact that, unlike newspapers "of record" such as the *New York Times*, the black press of an earlier time remains almost entirely *un*-indexed. Foraging thorough miles of microfilm to get basic information can prove a *mal de mer*–inducing process.

The writing of this book often took on the form of a detective investigation: searches through phone books in out-of-the-way locales, perusals of genealogical records and attempts at verifying apocrypha that has over the years acquired the patina of literal truth. Time is running out in which to gain first-hand accounts from witnesses to and participants in crucial events in the history of black show business. I found it both surprising and frustrating, for example, that in Los Angeles, where Billy McClain (see Chapter 3) had died only forty years ago and where he had spent the last three decades of his life, I could not come up with a single individual aside from Leonard Reed (see Chapter 10) who had either known or heard of him.

Gaining historical perspective on African American practitioners of the popular arts is further complicated by the general cultural wraparound that surrounded Black America in the earlier part of the last century and has continued to prevail to some degree ever since then. First and foremost, there is the much smaller amount of African American work that was actually preserved in wax and on film. Thus, we tend to recall Fannie Brice, but not Florence Mills[9]; write theses about Victor Herbert, but not Will Marion Cook; and elevate W.C. Fields to a position of comedic importance at the expense of Bert Williams (whom Fields called the "funniest man I have ever seen and the saddest man I have ever met").

Tony Jackson: Inarguably the most important black artist who was not recorded for phonographic posterity, but clearly should (and could) have been, was New Orleans–born Jackson, repeatedly cited by Jelly Roll Morton as his main musical inspiration.[10] It is possible that pianist Jackson was every bit as much a founding father of jazz as was "Mr. Jelly Lord"—who never failed to stir up controversy on those periodic occasions when he claimed for himself the distinction of being the "Inventor of Jazz." Morton called his friend Tony Jackson "the greatest single-handed entertainer in the world" and deemed him "the man of a thousand songs,"[11] many of which he composed himself, including his most famous, "Pretty Baby" and the immortal "I've Got Elgin Movements in My Hips with Twenty Years' Guarantee."

"There was no [music] from any opera or any kind of show or anything that was wrote on paper that Tony couldn't play," contended Jelly Roll.[12] In his *Early Jazz*, Gunther Schuller writes that Morton's then rather avant garde "emphasis on notating his music, planning his recording dates in advance, and publishing his orchestrations, and his love of opera excerpts and ragtime music are all largely attributable to the influence of Tony Jackson."[13] "In *They All Played Ragtime* Jackson is described thusly by Rudi Blesh and Harriet Janis: "He was dark-skinned and of slender build, about five feet ten in height. A distinctive mark was a tuft in the middle of his head. His eyes were protruding and heavy-lidded; a receding chin made a prominent feature of his mouth. The mouth could open, though, in a most expressive grin, and the long-fingered hands that swung loosely with his arms were made for the piano."[14]

According to his contemporaries, Jackson's vocal style was likewise noteworthy for its amazing range and a falsetto register that he used for comedic effect.

In 1905 Jackson went to Chicago where he quickly became a favorite of club owners and audiences throughout the city at such spots as the Pekin and the Elite No. 1 for the next fifteen years or so, when he wasn't touring with the Whitman Sisters (see Chapter 2) or, towards the end of his life, operating a horse farm for a brief time in Kentucky. Jackson's death at an early age was attributable to a fluke medical incident. "He had been drinking black coffee and lemon when he was seized by hiccups, and nothing could relieve them," according to Rudi Blesh and Harriet Janis.[15] And despite eight weeks of attempts by doctors and nurses to save him, he died on April 21, 1921, at just about the time the *de facto* ban of the recording of blacks began to lift. Jackson and many more like him were simply not invited into white phonograph studios in any great numbers until after the Beatles-like success of blues singer Mamie Smith and her recording of "Crazy Blues" in 1921.

Because of the lack of recorded proof, we simply will never know if it was Tony Jackson who truly was the Father of Jazz and not Jelly Roll Morton — not to mention similarly unrecorded cornetist Buddy Bolden; also cited in *every* jazz history as a major progenitor of the musical form.

Willard Hamby: Orally transmitted tales still abound of a pianist by the name of Willard Hamby who worked with the Louis Armstrong and Earl

Hines bands in the late 1920s and who was good enough to have bested Art Tatum in a "cutting contest" in Cleveland sometime during the mid–1920s.[16] But Hamby, like Jackson and so many others, was never recorded and fell through the cracks of vinyl history. That there are no mentions of him in any of the commonplace jazz histories, doesn't obviate his importance. It is fortunate that a significant enough amount of Scott Joplin's effects (including the forerunner of recordings, the piano rolls) remained for musicologist Vera Brodsky Lawrence to work with to bring about the major Joplin renaissance in the early 1970s.

Contemporary researchers trying to piece together the life and times of even once-eminent figures such as Joplin often find themselves painstakingly putting together a puzzle consisting of personal effects scattered to the four winds decades ago, finally reclaimed through exhaustive detective work. After her work was complete, it took Lawrence more than a decade and innumerable rejections before she found a publisher interested in going to press with her collection of Joplin rags.

Blind Tom Bethune: Even when the information is there, it takes archeological zeal to get to it. For example, much of the information that follows regarding pianist Bethune was obtained from a biographical pamphlet (see appendum) sold at Bethune concerts in the late 1880s and which I was fortunate to find listed — and subsequently bought — in a rare books auction catalogue. Certainly no more bizarre case history exists in all the annals of American show business than Bethune — regardless of ethnic classification. Born sightless and a slave in 1849, Bethune, according to one anonymous source, "manifested in his infancy so entire a want of intellect as to induce the belief that he was idiotic as well as blind." "His first manifestation of interest in anything," noted the same writer, "was his fondness for sounds; the first indication of capacity, his power of imitating them."[17]

Blind Tom was four when his master purchased a piano for his daughters, but the person who ultimately got the most use out of the instrument was Thomas, a.k.a. Blind Tom. One night, in a manner abundant in the lore of so-called *idiot savantry*, the slavemaster was awakened by the sound of music emanating from the common room. It was Tom playing at a level of expertise far beyond that of his formally trained daughters. Shortly thereafter the boy was taken to a local music store where he heard a pianist play an unpublished work; forthwith, the boy sat down and immediately played back the composition. (Thirteen years later when reminded of the incident, Bethune sat down and again rendered an accurate encore of the work that he had not heard in all the years in between.) Bethune also, according to the *Fayetteville Observer*, played "Fisher's Hornpipe" with one hand and "Yankee Doodle" with the other and sang "Dixie" all at once.[18]

It was soon obvious to the owner, General James Bethune, that Tom was some kind of genius, and he hired a professional instructor to teach the boy. The instructor stayed but a short while, however; there was no need for his services, he soon announced, stating that Blind Tom had far more expertise than the teacher himself possessed. It developed that he had but to hear any musical selection once in order to play it back perfectly—followed by accurate retention of the piece.

When he was seven, under the management of General Bethune, Blind Tom made his concert debut in Columbus, Georgia, to thunderous applause. Immediately, fakery was suspected and experts came from all over with music tests devised to fool the boy, but he passed each one with flying colors; going so far on one occasion as to play Beethoven's "Concerto No. 3"—after learning it by ear—standing up and with his back to the piano, i.e., his left hand played the right hand part and vice versa. Tom drew the attention of scientists from all over and was written about in such works as *Idiocy and Its Treatments* (1866) by the French physician Edouard Séguin. According to neurologist Edward Sacks in his 1995 book *An Anthropologist on Mars: Seven Paradoxical Tales*: "Although Tom was usually called an idiot or imbecile, such posturing and stereotypes are more characteristic of autism — but autism was only identified in the 1940s and was not a term or even a concept, in the 1860s."[19]

It was later advanced by one historian that Blind Tom's mental incapacitation might have been less extreme than surmised and that his blindness could have been curable by surgical means.[20]

An excellent mimic, Bethune also effected vocal simulations of such as the harp, guitar, banjo and — as listed in a playbill — "a Dutch woman, and hand organ." By 1873 Tom could play 3000 works from memory; by 1876, 5000, including those of Liszt, Gottschalk, Rossini, Bach, and Verdi in addition to his own compositions which he spontaneously composed while improvising at the keyboard, e.g. "Rainstorm," "The Battle of Manassas," and "Imitation of the Sewing Machine"— programmatic names given the pieces by his managers. Indeed, Blind Tom Bethune soon did have a number of agents and handlers who took a Barnum-like interest in him, for the word of the youth's musical prowess spread like wildfire. Here is part of a review from a 1869 issue of the *Baltimore Sun*: "We enjoyed an opportunity last night to hear the performances of the blind Negro boy called 'Tom,' at Carol Hall and though prepared for something uncommon, all expectations were surpassed by the reality. Nay, more, all preconceived ideas of music as a science, an art or an acquisition were thoroughly baffled, and a new question thrust upon us as what music really is in the economy of nature."[21]

Blind Tom was to become a major concert attraction both here and abroad: He played at the White House before President Buchanan and in widely heralded engagements throughout Europe, including some performances before royalty. Given the circumstances of Tom's servitude, he was increasingly exploited by his owners to a degree that made the later mistreatment of blacks on the 1920s T.O.B.A. vaudeville circuit seem absolutely beneficent by comparison. Although blacks were granted their freedom by the Emancipation Proclamation Act of 1863, the Bethune family was able by quasi-legal trickeries to retain ownership of Tom until 1887. This may have accounted for his reputed status as "The Last Slave Set Free by order of the Supreme Court of the United States," according to one undated playbill.[22] Bethune never owned any of the copyrights to his own works until after an 1887 court battle waged on behalf of his mother, Charity. And, indeed clashes over the spoils continued even after Blind Tom's death in 1908 in Hoboken, New Jersey, where he had retired — still famous, but broken in spirit. This enigmatic figure continues to challenge more traditional notions of genius and musical ability nearly a century later.

Unlike the fate that befell Blind Tom Bethune — perhaps as much for reasons of physical infirmity as race — many African American producers and actor managers, because they had a unique product to "sell," were able to secure a degree of creative autonomy and economic control for themselves long before blacks in other fields could do so. (Note: Since the publication of the first edition of this book, there have been several well-wrought retrospectives on Blind Tom, including a major biography, *The Ballad of Blind Tom, Slave Pianist* by Diedre O'Connell; a CD of his compositions, *John Davis Plays Blind Tom*; and a dramatization of his life on public television.)

In the latter half of the 19th century, a number of blacks owned and operated "all-colored" minstrel companies. Brooker and Clayton's Georgia Minstrels and Lew Johnson's Plantation Minstrels (sometimes billed as the Black Baby Boy Minstrels and Lew Johnson's Original Tennessee Jubilee Singers) were quite successful at giving whites entrepreneurs a run for their money.[23] And as minstrelsy began to evolve into what eventually came to known as vaudeville, around the turn of the century, here too early economic parity was obtained to by blacks such as Billy McClain (see Chapter Three).

S.H. Dudley: This performer, famed for his act-with-a-mule-turned-prominent theater mogul, started up his own black vaudeville circuit at least a decade before the founding of the more well-known T.O.B.A. Other important entrepreneurs included: Aubrey Miller and Flournoy Miller (of *Shuffle Along* fame); Irvin C. Miller (brother of Flournoy), and the combine of Bert Williams–George Walker–Jesse Shipp–Will Marion Cook (see Chapter One).

Black Patti: One of the most fascinating of all the black-owned companies was the long-running Black Patti's Troubadours, which starred Patti herself, born Sissieretta Jones, but renamed Patti in honor of the famed white opera diva, Adelina Patti. The Troubadour company managed the rather remarkable feat of mixing low comedy with Patti's high opera in a troupe that criss-crossed the U.S. from 1896 up through 1910, after which time occurred the singer's mid-career switchover to lady evangelist.

Tutt and Whitney: And then there was the wildly enterprising team of Indiana brothers Salem Tutt Whitney and J. Homer Tutt, the most prolific African American producing-writing-acting team of their day. Between 1910 and 1925, the two men oversaw and/or appeared in excess of forty touring revues and musical comedies. Up until the time of their 1929 *Deep Harlem*, however, the closest the two had ever gotten to Broadway legitimacy was their *Oh Joy*, which ran for four weeks in 1923 at New York's Bamboo Isle Theater, then located at Broadway and 57th Street.

Tutt and Whitney weren't the only important names connected with *Deep Harlem*. The score was by—in addition to Tutt—Joe Jordan (who had written the Fannie Brice signature tune, "Lovie Joe," with Will Marion Cook) and Henry Creamer ("After You've Gone," "'Way Down Yonder in New Orleans"); the libretto was by the producing-performing brothers. Orchestrations for the most part were by the Broadway arranger Will Vodery, a *Ziegfeld Follies* mainstay who also orchestrated much of George Gershwin's "serious" as well as pop material.

The Tutt-Whitney production was the latest addition to the small but steadily expanding list of black shows with their sights set on Broadway— starting out in 1903 with *In Dahomey*, the Bert Williams and George Walker hit; hitting its stride with *Shuffle Along* in 1921; and maintaining visibility into the late 1920s with the appearance of the long-running *Blackbirds of 1928* starring Bill "Bojangles" Robinson and Adelaide Hall. By the time of *Deep Harlem*, such shows had been especially vogueish on Broadway for several seasons with productions like *Dixie to Broadway* (1924), the 1927 edition of the popular revue *Runnin' Wild*, and *Rang Tang* (also '27). That all of these shows were musicals shouldn't come as a surprise; what was expected of blacks on the Great White Way in the 1920s was nothing more or less than the stereotype of the laughing, shuffling, pain-free, chicken-stealing black that had been the lot of African American entertainers ever since the clichés were forged for them by whites in minstrels shows of the 19th century. Even the implication that blacks had *romantic* sex lives, as was implied by a controversial kissing scene in 1921's *Shuffle Along*, was seen as an affront to white theatergoers, although not enough of one to hamper the production's lengthy run of 504 performances. Unquestionably, the team of Tutt and Whitney wanted something more for *Deep Harlem* than for it to be just another formula "plantation musical." Perhaps not a great deal more than that, but clearly *some* measure of seriousness.

If there was a "message" to the show, it was that American blacks possessed something beyond the frivolous disposition that was supposedly an intrinsic part of their nature; that black men and women's souls were infused with some degree of humanness; a capacity for emotion and feeling that existed, if for no other reason, as a result of the damage done to their souls by the forced diaspora that landed them in North America in the first place. And so, while act two of *Deep Harlem* adhered to the black musical formula — taking place in a Harlem nightclub and spotlighting the chorus line from the popular Connie's Inn — act one was anything but typical. The story began in the Kingdom of the Cushites, a once noble African tribe, now defeated in war and abducted into slavery. The action follows this group of Abyssinians on their forced march through the African desert and the jungle, and finally to the slave ship and a long and perilous ocean voyage. The remainder of act one depicts their experiences in slave markets and on pre–Civil War plantations and, finally, in the Savannah, Georgia, of the 1920s.[24]

This break with tradition, though, was apparently not to be endured. The day following *Deep Harlem's* 1/7/29 opening, the *New York Times* deemed the show to be nothing much more than "an abundance of flappy canvas scenery." Most of New York's many newspaper drama critics lambasted it in similar fashion. But at least one critic, Arthur Ruhl, writing in the *Herald-Tribune*, was sympathetic with the show's intentions:

> [Salem Tutt] Whitney (with the cavernous voice of an old-fashioned Southern Negro preacher) had the air throughout his work of being somewhat a philosopher and of letting his more or less solemn thoughts about the history and present thoughts about his race come to the front as much as he thought practicable in a musical show on Broadway.... It was interesting ... because of its attempts to make something out of what wide-awake Negro minds have been thinking of possibilities for genuine black drama, and in its very ingenuousness there was a kind of charm which is generally quite drowned out by the hullabaloo and brassy cocksureness that Broadway has come to expect and demand from black shows.[25]

Tutt and Whitney's production managed only to play out the week — opening on a Monday and closing on the following Saturday night. But Ruhl persisted in his defense of the production. A day after the show closed, the *Herald-Tribune* ran a long article by the critic expressing dismay with both the show's failure and with his fellow New York critics. *Deep Harlem* was clearly striving to be a little different from other black entertainments, Ruhl felt, and in doing so deserved some credit and a wide berth. The article went on to suggest that New York would never let black shows be different, that all the local critics would permit in a black musical was "meaningless whirling and fizzing with 'pep.'"[26]

In addition to his theatrical endeavors, Salem Tutt Whitney (the older brother of the Tutt and Whitney team) wrote a theatrical column, "Timely Topics," that appeared regularly for sixteen years in the *Chicago Defender* newspaper up until the time of his 1934 death at age 65. A common theme in Whitney's column was the racial stereotyping that had long since been a condition of employment for most African American performers, and the only sure cure for which was seeking work outside the borders of the U.S. Fully half of the biographical figures dealt with in the main part of this book — Will Marion Cook, Billy McClain, Valaida Snow, Nora Ray Holt and Hazel Scott — spent a significant part of their most productive years outside the country, and nearly all of them wrote letters back home extolling the advanced racial attitudes prevalent elsewhere.

Inarguably the most famous black show biz expatriate of the day was Josephine Baker, who travelled abroad to Paris for her first time in 1925, with the *Revue Nègre*, and wreaked such pleasant havoc that to this day France has never quite recovered.

Layton and Johnstone: Two expatriates somewhat passed over in coverage on the subject, but in their own less dramatic way nearly as popular in England as *la Baker* was in France, was the dapper team of "American Duetists" Turner Layton and Clarence "Tandy" Johnstone. The two teamed up in 1924 and probably never dreamed that their partnership would prove any more lasting than most such show biz "marriages of convenience."

Turner Layton was by far the more accomplished and experienced of the two, already having co-written such popular standards as "After You've Gone," "Dear Old Southland," and "'Way Down Yonder in New Orleans" before meeting up with Johnstone, an ex–Tammany Hall political functionary-turned-chiropodist. Layton would play the piano and sing, and Johnstone, as often as not leaning on the piano on one elbow, would harmonize along with him on such popular tunes of the day as "I Wonder Where My Baby Is Tonight," "Get Out and Get Under the Moon," "What'll I Do," and "All Alone" in an engaging style that wasn't quite jazz, not quite schmaltz, but that presentationally was perhaps much more "sophisticated" than the work of most African American entertainers of that time. The duo wore tuxedos (a possible first for blacks on stage), bore no traces of the minstrelsy tradition, and were as up-to-date as any act around in the early 1920s. In short order, Layton and Johnstone became a top attraction in the U.S. on the millionaire New York–Florida private party circuit. The team then decided to try Europe, and were lucky enough to almost immediately secure an engagement in 1924 at London's popular Café de Paris where at first they did not attract any special attention. But subsequently they were given the imprimatur of the Prince of Wales*, after he spotted them in a musical revue, and the team took off. Overnight, all of London, royalty included, wanted to see them; this was followed by equal success on "The Continent."

---

*Up through the 1920s, the stamp of royal approval played a significant role in the thriving careers of a number of African American expatriate performers, including Will Marion Cook, Valaida Snow, and Nora Ray Holt.

Between 1924 and 1935, Layton and Johnstone made hundreds of recordings, all of them in their popular piano-and-two-voices format, and earned between them each year between 65,000 and 180,000 dollars. Finally, it all came to an end in 1935 when Layton, now 44, and his somewhat older partner were dashed apart, apparently upon the shores of Clarence Johnstone's increasingly profligate ways. In 1934 he made headlines over his affair with the beautiful platinum blonde wife of British violinist Albert Sandler, who won a $12,500 settlement from the singer as a result. Johnstone's subsequent divorce from his wife Stella in order to marry the former Mrs. Sandler, Raymonde Defly Demery, ignited more press coverage, followed in 1936 by news reports that the once wealthy entertainer had declared bankruptcy, having lost nearly a quarter million dollars on bad investments. Soon thereafter, Layton and Johnstone were both in the news announcing the breakup of a musical partnership that had kept Europe and Great Britain entertained for nearly fifteen years. On May 31, after their last performance together, at London's Empire Theatre, the two held court in separate dressing rooms announcing their plans for the future. Said Mr. Johnstone: "I cannot say how sorry I am, but if Mr. Layton thinks he can do better for himself, there is no more to be said."

Layton, in turn, said he hoped Johnstone would have good luck in the future. But Johnstone, once the owner of a touring car that was a replica of one owned by King Edward V, was not to fare nearly as well as did Layton following the split-up of the team: After a brief, uneventful pairing with singer Jules Bledsoe, the original "Joe" of *Showboat*, Johnstone returned to America and soon disappeared into obscurity as a bellhop at a New York City hotel. Layton, no doubt helped out by what must have been considerable song royalties, remained a familiar figure on Great Britain's entertainment scene. He died on February 6, 1978, at age 86.[27]

In the liner notes for one of several Layton and Johnstone collections released in England since then, British critic Brian Rust wrote that there was "just some extra quality about the 'quaint and amusing negroes' [sic] that made them variety bill toppers for eleven years without changing their act, in a world hungry for constant change. Sophistication? The other double acts were all that. Musicianship? The others had plenty. Novelty — the fact that they were Negroes? You can't see that on a record. What the records do demonstrate is that this was indeed a quality act that had an indefinable something that can only be determined by listening."[28]

All-Black Cast Cinema: Unlike the phonographic medium (after blacks were finally let into recording studios en masse around 1920), film long continued to be a problem medium where African Americans were concerned. For aside from the mainstream exceptions such as Ethel Waters, Louis Armstrong et al., only a handful of significant black entertainers from earlier in the last century were captured on film for posterity. The uproar that arose when the great Bert Williams made his film debut in 1914 in *Darktown Jubilee* goes a long way toward illuminating why this happened.

"[*Darktown Jubilee*], which some contend was the 'first all–Negro'-cast movie ... was certainly the first film in which an established black star played a leading role, and Williams' appearance in top hat and zoot suit (instead of the raggedy outfit he usually donned on stage), without blackface makeup, apparently was too much for the mixed audience at its Brooklyn opening. The film was greeted with catcalls from whites and nearly precipitated a race riot. Subsequently it was boycotted by most distributors."[29]

There were some notable exceptions to this blackout on blacks in film. An "all-black" movie industry sprang up in Chicago in 1909 and continued to thrive and provide employment opportunities for African American entertainers until the 1950s. Among them were: Comic Sandy Burns—who along with Sam Russell comprised one-half of the popular two-man comedy team Ashes and Bilo—put in an appearance with Russell and Tim Moore of TV's *Amos 'n' Andy* in the 1923 silent *His Great Chance*; *The Brand of Cain*, a 1935 talkie by pioneer black filmmaker Oscar Micheaux, also featured Burns.

Anita Bush: The founder of the black theatre troupe, the Lafayette Players, Bush was an actress who apparently never got her chance to show what she could do in the mainstream cinema, but was employed in two films by an early company which specialized in black fare, Norman Films: *The Crimson Skull* (1921) and *Bull Doggers* (1923). Both also featured famed black cowboy and father of rodeo bulldogging, Bill Pickett (the subject of a 1994 U.S. stamp).*

Laura Bowman: An actress of artistic stature equal to that of Bush, Bowman also got the overwhelming portion of her screen exposure in all-black productions, including a number of works by filmmaker Oscar Micheaux, who seems to have been the man to see if you were black and wanted to work in the movies.

It is Micheaux's *Ten Minutes to Live* (1932), with his filming of the act of Gallie DeGaston and George Williams, that affords us what must rank as the most accurate capturing on film of how an early black vaudeville comedy team must have looked and sounded. After checking out Brown and DeGaston's pun-filled word play, which sometimes approaches almost delirious Shakespearean heights,[30] one comes away with some sense of what Moss and Frye ("How high is up?" ... "Up where? ... "Up anywhere!"), Burns and Russell, Harris and Holly ("You pull, my end will follow"), Glenn and Jenk-

---

*The Black Heritage stamp—which incorrectly depicted Pickett's brother instead—was quickly withdrawn. The few which did "go public" were immediately worth a small fortune.

ins (a streetsweeping act), the Jones Brothers (one wore a large alarm clock on his arm) and hundreds of other acts like them must also have been like.

The beloved (and talkative comedy) team of Butterbeans and Susie might have appeared in some sound film whose existence has somehow eluded this author, but at least their movements were captured on film in the 1926 silent Colored Motion Picture Producers of America release, *Nine Lives*.*

Fortunately, the work of the two greatest comics that black vaudeville ever produced — Pigmeat Markham and Moms Mabley — was featured in numerous all-black film productions. But one comes away from viewing much of their screen work with the feeling that you probably had to have "been there" live. Such performers relied heavily on give and take with their audiences, and little of the alchemical performing magic they possessed is apparent in their audience-less, statically filmed 1940s movies *Junction 88* (Markham) and *Boarding House Blues* (Mabley). If the kind of film technology that captured Richard Pryor's live performances so effectively in more recent times had been around back then, we would have a much better sense of why Moms and Pigmeat are held in such awe by those who still remember witnessing them perform in their prime.

Evelyn Preer: It was filmmaker Oscar Micheaux who afforded most of the film opportunities for actress Preer, who surely must qualify as the first example — regardless of race — of what has since come to be known in the entertainment industry as a multi-media entertainer. In the 1920s when most entertainers were getting their feet wet in one medium alone, Preer was firmly established not only as a film star, but also on recordings, in vaudeville and on the legitimate stage. (Preer's biggest multi-media competition Ethel Waters was still years away from working legit.)

Mississippi native Preer toured the Orpheum and other vaudeville circuits in the teens; then, simultaneous to her work with the Lafayette Players in the 1920s, she appeared on Broadway as the star of such productions as *Lulu Belle* (1926), *Rang Tang* (1927), and the '27 dramatization of DeBose Heyward's novel *Porgy*. All the while, she also managed to record numbers with such major jazz stars of the day as Duke Ellington, Red Nichols, Fletcher Henderson and Clarence Williams. So prolific was Ms. Preer on discs that she had to resort to a number of pseudonyms to account for all of the "sides" she was cutting. Among the other names she recorded under were Evelyn Thompson (her married name), Hotsy Jarvis, Sinclair Franks and Radio Red. Nineteen twenty-eight found the Lafayette Players, along with Ms. Preer and her husband, actor Edward Thompson, relocated to Los Angeles, a pioneer-

---

*It should be noted that like most silent films, in all likelihood the majority of the black-cast films have disappeared-perhaps forever. The author can verify the existence of but a few of the titles noted.

ing move made by all concerned not just with hope of stage work, but film opportunities as well.

The actress' film activities had actually begun a decade earlier when she established herself as Micheaux's leading lady — she played Dietrich to his von Sternberg — in *The Homesteader* (1918), *The Brute* (1920), *The Gunsaulus Mystery* (1921), *Birthright* (1924) and at least a half-dozen others, copies of which, for the most part, are believed to no longer exist. However, Micheaux's *Within Our Gates* (1920), long thought to have also vanished, was recently (1993) discovered in Spain and was soon shown at New York's Lincoln Center. In attendance was Preer's daughter, Sister Francescia Thompson, Ph.D., theatrical historian and leading scholar on the Lafayette Players.

One of the busiest actresses in Hollywood circa 1928 to 1932 — by the early 1930s she was also heard on radio — Preer appeared not only in numerous black-cast comedy shorts, but also in major studio features. Shortly after shooting her last feature, *Blonde Venus* (from which she was eventually cut), Preer died of pneumonia in Los Angeles on November 18, 1932.[31]

In his 1930 book *Black Manhattan*, James Weldon Johnson included Evelyn Preer on a small, select list of the most distinguished African American artists of the day. Of those he saluted (including Bill Robinson, Eubie Blake, Ethel Waters, and Noble Sissle), perhaps only Preer and one or two others would strike an unfamiliar chord with most knowledgeable readers of today. Such anonymity would probably not be the case had she not died in 1932 at the height of her career. Preer, like Laura Bowman and Anita Bush, was carrying on the tradition established by the mid–1800s by black tragedian Ira Aldridge; her lineage includes such other distinguished players as Charles Gilpin, Rose McClendon, Paul Robeson, Richard B. Harrison and Frank Wilson.[32]

Willie Covan and Marie Bryant: Seemingly content and happy just to be working and not to break out into the forefront of mainstream movies, some black professionals chose not to force the issue when it came to a film career. Thus, to those "in the know," it has almost become a cliché to cite the important shadow roles played by dancers-turned-dance-coaches Willie Covan and Marie Bryant in the evolution of the Great American Movie Musical. Covan began dancing professionally as a youth in mining camps in the west and ended up starring on Broadway in the 1920s. Another claim to fame was his behind-the-scenes activity as a teacher and choreographer for Metro-Goldwyn-Mayer during the 1940s. He was never given proper credit for his work at the time (especially with Eleanor Powell), but it is now generally conceded that the Golden Era of MGM musicals would have been somewhat less golden were it not for Covan's contributions. Recalled Los Angeles tapper Frances Nealy: "Willie Covan had a studio across from primarily black Jefferson High on the east side of L.A. on 41st Street; you'd see all these white kids coming over to take classes from him at his studio; and limos pulling up there letting out all these actresses. Judy Garland was one of them."[33]

Marie Bryant, who died in 1978, is spoken of in tones of hushed reverence by her peers. A triple threat artist (dancer, choreographer, singer), Bryant choreographed for films, appeared in the legendary Duke Ellington stage musical *Jump for Joy* and was one of the stars of the memorable jazz film *Jammin' the Blues*. Circa 1935 through 1955 she also appeared on most of the major night club and theater stages in the U.S. A black pioneer in the white film industry, like Willie Covan, Bryant choreographed unbilled for a number of film stars, perhaps most notably Betty Grable.

Jester Hairston: Also not receiving proper screen credit for his work in the 1930s and '40s was actor-choral director-composer Jester Hairston, whose life and times seem to illustrate the premise that the degrees of "separation" between African American entertainment professionals, to recall playwright John Guare, might not be "six," but perhaps two. Like Frances Williams he has been publicly and/or personally associated with many of the other biographical subjects in this book (including Williams). Also, like Williams, Hairston's career seems to illustrate the principle that if you wait around long enough in life, you just might end up a regular on a sitcom. Williams appeared on the highly praised *Frank's Place* for two seasons, and Hairston had a seven-year run on the popular *Amen*.

A 1929 music graduate of Tufts University in Boston, Hairston (born 1901) afterward attended Juilliard for two years, followed by a long association with the renowned Hall Johnson Choir. Hairston has sung background music in many films (*Green Pastures*, *St. Louis Blues*) and also arranged choral music for Russian composer Dimitri Tiomkin for movies such as *Lost Horizon* and *Duel in the Sun*, but never received screen credit. (Hairston also sometimes supported himself with small or extra parts in Tarzan movies.) For sixteen years Hairston was a member of the *Amos 'n' Andy* radio and TV stock companies.

But these credits are not the reasons Jester Hairston will be remembered by history: Until his death in 2000, Hairston was the last surviving member of the small group of the first artists — Nathaniel Dett, Eva Jessye, H.T. Burleigh, Rosamund Johnson et al. — who earlier in the last century devoted themselves to the task of explicating and popularizing the great African American music form of the spiritual. When partisans deem jazz "the one true American art form," what they mean to say or *should* say instead is "The Spiritual" — out of which jazz, blues, etc. spring and are only sub-species of the real thing.

In between his radio, film, TV and recording and live choral work, Hairston was awarded five honorary doctorates. As one reporter wrote of him in the 1990s, "His life reflects not only the changes in show business but a changing America."[34] This is especially true as it relates to his moving front and center as an African American ready to take proper credit for his artistic contributions.

*   *   *

In the introduction to a collection of his essays, James Baldwin recalled the day in 1940 when he was introduced to the world of black performing arts:

> I walked into music. I had grown up with music, but now, on Beauford's [Delaney] small black record player, I began to hear what I had never dared or been able to hear. Beauford never gave me any lectures. But, in his studio and because of his presence, I really began to *hear* Ella Fitzgerald, Ma Rainey, Louis Armstrong, Bessie Smith, Ethel Waters, Paul Robeson, Lena Horne, Fats Waller. He could inform me about Duke Ellington and W.C. Handy and Josh White, introduce me to Frankie Newton and tell tall tales about Ethel Waters. And these people were not meant to be looked on by me as celebrities, but as a part of Beauford's life and as part of my inheritance.[35]

At one time in Black America — as evidenced by Baldwin's epiphany at the hands of African American painter Beauford Delaney — the achievements and adventures of black entertainers were the stuff of orally transmitted folk tales. But mass media, and even academic recognition of this world of black art and entertainment has been a long time coming. I discovered this a while ago when I came across numerous fleeting references to Will Marion Cook in jazz and theatre histories, and had begun to suspect that here was one of the great figures of American music. But I could find no readily available books or writings that would put this into perspective for me; no overviews of the world of African American entertainment; no doctoral dissertations about Cook; nor significant entries in reference works to confirm this suspicion. Twenty years later it still seems to me that there is precious little attention paid by cultural historians of either race to the mirror world of black show business out of which Cook primarily operated. One reason for this lack is the dominant, still-prevailing white attitude that tends to regard black artistic expression as precipitated more by Eros than Agape, and therefore unworthy of exegesis.[36] This is complicated by the fact, as acknowledged by many blacks, that entertainment in general has played an overly co-optive, indeed repressive role in American history, i.e., the happy singing-and-dancing performers tend to cover up the harsh truths of hundreds of years of racism. At the same time, the enthusiasm many whites have exhibited for African American entertainers has always had a negative undertone: Because black performers are too often regarded as "forces of nature" rather than artists, "blackness" can easily be co-opted by whites as a stylistic affectation. There is currently no better example of this than the chain of House of Blues *faux* sharecropper cabin night clubs. The white audiences for whom these clubs are designed — who would never dream of setting foot in the actual habitat of a black sharecropper — can walk into this reproduction without fear that their racial world view will challenged in any way. They've come to get "blackness," not the complex history of suffering and triumph that created the blues. The fact that the various clubs hold off-hours symposiums for schoolchildren about the history of black music does not, in my estimation, mitigate against the fraudulence of the House of Blues "experience" itself. Audiences diverted by such spectacles have no use for the likes of Will Marion Cook — a singular individual, not a musical perfume to apply when needed.

I set out on my own to try and find out what I could about Will Marion Cook; and when I was finished I came to the conclusion that he was a revolutionary musician whose contributions paved the way for (and were the equal of) Ellington and Gershwin. Beyond that, Cook was a groundbreaking theatrical showman and, perhaps just as importantly, a racial crusader who waged a highly public lifelong battle against discrimination. So important and integral a figure to African American show business was Cook, in fact, that one cannot "get to him" without opening the door on a fascinating world that many blacks and nearly all whites (myself included) never even knew existed. Every chapter herein was born, in some way or another, out of my exposure to Cook. I hope that this book has in some small way helped to usefully illumine the contributions of African American entertainment professionals to interested parties of all races.

Appendix 1
*A Biographical Sketch of Blind Tom Bethune**

In addition to the biographical section, this sketch also contains a number of testimonials by prominent musicians and public figures as to the veracity of the claims made about Blind Tom's gifts, as well as numerous press reviews from the U.S. and abroad.

Blind Tom: The Great Negro Pianist

The performance and the character of the child generally attract so little attention, or the remembrance of them is so obscured by the lapse of time before the achievements of the man have made them subjects of interest, that it is always difficult, and often impossible, to gratify the curiosity naturally felt, to know the traits, qualities, and actions, which people imagine must have stamped the child as remarkable, as in the man they have been developed into powers which have lifted him to fame. Such, however, has not been the case with the subject of this sketch. His peculiarities were so singular, and some of them apparently so incompatible with others, as to attract attention in his early infancy; his powers so wonderful, even in their first manifestations, as to astonish and bewilder all who witnessed them. Those who did not witness, did not believe; or rather they could not conceive; for after making all due allowance for what they conceived the marvelous in narration, their powers of conception, of what was possible to such a being, fell far short of the truth; and it may be safely asserted that, to this day, no matter what they may

---

*Reprinted from: *Songs, Sketch of the Life, Testimonials from the Most Eminent Composers, and Opinions of the American and English Press, of Blind Tom the Marvelous, Musical Prodigy, The Negro Boy Pianist Whose Recent Performances at the Great St. James' and Egyptian Halls, London, and Salle Hertz, Paris, Have Created Such a Profound Sensation*, by Anonymous (New York: French & Wheat, Book and Job Printers, 1876).

have read or heard, or what they may have been led to expect, none have heard him for the first time, without a feeling of astonishment, and an involuntary acknowledgment to themselves that the reality had exceeded the expectations they had formed, and that "the half had not been told them."

Speculations have been made and theories formed without number, as to the source and the nature of these wonderful powers; it forms no part of the purpose of the writer to speculate or theorize; it is proposed to furnish facts and leave others to form their own theories and make their own speculations.

Thomas Greene Bethune (his parents having taken for him and themselves the name of their former owner), better known to the public as "Blind Tom," was born within a few miles of the city of Columbus, in the county of Muscogee and State of Georgia, on the 25th day of May, 1849. His parents are common field hands of the pure negro blood, with nothing to distinguish them from the mass of their race, except that his mother — a small woman of fine form — has remarkably small feet and hands, is of an active, merry temperament, and quick in her movements.

Tom was born blind, and, learning nothing from sight, manifested in his early infancy so entire a want of intellect as to induce the belief that he was idiotic as well as blind. His imbecility and helplessness secured for him the sympathy and care of the family in his infancy; when he began to walk and run about the yard, his amusing peculiarities made him a pet. His first manifestation of interest in anything was his fondness for sounds; the first indication of capacity, his power of imitating them. Musical sounds exerted a controlling influence over him; but all sounds, from the soft breathings of the flute to the harsh grating of the corn-sheller, appeared to afford him exquisite enjoyment.

He talked earlier than other children; and he talked no "baby talk." He uttered his words clearly and distinctly, attaching no meaning to them, but seeming to consider them merely sounds, which he imitated, as he did all others that he heard. Whatever words were addressed to him, whether in the form of a question, a command, a request, or as matter of information, he simply repeated in the tones in which they had been uttered; and would repeat not only them, but conversations he had heard — sometimes for hours at a time; yet, long after he was in possession of a vocabulary, with which, if he had known its use, he might have sustained a respectable conversation upon any ordinary topic, he never attempted to express by words an idea, a feeling, or a want. His wants he expressed by a whine, which those about him had to interpret as best they could.

The first effort to teach him was made one evening when the family was at supper (Tom, as usual at meal times, being present), when his owner, upon being informed that his mother, as an excuse for not teaching him something, had said he had not sense enough to learn anything, replied, "That is

SONGS,

Sketch of the Life,

TESTIMONIALS

FROM THE

MOST EMINENT

COMPOSERS,

AND OPINIONS

OF THE

AMERICAN & ENGLISH

PRESS,

OF

BLIND TOM

THE MARVELOUS MUSICAL PRODIGY,

THE NEGRO BOY PIANIST

WHOSE RECENT PERFORMANCES AT THE

Great St. James' and Egyptian Halls, London, and Salle Hertz, Paris,

HAVE CREATED SUCH A PROFOUND SENSATION.

Rare playbill for composer Blind Tom Bethune.

a mistake. A horse or a dog may be taught almost anything, provided you always use precisely the same terms to express the same idea. Show him what you mean, and have the patience to repeat it often enough. Tom has as much sense as a horse or a dog, and I will show you that he can be taught." He thereupon arose from the table, and approaching Tom, said to him, "Tom, sit down." Tom, of course, as was expected, stood still and repeated the words. He repeated the order and sat him down upon the floor. He then said to him, "Tom, get up." Tom sat still and repeated the order. He then repeated the order and lifted Tom to his feet. He then ordered Tom to sit down, which he did promptly — to get up, and he sprang to his feet. From that time there was matter of new interest about Tom. Everybody began to teach him something. It was soon discovered that he forgot nothing. Present to him any number of objects one after another, tell him the name of each as you presented it, he would put his hand upon it, smell of it, and pronounce its name; then present them in any order you pleased, and, after feeling and smelling of each as it was presented, he would, without fail, give its appropriate name. It was astonishing and interesting to test and to witness the exercise of this power, and, in consequence, Tom speedily learned to distinguish many things and call them by name.

He was perfectly delighted by cries of pain. When his mother whipped any of the older children he would laugh and caper, and rub his hands in an ecstasy of enjoyment; and soon would be found whipping himself, and repeating the words of the mother and the cries of the child. He enjoyed so highly the crying of children that he would inflict pain upon them, for the pleasure of hearing them cry; and a constant watch had to be kept on him when he was about younger children. He once choked a younger brother nearly to death, and at another time burnt an infant sister so badly as to produce fears of a fatal result. To this day any exclamation or expression indicative of pain gives him great pleasure; and though he will express sympathy for the sufferer, and prescribe remedies for his relief, he cannot restrain his expressions of pleasure. Doubtless it is the strength and the intensity of expressions given to sounds produced by pain that afford the enjoyment.

His mother usually did the churning; and when she was engaged in that employment, when he was unable to reach the top of the churn of ordinary size, he would whine and tug at her, until she would stand him on a stool and permit him to go to work. He did all the churning for the family as long as he remained at home, and was perhaps the only person who ever sought it as a source of pleasure.

Unlike other children, he delighted in being out of doors and alone at night, and unless prevented by being shut up in the house, would go into the yard, where he would go around a circle in a sort of dance, accompanying his motion sometimes with a monotonous hum, sometimes repeating conversations he had heard; then he would stop and whirl round like a top, rubbing his hands together, convulsed with laughter, as if he had found something which irresistibly moved him to mirth. This propensity to be out of doors was indulged by his parents the more readily, because, if they kept him in the house, he resorted to all the means in his power to make a noise. He dragged the chairs of the floor, rattled the dishes, beat the tin pans, and, unless closely watched, pinched or bit the younger children to make them cry. If they put him to bed they secured but little relief, for he would roll and twist himself into all sorts of shapes, and laugh and talk for hours, and frequently, unless the door was securely fastened, would get up after everybody was asleep, and go out to amuse himself in the yard.

His power of judging of the lapse of time was as remarkable as his power of remembering and imitating sounds. Those who are familiar with clocks which strike the hours, have observed that, a few minutes before the clock strikes, there is a sharp sound, different from and louder than the regular ticking. There was a clock in the house; and every hour in the day, just precisely when that sound was produced, Tom was certain to be there, and remain until the hour was struck. At one time the striking machine got out of order, but every hour, just at the time, he was there to listen; and as soon as the time for the clock to strike had passed, he would set up a cry and leave.

He exhibited his wonderful musical powers before he was two years old. When the young misses of the family sat on the steps, of an evening, and sang, Tom would come around and sing with them. One of them one evening said to her father:

"Pa, Tom sings beautifully, and he doesn't have to learn any tunes; he knows them all; for as soon as we begin to sing, he sings right along with us."

Very soon she said:

"He sings fine seconds to anything we sing."

His voice was then strong, soft, and melodious. Just before he had completed his second year, he had the whooping-cough from the effects of which his voice underwent an entire change: it became and continued for years exceedingly rough and harsh, though it did not affect the taste or correctness of his singing.

He was a little less than four years of age when a piano was brought to the house. The first note that was sounded, of course, brought him up. He was permitted to indulge his curiosity by running his fingers over and smelling the keys, and was then taken out of the parlor. As long as any one was playing he was contented to stay in the yard, and dance and caper to the music; but the moment it ceased, having discovered whence the sounds proceeded, and how they were produced, he was anxious to get to the instrument to continue them. One night the parlor and the piano had been left open, his mother had neglected to fasten her door, and he had escaped without her knowledge. Before day, the young ladies awoke, and, to their astonishment, heard Tom playing one of their pieces. He continued to play until the family at the usual time arose, and gathered around him to witness and wonder at his performance, which, though necessarily very imperfect, was marvelously strange; for, notwithstanding this was his first known effort at a tune, he played with both hands, and used the black as well as the white keys.

After a while he was allowed free access to the piano, and commenced playing everything he heard. He soon mastered all of that, and commenced composing for himself. He would sit at the piano for hours, playing over the pieces he had heard, then go out, and run and jump about the yard a little while, come back and play something of his own. Asked what it was, he replied, "It is what the wind said to me," or "what the birds said to me," or "what the trees said to me," or what something else said to him. No doubt what he was playing was connected, in his mind, with some sound or combination of sounds proceeding from those things, and not infrequently the representation was so good as to render the similarity clear to others.

There was but one thing which seemed to give Tom as much pleasure as the sound of the piano. Between a wing and the body of the dwelling there is a hall, on the roof of which the rain falls, from the roof of the dwelling, and runs thence down a gutter. There is, in the combination of sounds produced by the falling and running water, something so enchanting to Tom, that, from his early childhood to the time he left home, whenever it rained, whether by day or night, he would go into that passage and remain as long as the rain continued. When he was less than five years of age, having been there during a severe thunderstorm, he went to the piano and played what is now known as his Rain Storm, and said it was what the rain, the wind, and the thunder said to him. The perfection of the representation can be fully appreciated by those only who have heard the sounds [made] by the falling of the water upon the roofs; and its running off through the gutters.

There was in the city of Columbus a German music teacher, who kept pianos and music for sale. The boys about the city having heard much of Tom, sometimes asked the boys of the family to take him to town, that they might hear him; upon these occasions they asked permission of this man to use one of his pianos, and though he would grant the permission, he would not hear him. If he was engaged he would send them to the back part of the store, which was a very deep one; if he had nothing to do, he would walk out into the street. When Tom was about eight years of age, a gentleman having obtained permission to exhibit him, hired a piano of this man and invited him to visit his concert. He indignantly rejected the invitation.

The man, however, succeeded in awakening the curiosity of the wife of the musician sufficiently to induce her to attend, and she gave her husband such accounts that he went the next night. After the performance was over, he approached the man and said:

"Sir, I give it up; the world has never seen such a thing as that little blind negro, and will never see such another."

Encouraged by this, the exhibitor the next day applied to him to under-take to teach Tom. His reply was:

"No, sir; I can't teach him anything; he knows more of music than we know, or can learn — we can learn all that great genius can reduce to rule and put in tangible form; he knows more than that; I do not even know what it is, but I see and feel it is something beyond my comprehension. All that can be done for him will be to let him hear fine playing; he will work it all out by himself after a while, but he will do it sooner by hearing fine music."

It has been stated that Tom was born blind; in his infancy and for years the pupils of his eyes were white and apparently as inanimate as those of a dead fish. But nature pointed out to him a remedy which gradually relieved him from total darkness, and in process of time conferred upon him, to a limited extent, the blessings of vision.

When he was three or four years of age, it was observed that he passed most of his time with his face upturned to the sun, as if gazing intently upon it, occasionally passing his hand back and forth with a rapid motion before his eyes; that was soon followed by thrusting his fingers into his eyes with a force which appeared to be almost sufficient to expel the eye-balls from their sockets; from this he proceeded to digging one of them with sticks, until the blood would run down his face. All this must have been pleasant to him, or he would not have done it; and there is no doubt that he is indebted to the stimulus thus applied to his eyes, for the measure of sight he now enjoys. When five or six years of age, a small, comparatively clear speck appeared in one of his eyes, and it was discovered that within a very small space he could see any bright object. That eye has continued to clear, until he is now able to see luminous bodies at a distance, and can distinguish small bodies by bringing them close to his eye. Persons that he knows well, he can distinguish at the distance of a few feet, and it is hoped that in process of time his sight will so far improve, as to relieve him from many of the difficulties to which he is subject.

The mere technicalities of music Tom learns without difficulty. Its sub-stance he seems to comprehend intuitively. To teach him the notes, it was necessary only to sound them, and tell him their names. With the elements and principles of music he seemed familiar, long before he knew any of the names by which they were indicated; as a man going into a strange country may be perfectly acquainted with the appearance and nature of the material objects which meet his view, without knowing the names applied to them by the people.

Considering that in his early life he learned nothing, and later but little from sight, that he is possessed by an overmastering passion, which so per-vades his whole nature as to leave little room for interest in anything else, and gratification of which has been indulged to the largest extent, it is not surprising that, to the outside world, he should exhibit but few manifestations of intellect as applicable to any of the ordinary affairs of life, or that those who see him only under its influence should conclude that he is idiotic.

The elegance, taste and power of his performances, his wonderful power of imitation, his extraordinary memory — not only of music, but of names, dates and events — his strict adherence to what he believes to be right, his uniform politeness, and his nice sense of propriety, afford to those who know him well, ample refutation of this opinion.

Tom sometimes indulges in some strange gymnastics upon the stage, which are considered by many a part of his stage training. So far from this being the case, it is but a slight outcropping of his usual exercises. If those who see him upon the stage could witness his performances in his room, and the enjoyment they afford him, they would perhaps regret the necessity of his restraint in public. He never engaged in the plays of children or manifested any interest in them. His amusements were all his own. With a physical organization of great power and vigor, and an exuberance of animal spirits, he naturally sought physical exercise; compelled by want of sight to limit himself to a small space, he put himself in almost every conceivable posture, and resorted to those exercises which required the most violent physical exertion. They are now necessary certainly to his enjoyment, perhaps to his health.

Tom has been seen probably by more people that any one living being. He has played in almost every important city in the United States and in a great many smaller towns — and everywhere to good houses except in Boston — in Paris and most of the principal cities of England and Scotland; and everywhere he has astonished and please those who have heard him. Those who have observed him most closely, and attempted to investigate him most fully, pronounce him "a living miracle," unparalleled, incomprehensible, such as has not been seen before, and probably will never be seen again.

Appendix 2
A Selected Demas Dean Discography*

8/1922, New York. *Lucille Hegamin*: "Voodoo Blues"/"You Can Have Him I Don't Want Him Blues." Accompanied by Her Blue Flame Syncopators feat. Dean, John Anderson, Don Redman, Cyril Fullerton, Sterling Conaway or Maceo Jefferson, George Barber. Both released on Arto 9169, Bell P-169, Globe 7169.

9/1922, New York. *Lucille Hegamin*: "Beale Street Mama (Why Don't You Come Back Home?)"/"Aggravatin' Papa (Don't You Try to Two-Time Me)." Same personnel as 8/22. Both released on Cameo 270, Lincoln 2019.

10/1922, New York. *Lucille Hegamin*: "Papa, Papa"/"He May Be Your Man, But He Comes to See Me Sometimes." Same personnel as 9/22. Both released on Cameo 287.

3/1923, New York. *Lucille Hegamin*: "Waitin' for the Evening Mail"/"Now That You Got Him Can You Hold Him?" Accompanied by Her Blue Flame Syncopators, believed to be Dean and same personnel as 8/22. Both released on Cameo 343, Lincoln 2056.

8/9/26, New York. *Savoy Bearcats*: "Stampede"/"How Could I Be Blue?" Personnel: Dean, Gilbert Paris, James Reevy, Carmelo Jari (Jejo), Otto Mikell, Ramon Hernandez, Leon Abbey, Joe Steele, Freddy White, Harry Edwards, Willie Lynch. Both tracks unreleased.

8/23/26, New York. *Savoy Bearcats*: "Senegalese Stomp"/"Nightmare"/"Bearcat Stomp." Same personnel as 8/9/26. First two tracks released on Victor 20182; final track on Victor 20307.

---

*Information for this discography was extrapolated from several sources; including Brian Rust's *Jazz Records, 1897–1942* (New Rochelle, NY: Arlington House, 1978) and R. M. W. Dixon and J. Godrich's *Blues and Gospel Records 1902 to 1942* (Middlesex, England: n.p., 1963).

10/11/26, New York. *Savoy Bearcats*: "Stampede"/"Hot Notes"/"How Could I Be Blue?"/"Senorita Mine." Personnel same as 8/9/26. First two tracks released on Victor 20460; third track on Victor 20307; final track unreleased.

12/1926, New York. *Rosa Henderson*: "Git Goin'"/"Someday You'll Come Back to Me" Accompanied by Dean and Porter Grainger, piano. Both released on Paramount 7159, Perfect 119.

2/9/28, New York. *Bessie Smith*: "Thinking Blues"/"Pickpocket Blues"/"I Used to Be Your Sweet Mama." Personnel: Dean, Charlie Green, Fred Longshaw. First and third tracks released on Columbia 14292-D, Parlophone R-2483 (GB); second track released on Columbia 14304-D.

2/21/28, New York. *Bessie Smith*: "Standing in the Rain Blues"/"It Won't Be You"/"I'm a Cheater." Personnel: Dean, Charlie Green, Fred Longshaw. First two tracks released on Columbia 14338-D; final track unreleased.

6/21/28, New York. *Adelaide Hall*: "Baby"/"I Must Have That Man." Accompanied by Lew Leslie's Blackbirds Orchestra feat. Personnel: Dean, Pike Davis, Herb Fleming, Carmelo Jejo (Jari), Albert Socarras, Ramon Usera, George Rickson, Benny James, Henry Edwards, Jesse Baltimore. Both released on Brunswick 4031.

8/14/28, New York. *Lew Leslie's Blackbirds Orchestra*: "Bandana Babies"/"Magnolia's Wedding Day." Same personnel as 6/21/28. Both released on Brunswick 4030.

9/10/29, Hayes, Middlesex England. *Noble Sissle and His Orchestra*: "Kansas City Kitty"/"On the Lazy Amazon"/"Camp Meeting Day"/"Miranda." Personnel: Dean, Pike Davis, James Reevy, Buster Bailey, Rudy Jackson, Ralph Duquesne, Ramon Usera, Juice Wilson, William Rosamand, Lloyd Pinckney, Warren Harris, Henry Edwards, John Ricks, Jesse Baltimore. First track released on HMV B-5731 (GB); second track unreleased; third track released on HMV B-5709 (GB); final track released on Electrola (Germany) EG-1560.

10/10/29, Hayes, Middlesex England. *Noble Sissle and His Orchestra*: "I'm Crooning a Tune About June"/"Recollections"/"You Want Lovin' and I Want Love"/"Yet You Forget." Same personnel as 9/10/29. First track released on HMV B-5731, Electrola EG-1713; second and third tracks released on HMV B-5723; fourth track unreleased.

2/24/31, New York. *Noble Sissle and His Orchestra*: "Got the Bench, Got the Park"/"In a Café on the Road to Calais"/"Loveless Love." Personnel: Dean, Sidney Bechet, Tommy Ladnier, Billy Burns, Rudy Jackson, Ralph Duquesne, Ramon Usera, Lloyd Pinckney, Frank Ethridge, Edward Coles, Jack Carter. First and third tracks released on Brunswick 6073, Supertone S-2173; Melotone M-12444 ("Loveless" only); second track unreleased.

4/21/31, New York. *Noble Sissle and His Orchestra*: "Basement Blues"/"Wha'd Ya Do to Me?"/"Roll On, Mississippi, Roll On." First track released on Brunswick 6129; final two tracks released on Brunswick 6111.

8/15/34, Chicago. *Noble Sissle and His International Orchestra*: "Under the Creole Moon"/"The Old Ark Is Moverin'"/"Loveless Love"/"Polka Dot Rag." Personnel: Dean, Wendell Culley, Clarence Brereton, Chester Burrill, Sidney Bechet, Harvey Boone, Ramon Usera, James Tolliver, Oscar Mandera, Harry Brooks, Howard Hill, Edward Coles, Jack Carter, Billy Banks, Lavaida Carter. First two tracks released on Decca 153, final two on Decca 154.

3/11/36, New York. *Noble Sissle and His Orchestra*: "That's What Love Did to Me"/"You Can't Live in Harlem"/"I Wonder Who Made Rhythm"/"Tain't a Fit Night Out for Man or Beast"/"I Take to You"/"Rhythm of the Broadway Moon." Personnel: Dean, Wendell Culley, Clarence Brereton, Chauncey Haughton, Gil White, Jerome Pasquall, Jimmy Miller, Jimmy Jones, Wilbert Kirk, Chester Burrill, Sidney Bechet, Oscar Mandera, Harry Brooks, Billy Banks, Lena Horne. First and second track released on Decca 778; third and fourth tracks released on Decca 766 (or Columbia DB-5032 & Columbia FB-1493 [GB]); final two tracks released on Decca 847 (or Columbia DB-5032 & Columbia FB-1493 [GB]).

4/14/37, New York. *Noble Sissle and His Orchestra*: "Bandana Days"/"I'm Just Wild About Harry"/"Dear Old Southland"/"St. Louis Blues." Personnel same as 3/11/36 except Erskine Butterfield replaces Brooks. First two tracks released on Variety 552; third tracks released on LPs CBS CL-2102, BGP-62232; final track unreleased.

Appendix 3
"Negro Dance,"
by Nora Douglas Holt

Following four pages: Most of Nora Holt's personal effects, including her music scores, were lost while in storage during her long European sojourn. This is a rare surviving example of her composition — possibly the only surviving score by Holt — which was printed in her influential publication "Music and Poetry."

Negro Dance

N. DOUGLAS HOLT
Op. 25, No. 1.

Copyright, MCMXXI, by Holt Publishing Co. Chicago, Ill.

Negro Dance 4-2

Negro Dance 4-3

Negro Dance 4-4

RAYNER, DALHEIM &C.
MUSIC PRINTERS &C.
CHICAGO

Chapter Notes

All African American newspapers quoted are national editions of same and are generally available on microfilm at larger university research facilities and public libraries.

Preface

1. Dailey Paskman, *"Gentlemen, Be Seated!" A Parade of the American Minstrels* (New York: Clarkson N. Potter, 1976), pp. 173–74. Among the several works consulted regarding the evolution of minstrelsy, this revised edition of the seminal 1928 book on the subject proved invaluable, and contains the observation by the author: "It is to the Negro that the white minstrel owes everything, for without the presence of the black race in this country American minstrelsy would never have existed." Also helpful was Redd Foxx and Norma Miller's *The Redd Foxx Encyclopedia of Black Humor* (Pasadena, CA: Ward Ritchie Press, 1977).

2. Liner notes, "A Tribute to Black Entertainers" (Columbia/Legacy C2K 52454).

3. "'Dixie' Written by Blacks Scholars Suggest in Book," *Jet*, November 1, 1993, p. 10 — a news feature regarding the book *Way Up North in Dixie: A Black Family's Claim to the Confederate Anthem* by Howard Sacks and Judith Sacks (Washington, DC: Smithsonian Institution Press, 1991).

4. LeRoi Jones, *Blues People: Negro Music in White America* (New York: Morrow, 1963), p. 100. Jones draws the distinction between jazz and blues recordings, crediting the Original Dixieland Jazz Band, a white group, with having made the first authentic jazz records three years earlier, in 1917.

5. Peter M. Bergman, *The Chronological History of the Negro in America* (New York: Harper & Row, 1969), pp. 387–90.

6. Frank C. Taylor, with Gerald Cook, *Alberta: A Celebration in Blues* (New York: McGraw-Hill, 1987), p. 39.

7. Foxx and Miller, *The Redd Foxx Encyclopedia of Black Humor*, pp. 3–6.

8. Paskman, pp. 28–31. Paskman writes, "[E]thnological research proves that Africa actually possessed an instrument known as the 'banjar,' made of a large gourd, with a neck of wood attached, and fitted with four strings. It is quite possible that this primitive banjo came to America in the earliest days of Negro slavery."

9. Jones, pp. 82–86. cf. also Alec Wilder, *American Popular Song* (New York: Oxford, 1972), pp. 7–8. Regarding the evolution of popular music, Wilder quotes the book's editor James Maher as follows: "[Imagine] the following performing at the edge of Echo Canyon in Grand Canyon National Park: The Fisk Jubilee Choir richly intoning their heroic 'spirituals'; Scott Joplin, Ben Harney, and Eubie Blake playing ragtime piano with its broad spectrum of the vigorous and the academic...." And so forth for nearly a page, with the overwhelming number of contributors to Maher's historical analogy being African American, then concluding with the observation, "Imagine this great mélange of sounds pouring down into the canyon, mixing below, then returning in a single echo and you may get some idea of what happened as American popular music achieved a native idiom between 1890 and World War I."

10. John Lovell, Jr., *Black Song: The Forge and the Flame* (New York: Macmillan, 1972), pp. 402–25. cf. also Maude Cuney-Hare, *Negro Musicians and Their Music* (Washington: Associated Publishers, 1936), pp. 239–41.

11. Mel Watkins, *On the Real Side: Laughing, Lying, and Signifying — The Underground Tradition of African-American Humor That Transformed American Culture, from Slavery to Richard Pryor* (New York: Simon & Schuster, 1994), pp. 88, 148.

12. U.S. Census Bureau, 1910 census survey.

13. Harry Birdoff, *The World's Greatest Hit: Uncle Tom's Cabin* (New York: S.F. Vanni Publishers and Booksellers, 1947), pp. 306–10.

14. *Ibid.*, p. 225. The precedent-shattering black

performer who assumed the role of Uncle Tom with the Gustav Frohman Company, circa 1875, was the beloved Sam Lucas. In 1913 the 72-year-old actor became not only the first of his race to portray Tom on film, he was also the first black to have a leading role in a motion picture.

15. Carolyn Ione, *Pride of Family: Four Generations of American Women of Color* (New York: Summit Books, 1991), p. 151.

16. *American Theatre*, May 1991, p. 20. The estimate was made by Harriet Beecher Stowe's son.

17. Langston Hughes, *I Wonder as I Wander* (New York: Appleton Century Crofts, 1964), p. 116. Segregation held sway in the world of film exhibition, and in a most peculiar fashion, as Hughes writes in this second volume of his memoirs: "I could not help but think how impregnable Hollywood had been to Negroes, and how all over America the union of motion-picture operators did not permit Negroes to operate projection machines—not even in theaters in Negro neighborhoods. Negro-owned establishments had to employ white projectionists."

18. Clarence Muse and David Arlen, *Way Down South* (Hollywood: David Graham Fischer, 1932). Significant portions of this (regrettably) long out-of-print *roman à clef* are devoted to minute accounts of day-to-day life on the T.O.B.A., i.e., lodging, food, payroll, theater interiors, etc.

19. Jerry Ames and Jim Siegelman, *The Book of Tap* (New York: McKay, 1977), p. 92. Did message communication play a major role in the evolution of tap amongst slaves? Opinion of experts vary, with these authors taking the middle-ground position that it was not a key ingredient, but on the occasions when slaves had African signaling drums taken away from them by their masters, they would often revert to making sounds with their feet as a substitute.

20. James Weldon Johnson, *Black Manhattan* (New York: Alfred A. Knopf, 1940), p. 127.

21. Ann Charters, *Nobody: The Story of Bert Williams* (New York: Macmillan, 1970), p. 11. Fields' remark is a widely quoted one, appearing in nearly every book and article about the African American comedian.

Chapter 1

1. Rayford W. Logan and Michael R. Winston, *Dictionary of American Negro Biography* (New York: Norton, 1982), pp. 127–28. This is not to claim that Cook invented big band jazz, but that he was unarguably the first to successfully pull together the basic elements that went into its making. The very fact that he was the initial arranger to use saxophones in non–European music — documented elsewhere in this chapter — places him in the advance guard of the new music revolution. Elton C. Fax in Logan and Winston does a commendable job of contextualizing Cook's achievements: "Cook's excellent musical background combined with a drive to create a truly indigenous Negro music was bearing results." He goes on to term Cook's 1905 group, the Memphis Students, a "jazz band." Also: Osgood, p. 44. This first book published in the U.S. on the subject of jazz sees fit to include the name of Cook. Osgood writes of him in 1926: "These all-colored revues, which have been so much in vogue for three or four years past [i.e. *Shuffle Along*, etc.], are merely a development with the addition of costumes and scenery, of the shows that Will Marion Cook and his Clef Club used to give of a Saturday night in the years before that. Cook's men, all of whom could sing and play an instrument, were superb in such things as, for instance, his own best compositions, 'Swing Along' and 'Rain Song,' two numbers that entitle him to serious consideration as a composer of the best type of negro song. The rich voices and the *innate negro sense of rhythm* [italics mine] as expressed through the accompanying instruments made a combination thrilling to listen to."

2. Eileen Southern, *Biographical Dictionary of Afro-American and African Musicians* (Westport, CT: Greenwood Press, 1982), p. 386. Cf. also the didactic panel on Cook in "Beyond Category," the 1993–95 Smithsonian Institution traveling exhibit devoted to Duke Ellington: "In New York, Ellington surrounded himself with a circle of superior musicians, such as Will Marion Cook and Will Vodery. Cook gave Duke some advice that made a lasting impression: 'First you find the logical way, and when you find it, avoid it, and let your inner self break through and guide you. Don't try to be anybody else but yourself.'" (Original source unknown.)

3. Al Rose, *Eubie Blake* (New York: Schirmer, 1979), p. 42. Quotation from an interview with Eubie Blake conducted by Rose.

4. Edward T. James, ed., *Dictionary of American Biography Supplement Three, 1941–1945* (New York: Scribner's, 1945), p. 187.

5. James Weldon Johnson, *Along This Way: The Autobiography of James Weldon Johnson* (New York: Penguin, 1990), p. 173.

6. Duke Ellington, *Music Is My Mistress* (New York: Doubleday, 1973), p. 96. Cf. also Logan and Winston, *op. cit.*, p. 127. The violin-smashing incident is included in nearly every biographical entry on Cook; that is to say, the story has been repeated down the years on many dozens of occasions, but this writer has never been able to pin down the exact review that supposedly caused Cook to act as he did. Conductor Maurice Peress told me in a June 1995 phone interview that he has been led to believe that, in fact, the offending review — which Peress also never saw — trafficked in "the borrowed identity, typical of the time, of comparing blacks to their white counterparts; you had people being called 'the black this,' 'the black that.'" In Cook's case, says Peress, he was apparently likened to famed Hungarian violinist Eduard Reményi (1830–1898) and dubbed "The Black Reményi." "Cook was far too young and aware to

have been satisfied by something like this," says Peress. "In addition, I think he was bothered by having the fact that his race ever brought into the picture in the first place."

7. Morroe Berger, Edward Berger and James Patrick, *Benny Carter: A Life in American Music* (Metuchen, NJ: Scarecrow, 1982), v.1, p. 21.

8. Langston Hughes, Milton Meltzer and C. Eric Lincoln, *A Pictorial History of Black Americans*, fifth revised edition (New York: Crown, 1983), pp. 258–59.

9. Isadore Witmark and Isaac Goldberg, *From Ragtime to Swingtime: The Story of the House of Witmark* (New York: Lee Furman, 1939), pp. 195–97.

10. Johnson, *Along This Way, op. cit.*, p. 175.

11. Jervis Anderson, *This Was Harlem 1900–1950* (New York: Farrar, Straus, Giroux, 1982), p. 215. Letter to Van Vechten quoted.

12. *New York Times*, December 19, 1926, letter to the editor.

13. Mercer Cook, "Will Marion Cook: He Helped Them All," *Crisis*, October 1944, p. 323.

14. Thomas L. Riis, *Just Before Jazz* (Washington: Smithsonian Institution Press, 1989), p. 43. Letter from Johnson to William Graves.

15. Ramona Lowe, "Death of Will Marion Cook Seen End of Brilliant Era of Negro Show Life," *Chicago Defender*, July 28, 1944. Mitchell quoted in Cook obituary.

16. Riis, *op. cit.*, pp. 42–43.

17. Josef Skvorecky, *Dvorak in Love* (New York: Alfred A. Knopf, 1987), pp. 1–23. Chapter one of this *roman à clef* is primarily devoted to Cook.

18. *Ibid.*, author's acknowledgments.

19. *Ibid.*, p. 20: "The girls flew up and down while Will was grafting onto the polka sounds from — where, exactly, were they from?"

20. William S. McFeely, *Frederick Douglass* (New York: Norton, 1991), pp. 370–71.

21. Will Marion Cook, "Clorindy, the Origin of the Cakewalk," *Theatre Arts* (September 1947), p. 61. Cook writes: "I was barred…from the classes at the National Conservatory of Music because I wouldn't play my fiddle in the orchestra under Dvorak… Dvorak didn't like me anyway; Harry T. Burleigh was his pet." Burleigh (1866–1949) was a prominent African American composer-arranger especially noted for his setting of spirituals. Presumably this oft-reprinted article was intended for Cook's never-published memoir *A Helluva Life*.

22. For a description of this turn-of-the-century black Bohemian set, which operated out of New York's Marshall Hotel on West 53rd Street, see Johnson, *Along This Way, op. cit.* pp. 170–77.

23. Chris Goddard, *Jazz Away from Home* (New York: Paddington, 1979), p. 32. Arthur Briggs says that the orchestra was the Boston Symphony; however, inquiries made by the author to the orchestra's archivist indicate that Cook was never a member of the BSO. Presumably, a similar incident did occur, the details of which Cook imparted to Briggs, who, in turn, miscommunicated the name

of the orchestra to Goddard. The Boston Symphony's archivist wrote the author in June 1995: "It could be that the Cook you are looking for played with another Boston group of the time."

24. Will Marion Cook, *op. cit.*, pp. 61–65.

25. *Ibid.*

26. Foxx and Miller, *op. cit.*, p. 31.

27. Will Marion Cook, *loc. cit.*, pp. 61–65.

28. *Ibid.*, pp. 61–65.

29. *Ibid.*, pp. 61–65.

30. A professionally printed (published?) copy of the libretto for *Jes' Lak White Fo'ks* was deposited with the Library of Congress copyright office on June 15, 1900.

31. Charters, *op. cit.*, pp. 77, 83.

32. Eric Ledell Smith, *Bert Williams: A Biography of the Pioneer Black Comedian* (Jefferson, NC: McFarland, 1992), pp. 14–15.

33. Gerald Bordman, *The American Musical Theatre* (New York: Oxford, 1978), p. 190. *New York Times*, February, 19, 1903, review of *In Dahomey* quoted. The reviewer lavished an inordinate amount of space on the varying skin color of the principals, observing at one point, "One of the chorus girls clearly had blonde hair that wasn't peroxide." Bordman deemed *In Dahomey*, "one of the most important events in American Musical Theatre history."

34. *Life*, March 13, 1903, n.p. Review of *In Dahomey*.

35. Charters, *op. cit.*, p. 71.

36. *St. James Gazette*, May 18, 1903. Review of London production of *In Dahomey* by "A.C." This and other British reviews (unless otherwise noted) are cited by Jeffrey Green, "*In Dahomey* in London in 1903," *The Black Perspective in Music*, Spring 1983, pp. 23–40.

37. *The Globe*, May 18, 1903. Quoted in Jeffrey Green, "*In Dahomey* in London in 1903," *The Black Perspective in Music*, Spring 1983, pp. 23–40.

38. *Pall Mall Gazette* (London), May 18, 1903, p. 11. Review of *In Dahomey*.

39. Jeffrey Green, "*In Dahomey* in London in 1903," *The Black Perspective in Music*, Spring 1983, pp. 23–40.

40. *The Globe*, May 18, 1903. Quoted in Jeffrey Green, "*In Dahomey* in London in 1903," *The Black Perspective in Music*, Spring 1983, pp. 23–40.

41. George Bernard Shaw to Johnston Forbes-Robertson, December 21 and 22, 1903. In Dan H. Lawrence, ed., *Bernard Shaw; Collected Letters — 1898–1910* (New York: Dodd-Mead, 1965), pp. 384–85.

42. *Daily News* (London), May 16, 1903; interview with Cook. Quoted in Jeffrey Green, "*In Dahomey* in London in 1903," *The Black Perspective in Music*, Spring 1983, pp. 23–40.

43. Bordman, *op. cit.*, p. 218.

44. Rose, *loc. cit.*, p. 42. Quotation from an interview with Eubie Blake by Rose.

45. Rose, *op. cit.*, pp. 42–43.

46. Logan and Winston, *loc. cit.*.

47. Dave Dexter, Jr., *The Jazz Story: from the*

'90s to the '60s (Englewood Cliffs, NJ: Prentice-Hall, 1964), p. 57.

48. J.C. Thomas, *Chasin' the Trane: The Music and Mystique of John Coltrane* (New York: Doubleday, 1975), p. 31.

49. Southern, *Biographical Dictionary of Afro-American and African Musicians, op. cit.*, p. 82.

50. Charles Schwartz, *Gershwin: His Life and Music* (New York: Bobbs-Merrill, 1973), pp. 74–78. It is unfortunate that nearly every reference to the so-called 1924 Aeolian Hall concert by Whiteman deems it the first time that jazz music was ever played in a concert hall, when in fact James Reese Europe did the honors in 1912. In a biography of Gershwin, Charles Schwartz provides a perfect example of the historical inaccuracies surrounding both events. Unlike most other writers, however, he is at least aware of the fact that it had been done before Whiteman when soprano Eva Gauthier devoted at least a portion of her ostensibly classical recital to performing Gershwin, Kern and Berlin (all with Gershwin at the piano) a year earlier (1923). Additionally, there is little question that the 1912 concert was far jazzier than the 1924 affair. On February 12, 1913, James Reese Europe headed another Clef Club Concert at Carnegie featuring a mixture of old (Cook's "Swing Along" and "Rain Song" again) and new material. In 1914, Europe oversaw a third similar concert at Carnegie, this time as the head of his newly formed National Negro Symphony Orchestra.

51. Robert Kimball and William Bolcom, *Reminiscing with Sissle and Blake* (New York: Viking, 1973), p. 57. Configuration of orchestra taken from advertisement for another Clef Club concert of the previous year. The array of instruments brings to mind the musical experiments of "classical" composer Louis Moreau Gottschalk, deeply influenced by African rhythms, and who in mid–19th century Cuba presented a concert consisting of a military band, a Caribbean drumming group, a choir of 200, 68 clarinetists, 33 tuba players and sundry other players adding up to a grand total of 650.

52. Eileen Southern, *Readings in Black American Music* (New York: Norton, 1971), p. 225. Article by Europe appearing in *Literary Digest*, April 26, 1919. Quoted in Southern.

53. Peress on a 1989 NPR radio broadcast.

54. Sidney Bechet, *Treat It Gentle* (London: Cassell, 1960), p. 126.

55. Bechet, pp. 126–27.

56. Bechet, *op. cit.*, p. 127. Ansermet's review quoted by Bechet.

57. John Chilton, *Sidney Bechet: The Wizard of Jazz* (New York, Oxford, 1987), pp. 36–37. From the July 4, 1919, London debut performance program reprinted in Chilton.

58. Bechet, *op. cit.*, p. 128.

59. Chilton, *op. cit.*, p. 38. Quotation of Bechet from *Storyville Magazine*, no. 78 in Chilton.

60. "Abbie Mitchell Proves She Is One of the Greatest Actresses on Stage Today," *Pittsburgh Courier*, August 4, 1928.

61. Goddard, *op. cit.*, pp. 32, 53–59. Most jazz histories are unstinting in their praise of Cook and his contribution to the evolution of big band jazz, and Goddard in *Jazz Away from Home* (a survey of jazz musicians working in Europe in the earlier part of the 20th century) is typical. All the more ironic, then, that Cook should turn out to be such a relatively obscure cultural figure in the U.S.

62. James Lincoln Collier, *Duke Ellington* (New York: Oxford, 1987), pp. 100–02. Collier recounts the frustration of music critic Robert Darrell in the face of Ellington's refusal to admit familiarity with Eurocentric music as was assumed by Darrell, who was writing "serious" criticism of Ellington's work in the early 1930s.

63. Peter Gammond, ed., *Duke Ellington: His Life and Music* (New York: Da Capo, 1978), p. 54. From reprint in Gammond of three-part July 1944 *New Yorker* magazine profile of Duke Ellington by Richard O. Boyer.

64. *Ibid.*, p. 54.

65. Ellington, *op. cit.*, p. 95.

66. Norman Katkov, *The Fabulous Fanny: The Story of Fanny Brice* (New York: Alfred A. Knopf, 1953), p. 65.

67. *Ibid.*, p. 65.

68. For some insight into Cook's feelings about the turn black Broadway was taking, see: "W.M. Cook: Deplores 'High Yellow' Revues," *Chicago Tribune* (Paris edition), November 18, 1925.

69. Mercer Cook, "Will Marion Cook: He Helped Them All," *Crisis*, October 1944, p. 323.

70. Ramona Lowe, "Death of Will Marion Cook Seen as End of Brilliant Era of Negro Show Life," *Chicago Defender*, July 28, 1944. Cook's obituary quotes him as saying to Ziegfeld, "Here's a man [Vodery] who can do it better than I."

71. Liner notes by Noble Sissle. "Yamakraw," James P. Johnson (Folkways FJ 2842), 1962.

72. Edward Jablonski, *Harold Arlen: Happy With the Blues* (New York: Doubleday, 1961), p. 43.

73. "Will Marion Cook Writes New Song," *Amsterdam News*, June 19, 1938. It seems as if African American entertainers were forever being compared to the French singer; for example, in her autobiography *His Eye Is on the Sparrow*, Ethel Waters quotes the Chicago newspaper headline "Ashton Stevens Finds Yvette Guilbert of Her Race in Ethel Waters."

74. Mercer Cook, *loc. cit.*, "Will Marion Cook: He Helped Them All," *Crisis*, October 1944, p. 323.

75. *Ibid.*

76. Anderson, *op. cit.*, p. 33.

77. Johnson, *Along This Way, loc. cit.*, p. 173.

78. Mercer Cook, *loc. cit.*

79. Logan and Winston, *op. cit.*, p. 129. Handy quoted from unspecified source.

Chapter 2

1. *Chicago Defender,* June 18, 1910, letter to the editor.

2. Muse, Clarence, and David Arlen. *Way Down South* (Hollywood: David Graham Fischer, 1932), p. 16.

3. Gary Giddins, "Dinah Washington: The Once and Future Queen," *Village Voice*, February 9, 1988, pp. 85–6.

4. Marshall and Jean Stearns, *Jazz Dance: The Story of American Vernacular Dance* (New York: Macmillan, 1968), p. 85. Cf. also Edward Thorpe's comments on the Whitmans in *Black Dance* (Woodstock, NY: Overlook Press, 1990), p. 72.

5. *Ibid.*, p. 85.

6. Joan R. Sherman, "Albery Allson Whitman: Poet of Beauty and Manliness," *College Language Association Journal*, December 1971. Whitman's other works include *Essays on the Ten Plagues and Miscellaneous Poems* (c. 1871), *Leelah Misled* (1873), *The Rape of Florida* (1884), *Drifted Leaves* (1890) and *An Idle of the South* (1901).

7. *Ibid.*, p. 127.

8. *Ibid.*

9. Telephone interview with Ernestine Lucas, July 1994.

10. Perry Bradford, *Born with the Blues* (New York: Oak, 1965), p. 19. While no representative films or phonograph records of the sisters' act are known to have been made, at least two sides were cut by Essie Whitman in New York on October 1921 for W.C. Handy's popular Black Swan label: "Sweet Daddy It's You I Love" b/w "If You Don't Believe I Love You." Whitman was accompanied by a top-flight jazz band featuring Fletcher Henderson on piano and banjo. (The former title could be a variant title of "Think of Me Little Daddy," written by Bert Whitman and recorded by Wilbur Sweatman's Original Jazz Band around this same period.) In a 1927 *Pittsburgh Courier* article, the highly determined sister Mabel of the Whitman Sisters said that she and her siblings were on their way to Hollywood to take a crack at movies. If they arrived there, their dreams of the silver screen did not come true. There was also talk of a recording contract to involve all the sisters, but as far as is known, only Essie Whitman finally made it into the studio for one session.

11. "Beautiful Whitman Sisters Won International Acclaim on Stage," *Ebony*, March 1954, p. 57.

12. Henry T. Sampson, *Blacks in Blackface* (Metuchen, NJ: Scarecrow, 1980), p. 103.

13. Stearns and Stearns, *op. cit.*, p. 86

14. Sampson, *op. cit.*, p. 102.

15. Muse and Arlen, *op. cit.*, pp. 66–67.

16. Henry T. Sampson, *The Ghost Walks: A Chronological History of Blacks in Show Business.* Metuchen, NJ: Scarecrow, 1988, p. 245. However, in a 1995 letter to me from the Whitmans' relative Ernestine Lucas, she writes, "I still hold to my theory that Albery Whitman *could not* have left so large a sum of money as the article indicates ... I wouldn't put it past the 'girls' to have started the rumor as a ploy for 'human interest.'" (Lucas is the author of a family history containing extensive information regarding Albery and his daughters.)

17. Telephone interview with Ernestine Lucas, July 1994.

18. Stearns and Stearns, *loc. cit.*, p. 86.

19. *Ibid.*

20. Sherman, *op. cit.*, p. 128.

21. Ian Carr, Digby Fairweather and Brian Priestley, *Jazz: The Essential Companion* (New York: Prentice-Hall, 1987), p. 252; entry by Fairweather.

22. Nat Shapiro and Nat Hentoff, *Hear Me Talkin' to Ya* (New York: Dover, 1966), p. 88.

23. Rudi Blesh and Harriet Janis, *They All Played Ragtime* (New York: Oak, 1966), 173. Quoted from *Stage Magazine*, date unknown.

24. Muse and Arlen, *op. cit.*, p. 67.

25. "Whitman Sisters' Tent Theatre At Forty-Sixth Street and Wabash Avenue," *Pittsburgh Courier*, August 20, 1927. The same week found Nora Holt (see Chapter Five) on the Saturday midnight bill at Chicago's Apollo Theater.

26. Sampson, *Blacks in Blackface, op. cit.*, p. 105. Quoted from a 1931 issue of the *Baltimore Afro-American.*

27. Tony Langston, *Chicago Defender*, June 21, 1924. Review of *Romping Through.*

28. Tony Langston, "Whitman Sisters Change at Grand," *Chicago Defender*, June 28, 1924.

29. Butterbeans and Susie; the duo whose real names were Jodey and Susie Edwards and who were married in real life, were famed for their put-upon wife-triflin' husband comedy presentation. Their act also spotlighted Susie's warm, expressive blues singing.

30. "Whitmans Meet Coolidge," *Chicago Defender*, July 3, 1926. The meeting with the president, while the Sisters were playing to standing room only at D.C.'s Howard Theater, was arranged by the city's Crispus Attuck's Press Association. Along for the White House visit was Princess Wee Wee — the "World's Smallest Perfect Woman" — whose presence was said to have give President Coolidge "great pleasure."

31. "'Pioneers Pay Price' Says Mabel Whitman," *Chicago Defender*, September 27, 1924. Original interview with Whitman which appeared in the September 24 *Pittsburgh Courier* reprinted as a news story.

32. *Baltimore Afro-American*, January 19, 1929. Reprinted in Sampson, *Blacks in Blackface.*

33. Stearns and Stearns, *op. cit.*, p. 87.

34. "Mae Whitman, 'Boss' of the Famed Musical Hit, Is Show Game's Most Original Woman," *Pittsburgh Courier*, March 13, 1930.

35. "Mabel of Whitman Sisters Has a Word to Say; Listen," *Chicago Defender*, September 29, 1934, p. 8.

36. For an especially enlightening series of articles about African American entertainment professionals' struggles to attain their fair share of dignity and economic rewards — even from very early on — see a series of articles by the *Chicago Defender*'s music and drama critic, Sylvester Russell, which began in the 8/27/10 issue of the paper

and continued in the three subsequent issues (national ed.).

37. Muse and Arlen, *loc. cit.* In addition, Marshall and Jean Stearns point out in their book *Jazz Dance*, "Wherever and whenever [the Whitmans] saw a talented youngster on their tours, they collared them — with his parents' permission — and literally raised and educated him in their family troupe"; nor, they noted, did she allow smoking, drinking or cohabitation amongst her charges.

38. Stearns and Stearns, *op. cit.*, p. 91.

39. *Ibid.*

40. *Ibid.*, p. 89.

41. *Ibid.*, p. 90.

42. *Ibid.*, p. 89.

43. *Ibid.*, p. 90.

44. *Ibid.* Paraphrase of Alice Whitman's description in Marshall and Jean Stearn's *Jazz Dance*.

45. *Ibid.*, p. 89.

46. "Success of Pops and Louis Keep Whitman Sisters Idle," *Chicago Defender*, May 5, 1934.

47. "Mabel of Whitman Sisters Has a Word to Say; Listen," *Chicago Defender*, September 29, 1934, p. 8.

48. *Ibid.*

49. *Ibid.*

50. Stearns and Stearns, *op. cit.*, p. 91.

Chapter 3

1. U.S. Bureau of Census, 1910 census survey. There were also in the African American category: 1,279 actors, 12 stage carpenters, 321 stage hands, 50 fortune tellers and hypnotists and 5,804 musicians. Census reprinted in Henry T. Sampson's *Blacks in Blackface* (Metuchen, NJ: Scarecrow, 1980), p. 9.

2. Typescript, "Comedy Genius Billy McClain," by Zeke Blossom, circa 1902, New York Public Library, Billy Rose Theatre Collection.

3. Tom Fletcher, *The Tom Fletcher Story: 100 Years of the Negro in Show Business* (New York: Burdge, 1954), p. 91.

4. *Ibid.*, p. 93. Advertisements reprinted in *100 Years of the Negro in Show Business*. Also, description drawn from: Thomas L. Riis' *Just Before Jazz* (Washington: Smithsonian Institution Press, 1989), pp. 22–24; Fletcher, *op. cit.*, pp. 29, 53–54, 94; "Scottish Dances Held at Old Ambrose Park," *Brooklyn Eagle*, September 4, 1940.

5. Sampson, *Blacks in Blackface, op. cit.*, p. 400. Before his ascent to the throne of operetta king, Herbert also was musical director for at least one other early musical featuring the talents of African American entertainers: *The Gold Bug*, starring Bert Williams and George Walker.

6. *New York Times*, May 26, 1895, II, p. 16. Reprinted in Riis, 23.7. Fletcher, *loc. cit.*

7. Fletcher, Tom. *The Tom Fletcher Story: 100 Years of the Negro in Show Business* (New York: Burdge, 1954), p. 91.

8. Typescript, "Comedy Genius Billy McClain, *op. cit.*

9. Sampson, *Blacks in Blackface, loc. cit.* Quotations from McClain letter in the *Indianapolis Freeman*, April 2, 1910. Reprinted in Sampson.

10. Mel Watkins, *On the Real Side: Laughing, Lying, and Signifying — The Underground Tradition of African-American Humor That Transformed American Culture, From Slavery to Richard Pryor.* New York: Simon & Schuster, 1994, 111. Lew Johnson operated for three decades from the mid–1860s onward. Watkins writes: "Some consider him the most successful black owner of the period."

11. For a brief but interesting history of blacks in the prizefight ring, see James Weldon Johnson's *Black Manhattan* (New York: Alfred A. Knopf, 1940), pp. 65–73.

12. Peter M. Bergman, *The Chronological History of the Negro in America* (New York: Harper & Row, 1969), p. 520.

13. Henry T. Sampson, *The Ghost Walks: A Chronological History of Blacks in Show Business* (Metuchen, NJ: Scarecrow, 1988), p. 236. Quotations from McClain letter in the *Indianapolis Freeman*, n.d.

14. *Ibid*, p. 241.

15. Fletcher, *op. cit*, p. 98.

16. Typescript, "Comedy Genius Billy McClain," *op. cit.*

17. Sampson, *The Ghost Walks, op. cit.*, p. 245, Facts surrounding McClain's detention drawn from March 1902 (unknown) newspaper article reprinted in Sampson.

18. McClain departed the U.S. in 1904 after remaining with the Smart Set company until sometime in 1904. Early 1905 found him in England and Scotland touring extensively; 1906 at the Folies Bergere; in 1910 he was still abroad and flourishing at the Brussels Exposition where he produced three attractions. In 1910 he wrote: "I am the first Negro to produce, play, sing, dance, and talk in French." Reprinted in Sampson, *Blacks in Blackface, loc. cit.*

19. This refers to Bert Williams and George Walker's 1903 Command Performance for the King of England with the *In Dahomey* company.

20. Sampson, *The Ghost Walks, op. cit.*, p. 351. Quotations from McClain letter in the *Indianapolis Freeman*, n. d. Reprinted in Sampson.

21. "McClain, Father of Cakewalk in Hollywood to Make Picture," *Chicago Defender*, March 3, 1935. From the news story: "Uncle Billy drew forth a yellowed clipping bearing the notation: 'London, 1906.' It was the program of the Oxford theater [*sic*] in the British metropolis where he was 'doing a single' at the time, a song and dance act. On the same bill was Fred Karno's 'A Football Game,' with an array of comedians including the rising young actor, Charlie Chaplin."

22. Sampson, *The Ghost Walks, op. cit.*, p. 379. Quotations from McClain letter in the *Indianapolis Freeman*, n. d. Reprinted in Sampson.

23. McClain also writes herein: "I will admit there are only two race men over here, and Sam

McVey is one, and you can guess the other one." This now antiquated, but once common phrase, implied that the subject of the appellation was intensely devoted to the betterment of the "race." Such an individual would have been deeply political and possess a keen awareness of all determinants playing upon the social and economic progress of African Americans. In his *Black Manhattan, op. cit.*, p. 73, J. W. Johnson describes McVey as one of "a trio of formidable Negro Heavyweights" (during the first decade of the century), along with Sam Langford and Joe Jeanette.

24. Sampson, *The Ghost Walks, op. cit.*, p. 512. Quotations from McClain letter in the *Indianapolis Freeman*, n. d. Reprinted in Sampson.

25. Sampson, *Blacks in Blackface, loc. cit.* Quotations from McClain letter in the *Indianapolis Freeman*, April 2, 1910, reprinted in Sampson.

26. Keith F. Davis, *The Passionate Observer: Photographs by Carl Van Vechten* (Kansas City, MO: Hallmark, 1993), p. 111.

27. According to Leonard Reed, a performer who worked in this McClain tent show. Interviewed Summer 1991, Los Angeles.

28. "Billy McClain Takes Over Buffalo Theater," *Chicago Defender*, December 4, 1926. The article went on to note that, among his many other accomplishments, McClain had "introduced [boxers] Jack Johnson and Sam McVey to the king of England."

29. Fletcher, *op. cit.*, p. 99. In "Billy McClain Takes Over Buffalo Theater," *Chicago Defender*, December 4, 1926. The unsigned article also notes — without any attempt at editorialization — that McClain "has just finished as physical instructor to Hiram W. Evans, Imperial Wizard of the K.K.K."

30. *California Eagle*, August 28, 1931.

31. "McClain, Father of Cakewalk in Hollywood to Make Picture," *Chicago Defender*, March 3, 1935. The film was a short entitled *Rhapsody in Black* not to be confused with the Broadway musical of the same title. In *Frame By Frame: A Black Filmography*, the partially animated ten-minute film is described as a "sing-along with Negro spirituals."

32. Fletcher, *op. cit.*, p. 100. Note: *Variety* incorrectly gave his age as 93; the date of death therein (January 28) is also at odds with Fletcher's.

Chapter 4

1. Arlene Croce, *The Fred Astaire and Gingers Book* (New York: Outerbridge and Lazard, 1972), p. 154.

2. Reid Badger, *A Life in Ragtime: A Biography of James Reese Europe* (New York: Oxford University Press, 1995), p. 161.

3. Badger, *op. cit.*, p. 5.

4. David Levering Lewis, *When Harlem Was in Vogue* (New York: Alfred A. Knopf, 1981), p. 14.

5. Lewis, *op. cit.*, 13.

6. Ethel Waters with Charles Samuels, *His Eye Is on the Sparrow* (New York: Doubleday, 1951), p. 166.

7. John Chilton's *Who's Who of Jazz* (Philadelphia: Chilton, 1972) gives the birth year as 1900; Rosetta Reitz in her liner notes for the album *Hot Snow* (Rosetta Records, RR 1305) states 1905 and the entry for *Notable Black American Women*, Jessie Charney Smith, ed. (Detroit: Gale Research, 1992), p. 1056, notes that "the year is variously given as 1900, 1903, and 1909." Inasmuch as Snow apparently graduated from high school in 1920, the year 1903 — which would make her 17 at the time — seems likely.

8. Interview with Demas Dean, Los Angeles, Spring 1990.

9. The spelling of her Christian name vacillated between "Valyda," "Valada" and the more common "Valaida."

10. *Black Musical Theatre: From Coontown to Dreamgirls* (Baton Rouge: Louisiana State University Press, 1989), pp. 147–48. The story told to me by my interviewee Demas Dean, *op. cit.*, is essentially in agreement with Woll's account.

11. The usual "take" on Waters' difficult personality is that it was the inevitable and nearly-forgivable result of her rough and tumble early years in black vaudeville. Frances Williams (see Chapter Ten), a close friend, nevertheless often felt what she described as a "paranoid" gaze often coming from Waters; Fayard Nicholas (see Chapter Eleven) relates several examples of Water's legendary irascibility.

12. Woll, *op. cit.*, p. 148.

13. When Snow first sang "'Till the Real Thing Comes Along," it was a slightly different song from the standard "Until the Real Thing Comes Along." Writers Alberta Nichols and Mann Holiner revised their original 1931 version in 1936.

14. Although I have not been able to find playbills to the effect that Snow performed her most famous routine in "Rhapsody," Demas Dean recalls her having done so. It is possible, though, that he was confusing this with seeing Snow do the routine on some other occasion; or that it was added later in the run or out of town while touring.

15. Interview with Demas Dean, Los Angeles, Spring 1990.

16. Interview with Demas Dean, *op. cit.*

17. Bobby Short, *Black and White Baby* (New York: Dodd, Mead, 1971), p. 84.

18. Carman Moore, title unknown, *Village Voice*, February 19, 1982, pp. 79–80.

19. Based on the fact that much of her early vaudeville work seems to have been done around the Tennessee area. One biographical entry has her "of a Baltimore family." Again, the fuzzy particulars may be a result of Snow's claim of having been of mixed race parentage.

20. Valaida Snow, "I've Met No Color Bar in London," *Chicago Defender*, October 7, 1934 (reprinted from *London Daily Mirror*, October ?, 1934). She writes, "As it happens I am strongly against marriage between the two races, despite

the fact that I myself am the result of such a fusion." Inasmuch as Snow's mother attended black Howard University (and was, thus, African American), the conclusion to be drawn from this statement is that her father was white.

21. Liner notes, *Swing Is the Thing*, Valaida Snow (DRG/Swing Records, SW 8455/56), 1984.

22. *Ibid.*

23. Robert Kimball and William Bolcom, *Reminiscing with Sissle and Blake* (New York: Viking, 1973), p. 176.

24. Stanley Dance, *The World of Earl Hines* (New York: Scribner's, 1977), p. 65.

25. Sally Placksin, *American Women in Jazz: 1900 to the Present—Their Words, Lives and Music* (New York (?): Wideview Books, 1982), p. 95. In general, Snow seems to have been a great favorite of other trumpet players. In Stanley Dance's *The World of Earl Hines*, the author quotes Louis Armstrong as having once said of Snow: "Boy, I never saw anything that great!"

26. "Cite Valaida Snow on Bigamy Charge," *Chicago Defender*, June 24, 1933, p. 1. In his "Swing Is the Thing" notes, Frank Driggs also cites her marriage to Brown.

27. Liner notes, *Swing Is the Thing*, Valaida Snow, *op. cit.*

28. *Chicago Defender*, June 5, 1920. Snow was billed as "Valyda the Sensation."

29. Perry Bradford, *Born With the Blues* (New York: Oak, 1965), p. 128.

30. Linda Dahl, *Stormy Weather: The Music and Lives of a Century of Jazzwomen* (New York: Pantheon Books, 1984), p. 81.

31. Clarence Muse and David Arlen, *Way Down South* (Hollywood: David Graham Fischer, 1932), p. 35. Writes Muse, "[H]is eyes snapped fire." In her autobiography *His Eye Is on the Sparrow*, Ethel Waters draws an especially harrowing portrait of the supremely racist and unlikable showman.

32. "Example for Circuit Using Our People," *Chicago Defender*, December 6, 1924. According to a survey in the theatrical column of Tony Langston, based on letters he had received from performers. A number of other theaters come under fire for similar conditions.

33. Brian Hammond and Patrick O'Connor, *Josephine Baker* (Boston: Little, Brown, 1988), p. 12.

34. *Ibid.* Quoted from the *New York Evening World*, date unknown. This review places Baker in the opening night cast of *Chocolate Dandies*, but according to *Josephine Baker*, "[A]lthough Josephine never appeared in the show in New York City, there have been many people who claimed they saw her in it there!" The Sissle-Blake production ended up running until the following May, and also provided steady work for another legend-in-the-making, the inveterate Elisabeth Welch (now past her 90th birthday and still performing as of this writing in 1995).

35. Snow appeared at the Plaza the same year as Nora Ray Holt (Chapter Eleven); or at least it was a "smart [and] typically British" club run by [an] Englishman, Sir Victor Sassoon" (in Shanghai) at which Holt worked—Snow was associated professionally with Sassoon in that city. In all likelihood he was the operator of the Plaza establishment.

36. Chris Goddard, *Jazz Away from Home* (New York: Paddington, 1979), p. 19. Ironically, this important work on expatriate black jazz musicians makes only passing reference to Snow (p. 278).

37. Valaida Snow, "I've Met No Color Bar in London," *Chicago Defender*, October 7, 1934 (reprinted from *London Daily Mirror*, October ?, 1934). Snow's article was run alongside a rebuttal by A. Ward, Secretary, Negro Welfare Association ("You've Just Been Lucky—Old Settler").

38. Liner notes, *Swing Is the Thing*, Valaida Snow, *op. cit.*

39. "Cite Valaida Snow on Bigamy Charge," *Chicago Defender*, *loc. cit.*

40. "Valaida Snow Acquitted on Bigamy Charge," *Chicago Defender*, November 4, 1933, p. 1.

41. *London Daily Express*, September 14, 1934. Review of *Blackbirds of 1934*.

42. Snow's features are: *L'Alibi* (France, 1938) and *Pieges* (France, 1939). There are also two soundie shorts with Snow singing the title tunes, "If You Only Knew" (1942) and "Patience and Fortitude" (1946). The riddle of why Snow claimed appearances in the other two apparently non-existent films, or whether her memory was simply faulty, has yet to be solved.

43. Liner notes, *Hot Snow*, *op. cit.*

44. Material on Snow's release is contained in her file at the Simon Wiesenthal Center for Holocaust Studies in Los Angeles. It should be noted that there is a revisionist school of thought regarding Snow's experiences during this period having to do with the performer's possible exaggeration of her wartime incarceration: Some contend that she was a drug dealer and being held in jail in a Nazi-occupied country. What is beyond questioning, however, is the fact that Snow was under some sort of house arrest during this time, and under conditions that clearly violated the Geneva Convention. It is understandable that under the circumstances she may not have been able to make the subtle distinction between a jail used for holding prisoners of war and a concentration camp.

45. Smith, *op. cit.*, pp. 1056–57.

46. Floyd G. Snelson, "Valaida Snow, Once Nazi Prisoner, Returns," *Chicago Defender*, April 24, 1943, p. 18. In *Stormy Weather: The Music and Lives of a Century of Jazzwomen*, *op. cit.*, p. 82, Linda Dahl writes: "Conflicting reports have circulated about various aspects of Valaida Snow's life, including her birth date, given in different sources as 1900, 1905 and 1909, and particularly concerning her experience during the early forties while in Scandinavia." Dahl cites several sources which contain differing accounts of Snow's World War II

travails. The story in the *Defender*, however, constitutes the more or less "official" and most common version. Perhaps some future full-length biography will reveal the reasons for her detention and her experiences at the hands of the Nazis. *Chicago Defender*, April 24, 1943; "Valaida Snow, Once Nazi Prisoner, Returns: And Scribe Finds Star Still Hep to the Jive."

47. Liner notes, *Hot Snow, op. cit.* "I Came Back from the Dead" (original source unknown) cited.

48. Interview with Fayard Nicholas, Woodland Hills, CA, 1991. This writer strongly suspects that the TV program Nicholas saw was ABC's *This Is Your Life*-type series, *The Comeback Story*, which ran for four months in the fall and winter of 1953. Others on this program, which saluted people who had come back from insurmountable odds, included Billie Holiday, George Shearing and ... Bobby Breen! In 1994, singer Diana Ross began pre-production on a TV movie based on Valaida's life.

49. Dahl, *op. cit.*, p. 257.

50. Interview with Clora Bryant, Long Beach, CA, January, 1995.

51. Maurice Peress' comments regarding Valaida Snow are from his June 21, 1995, letter to the author.

52. Liner notes, *Swing Is the Thing*, Valaida Snow, *op. cit.*

53. Liner notes, *Hot Snow, op. cit.*: "She was buried on her birthday in Brooklyn's Evergreen Cemetery"—Rosetta Reitz.

Chapter 5

1. Jessie Charney Smith, ed. *Notable Black American Women* (Detroit: Gale Research, 1992), p. 510. "Most Married Negroes," *Ebony*, October 1949. pp. 51, 53. Cited in Smith.

2. Sylvia G.L. Dannett, *Profiles of American Womanhood*, volume 2 (Yonkers, NJ: Educational Heritage, 1964), p. 146.

3. Lloyd Wendt and Herman Kogan, *Big Bill of Chicago* (New York: Bobbs-Merrill, 1953), p. 34.

4. Smith, *op. cit.*, p. 509.

5. Bruce Kellner, ed. *The Harlem Renaissance: A Historical Dictionary for the Era* (New York: Methuen, 1987), p. 172.

6. "Gotham Social Set Is Stirred by Charges Against Mrs. Ray," *Chicago Defender*, July 25, 1925, p. 1.

7. "Holt-Ray Wedding Styled Most Brilliant Affair," *Chicago Defender*, August 4, 1923, p. 4.

8. Kellner, *loc. cit.*, p. 172.

9. "Gotham Social Set Is Stirred by Charges Against Mrs. Ray," *loc. cit.*

10. "Mrs. Nora Ray Holt's Silence Ends; Tells Her Side of Married Life," *Chicago Defender*, February 6, 1926, p. 1. She is quoted as saying: "Before Mr. Ray and I married he promised to give me a joint tenancy in his real estate holdings and in January, 1924, I asked him to fulfill his promise, which he reluctantly did, and asked that I make him joint owner of my property, but as I had not promised a gift of that kind I refused and that was the incipiency of our disruption."

11. Bruce Kellner, ed., *Letters of Carl Van Vechten* (New Haven: Yale University Press, 1987), p. 87.

12. *Ibid.*

13. "Gotham Social Set Is Stirred by Charges Against Mrs. Ray," *loc. cit.*

14. "(Little Lena) The Mamma Who Can't Behave," *Heebie Jeebies*, August 1, 1925. Cited in Kellner, ed., *The Harlem Renaissance, op. cit.*, p. 173.

15. John S. Wright, *A Stronger Soul Within a Finer Frame: Portraying African-Americans in the Black Renaissance* (Minneapolis: University Art Museum, University of Minnesota), 1990 (exhibition catalog), p. 14.

16. *Ibid.*

17. This was by no means as socially progressive—nor as new—as it sounds, for black and tans entailed more than a touch of exploitation, and had been around since at least the turn of the century In his novel *The Autobiography of an Ex-Colored Man* (New York: Penguin, 1990 [reprint of 1912 edition]), James Weldon Johnson makes it clear that in New York City, such operations were already in existence at the turn of the century.

18. Written for the February 1925 issue of the left-leaning black publication *The Messenger*; it is reprinted in volume 1 of *Speech and Power*, edited by Gerald Early (Hopewell, NY: Echo Press, 1992), p. 56.

19. Carl Van Vechten; edited by Bruce Kellner, *Keep A-Inching Along: Selected Writings of Carl Van Vechten about Black Art and Letters* (Westport, CT: Greenwood Press, 1979), p. 104. Letter to Van Vechten from Holt quoted by the former in a letter.

20. Kellner, *Carl Van Vechten and the Irreverent Decades*, p. 223.

21. Carl Van Vechten, *Nigger Heaven* (New York: Alfred A. Knopf, 1926), p. 85. Currently, one of the most discussed novels of the 1920s. Clearly the reason for this is the "shocking" (increasingly so over the decades) title that Van Vechten chose for his proto-Harlem Renaissance study. Interestingly, he also chose the U.S. title for British novelist Ronald Firbank's *Sorrow in Sunlight* (published two years before *Heaven*): *Prancing Nigger*.

22. Carl Van Vechten, *Nigger Heaven, op. cit.*, p. 81.

23. Bruce Kellner, *Carl Van Vechten and the Irreverent Decades* (Norman, OK: University of Oklahoma Press, 1968), p. 218.

24. Van Vechten, *Nigger Heaven*, p. 82.

25. *Ibid.*, p. 84.

26. *Ibid.*, p. 179.

27. Martin Bauml Duberman, *Paul Robeson* (New York: Alfred A. Knopf, 1988), p. 74. Quotation from diary of Essie Robeson.

28. It is not now known, based on existing documents, whether or not Holt had secured employment before departing to Europe.

29. Dannett, *op. cit.*, p. 147. Quotation from review of Holt; *London Daily Express*, date unknown.

30. *Ibid.*

31. *Ibid.*

32. Kellner, *Carl Van Vechten and the Irreverent Decades*, loc. cit.

33. Kellner, ed., *Letters of Carl Van Vechten, op. cit.*, p. 90.

34. Dannett, p. 147.

35. *Ibid.*

36. *Ibid.*, p. 148.

37. Kellner, *Carl Van Vechten and the Irreverent Decades*, *op. cit.*, p. 237. Cf. also Langston Hughes' *The Big Sea* (New York: Hill and Wang, 1963), p. 254. Note: In Hughes' version of the anecdote, the woman is identified as a "well-known New York matron."

38. Arnold Rampersad, *The Life of Langston Hughes; Volume I: 1902–1941; I, Too, Sing America* (New York: Oxford University Press, 1986), p. 291.

39. Kellner, ed., *Letters of Carl Van Vechten, op. cit.*, p. 154.

40. Van Vechten, *Nigger Heaven, op. cit.*, p. 84.

41. Kellner, ed., *Letters of Carl Van Vechten*, p. 242.

42. Carl Van Vechten; edited by Bruce Kellner, *Keep A-Inching Along: Selected Writings of Carl Van Vechten about Black Art and Letters, loc. cit.*, p. 104.

43. *Ibid.*

Chapter 6

1. Russell and David Sanjek, *American Popular Music Business in the 20th Century* (New York: Oxford University Press, 1991), p. 15.

2. Chris Goddard, *Jazz Away from Home* (New York: Paddington, 1979), p. 32.

3. David Hadju, *Lush Life: A Biography of Billy Strayhorn* (New York: Farrar, Straus, Giroux, 1996), p. 19.

4. The "Old World" had, in fact, long registered an awareness of the integrity of the art — especially musical — of African Americans, going back at least as far as Czech composer Dvorak's "New World Symphony," written in 1893, and Swiss conductor Ernst Ansermet's essay praising musicians Sidney Bechet and Will Marion Cook (see Chapter One). But not until the late 1920s and early '30s when European intellectuals directed serious attention toward Armstrong and Ellington that the point began to be driven home in America.

5. Ellington, Duke. *Music Is My Mistress* (New York: Doubleday, 1973), p. 156. A variant on this (orig. source unknown) appears on a didactic panel in the traveling Smithsonian exhibit devoted to Ellington, "Beyond Category." It reads as follows: "Let's not go overboard. Pea is only my right arm, left foot, eyes, stomach, hands, only not my ego."

6. The character of the adolescent Frankie in Carson McCullers' play *Member of the Wedding* is especially indicative of this tendency. According to my 1994 interviewee Frances Williams, Ethel Waters initially refused the memorable role she eventually played because, she told Williams, "That child is a lesbian." And it wasn't until McCullers had made some changes in the play — unspecified by Williams— that Waters agreed to take on what arguably became the signature role of her career.

7. Barry Ulanov, *Duke Ellington* (New York: Creative Age Press, 1946), p. 219.

8. *Ibid.*

9. The surname "Strayhorn" may have derived from the Scots "Strachan" or the Northumberland variants "Strahan" or "Straughan"; however, *The Oxford Dictionary of Surnames* includes no information to this effect, nor does it contain any data on the unusual "Strayhorn" per se. A fairly common surname in certain areas of the East Coast and in the Midwest (Pittsburgh, Cincinnati, etc.), it is one which appears to overwhelmingly borne by African Americans. It could also be an early intentional or unintentional variant spelling on a slaveholder's family name; however, mitigating against this possibility is the fact that the author has discovered the birth record of one John S. Strayhorn, born in Scotland in 1871.

10. Lemuel Strayhorn is a character in Jerome Wideman's short story "Daddy Garbage" in the collection *Damballah* (New York: Avon Books, 1981).

11. Bill Coss, "Ellington & Strayhorn, Inc.," *Downbeat*, July 7, 1962, p. 22.

12. *Ibid.*

13. Nat Shapiro and Nat Hentoff, *Hear Me Talkin' to Ya* (New York: Dover, 1966), p. 237.

14. Stanley Dance, *The World of Duke Ellington* (New York: Scribner's, 1970), p. 34.

15. David Hadju, "Something to Live For," *The Village Voice* jazz supplement, June 23, 1992, p. 4.

16. Ulanov, *op. cit.*, p. 221.

17. Leonard G. Feather, "Billy Strayhorn — The Young Duke, " *Jazz Magazine*, volume 1, nos. 5 and 6 (1943), p. 13.

18. Mercer Ellington with Stanley Dance, *Duke Ellington in Person: An Intimate Memoir* (Boston: Houghton Mifflin, 1978), p. 80.

19. David Hadju, "Something to Live For," *op. cit.*, p. 4.

20. Ellington and Dance, *loc. cit.*

21. *Ibid.*

22. "Black Beauty," sub-titled "A Portrait of Florence Mills," was originally part of Ellington's 1929 suite "Black and Tan Fantasy." Strayhorn's performance of the number with the Cootie Williams Rug Cutters unit of the Ellington band was recorded on June 22, 1939. By casual estimate,

between circa 1938 and 1966 Strayhorn appeared on more than fifty of Ellington's commercial LP recordings (based on the 1966 Ellington discography written by Luigi Sanfilippo published by the Centro Studi Di Musica Contemporanea, Palermo, Italy).

23. John LaTouche was another homosexual who worked extensively with Ellington, including co-writing the Ellington musical *Beggar's Holiday.* LaTouche and Strayhorn (with and without Ellington) were creators of several "classics" of unrequited homosexual yearning including: "Something to Live For," "Daydream," "Lush Life" and "Love Like This Can't Last."

24. Ulanov, *op. cit.,* p. 224.

25. George, Don. *Sweet Man: The Real Duke Ellington* (New York: Putnam's, 1981), p. 78.

26. Ellington, *op. cit.,* p. 156.

27. *Ibid.*

28. Bill Coss, "Ellington & Strayhorn, Inc.," *Downbeat,* July 7, 1962, p. 22.

29. Ellington and Dance, *loc. cit.*

30. John Gill, *Queer Noises* (Minneapolis: University of Minnesota Press, 1995), pp. 74–75. In this book, John identifies a number of gay jazz musicians, including (in addition to Strayhorn), avant-guardists Sun Ra and Cecil Taylor. In the early 1970s, jazz critic Ralph J. Gleason wrote that in all his years on the jazz beat, he'd known of only one homosexual. It was probably Strayhorn.

31. Jay Weiser, "The Glass Closet," *The Village Voice* jazz supplement, June 23, 1992, p. 12.

32. *Ibid.*

33. Writes Strayhorn biographer David Hadju in the June 23, 1992, *Village Voice* jazz supplement, "[H]e made another compromise, the great compromise of his life: in order to be true to himself as a gay man, he sacrificed wide-scale public attention, giving up not only the physical accoutrements of fame but the satisfaction of being recognized by the people who listened to his music."

34. Derek Jewell, *Duke* (New York: Norton, 1977), p. 72.

35. Dance, *op. cit.,* p. 33.

36. Luigi Sanfilippo, *General Catalog of Duke Ellington's Recorded Music* (Palermo, Italy: Centro Studi Di Musica Contemporanea, 1966), p. 32. The date of the session was December 28, 1940.

37. Ulanov, *op. cit.,* p. 225.

38. Ulanov, *op. cit.,* p. 229.

39. George, *op. cit.,* p. 80.

40. As for Ellington's sexual preferences, he might best be described as a "screaming heterosexual," if the evidence in both Don George's and Mercer Ellington's memoirs is to be believed. So promiscuous is the picture of Ellington that emerges in both these books, that it is a wonder Ellington was still able to affect his prodigious musical output. Strayhorn biographer David Hadju writes in the *Village Voice* jazz supplement (June 23, 1992) that a myth persisted that Ellington and Strayhorn's relationship "was fundamentally extramusical, because they were really gay lovers."

41. Lena Horne and Richard Schickel, *Lena* (New York: Doubleday, 1965), p. 98.

42. "We'll Be Together Again," Lena Horne, Blue Note CDP 7243 8 28974 2 2. Strayhorn songs include: "Maybe," "Something to Live For," "Love Like This Can't Last," "A Flower Is a Lovesome Thing" and "You're the One."

43. Jay Weiser, "The Glass Closet," *The Village Voice* jazz supplement, June 23, 1992, p. 12.

44. Mercer Ellington with Stanley Dance, *Duke Ellington in Person: An Intimate Memoir* (Boston: Houghton Mifflin, 1978), p. 157.

45. Gill, *op. cit.,* p. 51. A signifier of Strayhorn's *differentness,* according to *Queer Noises* author John Gill, is the fact that he read the *New Yorker* magazine while in high school.

46. George, *loc. cit.,* p. 80. By "his friend," George means Strayhorn's lover.

47. *Ibid.*

48. Ulanov, p. 228.

49. *Ibid.*

50. According to Jay Weiser in "The Glass Closet," *The Village Voice* jazz supplement, June 23, 1992, p. 12.

51. Ulanov, *loc. cit.,* p. 228.

52. Liner notes, "Great Times: Piano Duets, Duke Ellington and Billy Strayhorn" (Riverside 475, n.d.).

53. Strayhorn and Ellington also recorded two duet tracks in 1946 for RCA Victor: "Tonk" and "Drawing Room Blues." They also performed a half-hour concert for TV, a pilot for the *Jazz Casual* TV series, but the tape seems to have been erased due to union regulations.

54. Liner notes, "Great Times: Piano Duets, Duke Ellington and Billy Strayhorn," *op. cit.*

55. Dance, *op. cit.,* p. 62.

56. David Hadju, "Something to Live For," *The Village Voice* jazz supplement, June 23, 1992, p. 4.

57. *Ibid,* p. 15.

58. Bill Coss, "Ellington & Strayhorn, Inc.," *Downbeat,* July 7, 1962, p. 22.

59. Gary Giddins, "Passion Flower," *The Village Voice* jazz supplement, June 23, 1992, p. 3. Giddins attributes the Ellington statement as being overheard by photographer-filmmaker Gordon Parks.

60. Liner notes, "Great Times: Piano Duets, Duke Ellington and Billy Strayhorn," *op. cit.*

61. David Hadju, "Something to Live For," *The Village Voice* jazz supplement, June 23, 1992, p. 5. Hadju writes: "Similarly, set designer Oliver Smith and arranger Luther Henderson recall Strayhorn composing substantial portions of the *show Beggar's Holiday,* which is, again, credited solely to Ellington."

62. "New Hit Lush Life is Not New," *Downbeat,* August, 12, 1949.

63. *Ibid.*

64. Ellington seemed not to have an aversion to performing "Lush Life" "live" and in person. "Lush Life" became a show piece for alto saxophonist Johnny Hodges. At a 1948 Carnegie Hall perform-

ance of the song, Ellington introduced it by saying—somewhat cryptically—"I don't know which is better, living a 'Lush Life' or singing about it."

65. New York deejay (and #1 Sinatra fan) Jonathan Schwartz temporarily drove a wedge between himself and Sinatra when he played the "Lush Life" outtake on his radio show.

66. Dance, *op. cit.*, p. 28.

67. Jewell, *loc. cit.*

68. Shortly thereafter, Ellington integrated "The Four Freedoms" into his "Second Sacred Concert," which premiered January 19, 1968.

Chapter 7

1. Richard A., Maynard, ed., *The Black Man on Film: Racial Stereotyping* (Rochelle Park, NJ: Hayden Book, 1974), p. 46.

2. Interview with Frances Williams, Los Angeles, CA, Summer 1994.

3. Margo Jefferson, "Great (Hazel) Scott," *Ms.* magazine, November 1973, p. 25.

4. Art Taylor, *Notes and Tones: Musician-to-Musician Interviews* (New York: Coward, McCann and Geoghegan, 1977), p. 254.

5. Margo Jefferson, "Great (Hazel) Scott," *loc. cit.*

6. *Ibid.*

7. *Ibid.*

8. "Hot Classicist," *Time*, October 5, 1942, p. 88.

9. Hollie I. West, "Hazel Scott Reflects," *The Washington Post*, July 4, 1970.

10. The song (also known as "F.D.R. Jones") celebrates the birth of an African American child into a New Deal society, where life could be better for him than it had been for previous generations. It was recorded at the time by several artists, including Ella Fitzgerald, the Mills Brothers, and Cab Calloway. Judy Garland sang the number in blackface in the 1941 film *Babes on Broadway*. In 1954 the song was recorded by its composer, Harold Rome.

11. Margo Jefferson, "Great (Hazel) Scott," *loc. cit.*

12. Including pop pianist Frankie Carle and classicist José Iturbi (accompanying Judy Garland in the film *Thousands Cheer*, etc.); the latter mined the gimmick to signify to his audiences that just because he was a serious classical musician didn't necessarily mean that he couldn't loosen up, get down and have some fun when the filmic occasion called for him to do so.

13. Donald Bogle, *Brown Sugar* (New York: Harmony Books, 1980), p. 104. Here is film critic Pauline Kael's description of Scott in the Vincente Minnelli film *I Dood It*: "...Hazel Scott at the piano [sings] the extraordinarily intense 'Jericho' number—which is in the hot, revivalist, jazzy style of '20s theatre."

14. Les Ledbetter, "Hazel Scott, 61, Jazz Pianist, Acted in Films on Broadway," *New York Times*, Oc-

tober 3, 1981. The 1940 review was quoted in the *New York Times*' Scott obit.

15. *Ibid.*

16. LeRoi Jones, *Blues People: Negro Music in White America* (New York: Morrow, 1963), p. 218.

17. Norma Jean Darden, "Hazel Scott: Up Tempo," *Essence* magazine, November 1978, p. 76.

18. "Hazel's Heart Belongs to Daddy," *Ebony*, November 1945, p. 29.

19. James Gavin, *Intimate Nights: The Golden Age of New York Cabaret* (New York: Grove Weidenfeld, 1991), p. 34.

20. "Hep Hazel,' *Newsweek*, November 29, 1943, p. 71.

21. *Ibid.*

22. Adam Clayton Powell, Jr. *Adam by Adam: The Autobiography of Adam Clayton Powell, Jr.* (New York: Dial Press, 1971), p. 225.

23. Gavin, *loc. cit.*

24. L. Davis and J. Cleveland, "Hi, Hazel!," *Collier's*, April 18, 1942, p. 16.

25. "Hot Classicist," *Time*, October 5, 1942, p. 88.

26. "Hep Hazel,' *Newsweek*, *loc. cit.*

27. L. Davis and J. Cleveland, "Hi, Hazel!," *loc. cit.*

28. Orson Welles and Peter Bogdanovich, edited by Jonathan Rosenbaum. *This Is Orson Welles* (New York: HarperCollins, 1992), p. 365. From the "Welles Career: A Chronology" section. "July 29, 1941. On this date, OW registers the title for this omnibus movie which ultimately goes into production in Mexico (in the fall) and Rio (February). At this time, however, all but one of the stories that are to make up the picture are considerably different from what is done later: (1) *Jazz Story*, a history of American jazz as told through the life of Louis Armstrong, scripted by Elliot Paul in collaboration with Duke Ellington (who will compose and arrange the score) as well as Armstrong, to feature Armstrong as himself and Hazel Scott as Lil Hardin Armstrong (Armstrong's first wife)." Note: It was Lil Hardin who gave Hazel's mother, Alma, her first break as a jazz musician after the latter arrived in America. Hazel would have in all likelihood played a substantial role in this project, which might have set her film career off in a different direction, instead of her eventual lot in movies of looking cute and tickling the ivories.

29. Donald Bogle, *Toms, Coons, Mulattoes, Mammies & Bucks* (New York: Continuum, 1989), p. 121. Bogle writes: "Because musical numbers were not integrated into the script, the scenes featuring blacks could be cut from the films without spoiling them should local (or southern) theaters owners feel their audiences would object to seeing a Negro. The whole procedure now seems ridiculous and archaic; it was but another way in which motion pictures catered to audience prejudices."

30. When singer Billie Holiday came under fire for playing a maid in her first major film, *New Orleans*, she wryly defended herself by asserting, "Yes, but she's a cute maid!"

31. Taylor, *op. cit.*, p. 266.

32. *Ibid.*

33. *Ibid.*, p. 267.

34. "The Powells," *Ebony*, May 1946, p. 35.

35. Thomas A. Johnson, "Adam Clayton Powell, 63, Dies in Miami," *New York Times* Biographical Edition, April 5, 1972, p. 849.

36. *Ibid.*

37. "The Powells," *Ebony, loc. cit.*

38. "Powell Weds Scott," *Life*, August 13, 1945, p. 30.

39. Powell, *op. cit.*, p. 227.

40. *New York Times*, October 13, 1945, p. 17.

41. Powell, *op. cit.*, p. 79.

42. *Time*, October 22, 1945.

43. *Ibid.*

44. Powell, *loc. cit.*

45. *Ibid.* Quoted in Powell.

46. *Ibid.*

47. *Ibid.*

48. *Ibid.*

49. *Ibid.* (Finally in 1952, African American singer Dorothy Maynor was allowed to concertize at the D.A.R. hall.)

50. Adam Clayton Powell, Jr., "My Life with Hazel Scott," *Ebony*, January 1949, p. 42. Powell: "Her contract with Columbia Concerts contains a very significant clause which says that if hotel accommodations for herself and party cannot be arranged without strings, the engagement is off."

51. Hollie I. West, "Hazel Scott Reflects," *loc. cit.*

52. Adam Clayton Powell, Jr., "My Life with Hazel Scott," *loc. cit.*

53. Louie Robinson, "Hazel Scott Comes Home Again to the Action," *Ebony*, March 1968, p. 96.

54. Hazel Scott on TV special *Brown Sugar*.

55. "Hazel Scott Awarded $250 in Discrimination Suit," *Variety*, April 26, 1950, p. 55.

56. Adam Clayton Powell, Jr., "My Life with Hazel Scott," *loc. cit.*

57. Powell, *op. cit.*, p. 248.

58. Norma Jean Darden, "Hazel Scott: Up Tempo," *loc. cit.*

59. Adam Clayton Powell, Jr., "My Life with Hazel Scott," *loc. cit.*

60. Walter Goodman, *The Committee; The Extraordinary Career of the House Committee on Un-American Activities* (New York: Farrar, Straus, Giroux, 1972), p. 290.

61. *Ibid.*

62. *Ibid.*

63. Bogle, *Brown Sugar, op. cit.*, 106.

64. Adam Clayton Powell, Jr., "My Life with Hazel Scott," *loc. cit.*

65. Norma Jean Darden, "Hazel Scott: Up Tempo," *loc. cit.*

66. *Ibid.* Scott: "Adam said in his autobiography that he subconsciously resented my career. I had to give up clubs."

67. *Ibid.* Scott: "Let a woman try it. It's the old boys-will-be-boys double standard."

68. Hazel Scott, "The Truth About Me," *Ebony*, September 1960, p. 137.

69. *Ibid.*

70. *Ibid.*

71. *Ibid.*

72. *Ibid.*

73. Thomas A. Johnson, "Adam Clayton Powell, 63, Dies in Miami," *New York Times* Biographical Edition, April 5, 1972, p. 849. Writes Johnson, "It was in March 1960 during the same year he took over the House committee, that Mr. Powell appeared on a television interview show in New York and triggered the events that were to destroy the effectiveness of the most powerful black elected official to date. Offhandedly, during a discussion of police corruption in Harlem, he called a 63-year-old Harlem widow, Mrs. Esther James, a 'bag woman,' or collector of graft for the police. ... During an eight-year legal battle, however, Mrs. James was awarded damages that ran as high as $575,000 but that were reduced on appeal to $55,787. Mr. Powell consistently refused to pay." Eventually, Powell fled the country to Bimini. Finally, with his debt satisfied and reelected to the 91st Congress, Powell returned to Harlem in March, 1968.

74. Hazel Scott, "The Truth About Me," *loc. cit.*, Scott writes: "When it became clear that I had timed my arrival to coincide exactly with the trial of my son's father, and that I refused to be used by anyone, the picture slowly began to change. Doors that had stood ajar slowly closed."

75. Louie Robinson, "Hazel Scott Comes Home Again to the Action," *loc. cit.*

76. Leonard Feather, An appreciation by jazz critic Feather, who produced Scott's first recordings, *Los Angeles Times*, October 11, 1981.

77. *Ibid.*

78. Powell, *op. cit.*, p. 228.

79. Louie Robinson, "Hazel Scott Comes Home Again to the Action," *loc. cit.*

80. Taylor, *op. cit.*, p. 259.

81. Margo Jefferson, "Great (Hazel) Scott," *loc. cit.*

82. Louie Robinson, "Hazel Scott Comes Home Again to the Action," *loc. cit.*

Chapter 8

1. Stuart Nicholson, *Ella Fitzgerald: Biography of the First Lady of Jazz* (New York: Macmillan, 1994), p. 148.

2. Maria Cole with Louie Robinson, *Nat King Cole: An Intimate Biography* (New York: William Morrow, 1971), p. 78.

3. Lena Horne and Richard Schickel, *Lena* (New York: Doubleday, 1965), p. 204.

4. Liner notes, "The Jazz Sides, Dinah Washington" (Mercury EMS-2–401), 1976. Illustrating just how permanent an impact Washington leveled on secular blues-based music, she was inducted into the *Rock and Roll* (italics mine) Hall of Fame in 1993, in the "early influences" category.

5. Donald Bogle, *Brown Sugar* (New York: Harmony Books, 1980), p. 215.

6. Dempsey J. Travis, *Autobiography of Black Jazz* (Chicago: Urban Research Institute, 1983), p. 497. Some of the material for this anecdote is drawn from Travis' account of the incident between Washington and a record company executive.

7. Liner notes, "A Slick Chick on the Mellow Side, Dinah Washington" (Emarcy 814 184–1), 1983. A more plausible variant of this incident is told by jazz trumpeter Donald Byrd, who informed writer Dee Dee McNeil in the magazine *The Soul and Jazz Record* (date unknown) that he once witnessed Dinah, upon her arrival in England, instruct a gaggle of reporters, "Tell Elizabeth, 'The Queen has arrived.'"

8. *Ebony*, June 1950, p. 59.

9. *Ebony*, March, 1964, p. 146

10. *Ebony*, November, 1956, p. 37.

11. Bill Crow, *Jazz Anecdotes* (New York: Oxford University Press, 1990), p. 294.

12. Nat Shapiro and Nat Hentoff, *Hear Me Talkin' to Ya* (New York: Dover, 1966), p. 247.

13. Ian Carr, Digby Fairweather and Brian Priestley, *Jazz: The Essential Companion* (New York: Prentice-Hall, 1987), p. 408. Fairweather: "Although she was ugly, there was beauty in her smile and in the gentle personality which accepted taunts from her audience with great good humor...."

14. *Ebony*, June 1950, p. 59.

15. Jess Stearns' '50s bestseller *The Search for Bridey Murphy* was about investigations into the central figure's past lives. One would suppose that what Chamblee meant was *The Three Faces of Eve*, a book and film from around the same period which dealt with multiple personalities.

16. Leslie Gourse, *Louis' Children: American Jazz Singers* (New York: Morrow, 1984), p. 226.

17. Travis, *op. cit.*, 193.

18. Interview with Leonard Reed, Los Angeles, 1985.

19. Anita O'Day with George Eells, *High Times Hard Times* (New York: Putnam's, 1981), p. 239.

20. Liner notes, "The Jazz Sides, Dinah Washington," *op. cit.*

21. Gary Giddins, "Dinah Washington: The Once and Future Queen," *Village Voice*, February 9, 1988, p. 85.

22. Ross Russell, *Bird Lives: The High Life and Hard Times of Charlie (Yardbird) Parker* (New York: Charterhouse, 1973), p. 331.

23. Travis, *op. cit.*, p. 308.

24. *Ibid.*, p. 304.

25. *Ibid.*

26. Under the headline "Only Her Hairdresser Knows For Sure," the following March 6, 1995, *Newsweek* news item illustrates how times have changes since the mid–1950s when Washington rocked her management back on their heels with her blonde hair: "Blondes may have more fun, but they definitely aren't all born that way. Ever since bleached rapper T-Box of platinum-selling TLC stepped up to the mike, urban tress-masters have noticed that black demand for golden locks has soared. Recording artists Mary J. Blige, Yo-Yo, Sandi Denton of Salt 'N' Pepa, Janet Jackson, actress Jada Pinkett, model Beverly Johnson, poet Nikki Giovanni and even gender-bending RuPaul have all hit the bottle (or wig)— as much for style as to challenge racial norms. 'This is one way of saying to mainstream society we can look good in anything you can,' says Pinkett. 'Maybe even better.'"

27. Ross Russell, *Bird Lives: The High Life and Hard Times of Charlie (Yardbird) Parker* (New York: Charterhouse, 1973), p. 81.

28. "The Jazz and Soul Record," undated clipping from author's collection.

29. Jack Schifmann, *Uptown: The Story of Harlem's Apollo Theatre* (New York: Cowles, 1971), p. 106.

30. Interview with Leonard Reed, Los Angeles, 1985.

31. "The Jazz and Soul Record," *op. cit.*

32. James Lincoln Collier, *Louis Armstrong: An American Genius* (New York: Oxford University Press, 1983), p. 317.

Chapter 9

1. Trevor Armbrister, "Don't Call Me Junior Anymore," *Saturday Evening Post*, February 13, 1965, pp. 89–93.

2. *Why Me? The Sammy Davis Story* (New York: Warner Books, 1989), p. 53. In this second volume of Davis' memoirs, he describes what he had to go through in the early 1950s to become the first black to both perform and live at Vegas' Old Frontier Hotel.

3. "America's Black Forum," TV interview, 1985.

4. Interview with Frances Nealy, Los Angeles, 1992.

5. Interview with Olga James, Los Angeles, 1993.

6. Davis got to keep only one-third of the money he received for *Golden Boy*. According to a November 13, 1964, *Life* magazine story, the rest went to his father and uncle— like most of his other earnings— under a long-term contract which did not expire until 1965.

7. Telephone interview with Arthur Penn, 1993.

8. Thomas Thompson, "Sammy Davis: An Extraordinary Star's Desperate Fight Makes *Golden Boy* a Broadway Hit," *Life*, November 13, 1964.

9. Arnold Shaw, *Sinatra, the Entertainer* (New York: Delilah, 1982), p. 82.

10. Kitty Kelly, *His Way: The Unauthorized Biography of Frank Sinatra* (New York: Bantam Books, 1986), p. 255.

11. Kelly, *op. cit.*, p. 327.

12. Kelly, *op. cit.*, p. 325.

13. Alex Haley, "*Playboy* Interview: Sammy Davis, Jr.," *Playboy*, December 1966.

14. Trevor Armbrister, "Don't Call Me Junior Anymore," *Saturday Evening Post, loc. cit.*

15. The weaknesses in the original were also alluded to in Howard Taubman's October 21, 1964, *New York Times* review of *Golden Boy*.

16. William Gibson, *Golden Boy* (New York: Random House, 1965), p. 7. The playwright quoting Elkins.

17. Trevor Armbrister, "Don't Call Me Junior Anymore, *Saturday Evening Post, loc. cit.*

18. Gibson, *loc. cit.*

19. Trevor Armbrister, "Don't Call Me Junior Anymore, *Saturday Evening Post, loc. cit.*

20. Telephone interview with Arthur Penn, 1993.

21. *Ibid.*

22. *Ibid.*

23. Martin Bauml Duberman, *Paul Robeson* (New York: Alfred A. Knopf, 1988), pp. 57–58.

24. Sammy Davis, Jr., and Jane and Burt Boyar, *Why Me? The Sammy Davis Story, op. cit*, p. 155.

25. Oriana Fallacci, *The Egotists* (New York: Tempo Books, 1969), p. 189.

26. Truman Capote, *Answered Prayers: The Unfinished Novel* (New York: Random House, 1987), p. 140.

27. Fallacci, *op. cit.*,186.

28. "Sammy Davis Balks at Role in *Sandpiper*," *Daily Variety*, August 31, 1964. The trade publication said the reason for Davis' departure was that he felt producer Marty Ransohoff had taken the whole point of his role out of the script by changing it. There were no specifics as to what the changes constituted.

29. Fallacci, *op. cit.*, 192.

30. The accident occurred as Davis was on his way back to Los Angeles from Las Vegas. News stories had the effect of pushing the Debbie Reynolds-Eddie Fisher nuptials off the nation's front pages. Davis was hospitalized in San Bernardino and spent four days in total darkness. During the time he received 500 telegrams and visits from such show business royalty as Frank Sinatra and Jack Benny. Two fans offered their own eyes for a transplant, unaware that such operations could not be performed.

31. Thomas Thompson. "Sammy Davis: An Extraordinary Star's Desperate Fight Makes *Golden Boy* a Broadway Hit," *loc. cit.*

32. *Ibid.* (According to a story in the February 13, 1965, *Saturday Evening Post*, Davis also had pasted up, along with hundreds of opening night telegrams, photos of John Kennedy, Queen Elizabeth, Audrey Hepburn and Mrs. Medgar Evers with a caption underneath: "You can kill a man, but you can't kill an idea.'

33. Radie Harris, "Broadway Ballyhoo" (column), *Hollywood Reporter*, October 24, 1964.

34. Trevor Armbrister, "Don't Call Me Junior Anymore, *Saturday Evening Post, loc. cit.*

35. Thomas Thompson, "Sammy Davis: An Ex-

traordinary Star's Desperate Fight Makes *Golden Boy* a Broadway Hit," *loc. cit.*

36. Trevor Armbrister, "Don't Call Me Junior Anymore, *Saturday Evening Post, loc. cit.*

37. *Ibid.*

38. Telephone interview with Arthur Penn, 1993.

39. Thomas Thompson, "Sammy Davis: An Extraordinary Star's Desperate Fight Makes *Golden Boy* a Broadway Hit," *loc. cit.*

40. Trevor Armbrister, "Don't Call Me Junior Anymore, *Saturday Evening Post, loc. cit.*

41. Thomas Thompson, "Sammy Davis: An Extraordinary Star's Desperate Fight Makes *Golden Boy* a Broadway Hit," *loc. cit.*

42. Howard Taubman, "Sammy Davis in a Musical *Golden Boy*," *New York Times*, October 21, 1964, p. 56

43. Thomas Thompson, "Sammy Davis: An Extraordinary Star's Desperate Fight Makes *Golden Boy* a Broadway Hit," *loc. cit.*

44. *Ibid.*

45. Hank Grant, "On the Air" (column), *Hollywood Reporter*, November 16, 1964.

46. "Sinatra Testifies Before U.S. Court," *New York Times*, November 11, 1964. The article offers no sense of why the grand jury was convened or the reason for the testimony.

47. Davis and Boyar, *op. cit.*, pp. 213–15. Davis' describes his brief fling with a Hollywood sect as dabbling and concludes with: "One morning after a 'coven' that wasn't quite fun and games, without anyone telling me to, I got some nail polish remover and took off the red fingernail" [the signifier of membership in a certain cult].

48. Bruce Jay Friedman, *The Collected Short Fiction of Bruce Jay Friedman* (New York: Donald I. Fine, 1995), p. 357.

Chapter 10

1. Unless otherwise noted, all quotes from the subject are from Spring 1990 interviews with the author.

2. It is interesting to note that *Shuffle Along* had a similar impact on Langston Hughes; i.e., drawing him to New York City. In his autobiography *The Big Sea*, he writes: "To see *Shuffle Along* was the main reason I went to Columbia. When I saw it, I was thrilled and delighted. From then on I was in the gallery of the Court Theatre every time I got a chance." (Hughes misremembers the name of the theater; it was actually The Colonial.) The show precipitated Hughes' going *to* college and Dean *leaving* the university.

3. "Travellin' Man, the Story of Demas Dean as told to Peter Carr," *Storyville Magazine* #72, August-September 1977, p. 210.

4. *Ibid.*

5. *Ibid.*

6. *Ibid.*

7. Thompson was born in Prescott, Arizona, in 1888, and died one hundred years later in Kansas.

8. Charles Champlin, "Life After *Frank's Place*," *Los Angeles Times*, October 18, 1988, pp. IV, 1.

9. Unless otherwise noted, all quotes from the subject are from summer 1994 interviews between the author and Williams.

10. From the tape of an TV interview shown at Williams' January 22, 1995, memorial service (original source unknown).

11. During the several years that I knew Williams, she was unable to find a copy of the letter — one of which she very proud. It surfaced after her death and was read at her memorial service.

12. Leonard Maltin, *Movie and Video Guide 1994* (New York: Signet, 1993), p. 1096.

13. British critic Richard Dyer, while implicitly acknowledging the premise of both Williams' and Robeson's negative "take" on the latter's career in films, ultimately feels the situation cannot be summed up quite so binarily: In his book *Heavenly Bodies* (New York: St. Martin's, 1986) he writes: "[T]he figure of Robeson still sets off arguments of black peoples, and there is still a striking disparity in the different ways he is perceived... There are different, white and black, ways of looking at or making sense of Robeson, but it would be a mistake to think that the white view is the one that stresses achievement, the black the one that stresses selling out."

14. Martin Bauml Duberman, *Paul Robeson* (New York: Alfred A. Knopf, 1988), p. 710. Williams quoted from unspecified oral history conducted in 1981 by Kim Fellner and James MacLachlan.

15. These were the words with which Williams concluded the 1992 interview with co-curator Les Wills and myself for the California Afro-American Museum audio installation.

16. *Los Angeles Sentinel*, January 12, 1995. Memorial by staff writer Libby Clark.

17. Related by Jackson at played at Williams' January 22, 1995, memorial service.

18. From the videotape of Angelou shown at Williams' January 22, 1995, memorial service.

19. From the videotape of Williams interviewed by Price; shown at her January 22, 1995, memorial service (original source unknown).

Chapter 11

1. Willie "The Lion" Smith and George Hoefer, *Music on My Mind: Memoirs of an American Pianist* (New York: Doubleday, 1964), p. 290.

2. Interview with Fayard Nicholas, Woodland Hills, CA, 1991. Note: In December 1991, the brothers received the prestigious Kennedy Center honors for their six decades-plus of achievement in the entertainment field. Inarguably, the Nicholases were the longest running team in show business. Active in every area of performance, they are best remembered today for their high energy specialty appearances in MGM and 20th Century–Fox musicals of the '30s and '40s.

3. *Ibid.*

4. *Ibid.*

5. Bruce Kellner, ed., *The Harlem Renaissance: A Historical Dictionary for the Era* (New York: Methuen, 1987), p. 83.

6. Jim Haskins, *The Cotton Club* (New York: Random House, 1977), p. 127.

7. Interview with Fayard Nicholas, *ibid.*

8. Kellner, ed., *op. cit.,* p. 213. The Lafayette company, which disbanded in Los Angeles in 1932, also had troupes in Philadelphia and Washington, D.C.

9. Ted Fox, *Apollo* (New York: Holt, Rinehart and Winston, 1982), p. 105.

10. George Schuyler, *Black No More* (New York: Macaulay, 1931), pp. 17–23. Most novels of the Harlem Renaissance place strong emphasis on this aspect of social life, with Schuyler's scathing satire *Black No More* coming down especially heavily on the hypocrisy of some white pub crawlers.

11. A reproduction of this map constitutes the end papers of Cab Calloway's autobiography (with Bryant Rollins) *Of Minnie the Moocher and Me* (New York: Crowell, 1976).

12. Fox, *op. cit.,* pp. 1, 22.

13. Ralph Cooper with Steve Daugherty, *Amateur Night at the Apollo* (New York: Harper-Collins, 1990), pp. 233–34. In 1982 the then decaying and mostly unused facility was taken over by the Harlem Urban Development Corporation, a state agency which in turn leased it to Inner City Broadcasting. The following year it was named a National Historic Landmark. In the years since then, its fortunes have steadily increased. It is now a lively TV production facility, in addition to continuing to serve as a live performance venue.

14. Fox, *op. cit.,* p. 67. Article in January (?) 1937 issue of the *New York World-Telegram.* Reprinted in Fox.

15. Curiously, no mention of Cooper's association with the theater is made in the more or less "official" memoir of the spot, *Apollo: The Story of Harlem's Apollo Theatre,* by the original owner's son, Jack Schiffman.

16. Liner notes by Langston Hughes for "A Night at the Apollo," Vanguard Records, 1954.

17. Fox, *op. cit.,* p. 7.

18. Fox, *op. cit.,* p. 67; article in January (?) 1937 issue of *New York World-Telegram.* Reprinted in Fox.

19. After the dissolution in Europe of her group the Creole Belles, Georgette Harvey (1883–1952) "lived in St. Petersburg for over a decade and was popular with members of Czar Nicholas's court," writes photograph curator Keith F. Davis in *The Passionate Observer: Photographs by Carl Van Vechten* (Kansas City, MO: Hallmark, 1993), p. 111.

20. Interview with Herb Jeffries, Woodland Hills, CA, 1991. Unless otherwise noted, all Jeffries' remarks are from this interview. Not long after his Chicago period, Jeffries made film history start-

ing in 1938 when he began appearing as a singing cowboy in a series of all-black-cast westerns. The brainchild of this former balladeer with the Earl Hines Orchestra, the films included *The Bronze Buckaroo* and *Harlem on the Prairie.* So successful were these "ten-day wonders" that they managed to break out of the black theater circuit for which they were originally intended and onto the screens as far afield as New York's Times Square Theatre.

21. Leroy Ostransky, *Jazz City: The Impact of Our Cities on the Development of Jazz* (Englewood Cliffs, NJ: Prentice-Hall, 1978). The chapter "Chicago: The Wide Open Black Belt" contains a number of interesting and useful statistics regarding the important period in American social and labor history known as The Great Migration.

22. Depiction of Dave's drawn from Dempsey Travis' *Autobiography in Black Jazz* (Chicago: Urban Research Institute, 1983), pp. 213–14.

23. "Cabarets," *Chicago Defender*, September 22, 1934.

24. Interview with Herb Jeffries, Woodland Hills, CA, 1991.

25. *Ibid.*

26. *Ibid.*

27. Travis, *op. cit.*, p. 221. Lyrics reprinted in Travis.

28. Writing under the pseudonym Juli Jones.

29. Sampson, Henry T. *Blacks in Blackface* (Metuchen, NJ: Scarecrow, 1980), pp. 44–46. In a table prepared by Sampson showing theaters owned and operated by blacks between 1910 and 1930, Chicago is shown as having six, New York none.

30. *Entertainment Tonight,* special Davis tribute, broadcast May 16, 1990.

31. Los Angeles' first major wave of African American settlers took place in the late 1880s after a federal ban on Chinese laborers; blacks arrived in their stead to work the farms around the L.A. area. The first densely populated black area of the city was the downtown Temple Street district. According to the Summer 1988 *Southern California Quarterly*, p. 416, "As more blacks arrived in the '20s, they were shunted south toward 'Mud Town' (probably named for the wildcat oil wells that dotted the fields of south central Los Angeles), otherwise known as Watts, which was annexed to the city of Los Angeles in 1926." Central Avenue most directly connected the older black district with Watts.

32. James Lincoln Collier, *Louis Armstrong: An American Genius* (New York: Oxford University Press, 1983), p. 221.

33. *Southern California Quarterly*, Summer 1988, p. 416. It was only with the coming of World War II, according to Gary Marmorstein, author of the article "Central Avenue Jazz," that Los Angeles became a major urban area of black population.

34. The Last Word, Down Beat and Jack's Basket Room were unquestionably the three most influential of all the many jazz-oriented Central Avenue clubs. At the Basket Room, the internationally famous, but seriously underemployed Charlie Parker sometimes worked for $25 a night.

35. Jack Kerouac, *On the Road* (New York: New American Library, 1955), p. 94.

36. Interview with Frances Nealy, Los Angeles, 1994.

37. *Ibid.*

38. Art Pepper and Laurie Pepper, *Straight Life: The Story of Art Pepper* (New York: Schirmer Books, 1979), pp. 47–48. Lee Young quoted.

39. Roy Porter with David Keller, *There and Back* (Baton Rouge: Louisiana State University Press, 1991), p. 65. Porter: "[At the Club Alabam], Lana Turner was on the scene a lot, because she had eyes for Mr. B."

40. *Ibid.*

41. Interview with Frances Williams, 1994, Los Angeles.

42. Observations regarding Hollywood club owners soliciting police assistance in closing down Central is a commonly held assumption that has been communicated in numerous interviews—by myself and others—with black musicians working on Central at the time. In my interview with Clora Bryant, in Long Beach, CA, in January, 1995, she too propounded this version of the events leading up to the end of Central Avenue as a popular L.A. entertainment district for blacks and whites alike.

43. Interview with Clora Bryant, Long Beach, CA, 1995.

44. Interview with Stephen Isoardi, Los Angeles, CA, 1994.

45. Interview with Frances Nealy, *loc. cit.*

46. Interview with Clora Bryant, *loc. cit.*

47. *Ibid.*

Chapter 12

1. Interview with Williams, Summer 1994.

2. Gail Cohee and Leslie Lewis, *Sisters of the Harlem Renaissance* (Martinsville, IN: Helaine Victoria Press, 1991).

3. Langston Hughes, *The Big Sea* (New York: Hill and Wang, 1963), pp. 225–26.

4. Carl Van Vechten, *Parties* (New York: Alfred A. Knopf, 1930), p. 33.

5. Daphne Duval Harrison, *Black Pearls: Blues Queens of the 1920s* (New York: Oxford University Press, 1988), p. 14.

6. George Chauncey, *Gay New York* (New York: Basic Books, 1994), p. 252. The author also cites an example of Bentley's scabrous parodic style ("Alice Blue Gown"): "And he said, 'Dearie, please turn around'/And he shoved that big thing up my brown./He tore it. I bored it. Lord How I adored it./My sweet little Alice Blue Gown."

7. Gladys Bentley, "I Am a Woman Again," *Ebony*, August 1952.

8. Judith Butler, author of *Vested Interests*, a

radical reconsideration of the subject of transvestism which has become a key work in the burgeoning "gender studies" field.

9. Gunther Schuller, *Early Jazz: Its Roots and Musical Development* (New York: Oxford University Press, 1968), p. 71. Schuller points out that "until the race record boom of the early 1920s, the main consumer was the white man." Note: As a result, the great black star Florence Mills, despite the fact that she did not die until 1927, made only one test recording—for Victor—in all of her career.

10. Quotes by Morton to this effect appear in such standard jazz histories as Rudi Blesh and Harriet Janis' *They All Played Ragtime* (New York: Oak, 1966), pp. 160–61; Gunther Schuller's *Early Jazz* (*op. cit.*), p. 138; and *Jazz: The Essential Companion* by Carr, Fairweather and Priestley (New York: Prentice-Hall, 1987), p. 252.

11. Schuller, *loc. cit.*; Morton quoted.

12. *Ibid.*; Morton quoted.

13. *Ibid.*

14. Blesh and Janis, *op. cit.*, p. 160.

15. Blesh and Janis, *op. cit.*, p. 16.

16. This sentiment came out in several musicians and entertainers I have interviewed over the years. Hamby's name was first posited to me by night club impresario Leonard Reed in the late 1980s; since then I have from time to time mentioned the name to others who were "on the scene" at the time Hamby was in Chicago to see what their reaction might be. It was invariably highly positive. The recollection of the "cutting" contest between Tatum and Hamby was told to me by Mifflin Campbell, a singer with the Chicago group The Peanut Boys, which via a series of personnel permutations eventually evolved into the popular Ink Spots.

17. Anonymous, *Songs, Sketch of the Life, Testimonials from the Most Eminent Composers, and Opinions of the American and English Press* (New York: French & Wheat, Book and Job Printers, 1876), p. 3. Information on Blind Tom's repertoire and other material on Blind Tom in this chapter (unless otherwise noted) is drawn from this source.

18. Howard Sacks and Judith Sacks, *Way Up North in Dixie: A Black Family's Claim to the Confederate Anthem. Washington* (Smithsonian Institution Press, 1991), p. 188. The May 19, 1862, edition of "*Fayetteville* [?] *Observer*" quoted.

19. *Ibid.*, pp. 188–90.

20. Ricky Jay (pseud. Richard J. Potash, *Learned Pigs and Fireproof Women* (New York: Warner Books, 1986), p. 80.

21. *Ibid.*, p. 75. Quoted in chapter on Bethune.

22. *Ibid.*, p. 81. Playbill reproduced therein. Presumably what this actually means is that Bethune was first a slave of and then was under guardianship of General Bethune after Emancipation Proclamation until this legal control of Tom was wrested away from him by the latter's sister in 1887. Thus, the phrase "The Last Slave Set Free" is something of a stretch.

23. Mel Watkins, *On the Real Side: Laughing, Lying, and Signifying—The Underground Tradition of African-American Humor That Transformed American Culture, From Slavery to Richard Pryor* (New York: Simon & Schuster, 1994), pp. 103–104.

24. Allen Woll, *Black Musical Theatre: From Coontown to Dreamgirls* (Baton Rouge: Louisiana State University Press, 1989), p. 129. Description drawn from Woll's account of *Deep Harlem*.

25. *New York Herald-Tribune*, January 30, 1929.

26. *New York Herald-Tribune*, February 4, 1929.

27. "'Tandy' Johnson, Stage Star, Must Pay $12,500 in Law Suit," *Chicago Defender*, June 1, 1935; "Star Admits Big Income in Quiz," *Chicago Defender*, March 14, 1936; "Layton and Johnstone Act Splits," *Chicago Defender*, June 1, 1935.

28. Liner notes, "American Duetists with Piano, Layton and Johnstone" (EMI Records, SHB 57, 1979).

29. Watkins, *op. cit.*, p. 192.

30. The comics, both working in blackface, toss about such repartee as: "Fresh air don't mean nothin' to me now. Give me less liberty, and more food than a whole lot of freedom of starvin' to death"; "Where there's a will there's a way"—"I've got the will to eat, but I can't find the way"; "Why did the boy stand on the burning deck?"—"It was too doggone hot to sit down."

31. Preer's name appears in the credits of *Blonde Venus*, but even her daughter, Sister Francescia Thompson, has not been able to spot her in the film. Inasmuch as newspaper advertisements in the black press mentioned the actress' name in conjunction with the film, in all likelihood Preer was in an early release print of the film, which is known to have been re-cut and even partially re-shot by von Sternberg after its initial release.

32. New York–born Ira Aldridge was noted for his *Othello*, which he debuted in Liverpool in 1827 opposite Charles Kean as Iago. For more than forty years he toured extensively in *Othello* and other plays throughout Britain and the Continent, and in the 1860s was received with great enthusiasm in Russia for his Lear. After settling in England in the early 1830s he never returned to America. He died in Poland in 1867.

33. Summer 1992 interview with Frances Nealy. At a taping for a summer 1988 episode of the "magazine"-style TV series *Photoplay*, a dozen of L.A.'s preeminent tap dancers reminisced in front of cameras for several hours for a segment which lasted only a few minutes when aired. Covan, in his early nineties, regaled a group of listeners—myself included—with how he'd learned to dance by listening to trains roaring and clickety-clacking through his boyhood Chicago. The career of Covan (who died in 1990) stretched all the way back to almost the very beginning of modern show business, but there he was only a few years ago still teaching master classes in dance—seated in a chair just like a tap Martha Graham.

34. *Washington Post*, "TV Week" section, January 8, 1989.

35. James Baldwin, *The Price of the Ticket* (New York: St. Martin's/Marek, 1985), p. x.

36. White show business history has been the subject of countless volumes, but there are only a handful of books which attempt to quantify and qualify the history of African American entertainment. Two of these works are very recent and ostensibly are on the subject of black comedy and tap dancing: Mel Watkins' *On the Real Side* (New York: Simon & Schuster, 1994) and Rusty Frank's *Tap!* (New York: Morrow, 1990). Both books tend also to present useful overviews of black show business per se. Rounding out the list are: Langston Hughes and Milton Meltzer's *Black Magic* (New York: Crown, 1967); *The Redd Foxx Encyclopedia of Black Humor* (Pasadena, CA: Ward Ritchie Press, 1977); Marshall and Jean Stearns' *Jazz Dance: The Story of American Vernacular Dance* (New York: Macmillan, 1968); and Tom Fletcher's *The Tom Fletcher Story: 100 Years of the Negro in Show Business* (New York: Burdge, 1954).

Bibliography

Ames, Jerry, and Jim Siegelman. *The Book of Tap*. New York: McKay, 1977.

Anderson, Jervis. *This Was Harlem 1900–1950*. New York: Farrar, Straus, Giroux, 1982.

Baldwin, James. *The Price of the Ticket*. New York: St. Martin's/Marek, 1985.

Bechet, Sidney. *Treat It Gentle*. London: Cassell, 1960.

Berger, Morroe, Edward Berger, and James Patrick. *Benny Carter: A Life in American Music*. Metuchen, NJ: Scarecrow, 1982.

Bergman, Peter M. *The Chronological History of the Negro in America*. New York: Harper & Row, 1969.

Birdoff, Harry. *The World's Greatest Hit: Uncle Tom's Cabin*. New York: S.F. Vanni Publishers and Booksellers, 1947.

Blesh, Rudi, and Harriet Janis. *They All Played Ragtime*. New York: Oak, 1966.

Bogle, Donald. *Brown Sugar*. New York: Harmony Books, 1980.

_____. *Toms, Coons, Mulattoes, Mammies & Bucks*. New York: Continuum, 1989.

Bordman, Gerald. *The American Musical Theatre*. New York: Oxford University Press, 1978.

Bradford, Perry. *Born with the Blues*. New York: Oak, 1965.

Calloway, Cab, and Bryant Rollins. *Of Minnie the Moocher and Me*. New York: Crowell, 1976.

Capote, Truman. *Answered Prayers: The Unfinished Novel*. New York: Random House, 1987.

Carr, Ian, Digby Fairweather, and Brian Priestley. *Jazz: The Essential Companion*. New York: Prentice-Hall, 1987.

Charles, Ray, and David Ritz. *Brother Ray*. New York: Dial Press, 1978.

Charters, Ann. *Nobody: The Story of Bert Williams*. New York: Macmillan, 1970.

Chauncey, George. *Gay New York*. New York: Basic Books, 1994.

Chilton, John. *Sidney Bechet: The Wizard of Jazz*. New York: Oxford University Press, 1987.

_____. *Who's Who of Jazz*. Philadelphia: Chilton, 1972.

Cohee, Gail, and Leslie Lewis. *Sisters of the Harlem Renaissance*. Martinsville, IN: Helaine Victoria Press, 1991.

Collier, James Lincoln. *Duke Ellington*. New York: Oxford University Press, 1987.

_____. *Louis Armstrong: An American Genius*. New York: Oxford University Press, 1983.

Cooper, Ralph, with Steve Daugherty. *Amateur Night at the Apollo*. New York: HarperCollins, 1990.

Crow, Bill. *Jazz Anecdotes*. New York: Oxford University Press, 1990.

Dahl, Linda. *Stormy Weather: The Music and Lives of a Century of Jazzwomen*. New York: Pantheon Books, 1984.

Dance, Stanley. *The World of Duke Ellington*. New York: Scribner's, 1970.

_____. *The World of Earl Hines*. New York: Scribner's, 1977.

Dannett, Sylvia G.L. *Profiles of American Womanhood, Vol. 2*. Yonkers, NJ: Educational Heritage, 1964.

Davis, Keith. *The Passionate Observer: Photographs by Carl Van Vechten*. Kansas City, MO: Hallmark, 1993.

Davis, Sammy, Jr., and Jane and Burt Boyar. *Why Me? The Sammy Davis Story*. New York: Warner Books, 1989.

de Barrios, Paul. *Jackson Street After Hours.* Seattle: Sasquatch Books, 1993.

Dexter, Dave, Jr. *The Jazz Story: from the '90s to the '60s.* Englewood Cliffs, NJ: Prentice-Hall, 1964.

Dixon, R.M.W., and J. Godrich. *Blues and Gospel Records 1902 to 1942.* Middlesex, England: n.p., 1963.

Duberman, Martin Bauml. *Paul Robeson.* New York: Alfred A. Knopf, 1988.

Dyer, Richard. *Heavenly Bodies: Film Stars and Society.* New York: St. Martin's, 1986.

Early, Gerald, ed. *Speech and Power.* Hopewell, NY: Echo Press, 1992.

Ellington, Duke. *Music Is My Mistress.* New York: Doubleday, 1973.

Ellington, Mercer, with Stanley Dance. *Duke Ellington in Person: An Intimate Memoir.* Boston: Houghton Mifflin, 1978.

Fallaci, Oriana. *The Egotists.* New York: Tempo Books, 1969.

Fletcher, Tom. *The Tom Fletcher Story: 100 Years of the Negro in Show Business.* New York: Burdge, 1954.

Fox, Ted. *Apollo.* New York: Holt, Rinehart and Winston, 1982.

Foxx, Redd, and Norma Miller. *The Redd Foxx Encyclopedia of Black Humor.* Pasadena, CA: Ward Ritchie Press, 1977.

Gammond, Peter, ed. *Duke Ellington: His Life and Music.* New York: Da Capo, 1978.

Gavin, James. *Intimate Nights: The Golden Age of New York Cabaret.* New York: Grove Weidenfeld, 1991.

George, Don. *Sweet Man: The Real Duke Ellington.* New York: Putnam's, 1981.

Gibson, William. *Golden Boy.* New York: Random House, 1965.

Gill, John. *Queer Noises.* Minneapolis: University of Minnesota Press, 1995.

Goddard, Chris. *Jazz Away from Home.* New York: Paddington, 1979.

Goodman, Walter. *The Committee; The Extraordinary Career of the House Committee on Un-American Activities.* New York: Farrar, Straus, Giroux, 1972.

Gordon, Max. *Live at the Village Vanguard.* New York: St. Martin's, 1980.

Gourse, Leslie. *Louis' Children: American Jazz Singers.* New York: Morrow, 1984.

Hammond, Brian, and Patrick O'Connor. *Josephine Baker.* Boston: Little, Brown, 1988.

Hanks, Patrick, and Flavia Hodges. *A Dictionary of Surnames.* Oxford, New Brunswick: Rutgers University Press, 1988.

Harrison, Daphne Duval. *Black Pearls: Blues Queens of the 1920s.* New York: Oxford University Press, 1988.

Haskins, Jim. *The Cotton Club.* New York: Random House, 1977.

Horne, Lena, and Richard Schickel. *Lena.* New York: Doubleday, 1965.

Hughes, Langston. *The Big Sea.* New York: Hill and Wang, 1963.

_____. *I Wonder as I Wander.* New York: Appleton Century Crofts, 1964.

_____, Milton Meltzer and C. Eric Lincoln. *A Pictorial History of Black Americans,* fifth revised edition. New York: Crown, 1983.

Ione, Carolyn. *Pride of Family: Four Generations of American Women of Color.* New York: Summit Books, 1991.

Jablonski, Edward. *Harold Arlen: Happy with the Blues.* New York: Doubleday, 1961.

James, Edward T., ed. *Dictionary of American Biography Supplement Three, 1941–1945.* New York: Scribner's, 1945.

Jay, Ricky (pseud. Richard J. Potash). *Learned Pigs and Fireproof Women.* New York: Warner Books, 1986.

Jewell, Derek. *Duke.* New York: Norton, 1977.

Johnson, James Weldon. *Along this Way: The Autobiography of James Weldon Johnson.* New York: Penguin, 1990 (reprint of 1933 edition).

_____. *Autobiography of an Ex-Colored Man.* New York: Penguin, 1990 (reprint of 1912 edition).

_____. *Black Manhattan.* New York: Alfred A. Knopf, 1940.

Jones, LeRoi. *Blues People: Negro Music in White America.* New York: Morrow, 1963.

Kael, Pauline. *5001 Nights at the Movies.* New York: Holt Rinehart Winston, 1982.

Katkov, Norman. *The Fabulous Fanny: The Story of Fanny Brice.* New York: Alfred A. Knopf, 1953.

Kellner, Bruce. *Carl Van Vechten and the Irreverent Decades.* Norman: University of Oklahoma Press, 1968.

_____, ed. *The Harlem Renaissance: A Historical Dictionary for the Era.* New York: Methuen, 1987.

_____, ed. *Letters of Carl Van Vechten.* New Haven: Yale University Press, 1987.

Kelly, Kitty. *His Way: The Unauthorized Biography of Frank Sinatra.* New York: Bantam Books, 1986.

Kerouac, Jack. *On the Road.* New York: New American Library, 1955.

Kimball, Robert, and William Bolcom. *Reminiscing with Sissle and Blake*. New York: Viking, 1973.

Klotman, Phyllis Rauch. *Frame by Frame: A Black Filmography*. Bloomington: Indiana University Press, 1979.

Logan, Rayford W., and Michael R. Winston. *Dictionary of American Negro Biography*. New York: Norton, 1982.

Lovell, John, Jr. *Black Song: The Forge and the Flame*. New York: Macmillan, 1972.

Lucas, Ernestine Garrett. *Wider Windows to the Past*. Springfield, OH: 1995. (Information on this family history which contains extensive information on Albery Allson Whitman and his daughters can be obtained by writing to: Ernestine G. Lucas, P.O. Box 1082, Springfield, Ohio 45501–1082.)

Maltin, Leonard. *Movie and Video Guide 1994*. New York: Signet, 1993.

McFeely, William S. *Frederick Douglass*. New York: Norton, 1991.

Muse, Clarence, and David Arlen. *Way Down South*. Hollywood: David Graham Fischer, 1932.

O'Day, Anita, with George Eells. *High Times Hard Times*. New York: Putnam's, 1981.

Osgood, Henry O. *So This Is Jazz*. Boston: Little, Brown, 1926.

Ostransky, Leroy. *Jazz City: The Impact of Our Cities on the Development of Jazz*, Englewood Cliff, NJ: Prentice-Hall, 1978.

Paskman, Dailey. *"Gentlemen, Be Seated!": A Parade of the American Minstrels*. New York: Clarkson N. Potter, 1976.

Pepper, Art, and Laurie Pepper. *Straight Life: The Story of Art Pepper*. New York: Schirmer Books, 1979.

Placksin, Sally. *American Women in Jazz: 1900 to the Present; Their Words, Lives and Music*. New York: Wideview Books, 1982.

Porter, Roy, with David Keller. *There and Back*. Baton Rouge: Louisiana State University Press, 1991.

Powell, Adam Clayton, Jr. *Adam by Adam: The Autobiography of Adam Clayton Powell, Jr.* New York: Dial Press, 1971.

Rampersad, Arnold. *The Life of Langston Hughes; Volume 1: 1902–1941; I, Too, Sing America*. New York: Oxford University Press, 1986.

Riis, Thomas L. *Just Before Jazz*. Washington: Smithsonian Institution Press, 1989.

Rose, Al. *Eubie Blake*. New York: Schirmer, 1979.

Russell, Ross. *Bird Lives: The High Life and Hard Times of Charlie (Yardbird) Parker*. New York: Charterhouse, 1973.

Rust, Brian. *Jazz Records 1897–1942*. New Rochelle, NY: Arlington House, 1978.

Sacks, Howard, and Judith Sacks. *Way Up North in Dixie: A Black Family's Claim to the Confederate Anthem*. Washington: Smithsonian Institution Press, 1991.

Sacks, Oliver. *An Anthropologist on Mars: Seven Paradoxical Tales*. New York: Knopf, 1995.

Sampson, Henry T. *Blacks in Blackface*. Metuchen, NJ: Scarecrow, 1980.

_____. *The Ghost Walks: A Chronological History of Blacks in Show Business*. Metuchen, NJ: Scarecrow, 1988.

Sanfilippo, Luigi. *General Catalog of Duke Ellington's Recorded Music*. Palermo, Italy: Centro Studi Di Musica Contemporanea, 1966.

Schifmann, Jack. *Uptown: The Story of Harlem's Apollo Theatre*. New York: Cowles, 1971.

Schuller, Gunther. *Early Jazz: Its Roots and Musical Development*. New York: Oxford University Press, 1968.

Schuyler, George. *Black No More*. New York: Macaulay, 1931.

Schwartz, Charles. *Gershwin: His Life and Music*. New York: Bobbs-Merrill, 1973.

Shapiro, Nat, and Nat Hentoff. *Hear Me Talkin' to Ya*. New York: Dover, 1966.

Shaw, Arnold. *Sinatra, the Entertainer*. New York: Delilah, 1982.

Shaw, Bernard. *Collected Letters.1898–1910*. New York: Dodd, Mead, 1965.

Short, Bobby. *Black and White Baby*. New York: Dodd, Mead, 1971.

Skvorecky, Josef. *Dvorak in Love*. New York: Alfred A. Knopf, 1987.

Smith, Eric Ledell. *Bert Williams: A Biography of the Pioneer Black Comedian*. Jefferson, NC: McFarland, 1992.

Smith, Jessie Carney, ed. *Notable Black American Women*. Detroit: Gale Research, 1992.

Smith, Willie "The Lion," and George Hoefer. *Music on My Mind: Memoirs of an American Pianist*. New York: Doubleday, 1964.

Songs, Sketch of the Life, Testimonials from the Most Eminent Composers, and Opinions of the American and English Press. New York: French & Wheat, Book and Job Printers, 1876 (see appendix A).

Southern, Eileen. *Biographical Dictionary of*

Afro-American and African Musicians. Westport, CT: Greenwood Press, 1982.

_____. *The Music of Black Americans.* New York: Norton, 1971.

_____. *Readings in Black American Music.* New York: Norton, 1971.

Stearns, Marshall, and Jean Stearns. *Jazz Dance: The Story of American Vernacular Dance.* New York: Macmillan, 1968.

Taylor, Art. *Notes and Tones: Musician-to-Musician Interviews.* New York: Coward, McCann and Geoghegan, 1977.

Taylor, Frank C., with Gerald Cook. *Alberta: A Celebration in Blues.* New York: McGraw-Hill, 1987.

Thomas, J.C. *Chasin' the Trane: The Music and Mystique of John Coltrane.* New York: Doubleday, 1975.

Thorpe, Edward. *Black Dance.* Woodstock, NY: Overlook Press, 1990.

Travis, Dempsey J. *Autobiography of Black Jazz.* Chicago: Urban Research Institute, 1983.

Ulanov, Barry. *Duke Ellington.* New York: Creative Age Press, 1946.

Van Vechten, Carl. *Keep A-Inching Along: Selected Writings of Carl Van Vechten about Black Art and Letters.* Westport, CT: Greenwood Press, 1979.

_____. *Nigger Heaven.* New York: Alfred A. Knopf, 1926.

_____. *Parties.* New York: Alfred A. Knopf, 1930.

Watkins, Mel. *On the Real Side: Laughing, Lying, and Signifying — The Underground Tradition of African-American Humor That Transformed American Culture, from Slavery to Richard Pryor.* New York: Simon & Schuster, 1994.

Welles, Orson, and Peter Bogdanovich. *This Is Orson Welles.* New York: HarperCollins, 1992.

Wendt, Lloyd, and Herman Kogan. *Big Bill of Chicago.* New York: Bobbs-Merrill, 1953.

Wideman, Jerome. *Damballah.* New York: Avon Books, 1981.

Wilder, Alec. *American Popular Song.* New York: Oxford, 1972.

Witmark, Isadore, and Isaac Goldberg. *From Ragtime to Swingtime: The Story of the House of Witmark.* New York: Lee Furman, 1939.

Woll, Allen. *Black Musical Theatre: From Coontown to Dreamgirls.* Baton Rouge: Louisiana State University Press, 1989.

Wright, John S. *A Stronger Soul Within a Finer Frame: Portraying African-Americans in the Black Renaissance.* Minneapolis: University Art Museum, University of Minnesota, 1990 (exhibition catalogue).

Index

ML
3556
.R36
2010